Wildlife Photographer of the Year

PORTFOLIO FOUR

Editor
HELEN GILKS

Picture Editor
PETER WILKINSON FRPS

Designer
GRANT BRADFORD

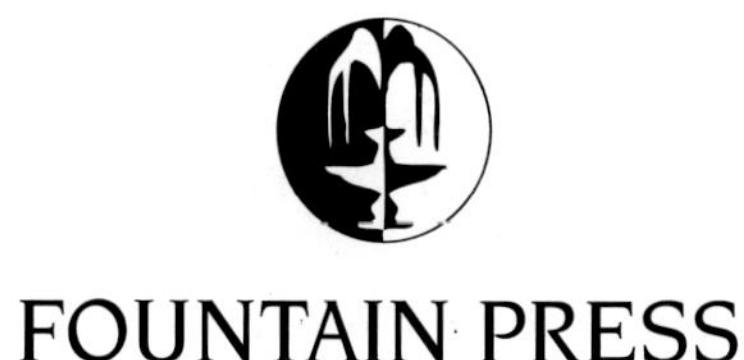

FOUNTAIN PRESS

Published by
FOUNTAIN PRESS LIMITED
Fountain House
2 Gladstone Road
Kingston-upon-Thames
Surrey KT1 3HD
England

Editor
Helen Gilks

Picture Editor
Peter Wilkinson

Design & Layout
Grant Bradford

Colour Origination
by Swift Graphics

Printed & Bound
in Italy
by poligrafici calderara

ISBN 0 86343 371 5

Contents

Foreword

Please turn these pages with all the care they so richly deserve and drink in the true meaning of each image. Each one a snapshot of our time as we draw towards the end of this sad century. Each one a tribute to the living world and the ingenuity of humankind. A tribute to the photographers' skill, to those who design, create and engineer cameras, and to those who craft the film and the chemicals which capture and develop the images. But think, too, though, of the living things that may be disturbed or destroyed by the mining for minerals, the making of chemicals and the feet of photographers. Yes, even photography has the power to destroy as it creates.

You hold in your hands a document of great beauty and importance. Will it become just another part of the archive of a dying world or will it begin to weave real magic?

The photographers have done their best, and they have had their reward – the chance to see for themselves. Now it's up to you. You can either close this book and your mind to the beauty and the problems it portrays. Or, you can lay it open at your favourite page and make your coffee table a podium from which to campaign for the changes that must come to create a new world order - when indigenous people, plants and animals will have equal rights with us to a fair share of this blue green planet.

David Bellamy

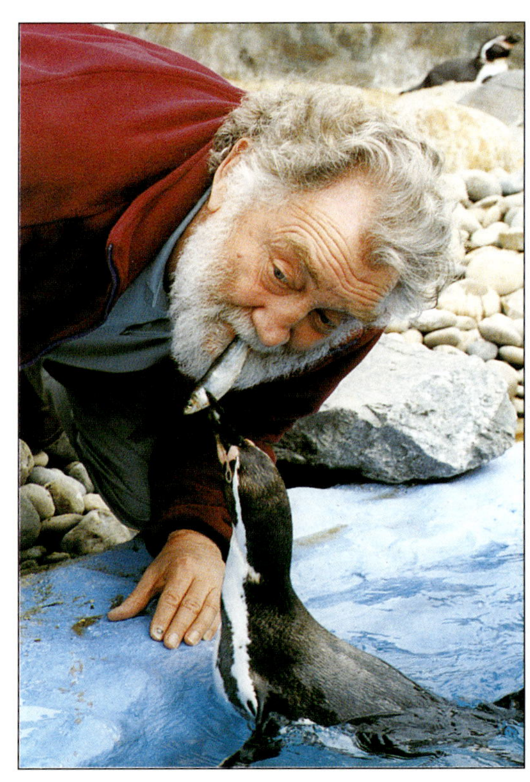

This book displays the winning and commended images from the Wildlife Photographer of the Year 1994 Competition, which has been organised for the eleventh year by BBC Wildlife Magazine and the Natural History Museum, London, and sponsored for the fifth year by British Gas.

The competition aims to find the best wildlife pictures taken by photographers worldwide, and through these images emphasise the beauty, wonder and importance of the natural world. A record number of more than 12,000 entries poured in from 50 different countries, and the work of photographers from 22 countries is represented in this book - testimony to the truly international status of the event.

Photographs, which had to be colour slides, were entered in 14 different categories which each carried a first prize of £1,000 and a runner-up prize of £500. Where competition was particularly fierce, the judges awarded a specially commended, or third prize. Other photos reaching the final stages of the judging were highly commended. In addition, the Eric Hosking Award was given for the best portfolio of pictures by a photographer aged under 27 years. A special competition was held for young photographers aged 17 years and under.

The winners gathered at the Natural History Museum in October for an awards ceremony compèred by Barry Paine. The prizes were presented by an array of celebrities from the field of natural history, the environment movement and entertainment: Chris Baines, David Bellamy, Virginia McKenna, Bill Oddie, Julian Pettifer, Andrew Sachs and Lady Scott. The junior prizes were presented by Simon King and Nick Davies. This awards ceremony marked the opening of the exhibition of winning and commended images at the Natural History Museum, where it is on display for four months. Two further exhibitions tour the UK visiting some 20 different galleries, museums and nature centres. Additional exhibitions go on display in Australia, France, Germany, Holland, Japan and the USA.

British Gas

Wildlife Photographer of the Year

1994

Over the years, the Wildlife Photographer of the Year Competition has stimulated some outstanding photographs from around the world and it continues to gain in international stature.

The photographs in this collection beautifully illustrate their creators' commitment to quality and to the environment, aspirations which British Gas is proud to share. As a world class company, we too are committed to excellence and have a long tradition of environmental responsibility.

This book is a superb tribute to those ideals. Our involvement, as sponsor of the competition for the last five years, has been a privilege.

Cedric H Brown
Chief Executive, British Gas

Comment

From Frans Lanting, a judge of this year's competition and overall winner of the event in 1991.

When I decided to devote my life to nature photography some 20 years ago, there were few role models. The visual documentation of the natural history of our planet was the domain of just a handful of people around the world. Today, this specialty has become a rapidly expanding field made up of professionals, amateurs, and every gradation between, all of whom offer us much to be inspired by.

The Wildlife Photographer of the Year Competition reflects this growth. It is establishing an international standard for excellence in nature photography just as the World Press Photo and Pictures of the Year awards have for international photo-journalism . Such recognition for distinguished achievement is, in my opinion, long overdue. In the past two decades, I have seen the number of my colleagues multiply at a time when human societies around the world are becoming ever more urbanised and fewer people have direct contact with the natural world. Society now depends in part on photographers and other image-makers for a vision of the Earth. Few of us could imagine a mountain gorilla or a humpback whale, for instance, without making mental reference to a photograph. We wouldn't know what they looked like nor would we have as clear an understanding of how they lived.

To those photographers who fear that 'everything has already been done', I offer a contrary view. There will always be new ground to break. In my own work around the world, I often come upon wild places and wild creatures that are virtually unknown outside a small circle of local people and scientific experts. Tropical forests in particular, which are under-represented in this competition, present a cornucopia of photographic possibilities, and will allow anyone with determination and vision to make significant contributions.

But one doesn't need to go to places no one else has been before to make memorable images. The way we photograph nature is always a reflection of how we relate to the natural world we know. And as these ideas evolve, so does our photography. I can't think of a better way to illustrate that notion than by referring to the image the judges of this year's contest declared the overall winner. A great deal of good photographs have been made of polar bears, yet this particular image does what an outstanding photograph is uniquely able to do. It shows something we are all familiar with in a striking new perspective. To see one of the greatest of wild beasts dwarfed by the immensity of its surroundings is not just powerful testimony to the survival skills of the polar bear, but a reminder, if we ever needed one, that it is the Earth itself which supports every living thing.

WINNERS 1984-1993

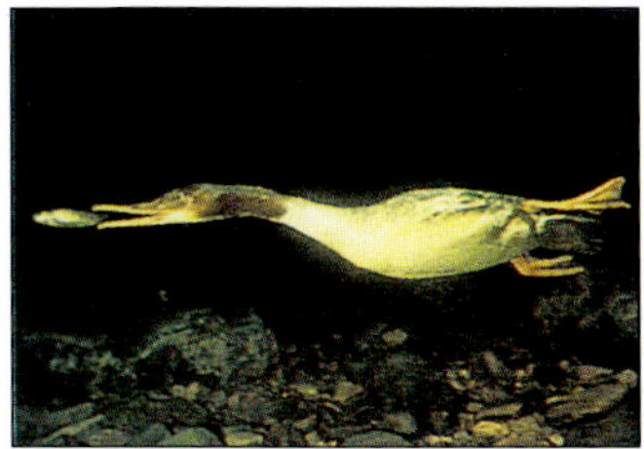

1984
Richard & Julia Kemp
United Kingdom

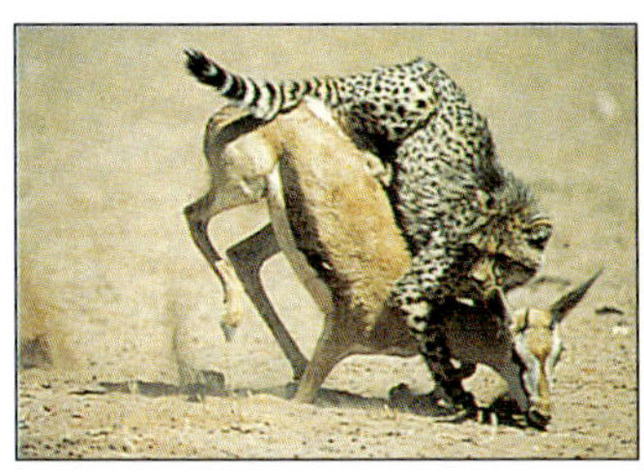

1985
Charles G Summers Jnr.
United States of America

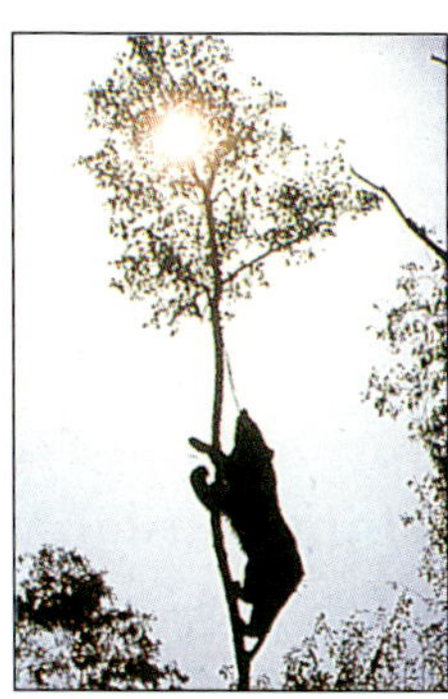
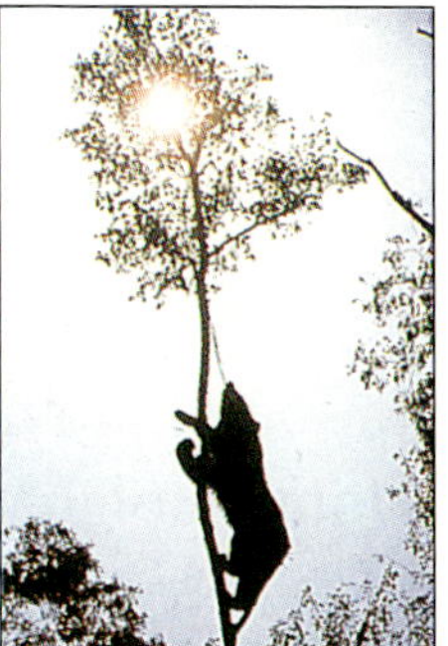
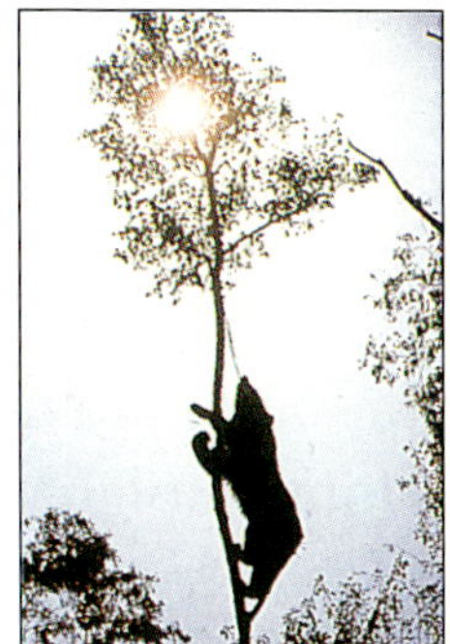

1986
Rajesh Bedi
India

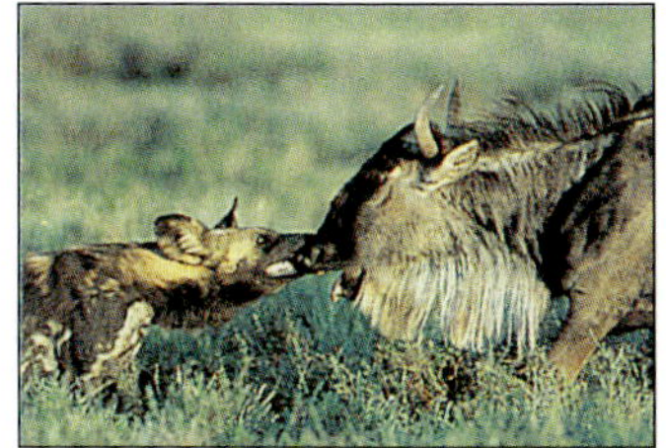

1987
Jonathan Scott
United Kingdom

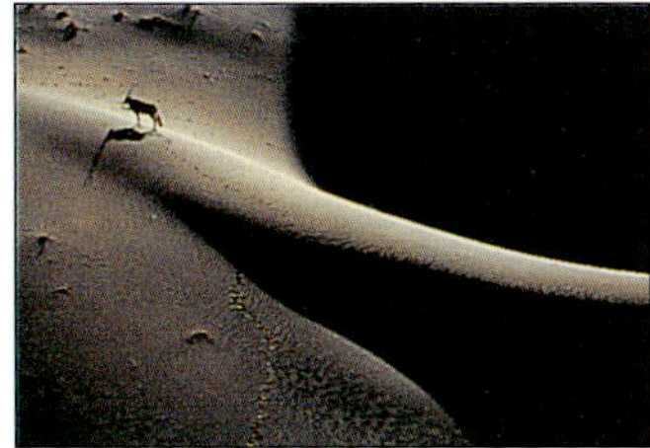

1988
Jim Brandenburg
United States of America

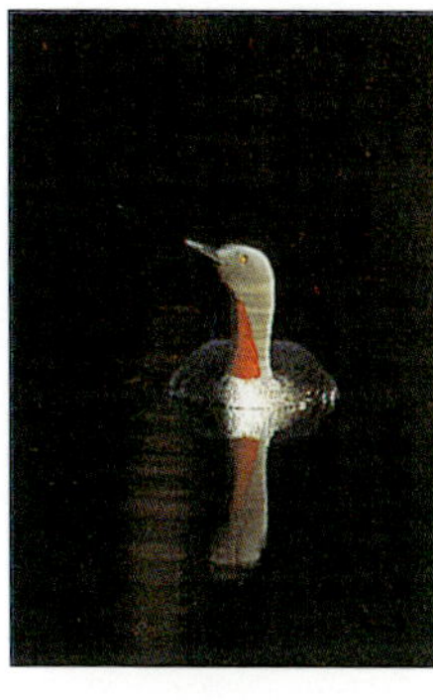

1989
Jouni Ruuskanen
Finland

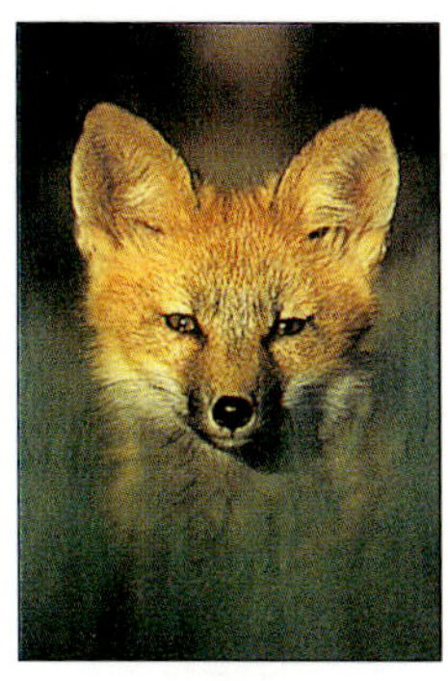

1990
Wendy Shattil
United States of America

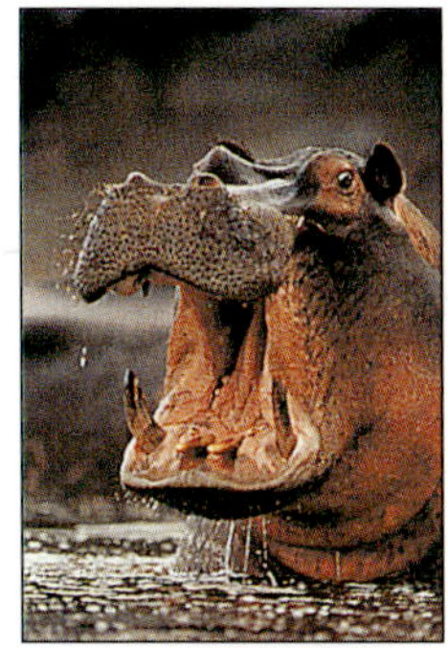

1991
Frans Lanting
The Netherlands

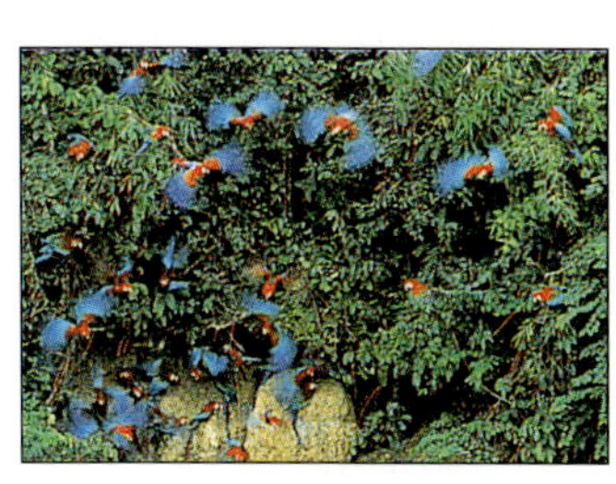

1992
André Bärtschi
Liechtenstein

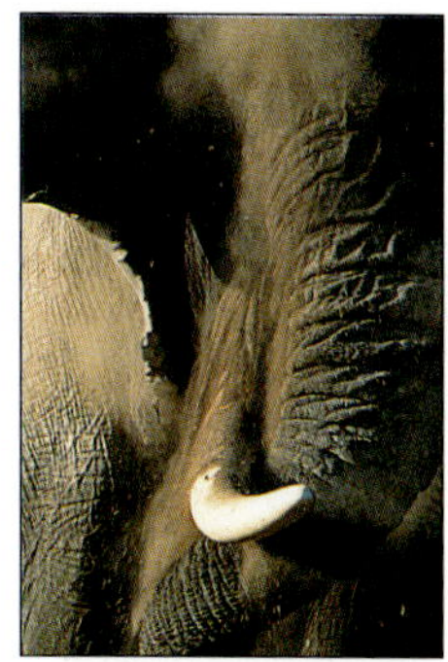

1993
Martyn Colbeck
United Kingdom

THE JUDGES

Heather Angel
Wildlife photographer

Dr Giles Clarke
Head of Exhibitions and Education at The Natural History Museum, London

Rosamund Kidman Cox
Editor of BBC Wildlife Magazine

Frans Lanting
Wildlife Photographer

Amanda Nevill
Head of the National Museum of Photography, Film and Television

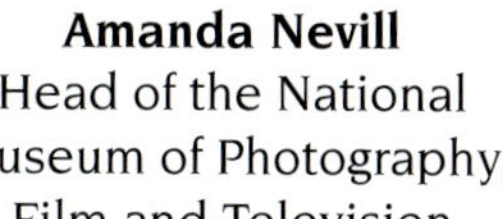

Bruce Pearson
Wildlife artist

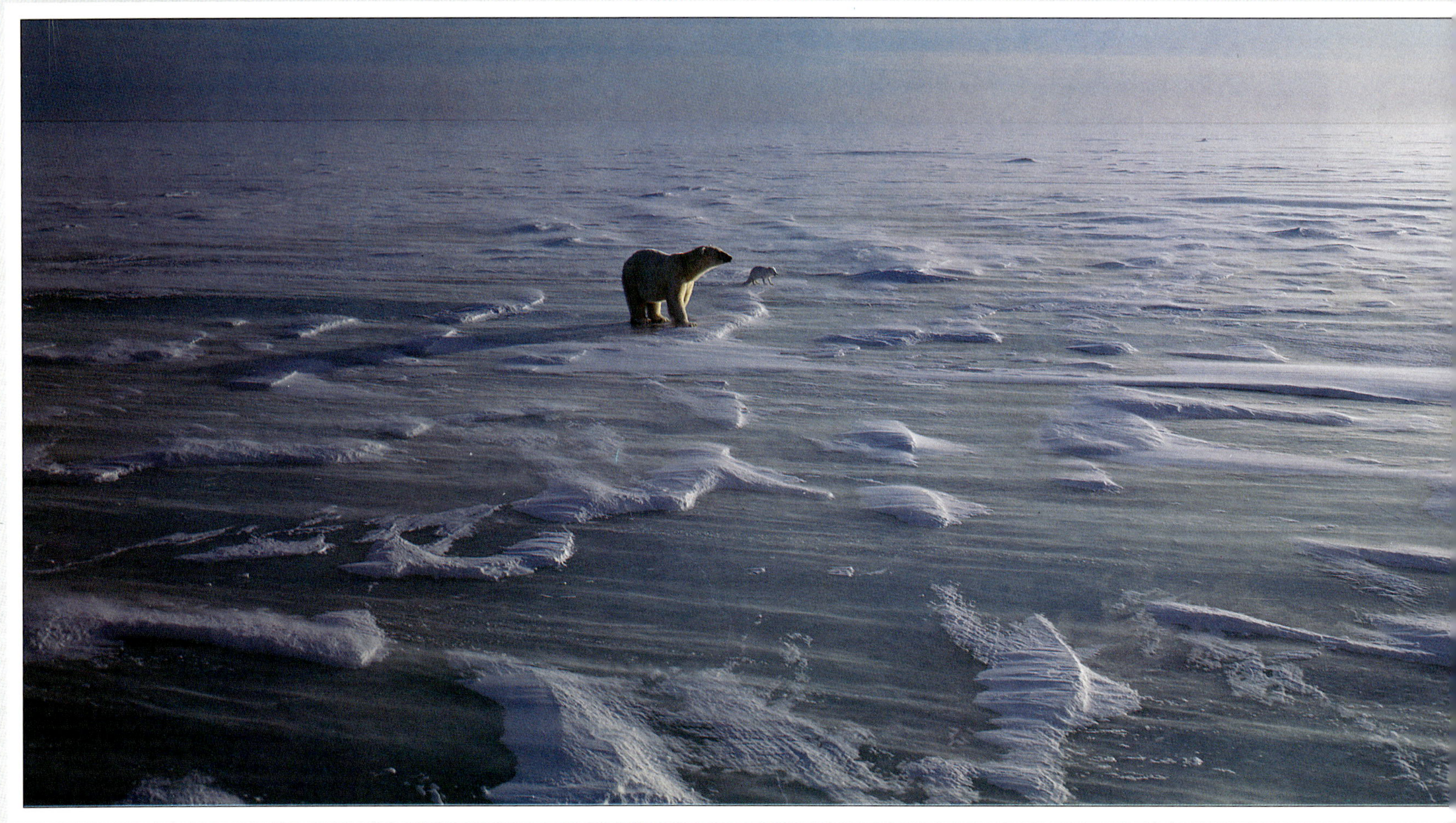

Wildlife Photographer of the Year

The 'Wildlife Photographer of the Year' title was awarded for the single image judged to be the most striking and memorable of all the photographs entered for the competition. The 1994 winner, Thomas Mangelsen, received the British Gas award – a bronze trophy of an ibis and a cheque for £5,000.

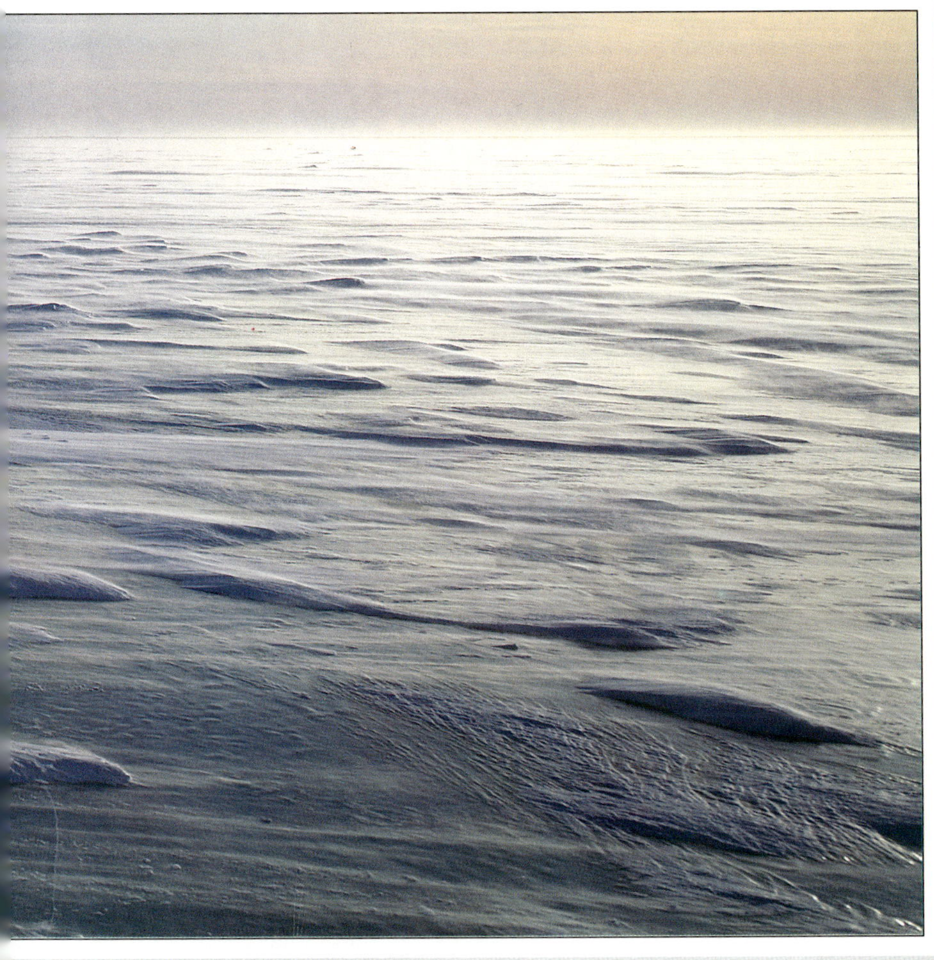

Thomas D Mangelsen
United States of America
WILDLIFE PHOTOGRAPHER OF THE YEAR
1994

Polar bear and Arctic fox, Hudson Bay

"For the past seven years I have spent November in Hudson Bay photographing the polar bears that congregate along the shores. The bears are waiting for the sea to freeze so that they can venture onto the ice to hunt seals, their main food. Arctic foxes are often seen with the bears, scavenging for leftovers. My aim was to capture the vast landscape and harsh conditions of the far north that is the home of these animals."

Fuji 617 Panoramic camera with Fujinon SW 105mm f8 lens; bean bag; 1/125sec at f11; Fujichrome Velvia

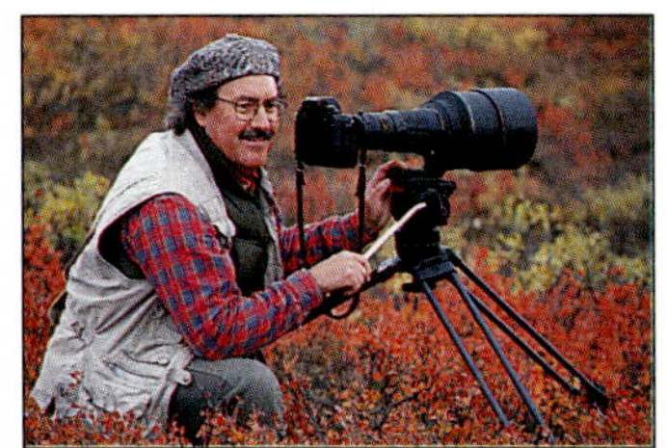

Thomas D Mangelsen

Thomas Mangelsen started taking photographs after graduating with a degree in biology. At first, he concentrated on the subjects he knew best - waterfowl along the river Platte where he grew up. Today he spends more than half the year travelling around the world to take pictures. He is interested in photographing all facets of nature, especially birds in flight, bears, and African wildlife. He believes that the key to taking fine-art nature photographs is a knowledge of animal behaviour and ecosystems combined with technical skill and creative imagination. Testimony to his success as a fine-art nature photographer are the nine galleries across the USA which sell prints of his photographs, and a book *Images of Nature - The Photographs of Thomas Mangelsen*. His pictures have also been widely published in nature books and magazines. In addition to his award-winning image, Thomas Mangelsen has a category runner-up prize and four highly commended images in this year's competition.

British Wildlife

This category was run for the first time in 1994, in association with BBC1's Good Morning series. The entries had to feature British plants or animals, photographed in wild or urban settings.

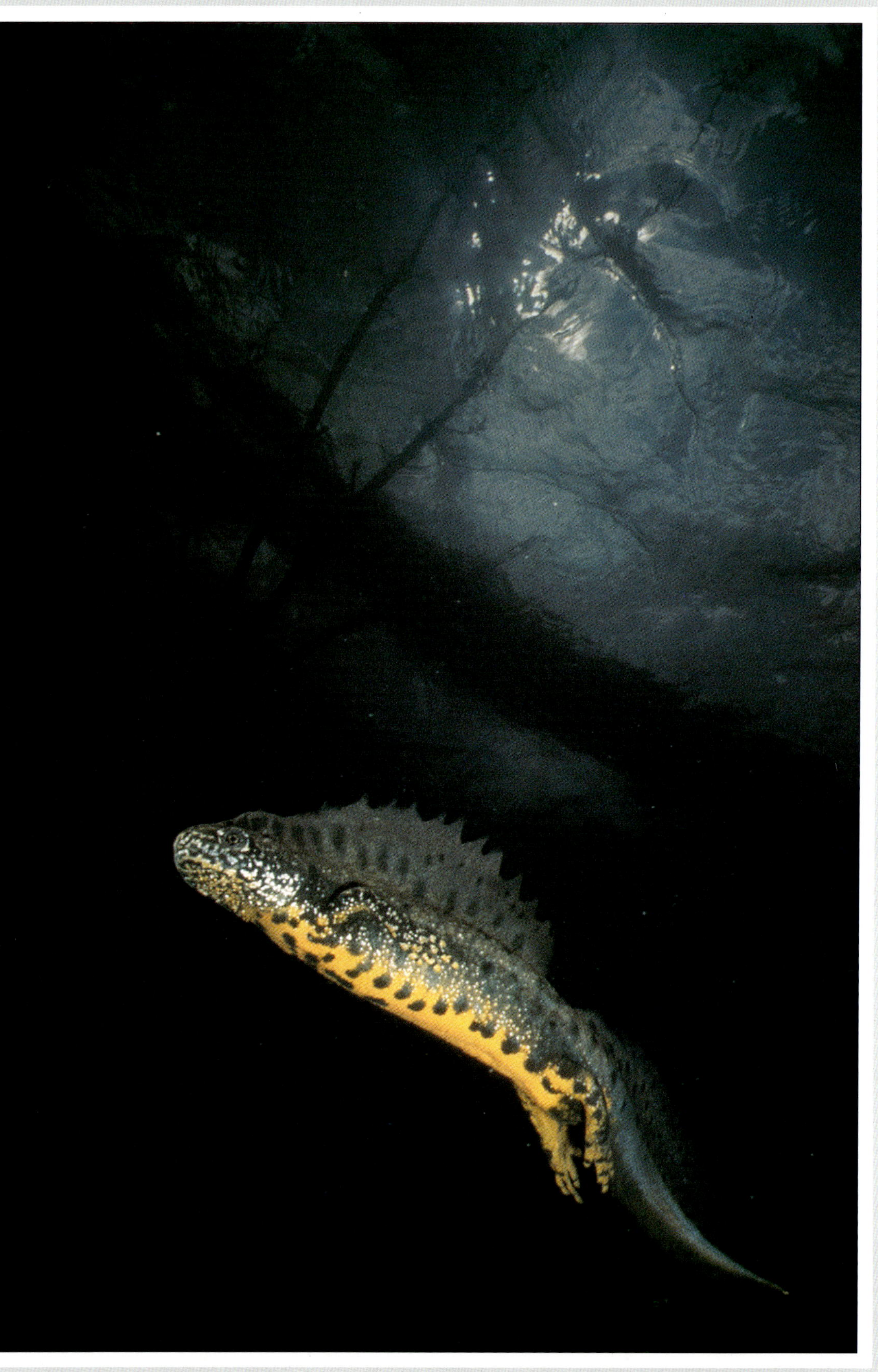

Alan James
England
WINNER

Male great crested newt

"I wanted to photograph a male in full mating colours against a background of sun breaking through the surface-water, specifically for this category. The picture was taken in a local quarry where I had observed male newts using submerged boulders as observation posts for prospective mates. I took more than 400 exposures in one day and achieved the image I had in mind by combining a frame of the newt with another of the sun on the water's surface."

Newt: Nikonos V with 28mm lens and close-up outfit; dual strobes; 1/90 sec at f16/22. Sunburst background: Nikonos V with 15mm lens; 1/90 sec at f16/22; Ektachrome 50

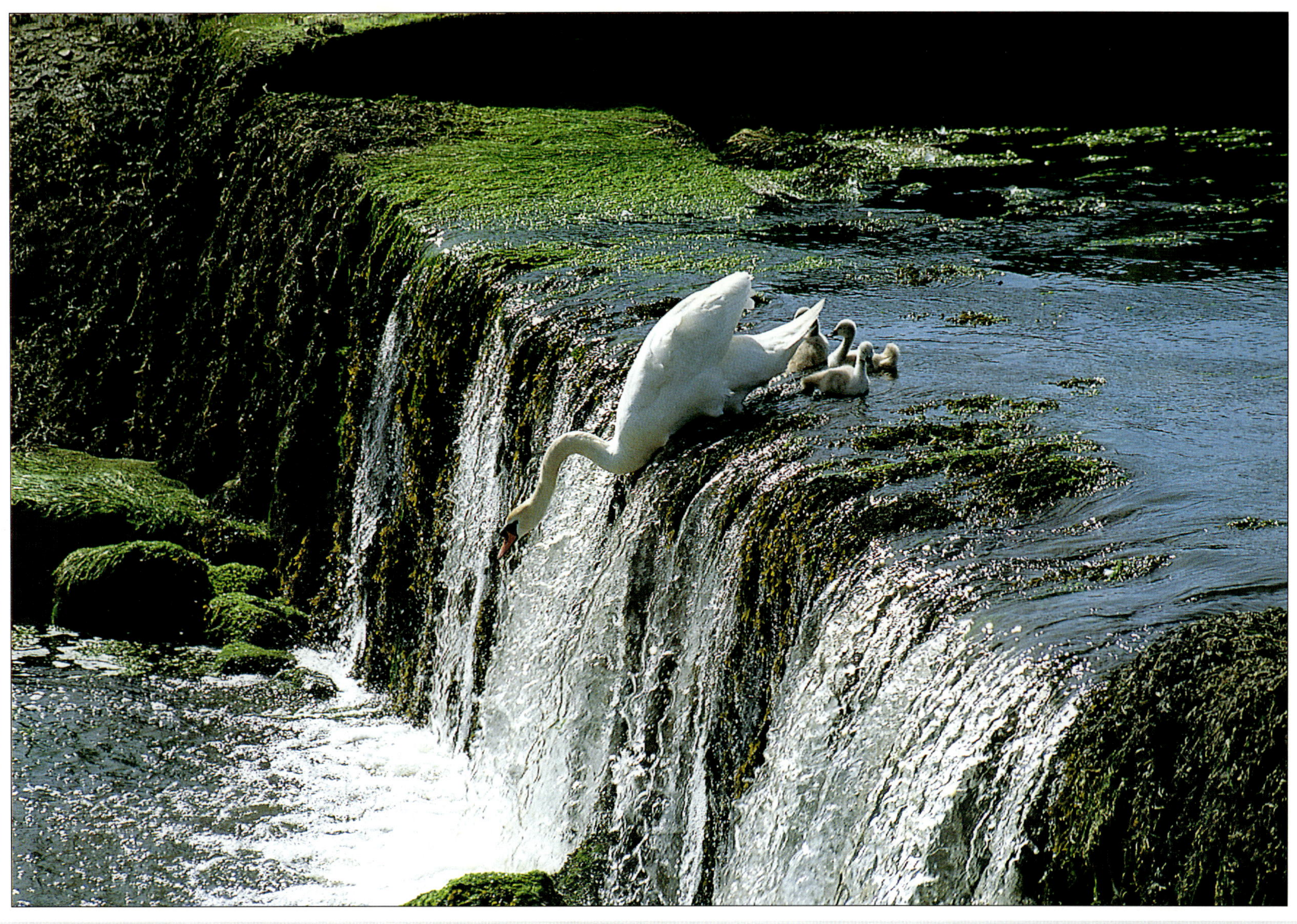

John Neil
England
SPECIALLY COMMENDED

Swan and cygnets at waterfall

"This picture was taken in Castletown harbour at low tide. The swan went over the waterfall, followed by the cygnets, to join her mate. Unfortunately, this was the last frame on the film so I wasn't able to record the cygnets' successful descent."

Nikon F4 with 80-200mm lens; Fujichrome Velvia

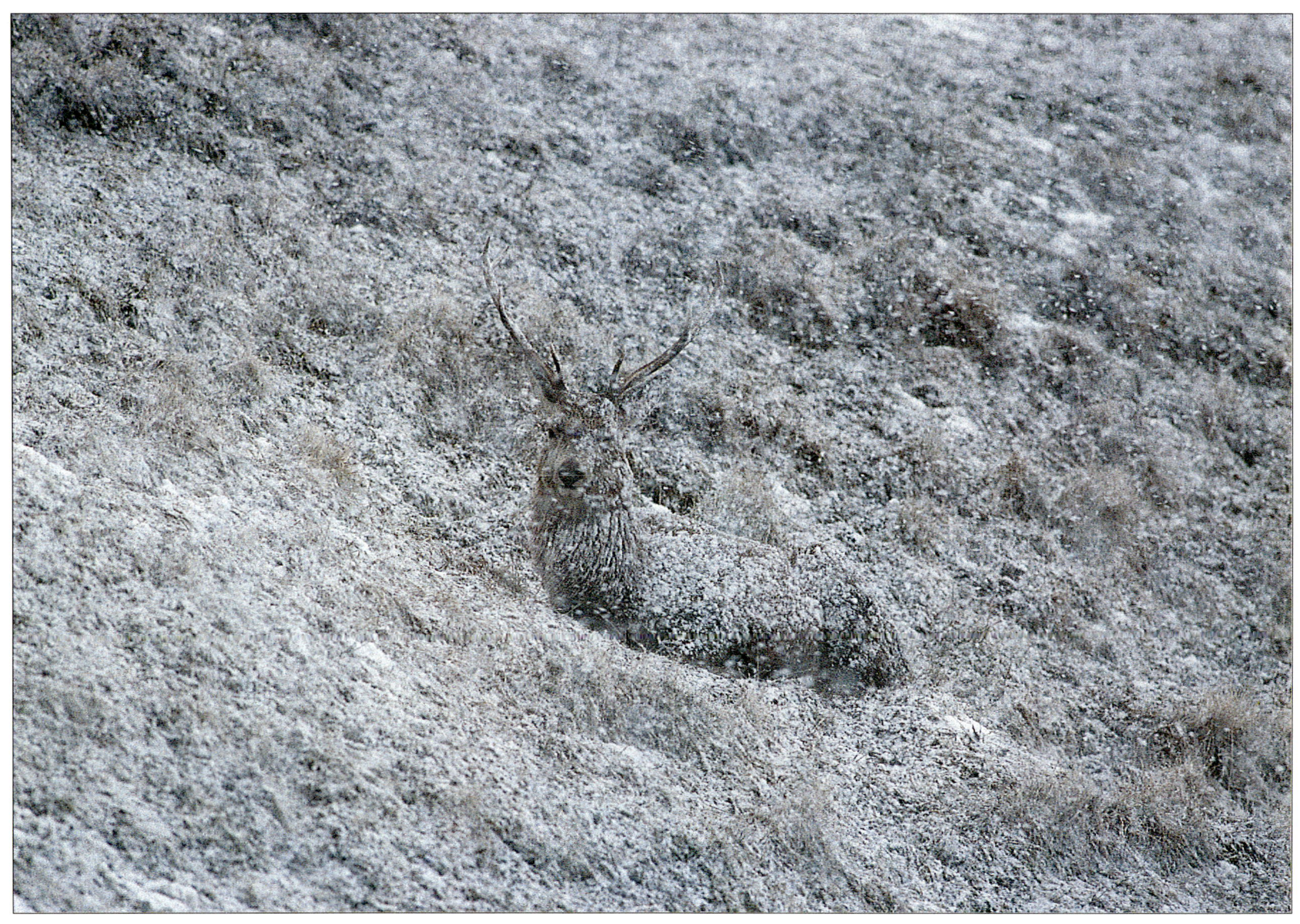

Peter Moore
Scotland
RUNNER-UP

Red deer stag

*"In early March, an exceptional fall of snow forced the red deer in the Highlands down to the glens to find food.
It was one of those wonderful Scottish days of bright sun, swirling wind and snow showers, and the deer were feeding not far from the road."*

Nikon F801 with 500mm lens and x1.4 extender; bean bag; auto at f5.6; Kodachrome 64

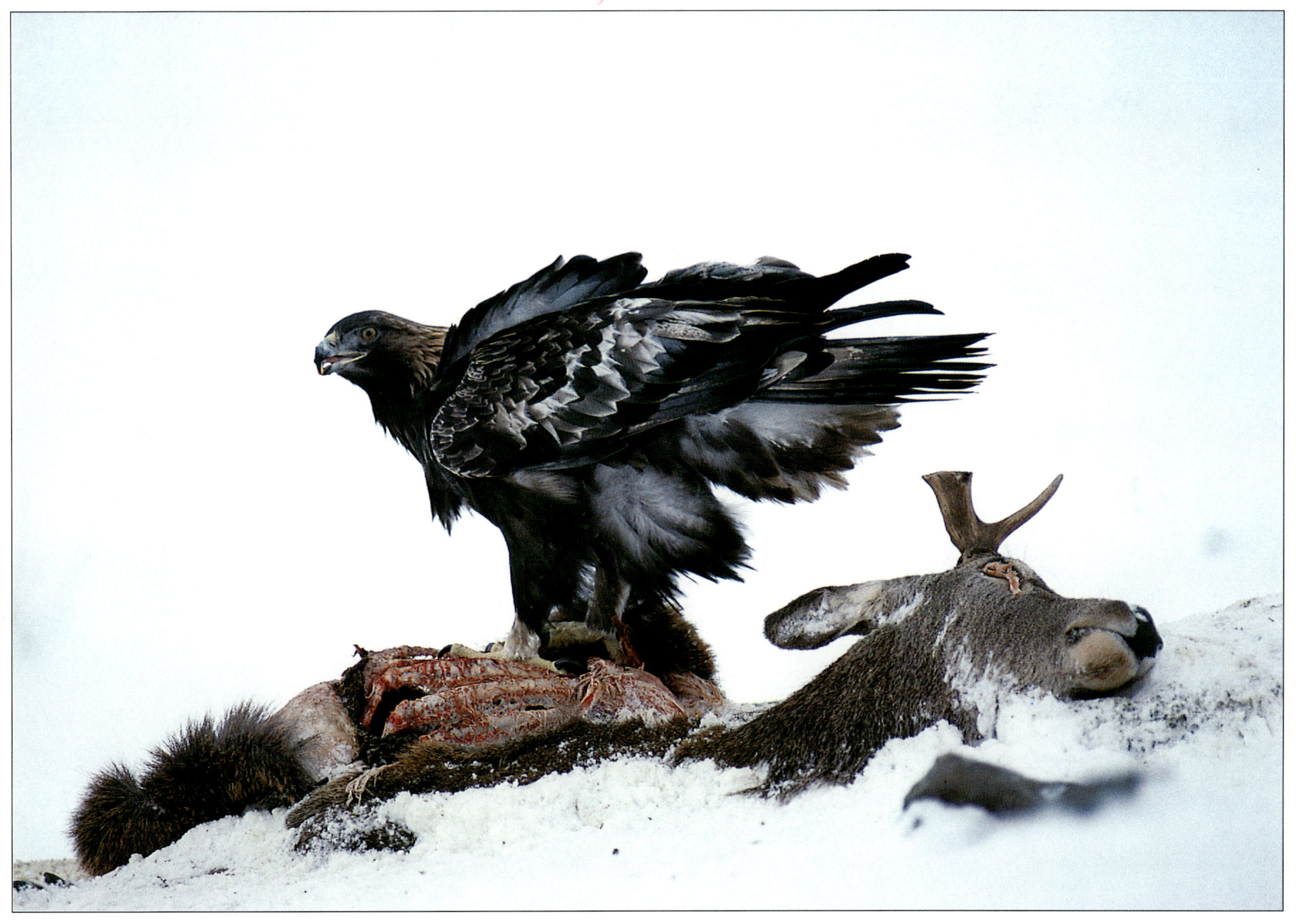

Laurie Campbell
Scotland
HIGHLY COMMENDED

Golden eagle feeding on carrion

" Eagles will feed on carrion when the weather makes hunting difficult. When harsh conditions arrived, I put out a deer carcass close to a hide I had built from rocks, six months previously. This is one of some 2,000 images of golden eagles I have taken over the past few years."

Nikon F4 with 300mm lens; tripod;1/250sec at f4; Kodachrome 64

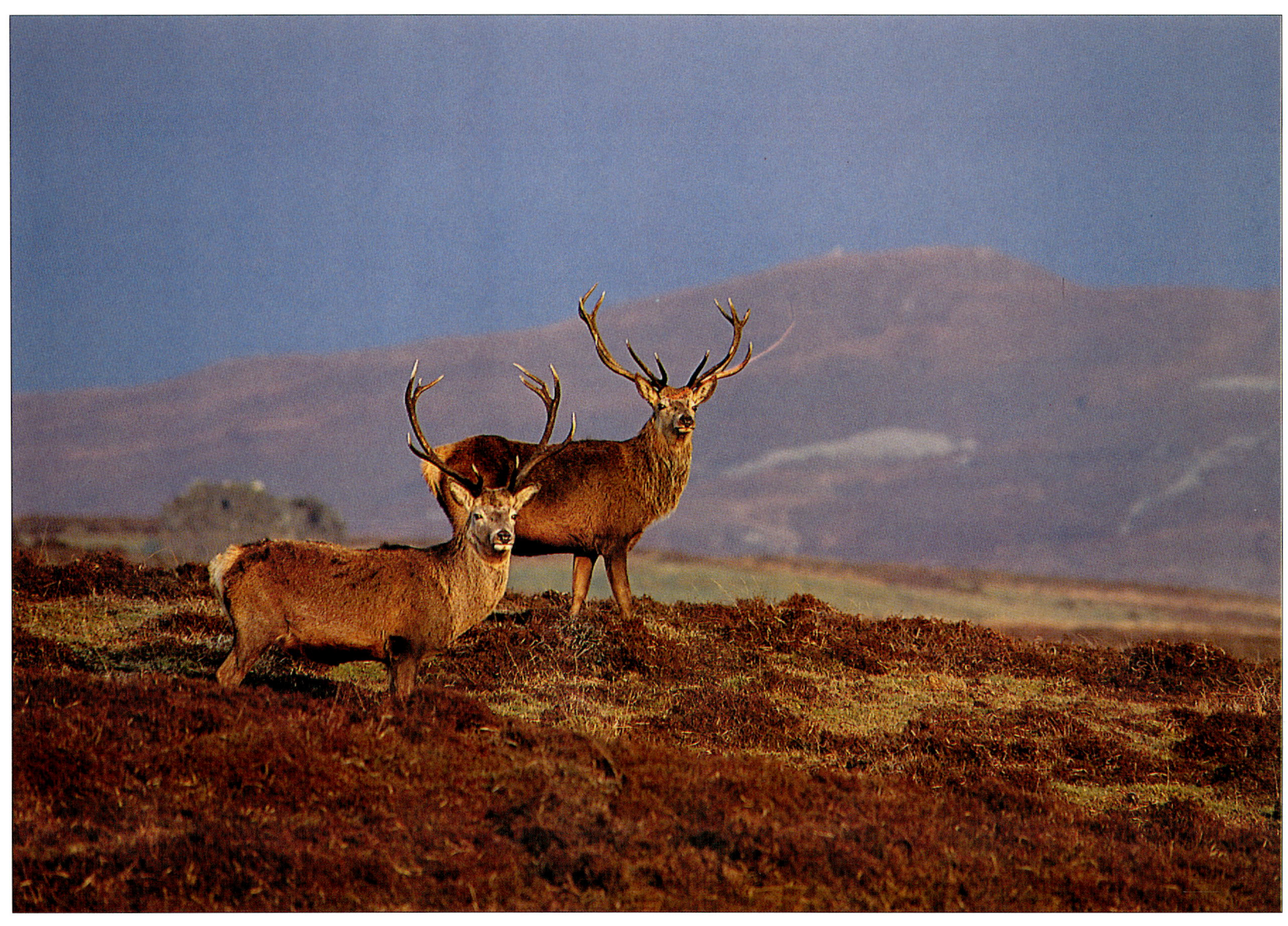

Paul Hicks
England
HIGHLY COMMENDED

Red deer stags

"I took this picture at a spot on the Isle of Islay where stags gather in winter. On this afternoon the sky cleared and the stags were beautifully lit by the winter sun. Getting the shot was mainly a matter of waiting for a chance to single out a pleasing composition from among the restless herd."

Nikon F4S with 300mm lens; tripod; 1/60sec at f8; Fujichrome Velvia

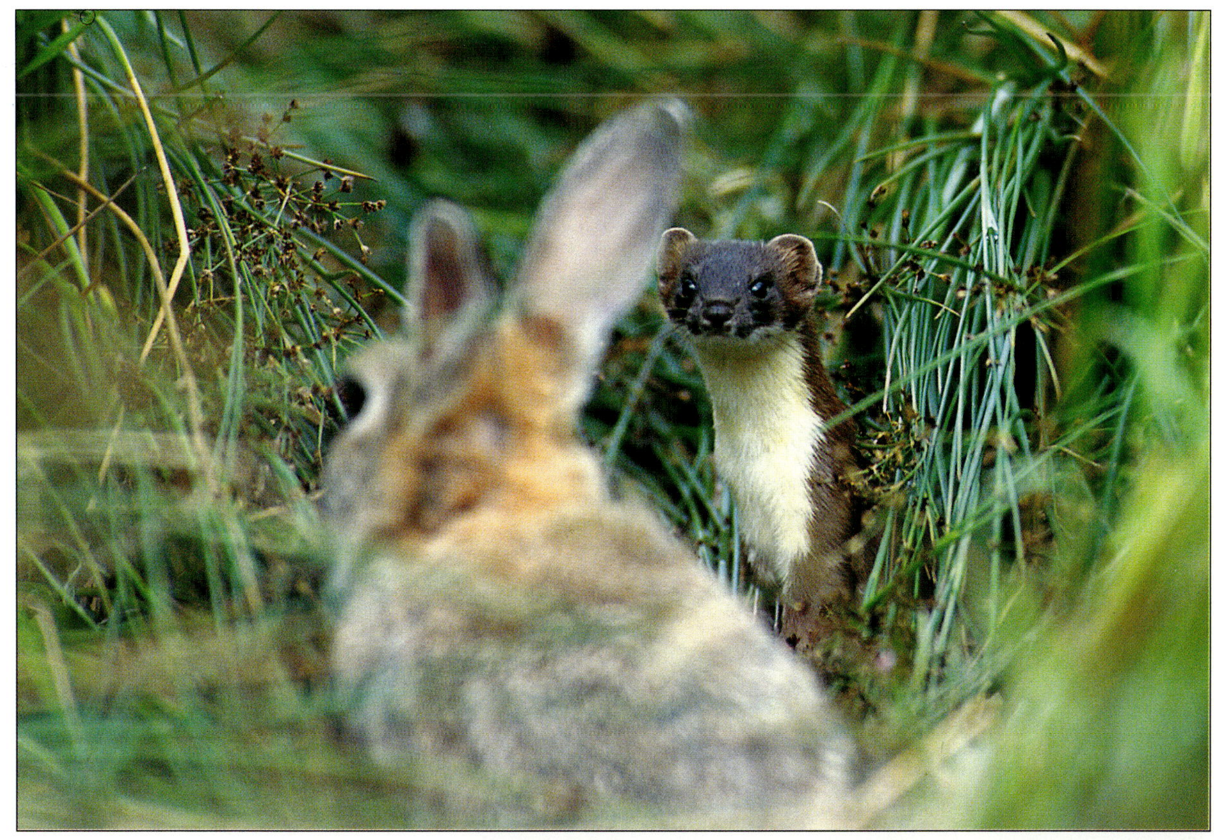

Brian Lightfoot
United Kingdom
HIGHLY COMMENDED

Stoat hunting rabbit

"I spotted this stoat hunting a rabbit along a roadside and, as luck would have it, they both stopped directly opposite me, the rabbit completely mesmerised by its hunter. Seconds later the stoat was on the rabbit's neck."

Nikon F4S with 500mm lens and extension tube; Fujichrome 100

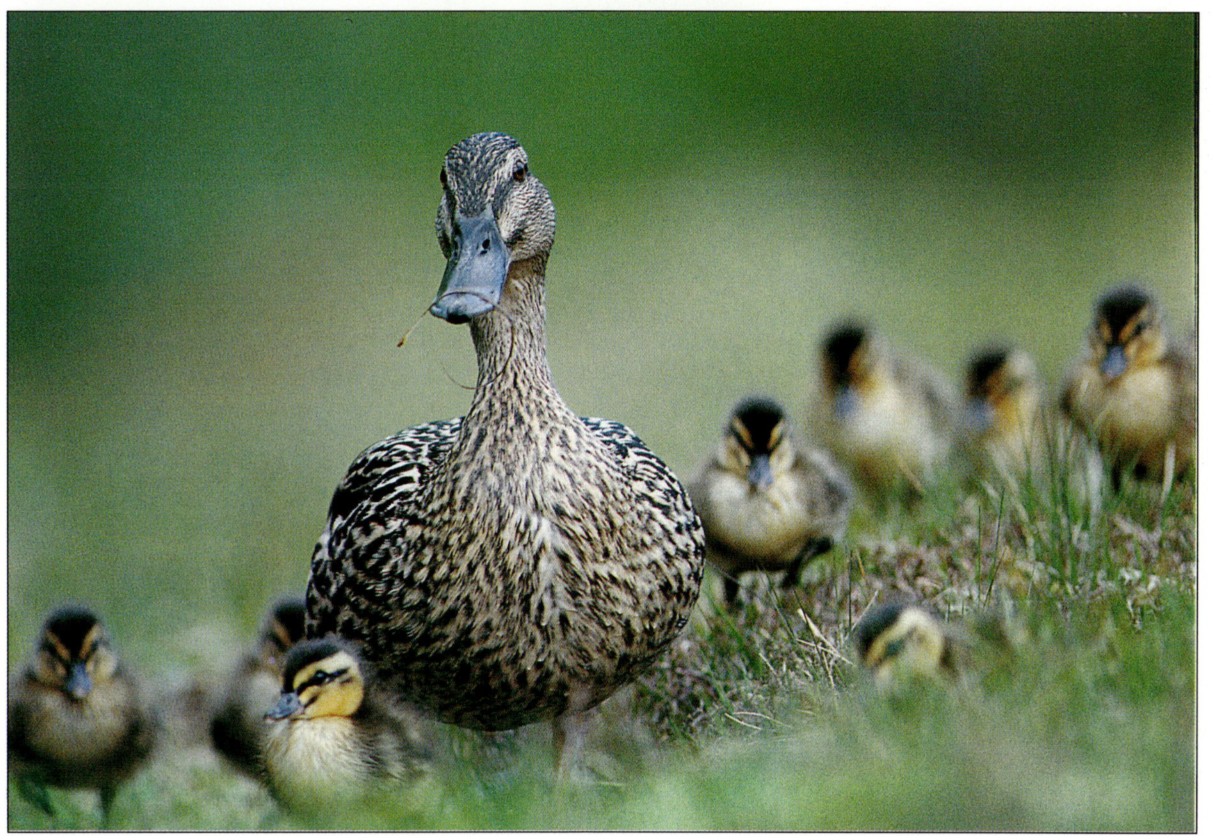

Laurie Campbell
Scotland
HIGHLY COMMENDED

Mallard with ducklings

"I came across these birds unexpectedly while out photographing mosses. Luckily, I had a long lens which allowed me to take some pictures from a distance without disturbing the birds. The duck is making her way from the nest site to water."

Nikon F3 with 600mm lens; tripod; 1/125 sec at f5.6; Kodachrome 200

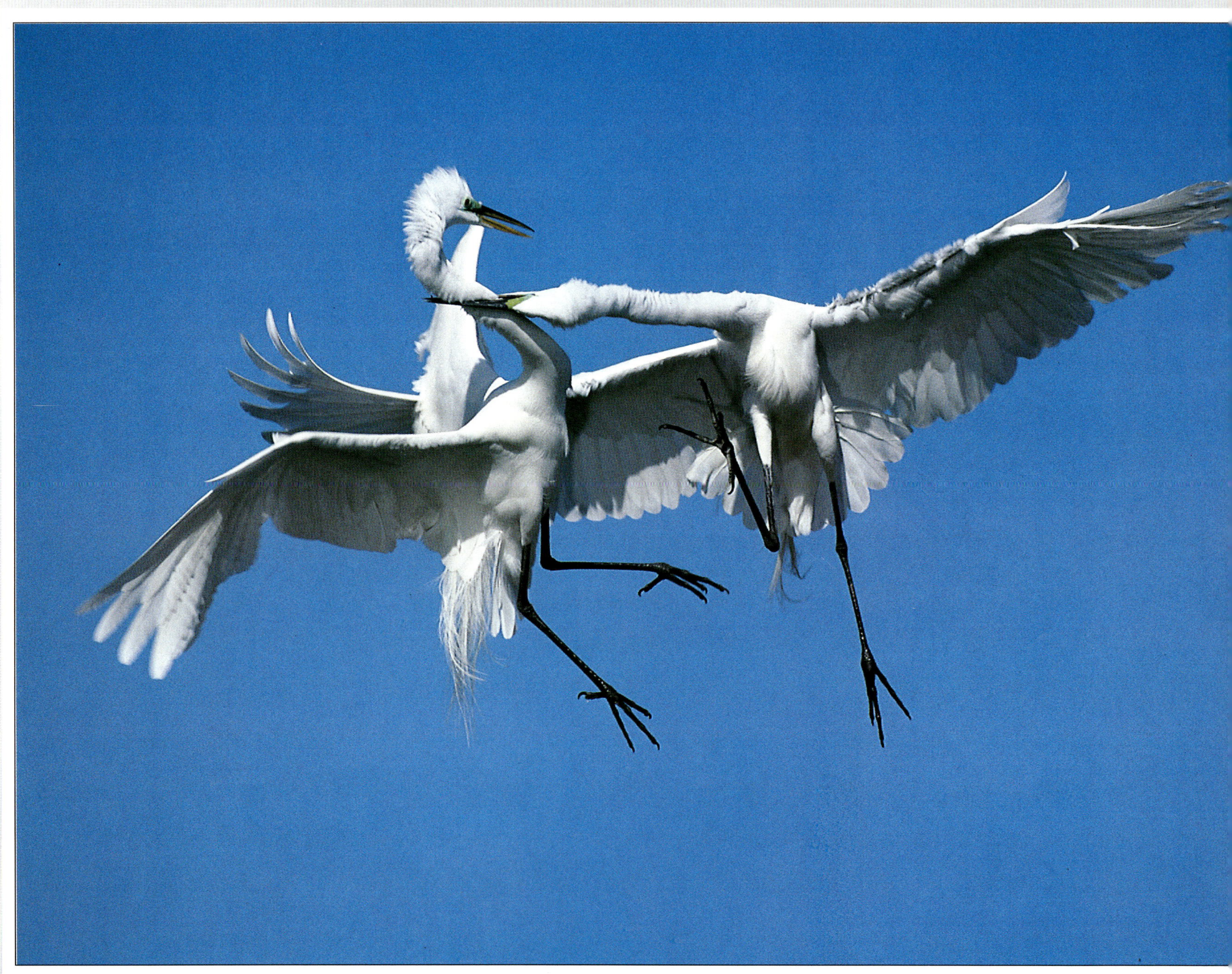

Animal Behaviour

- BIRDS -

This category is for photographs of birds actively doing something. The pictures are judged for their interest as well as their aesthetic appeal.

Mary Ann McDonald
United States of America
WINNER

Great egrets fighting

"Although great egrets usually seem serene and peaceful, during the breeding season, a calm scene can suddenly erupt into a flurry of feathers as males compete for mates and prime nesting sites. Fighting often begins in the trees or on the ground, and continues in the air until one of the birds is eventually driven off."

Nikon F4 with 500mm lens; tripod; 1/1,000 sec at f5.6; Kodachrome 64

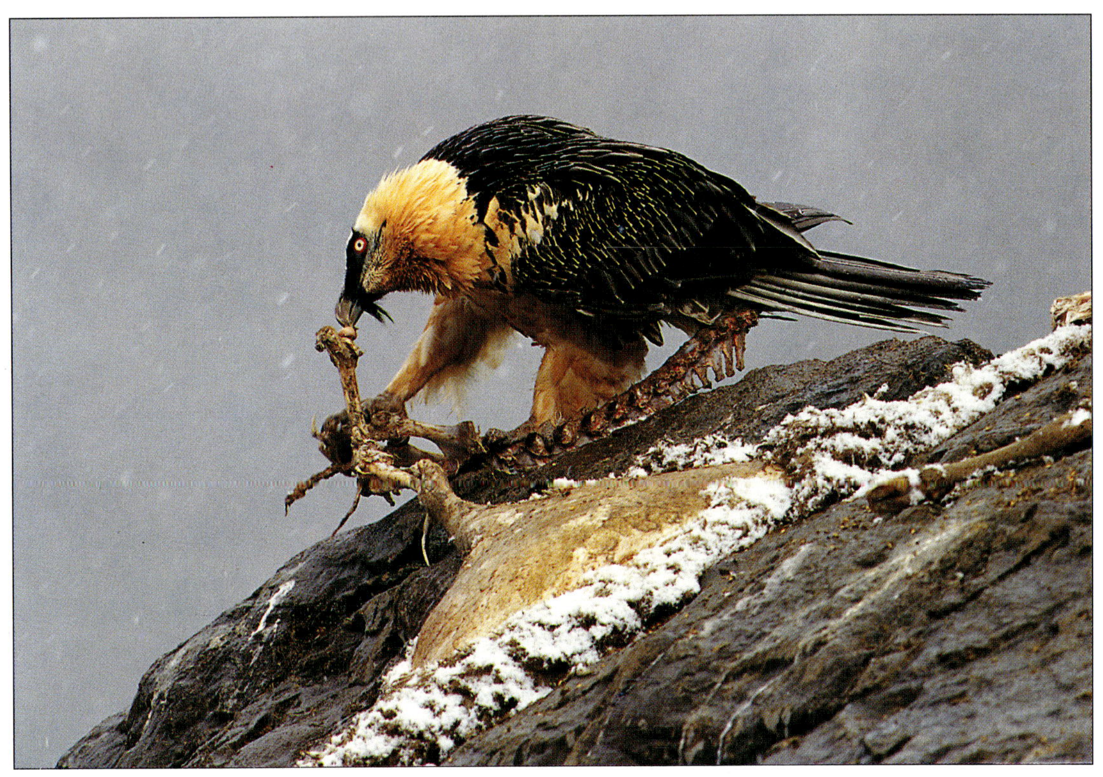

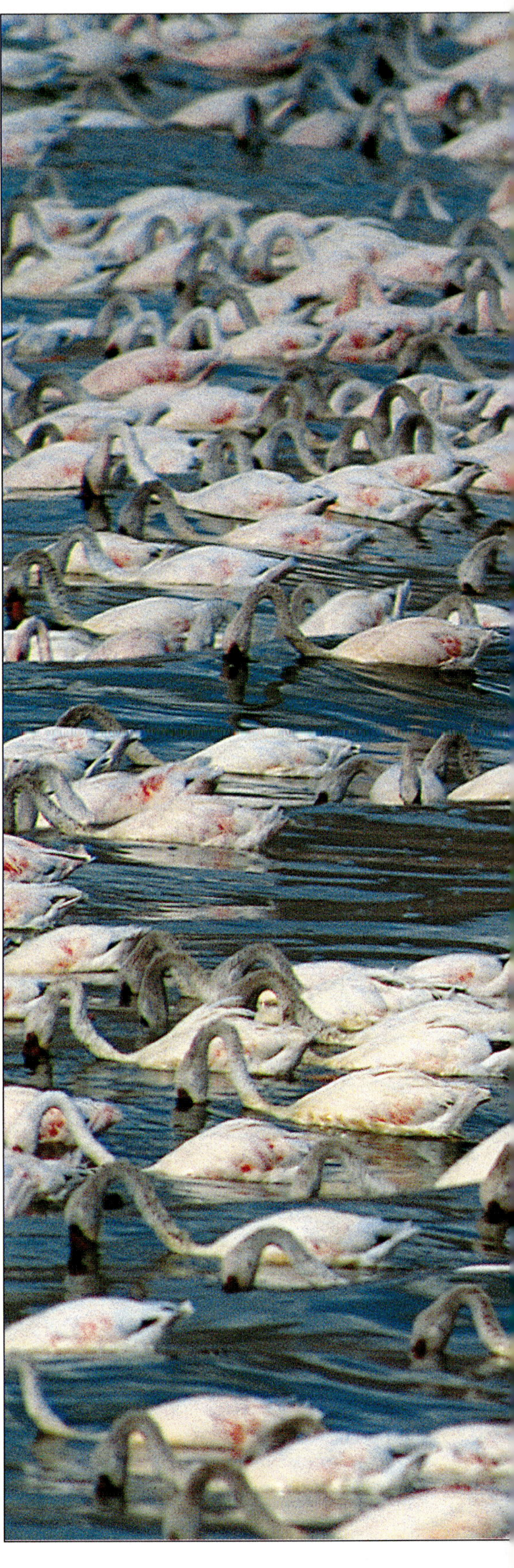

Francisco Márquez
Spain
RUNNER-UP

Lammergeier feeding

"The lammergeier is the most beautiful but most threatened species of vulture in Europe. It has the curious habit of feeding almost exclusively on bones. For many years I have been photographing them in the Pyrenees. On this occasion, a cold February day, I watched one extricating the bones from a sheep carcass which had been stripped previously by griffon vultures."

Nikon F4S with 500mm lens and x1.4 extender; tripod; Ektachrome Panther 100

Mike Hill
United Kingdom
SPECIALLY COMMENDED

Lesser flamingos feeding

"While on holiday in Kenya, I visited Lake Bogoria specially to photograph flamingos. Large concentrations along the shore, where they had gathered at a freshwater source, forced some of the birds out into deeper water to feed. Flamingos normally feed standing, filtering mud and water for algae through their beaks."

Nikon F4 with 600mm lens; bean bag; 1/125 sec at f8; Fujichrome Velvia

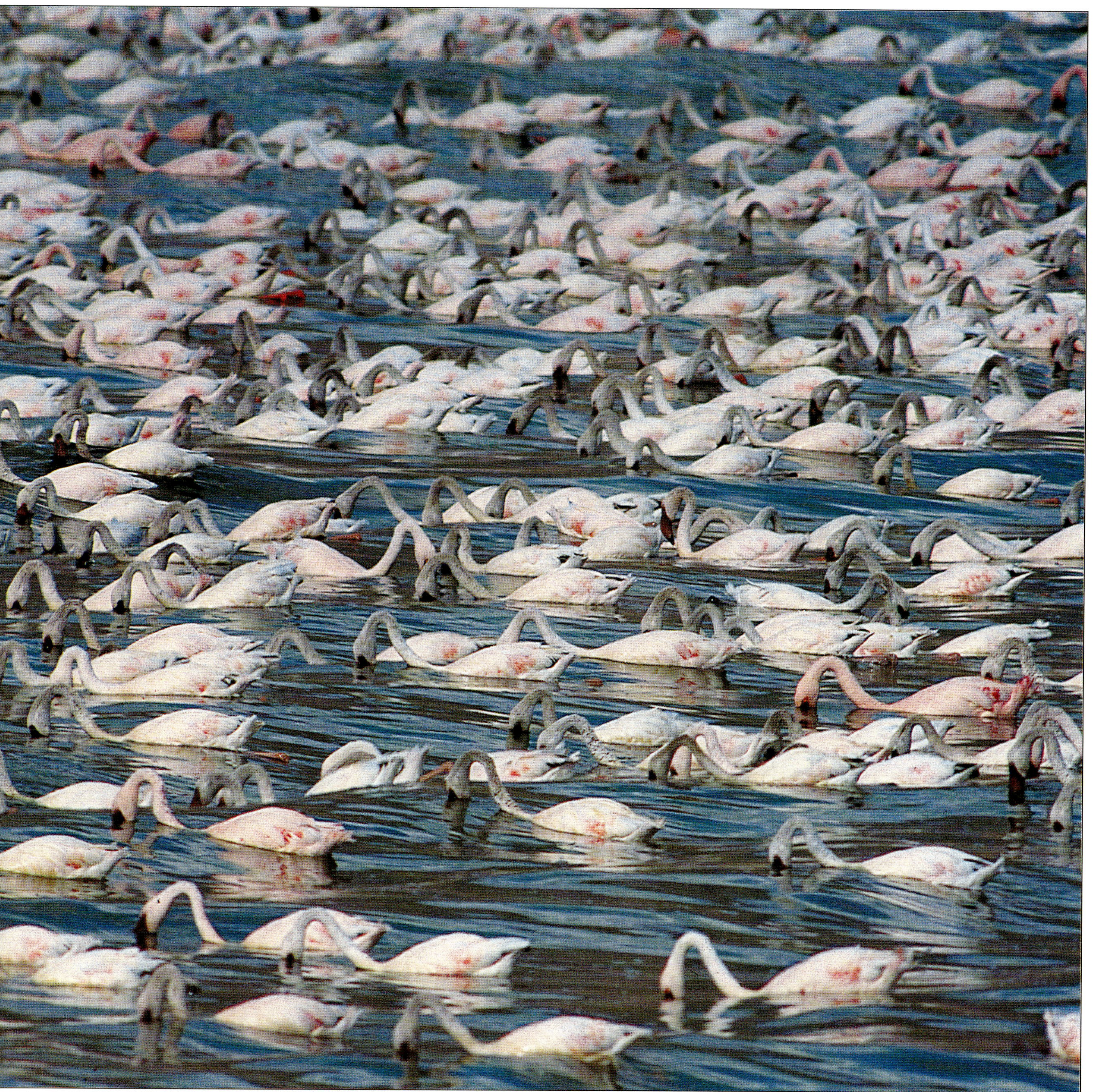

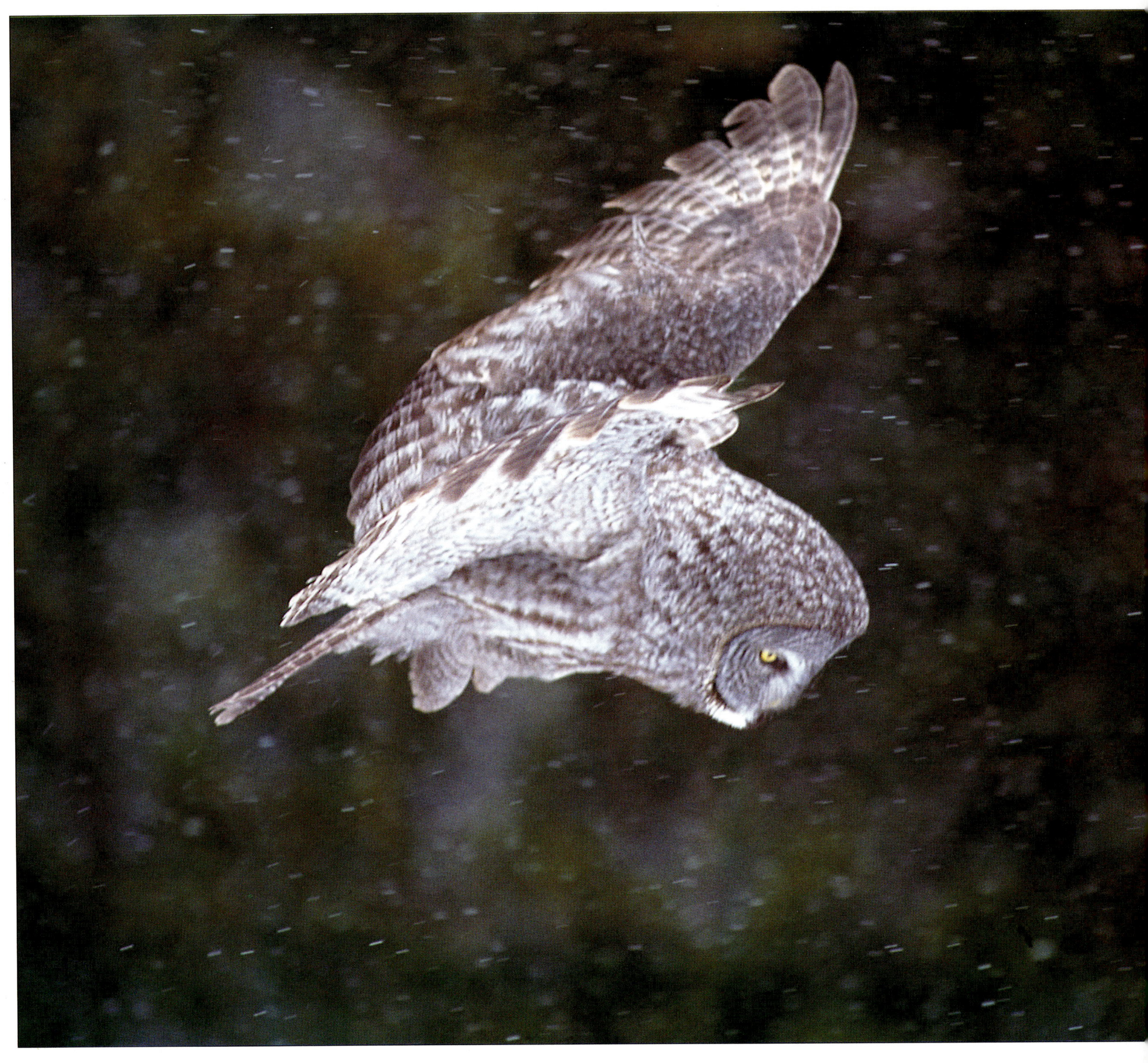

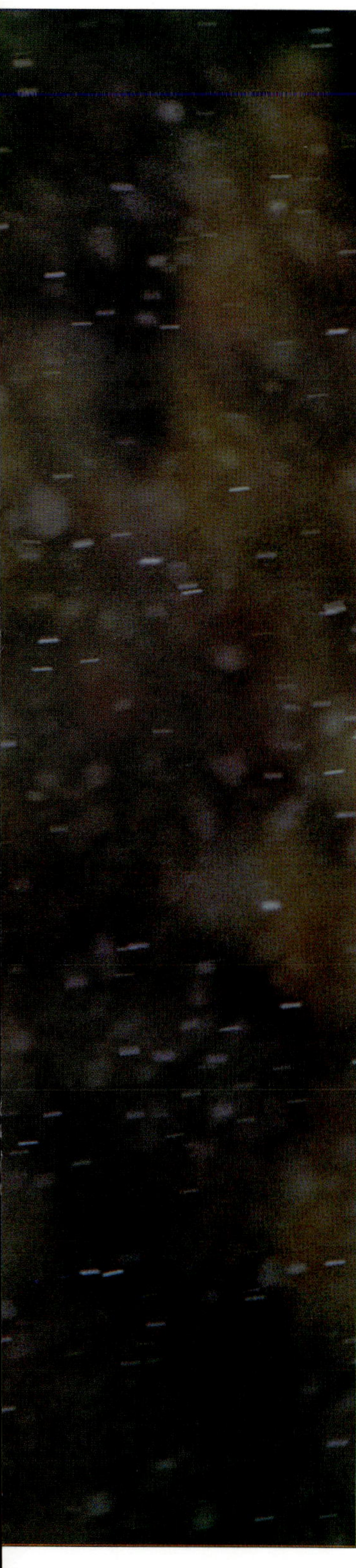

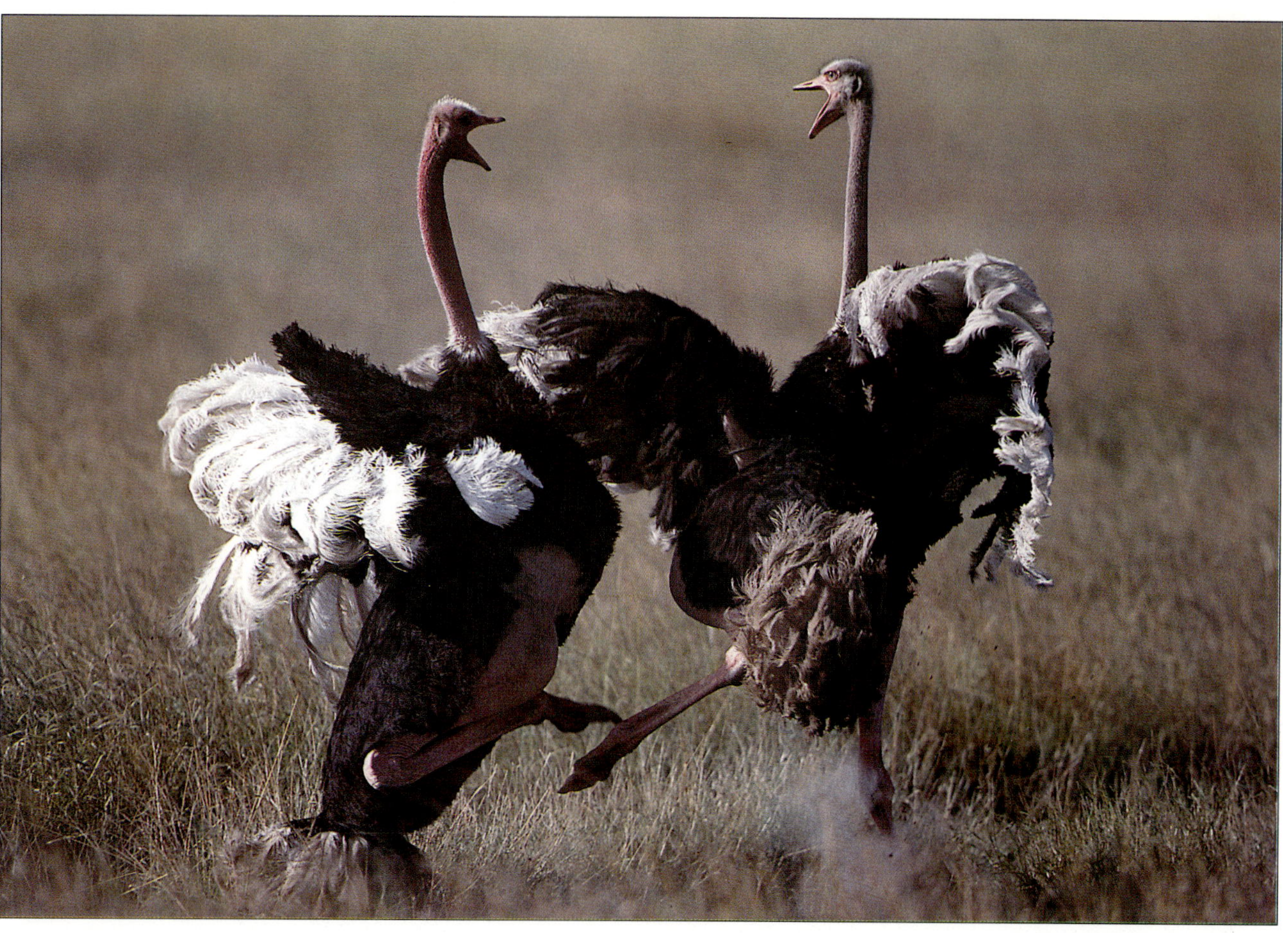

Rich Kirchner
United States of America
HIGHLY COMMENDED

Great grey owl hunting

"On a visit to Yellowstone National Park, I followed a pair of great grey owls for about five hours while they hunted for mice and other rodents. Here, one of the pair is hovering before diving to the ground after prey."

Nikon F4 with 500mm lens; tripod; 1/250sec at f4; Fujichrome Velvia rated at 80ASA

Anup Shah
United Kingdom
SPECIALLY COMMENDED

Ostriches fighting

"Two male and three female ostriches were peacefuly picking their way through the plain. Suddenly, the neck of one male turned from light pink to red. The other, apparently dominant, male noticed and moved in briskly. Face to face, feathers ruffled and wings waving, the two ostriches kicked out at each other. It was all over in no time; the dominant male had made his point and the subordinate ostrich knelt, face and neck on the ground. Soon the group moved on peacefully together."

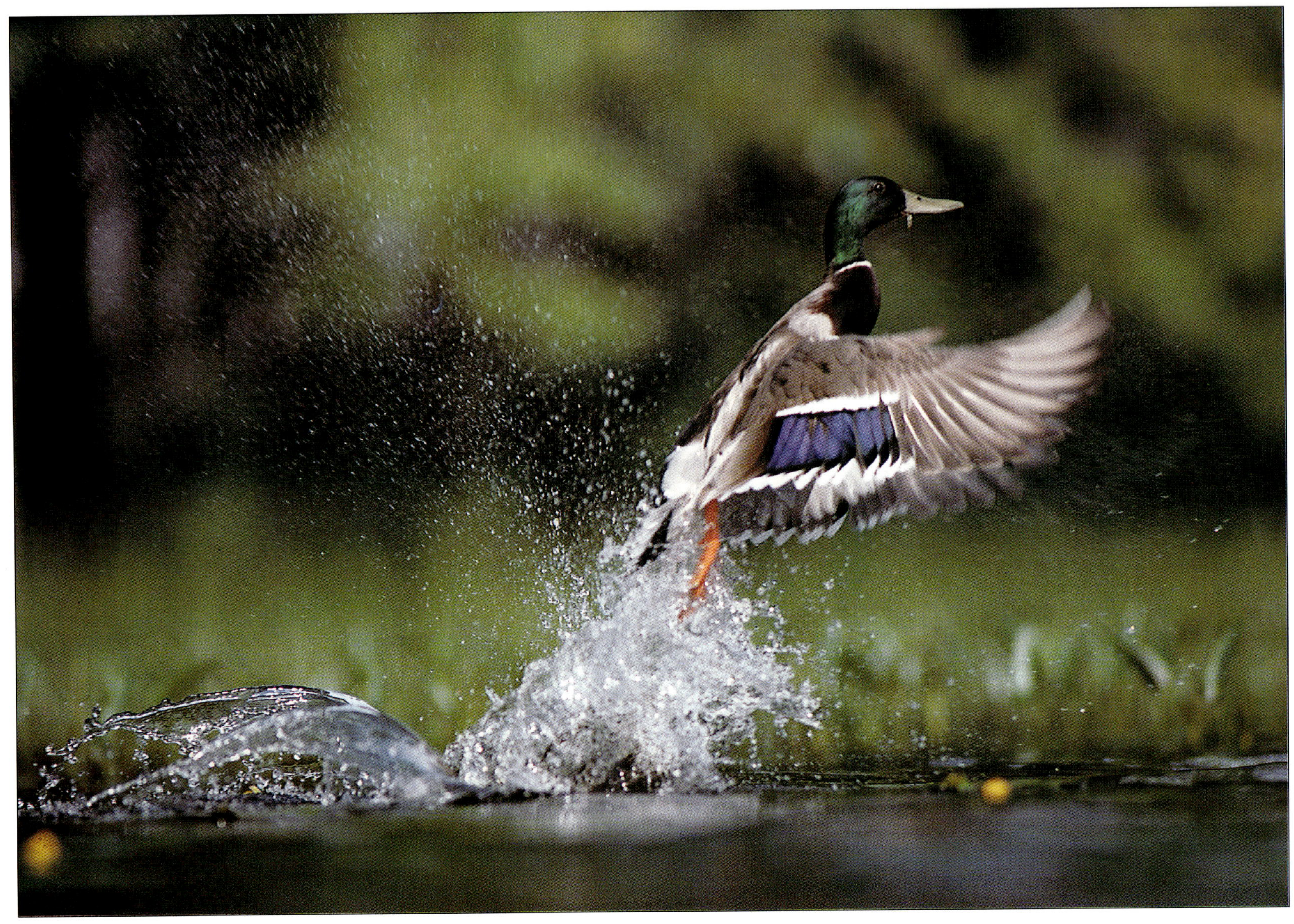

Scott Nielsen
United States of America
HIGHLY COMMENDED

Mallard duck taking flight

"To lift itself out of the water, the mallard, like other dabbling ducks, thrusts its webbed feet and slaps its wings against the water. Both these actions combine to produce a big splash – as can be seen in this picture."

Nikon F4 with 300mm lens; 1/2,000 sec at f2.8; Kodachrome 64

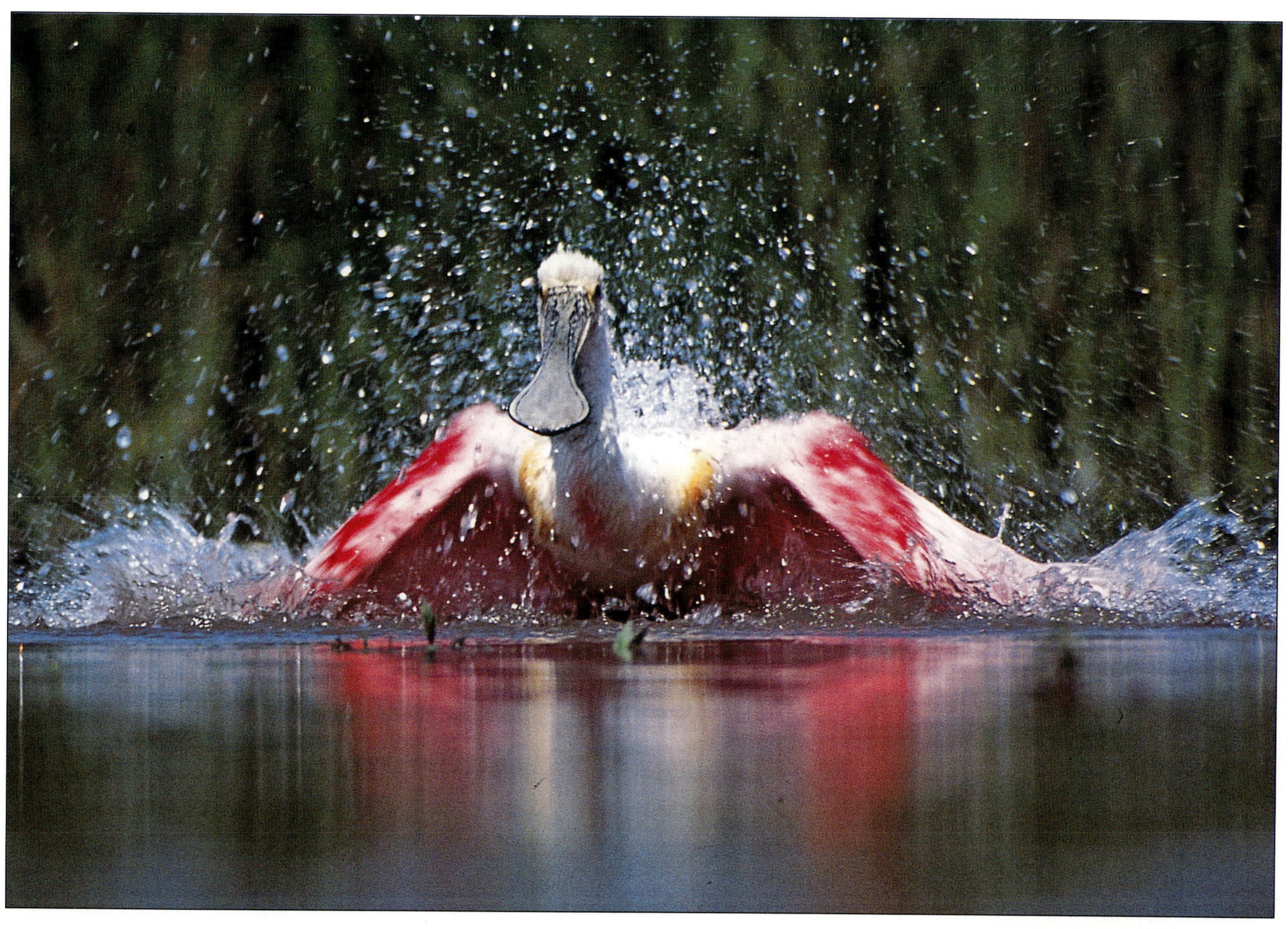

John Eastcott
& Yva Momatiuk
United States of America
HIGHLY COMMENDED

Roseate spoonbill bathing

"To take this picture we built a floating blind on a small Cajun fishing boat and placed it in a small tidal lagoon near a breeding colony of spoonbills. The temperature was in the high nineties, and we had to wait twenty-four hours before we were close enough to photograph a bathing spoonbill. The presence of a five-foot alligator made the birds somewhat skittish."

Canon EOS2 with 300mm lens and x2 and x1.4 extenders; Fujichrome Provia 100

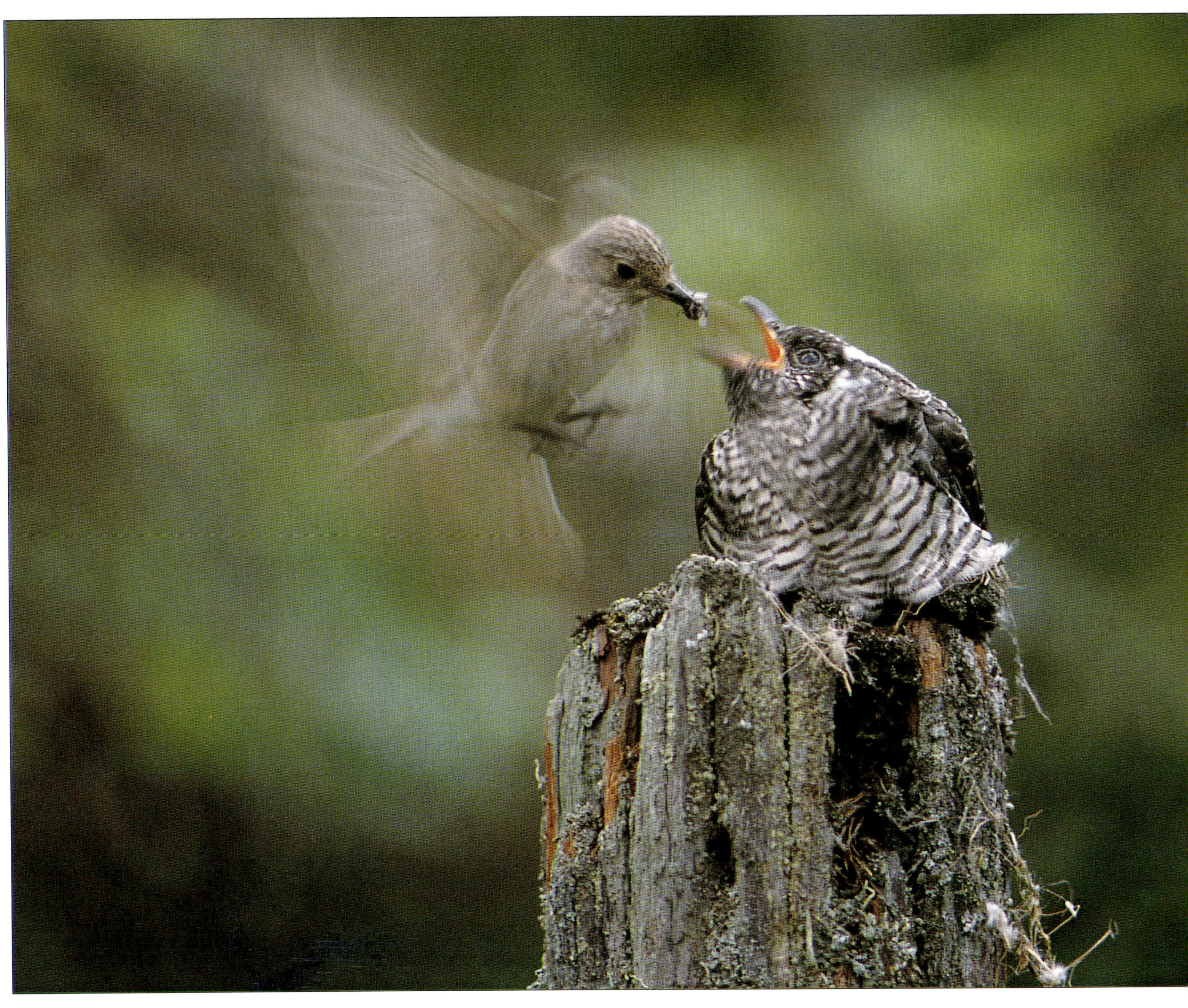

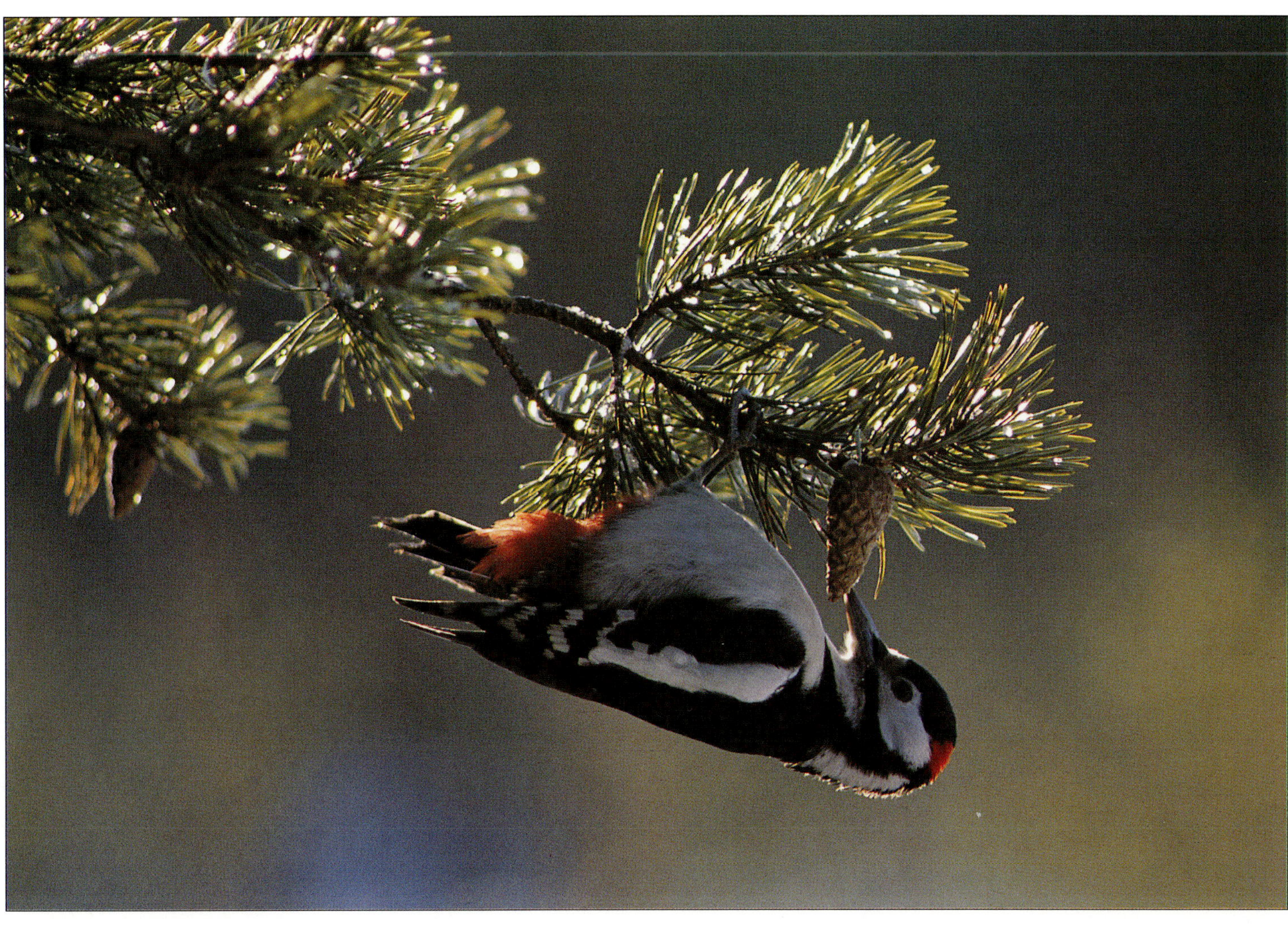

Risto Petäjämäki
Finland
HIGHLY COMMENDED

Flycatcher feeding cuckoo chick

"In June 1990, I built a hide to watch and photograph the development of a cuckoo chick. The cuckoo egg was laid in a flycatcher's nest. Shortly after it hatched, the chick ejected the flycatcher's eggs. It grew rapidly and was soon bigger than the flycatcher."

Canon AE with 400mm lens; tripod; Fujichrome 100

Risto Petäjämäki
Finland
HIGHLY COMMENDED

Great spotted woodpecker feeding

"I watched this woodpecker over several days. The bird frequently fed on pine cone seeds, returning several times to the same cone. I took the picture in March near Joutseno."

Canon AE with 400mm lens; tripod; Fujichrome 100

Klaus Sudbrack
Germany
HIGHLY COMMENDED

Long-tailed tit collecting feather

"One day, while walking in a wood, I noticed a long-tailed tit collecting feathers. Being an enthusiastic wildlife photographer, I always carry a camera. I had to wait almost three hours before I was lucky enough to get this photograph."

Canon EOS5 with 75-300mm lens; tripod; 1/350 sec at f6.7; Kodachrome Elite 100

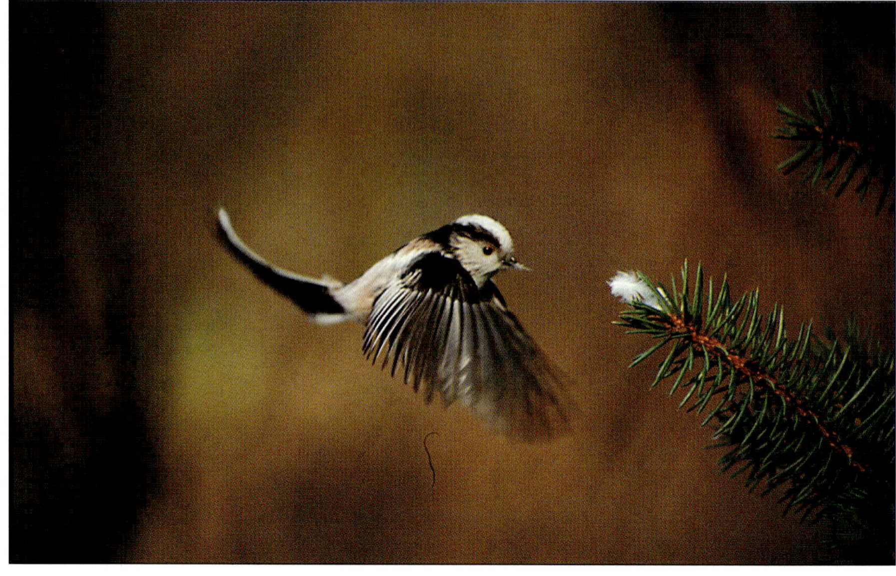

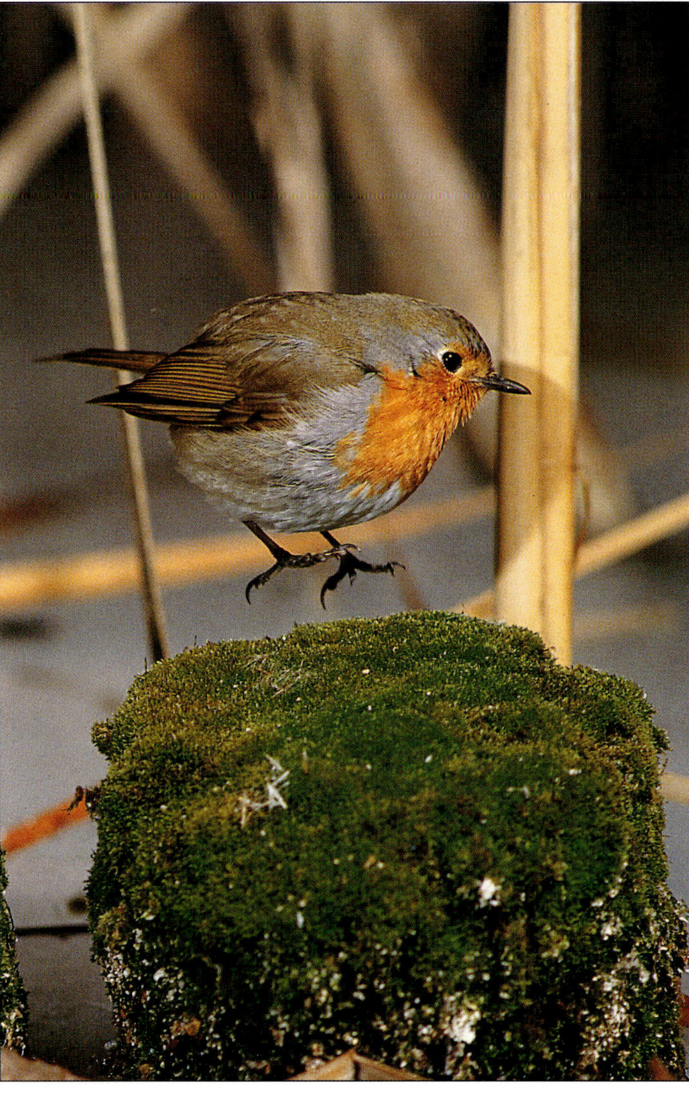

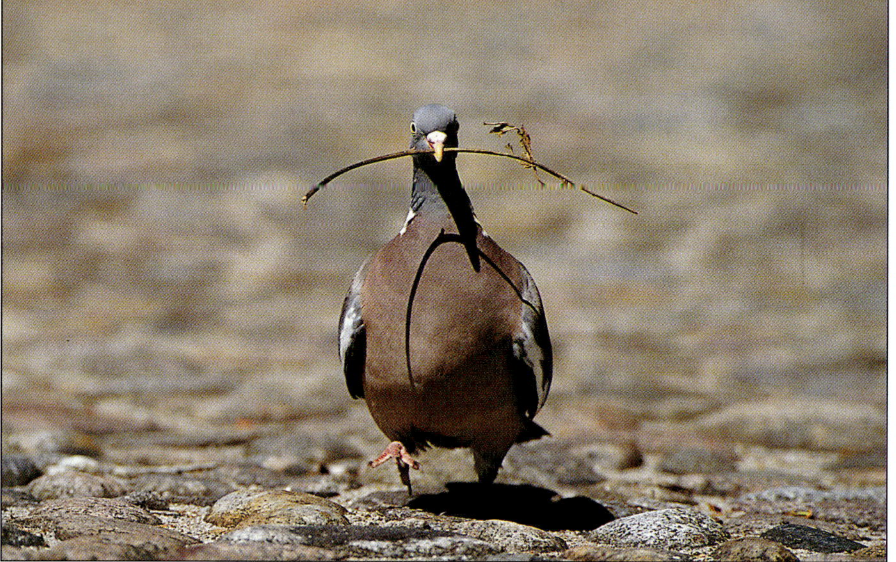

Ihász Zoltán
Hungary
HIGHLY COMMENDED

Robin hopping

"I photographed this robin for several days from a hide near the River Danube. It was several degrees below zero, and I put out food to attract the bird."

Asahi Pentax Z1 with 400mm lens; flash; tripod; 1/60 sec at f8; Fujichrome 100

Kent Larsson
Sweden
HIGHLY COMMENDED

Woodpigeon collecting nest material

"This woodpigeon was collecting material to make a nest in the only tree in a square in Tönder. Fortunately I had my camera in my car close by and was able to take lots of pictures."

Canon EOS1 with 300mm lens; monopod; 1/500 sec at f8; Fujichrome Professional 100

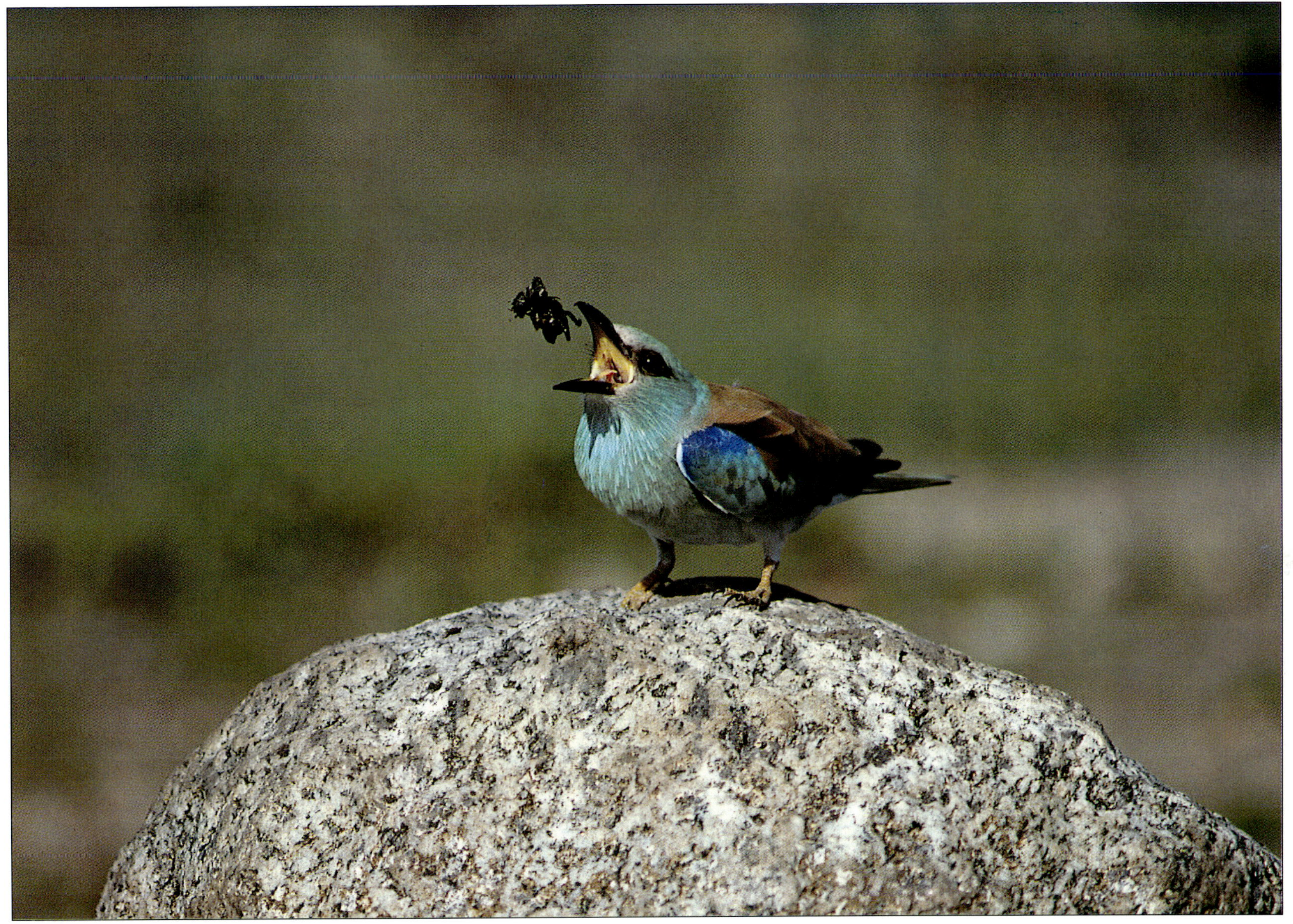

Mike Mockler
United Kingdom
HIGHLY COMMENDED

European roller

"I was leading a safari group in the Serengeti National Park, Tanzania, when I noticed a couple of European rollers. They seemed quite unconcerned about our vehicle so we moved closer. This roller caught a beetle and tossed it in the air a couple of times before swallowing it."

Nikon F4S with 600mm lens; bean bag; Kodachrome 64

Animal Behaviour

- MAMMALS -

Photographs entered in this category must show mammals actively doing something, and are judged for their interest as well as aesthetic appeal. The entries were particularly good this year, and the judges awarded five prizes.

Konrad Wothe
Germany
JOINT WINNER

Leopard at dusk

"I photographed this leopard in the Serengeti National Park, Tanzania, just after it had come down from the tree where it had been sleeping during the day. I wanted to capture a sense of movement. It was after sunset and quite dark at the time."

Canon EOS1 with 600mm lens; car mount; 1/15 sec at f4; Kodachrome 200

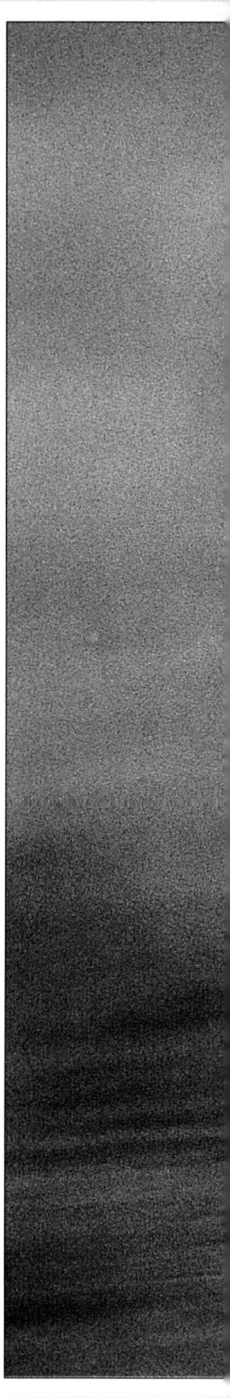

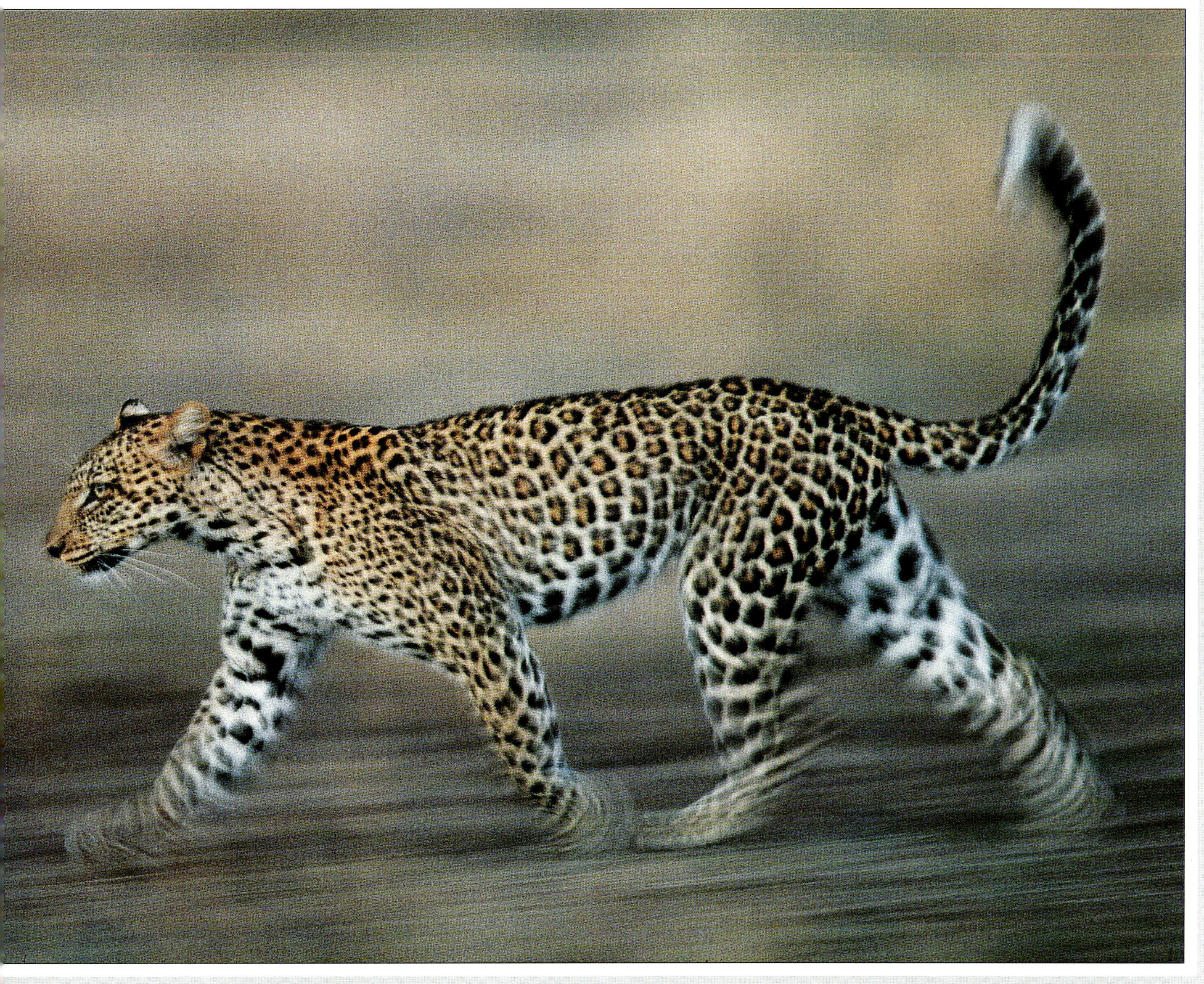

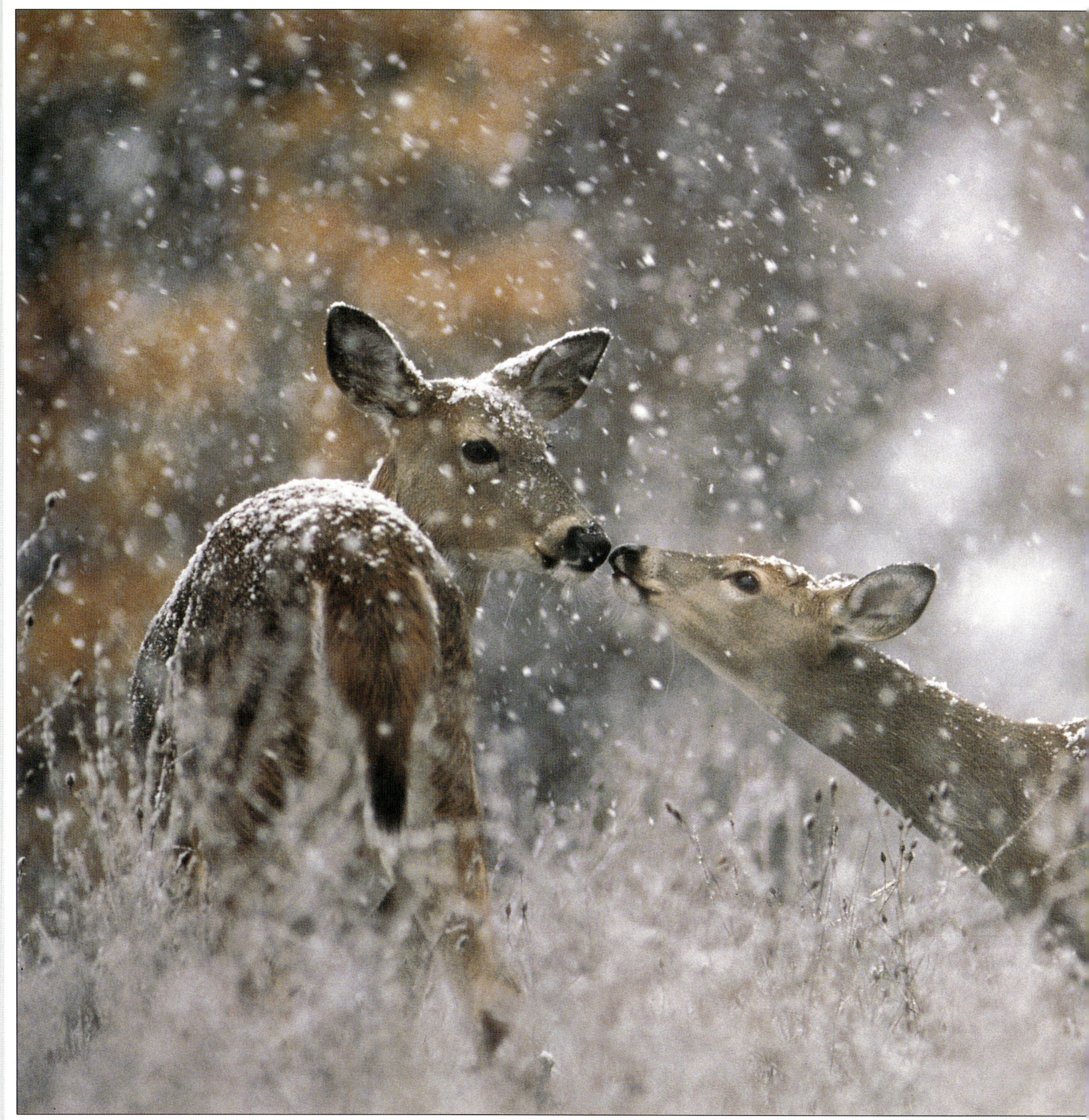

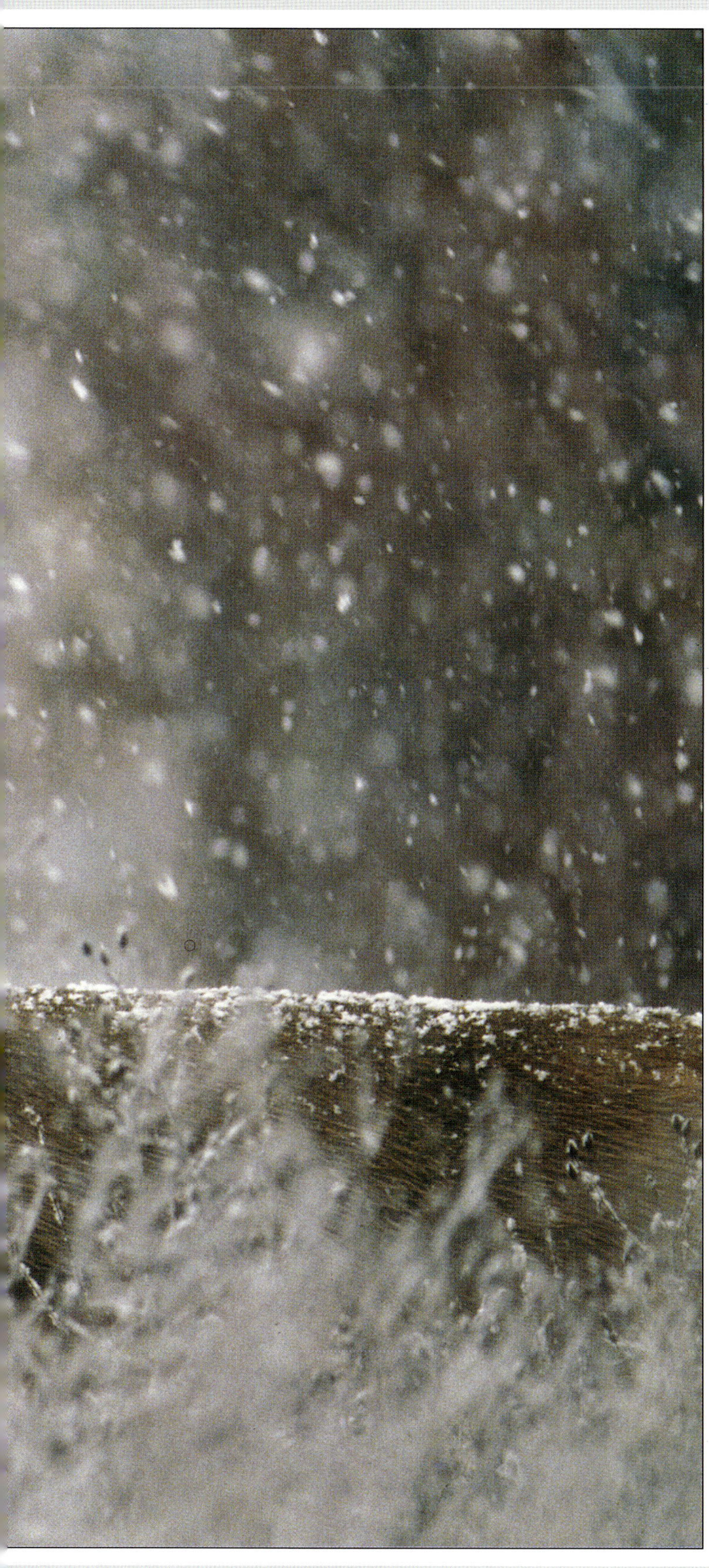

Carl R Sams II
United States of America
JOINT WINNER

White-tailed deer

"Since 1982, I have taken thousands of photos of a particular white-tailed deer family. This picture was taken in October and shows a fawn seeking reassurance from its mother, as it experiences snow for the first time. Just as I took this image I ran out of film, and having spent three hours in rain and sleet, my fingers were so cold I couldn't reload the camera."

Nikon F4 with 300mm lens; 1/250 sec at f2.8; Fujichrome 100 rated at 200

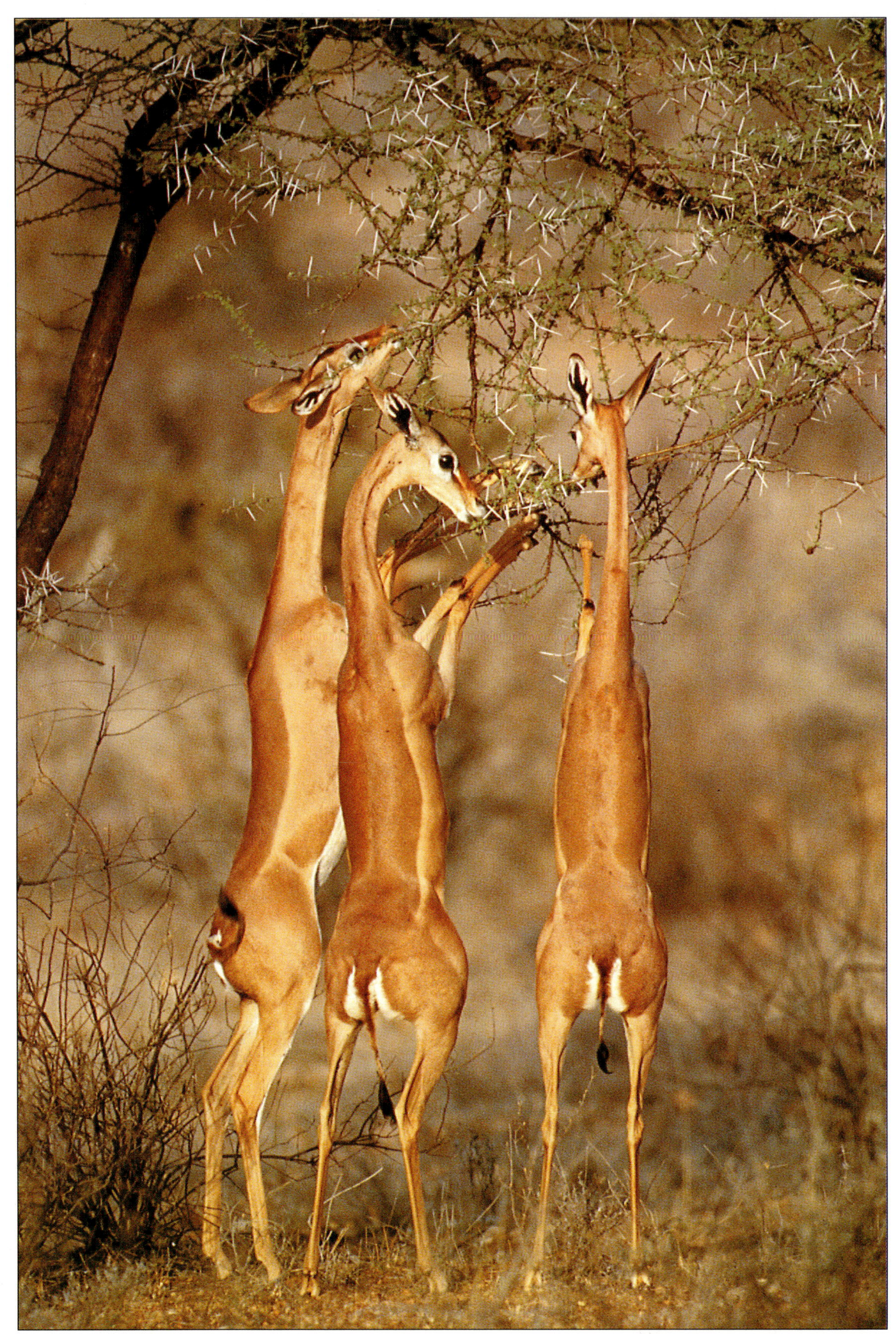

Renee Lynn
United States of America
HIGHLY COMMENDED

Gerenuk feeding

"Unlike any other antelope, gerenuk stand on their hind legs to feed. I couldn't resist the sight of these graceful creatures feeding together in beautiful morning light in the Samburu Reserve, Kenya."

Nikon F4 with 500mm lens; 1/500 sec at f4; Fujichrome 100

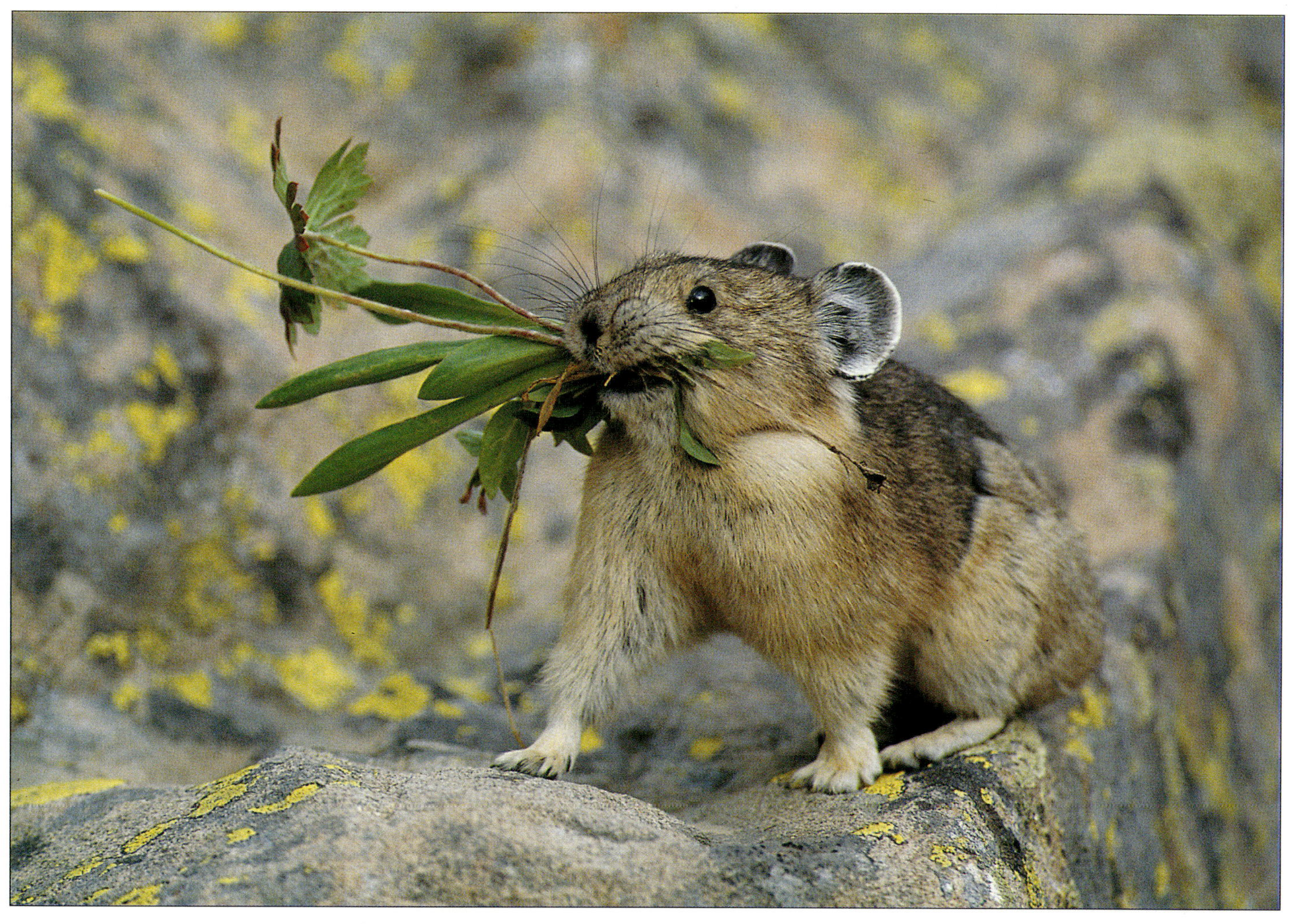

George D Lepp
United States of America
RUNNER-UP

Pika collecting food

"In summer, pika collect grasses and other plant material and store them in rocks next to their burrows to feed on in winter. This pika, in the Yankee Boy Basin near Ouray, Colorado, was busy at its task and ignored me ."

Canon EOS1 with 300mm lens and x2 extender; tripod; Fujichrome 100

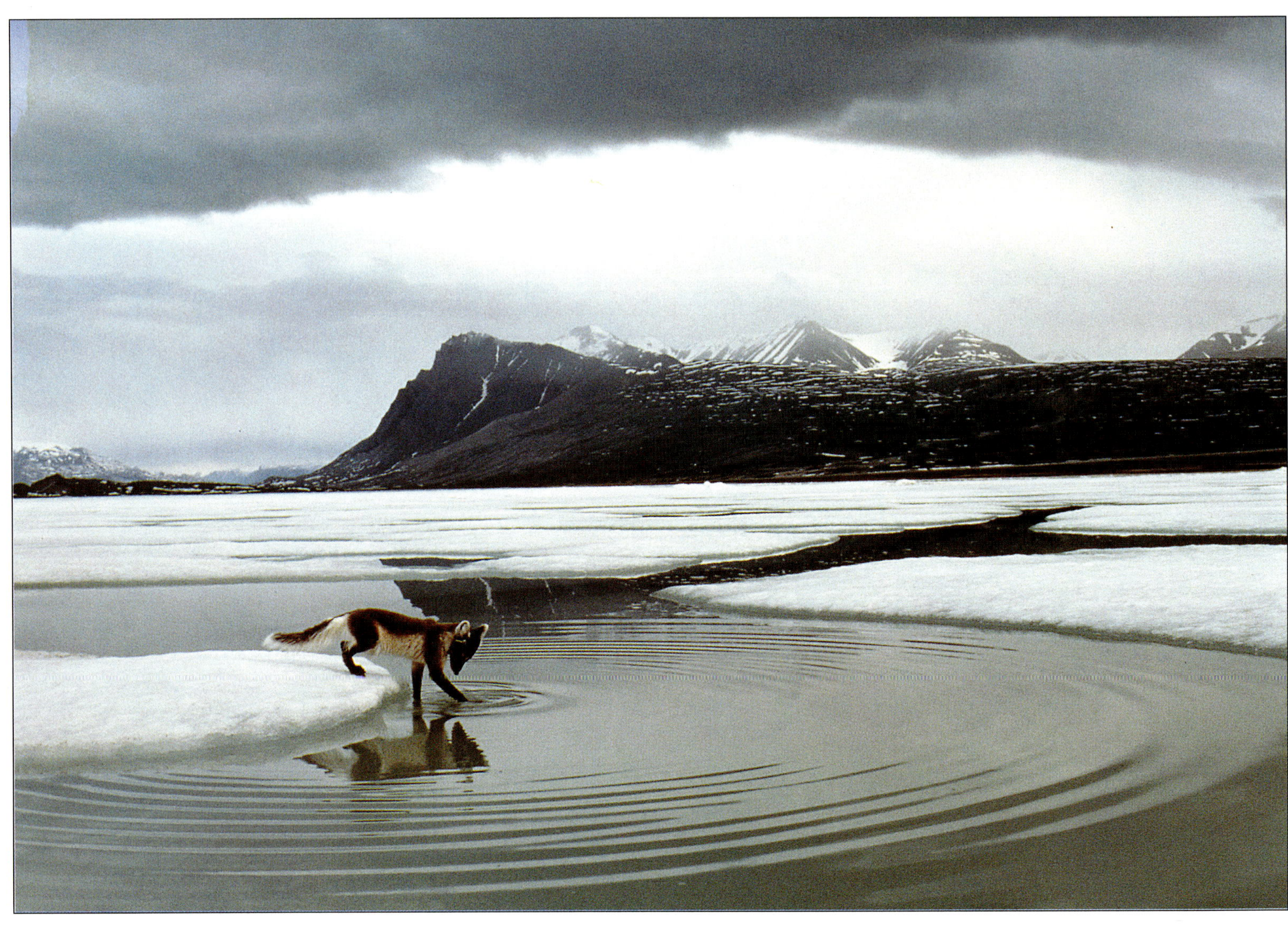

Jean-Louis Klein
& Marie-Luce Hubert
France
SPECIALLY COMMENDED

Arctic fox testing water

"Lemmings are an important food source for Arctic foxes, but in 1993 they were scarce, and the foxes were searching for arctic tern breeding colonies on the small islands along the coast of Greenland. As they searched, the foxes had to cross crevices and pools, which were getting larger as the ice melted. Here a fox dips his paw into a pool to see how deep it is."

Canon EOS1 with 80-200mm lens; 1/125sec at f4; Fujichrome 100

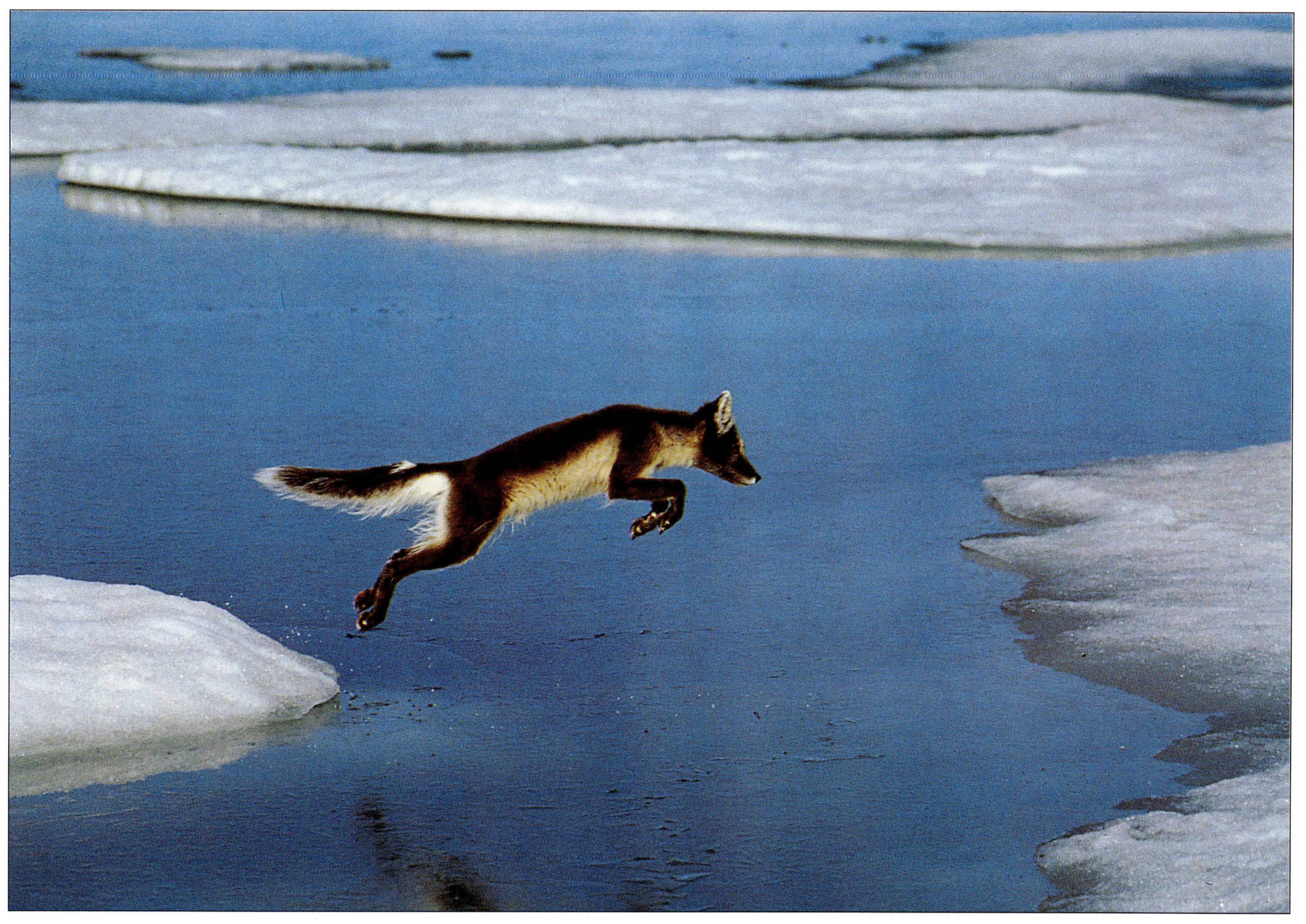

Jean-Louis Klein
& Marie-Luce Hubert
France
HIGHLY COMMENDED

Arctic fox jumping pool

"We followed Arctic foxes as they hunted for the nest sites of Arctic terns on the small islands along the coast. The pack ice was melting and the foxes had to jump over crevices and small pools of water as they searched."

Canon EOS1 with 80-200mm lens; 1/250 sec at f5.6; Fujichrome 100

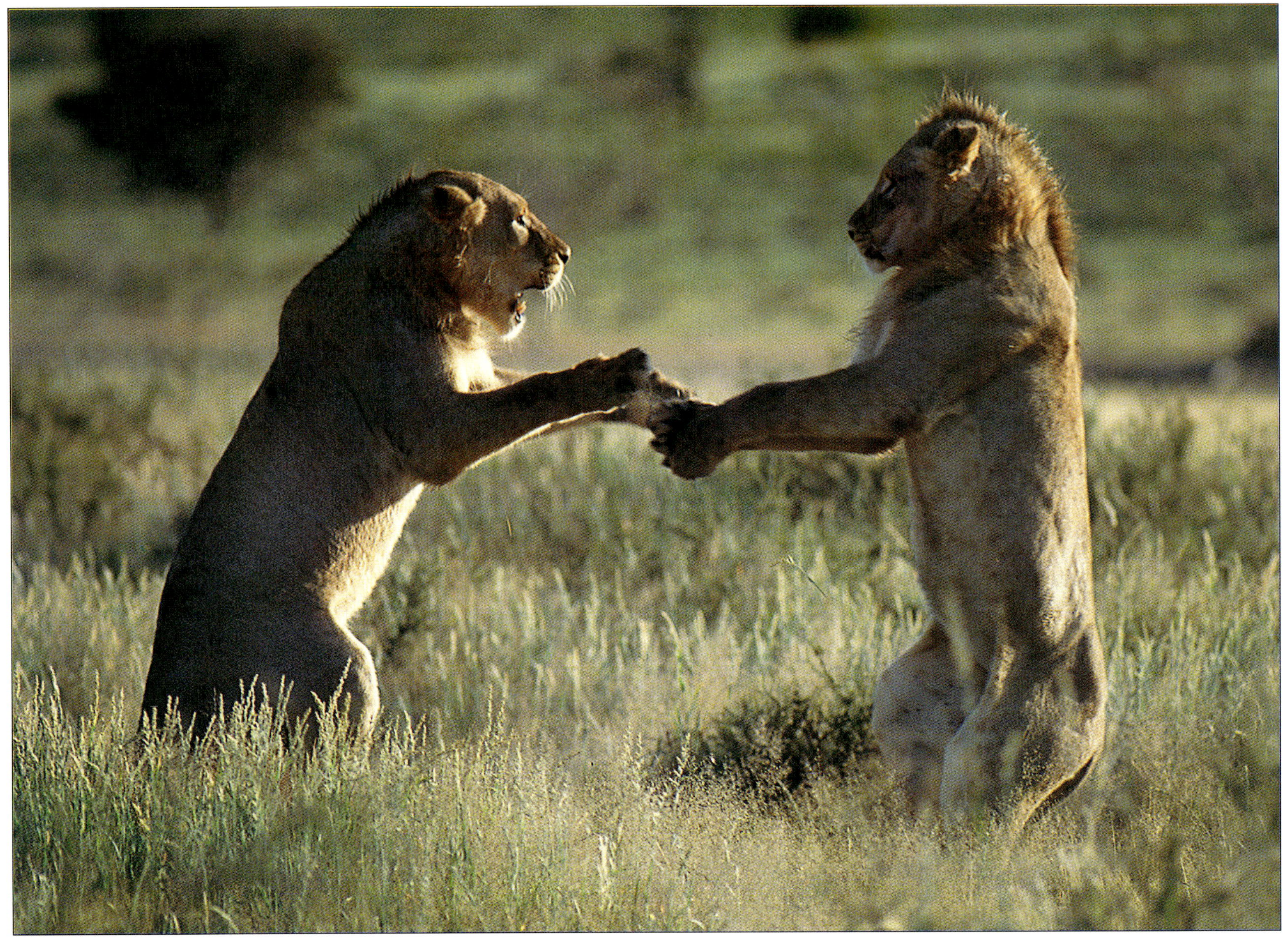

Tim Jackson
United Kingdom
HIGHLY COMMENDED

Lions play-fighting

"These two boisterous young lions featured in last year's exhibition, trying to kill porcupines. Since then, their manes have grown longer and they have firmly established themselves in the Kalahari as a territorial pair."

Nikon F801S with 300mm lens; bean bag; 1/500 sec at f4; Fujichrome

Erwin & Peggy Bauer
United States of America
SPECIALLY COMMENDED

Brown bears

"Despite appearances, these bears are courting not fighting. When they first met, they circled and pranced, and eventually the pawing-pushing dance began. It may have lasted as long as an hour."

Canon EOS1 with 600mm lens ; tripod; Kodachrome 200

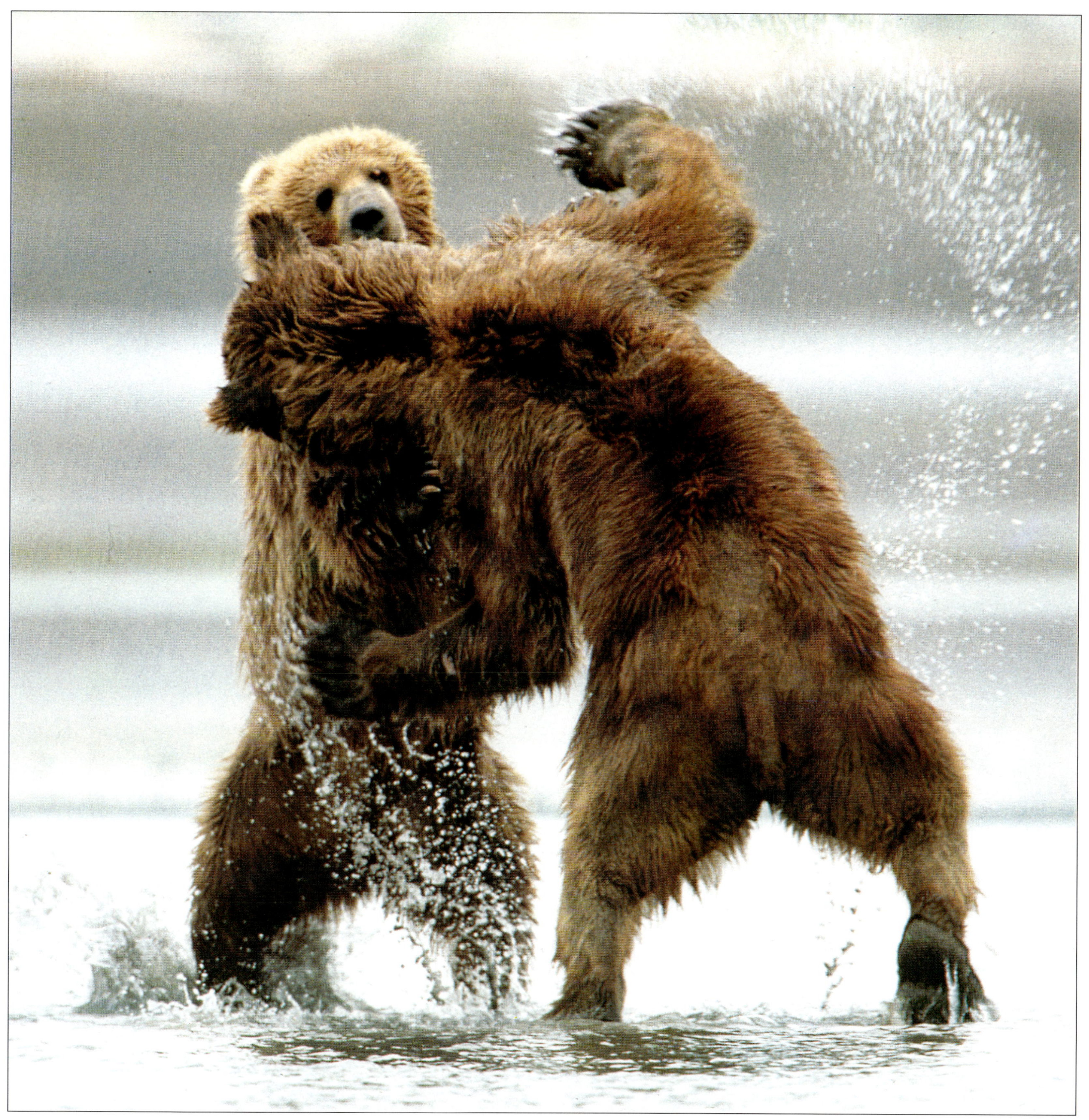

Jean-Louis Klein & Marie-Luce Hubert
France
HIGHLY COMMENDED

Arctic fox cubs playing

"During our trip to Greenland, we followed an Arctic fox and her two surviving cubs. Here they are playing close to their den. The mother was so hungry that one day she tore into our tent in her search for food, and we were forced to move into an old trapper's hut. A few hours later a polar bear appeared in the camp and destroyed food containers and two storage tents. Thanks to the fox, we were not in our tent!"

Canon EOS1 with 500mm lens; tripod; 1/125 sec at f5.6; Fujichrome Velvia

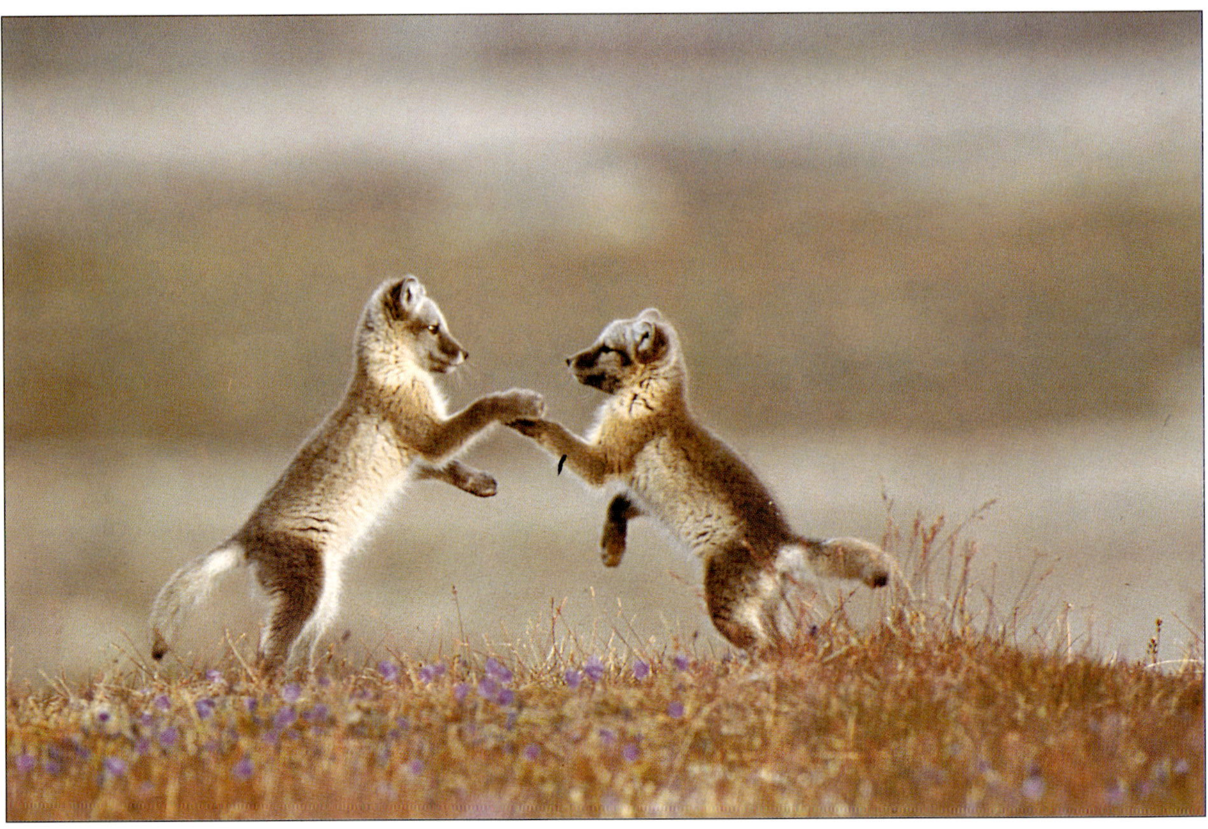

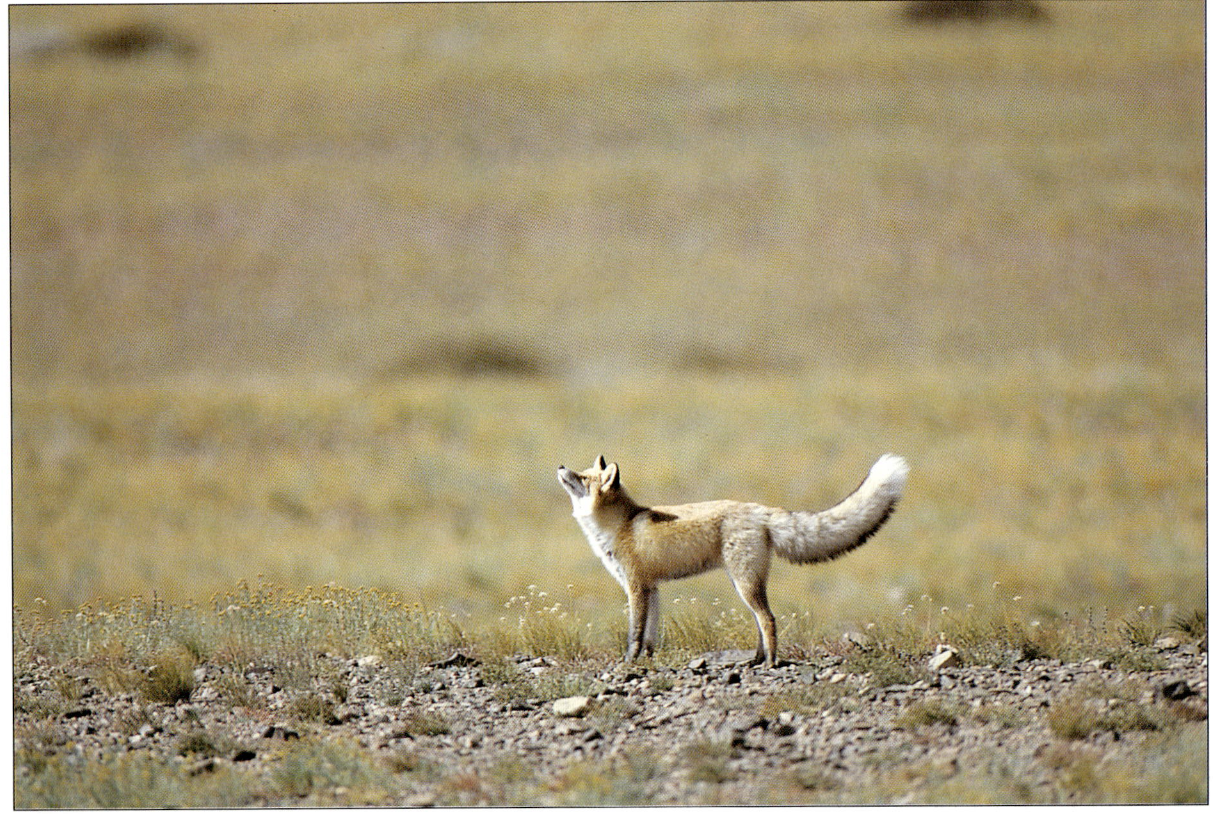

Gertrud & Helmut Denzau
Germany
HIGHLY COMMENDED

Red fox sniffing the air

"On the long drive between Ulan Batar and the Gobi Desert, we kept our camera at the ready for any unforeseen wildlife. The steppe is full of rodents and the animals that live off them. Eventually, we came across this fox and watched it hunt mice and grasshoppers. Most of the time its head was down, but at this moment, he raised it for a few seconds to sniff the air - or perhaps he was watching raptors in the sky."

Nikon F4 with 600mm lens; 1/500 sec at f4; Fujichrome 100

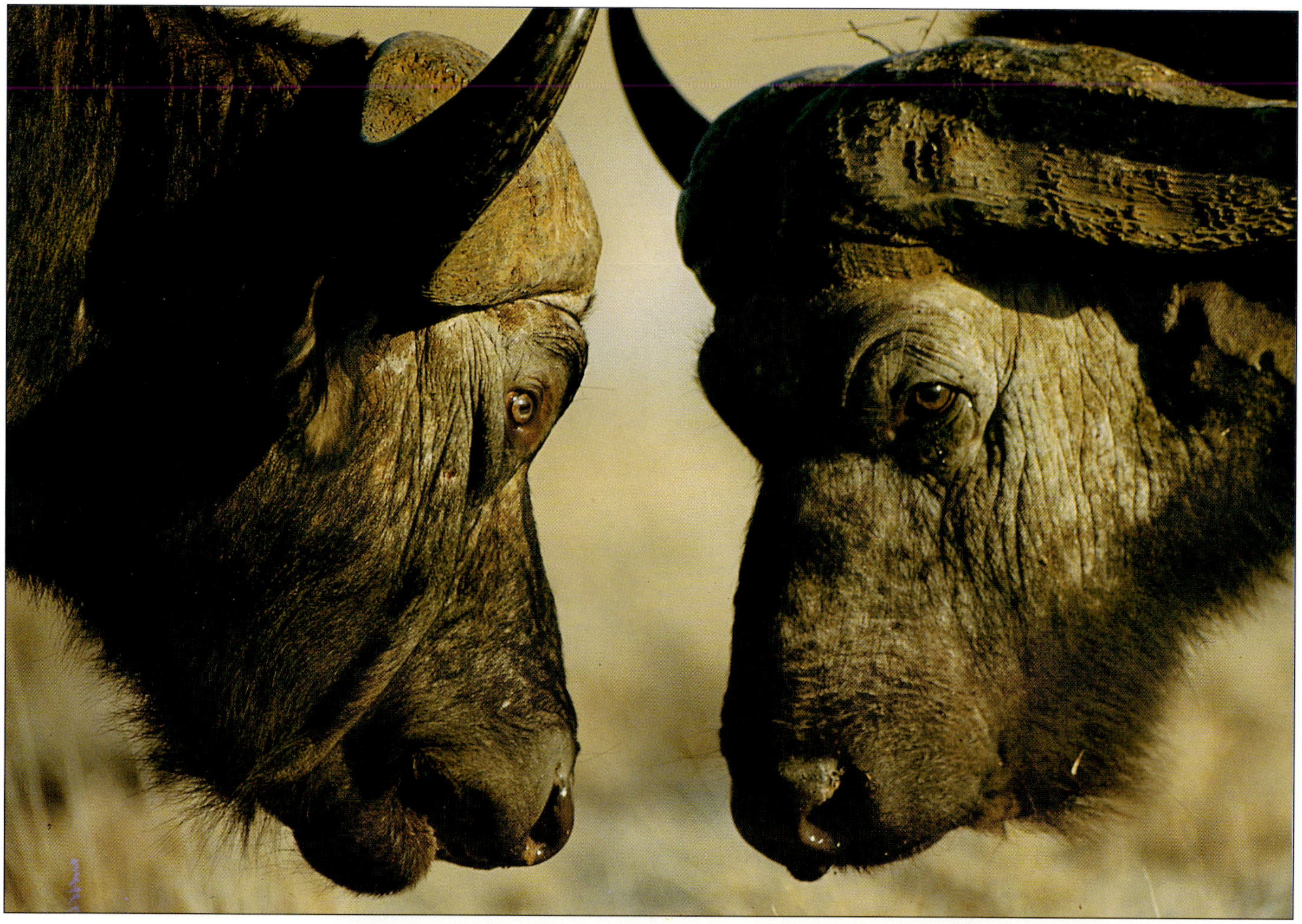

Karl Ammann
Switzerland
HIGHLY COMMENDED

Cape buffalo

"Recently, a herd of Cape buffalo has been returned to Samburu National Park in Kenya. These two bulls were out on the open short grass plain, tussling at regular intervals. They seemed to be playing rather than fighting. I used a long lens to get close into the action without disturbing them. Early morning sun reflected highlights in their eyes."

Nikon 8008S with 800mm lens; 1/250 sec at f5.6; Kodachrome 200

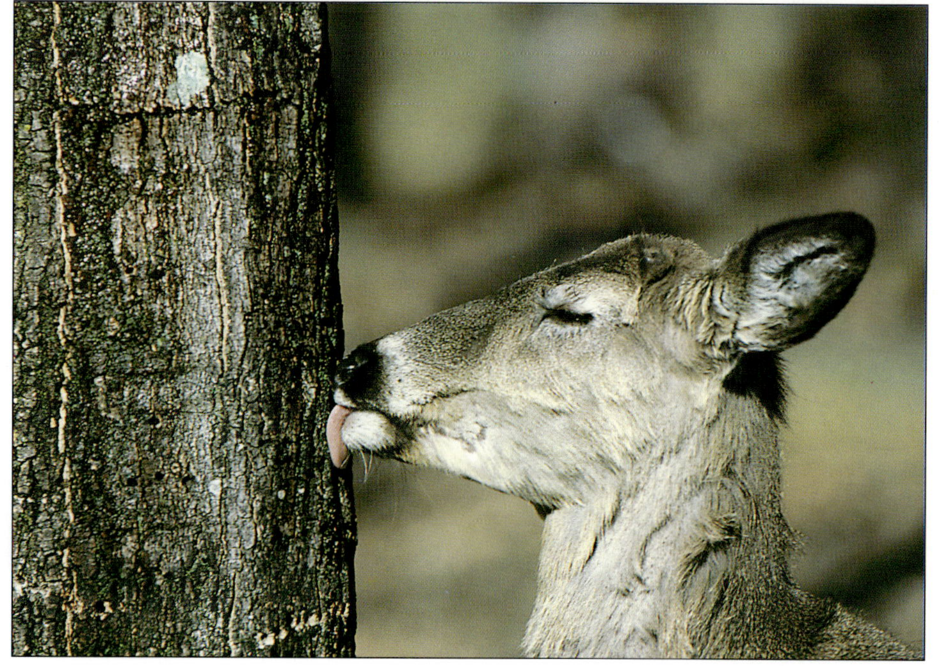

Daniel J Cox
United States of America
HIGHLY COMMENDED

White-tailed deer licking sap

"I photographed this deer, as it licked sap from a sugar maple tree, in the hardwoods of northern Minnesota. I had never seen this behaviour before."

Nikon F3 with 300mm lens; Kodachrome 64

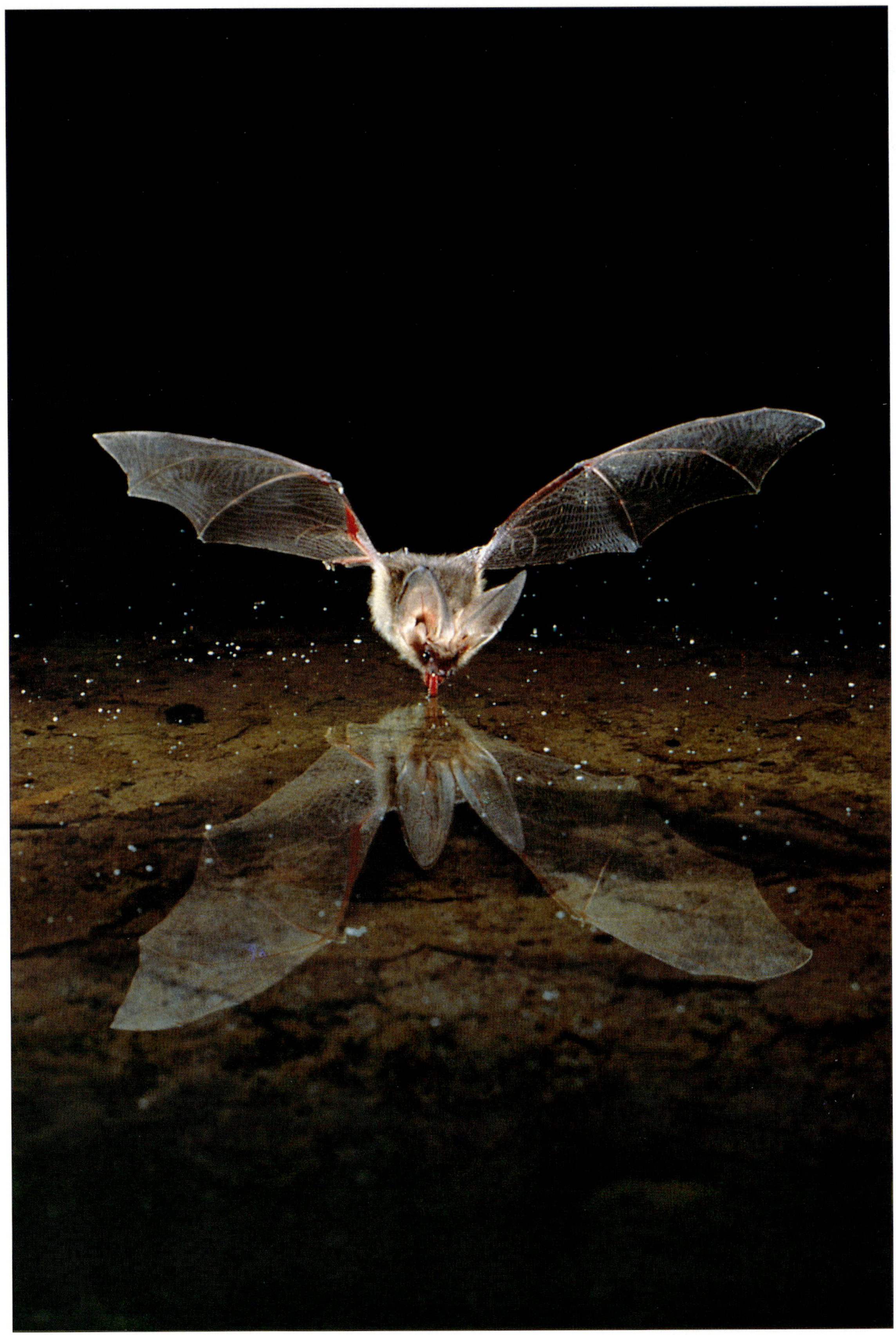

Claudio Calvani
Italy
HIGHLY COMMENDED

Long-eared bat drinking

"I am very interested in bats and, after a month's research in the Orecchiella Park, Tuscany, I found a place where long-eared bats came to drink."

Hasselblad 553; flash; f16; Fujichrome Velvia

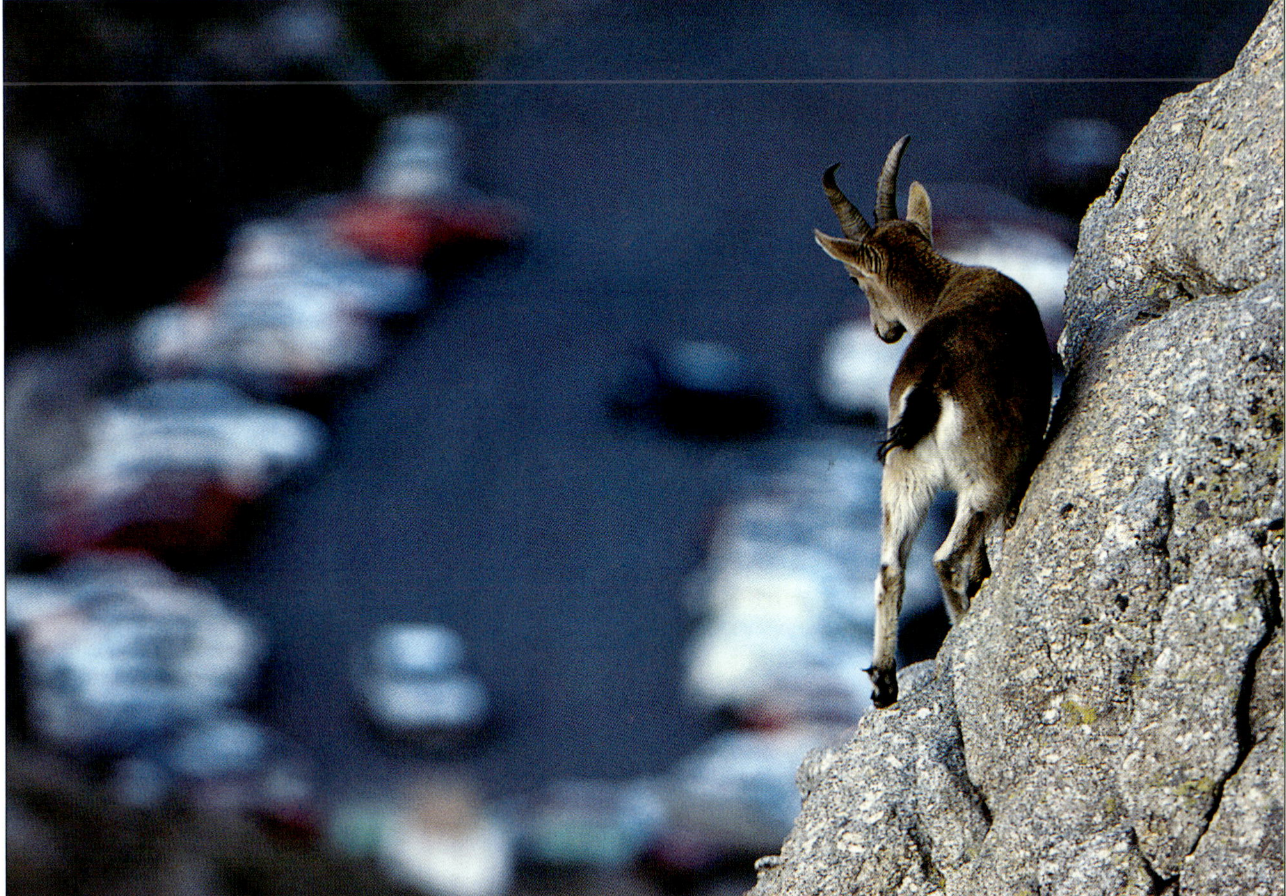

Roberto Travesi
Spain
HIGHLY COMMENDED

Mountain goat

"The wild goat Capra pyrenaira hispanica is an extraordinary climber, able to negotiate very steep cliffs. This can make the photograper's work difficult and, in bad weather conditions, dangerous. I took this picture in the Sierra Gredos mountains."

Canon T90 with 500mm lens and x1.4 extender; tripod; 1/60sec; Kodachrome 64

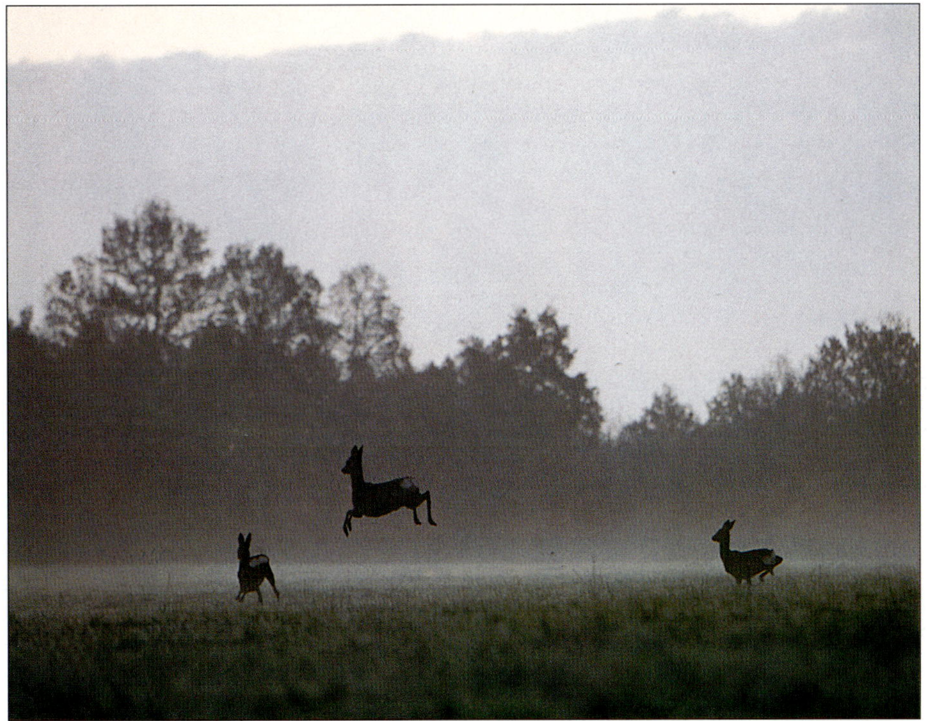

Pascal Bourguignon
France
HIGHLY COMMENDED

Roe deer running

"I took this picture very early one November morning in Haute-Marne. When the roe deer noticed me they started to run across the meadow. I took several shots and in each one, one of the deer was off the ground. I like to take pictures of animals in their habitat, with the animal occupying only a small part of the frame."

Canon EOS1 with 80-200 mm lens; 1/750 sec at f3.5; Kodachrome 200

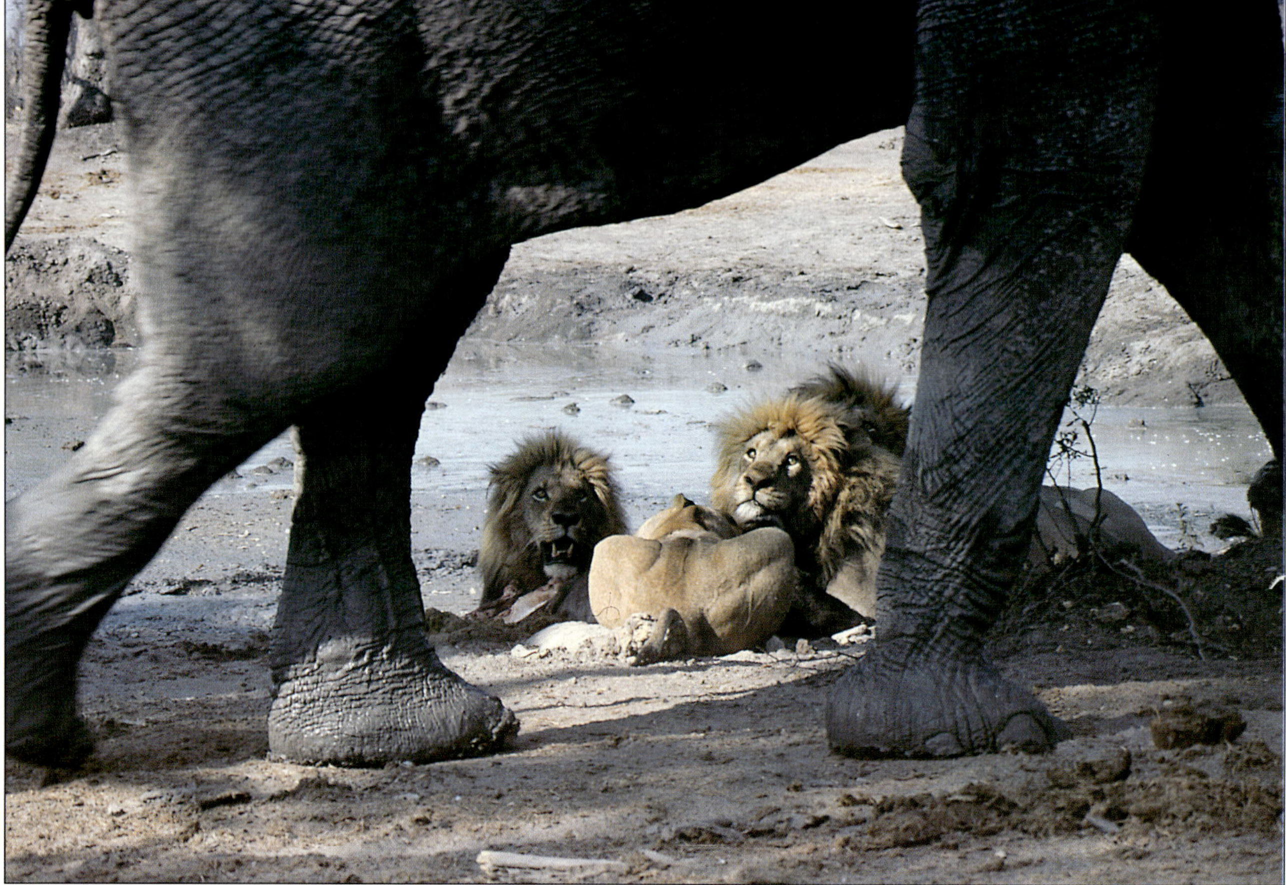

Bruce Cantle
Zimbabwe
HIGHLY COMMENDED

Lions and elephant

"It was the dry season at the time and this was the only waterhole in the Savuy area of the Chobe National Park, Botswana. These lions had killed a wildebeest and when the elephant came to drink, they were trying to keep it away from their kill. Usually elephants will chase lions if they are close."

Olympus OM10 with 120-600mm lens; 1/125 sec at f5.6; Kodachrome 64

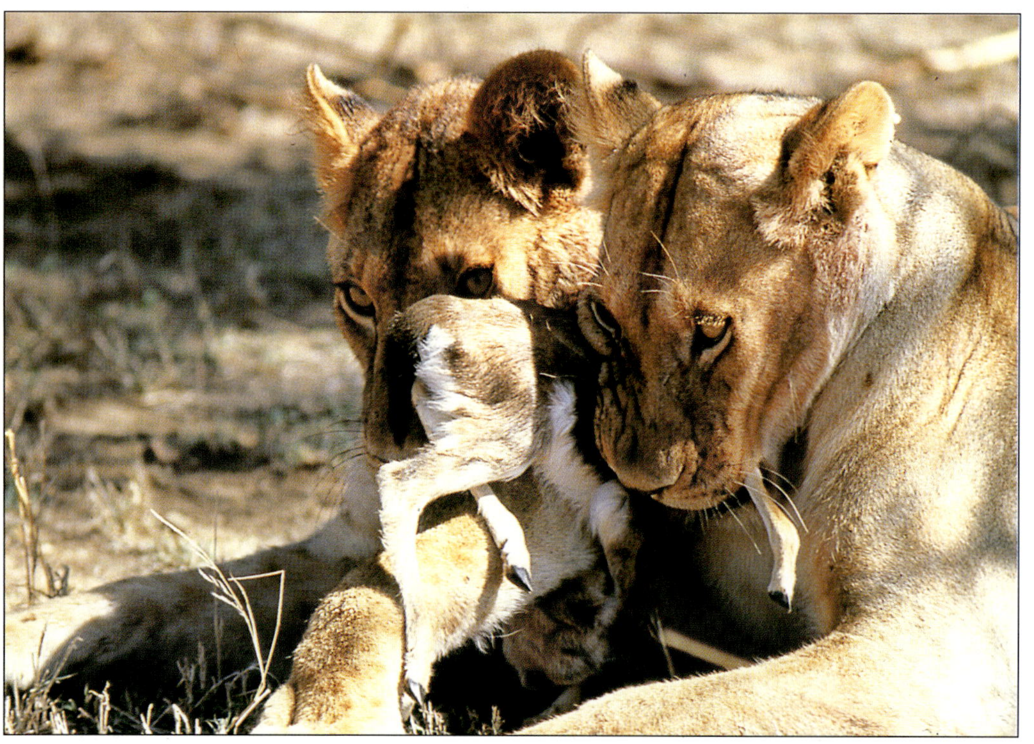

Tony Ord
United Kingdom
HIGHLY COMMENDED

Young lions with gazelle

"These two lions, a male and a female, were stalking a giraffe when a young Thomson's gazelle, separated from its mother, strayed nearby. At once, the two lions ran towards it and both took hold of it in their mouths. Neither moved for about 20 minutes. Finally, the female took it away and, without further resistance, ate it."

Nikon 801 with 300mm lens; car-mount tripod; Fujichrome 100

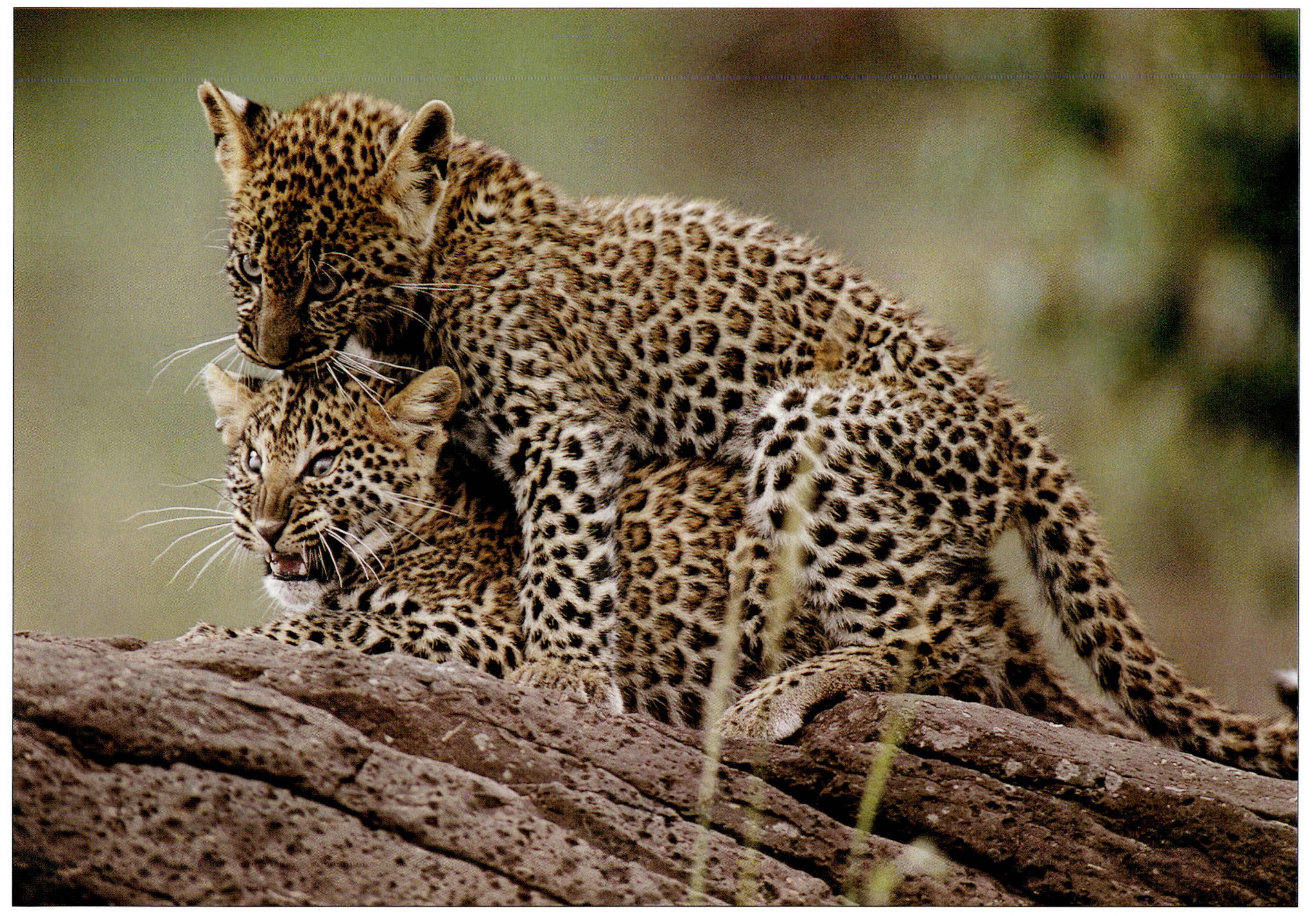

Fritz Pölking
Germany
HIGHLY COMMENDED

Leopard cubs playing

"These cubs are ones I've been following since their birth in November 1993. I spend two to three weeks at a time in the Maasai Mara following them and then return home for a few weeks before flying back to Kenya. In all, I must have taken some 30,000 slides of this leopard family."

Nikon F4 with 600mm lens; car-mount tripod; 1/250 sec at f4; Kodachrome 200

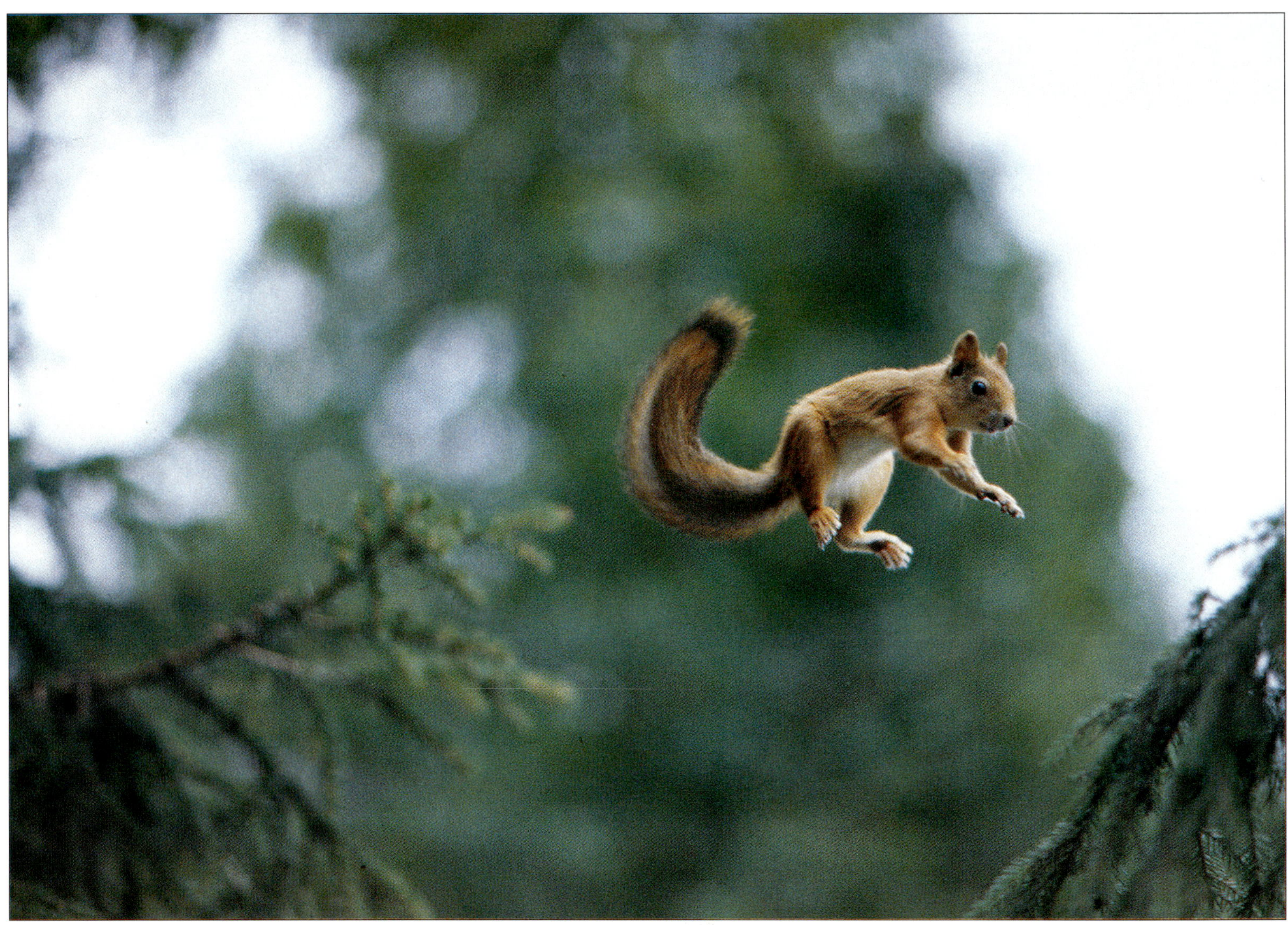

Hannu Hautala

Finland

HIGHLY COMMENDED

Squirrel

"I spent almost a month one summer in Kuusamo trying to get a good picture of a squirrel jumping - this is one of 800 attempts. It was difficult to get the fast-moving squirrel in focus because of the very narrow depth of field that results from using a long lens and fast shutter speed."

Canon EOS5 with 85mm lens; tripod; hide; 1/2,000 sec at auto; Fujichrome 400

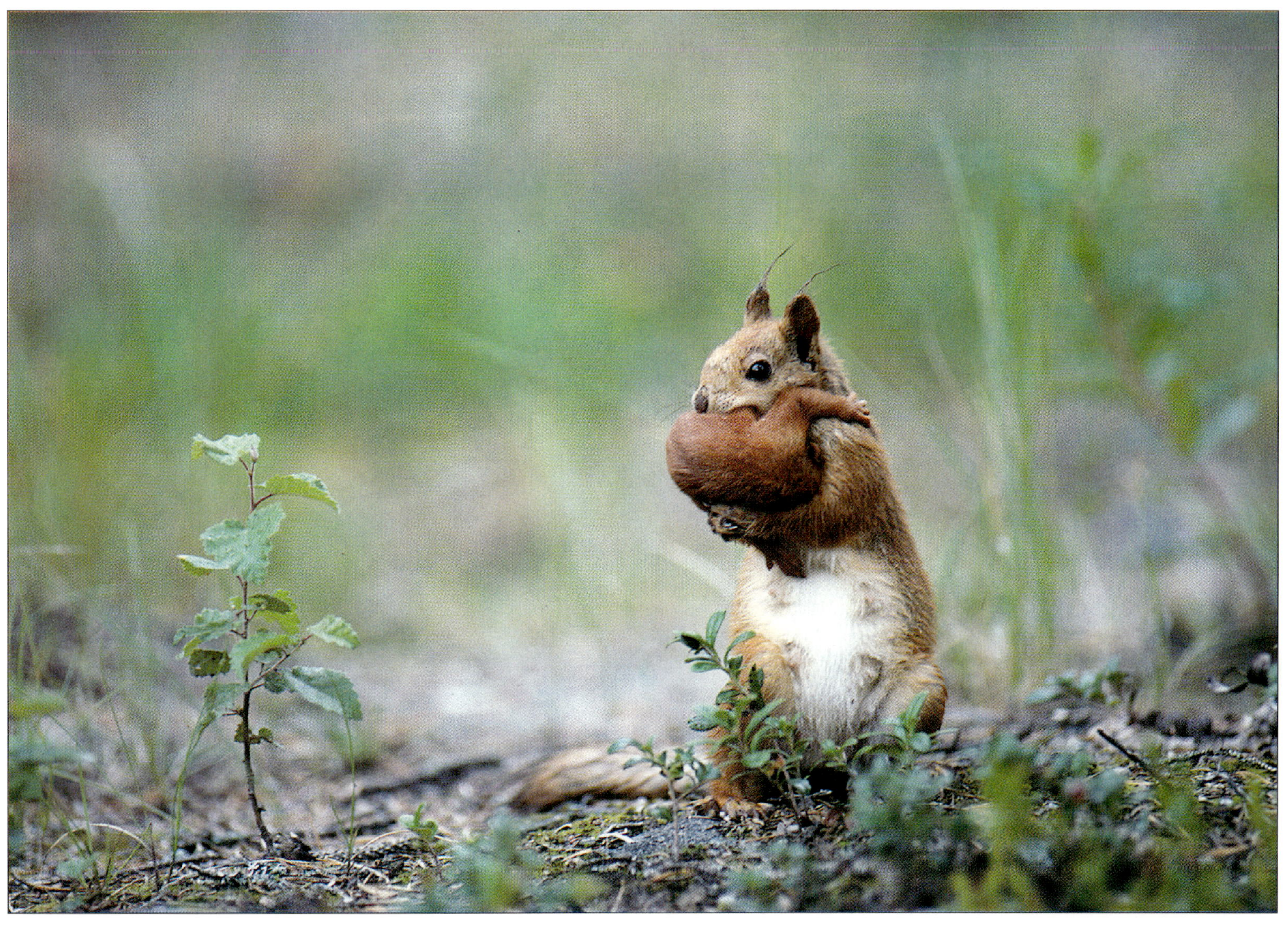

Seppo Määttä
Finland

HIGHLY COMMENDED

Red squirrel moving baby

"One afternoon in July, I was drinking coffee in the kitchen when I saw this squirrel carrying a baby in our garden. She was moving her young to a new home in our attic. I quickly got my camera and was able to photograph the squirrel as she moved her third baby."

Minolta with 300mm lens; Kodachrome 64

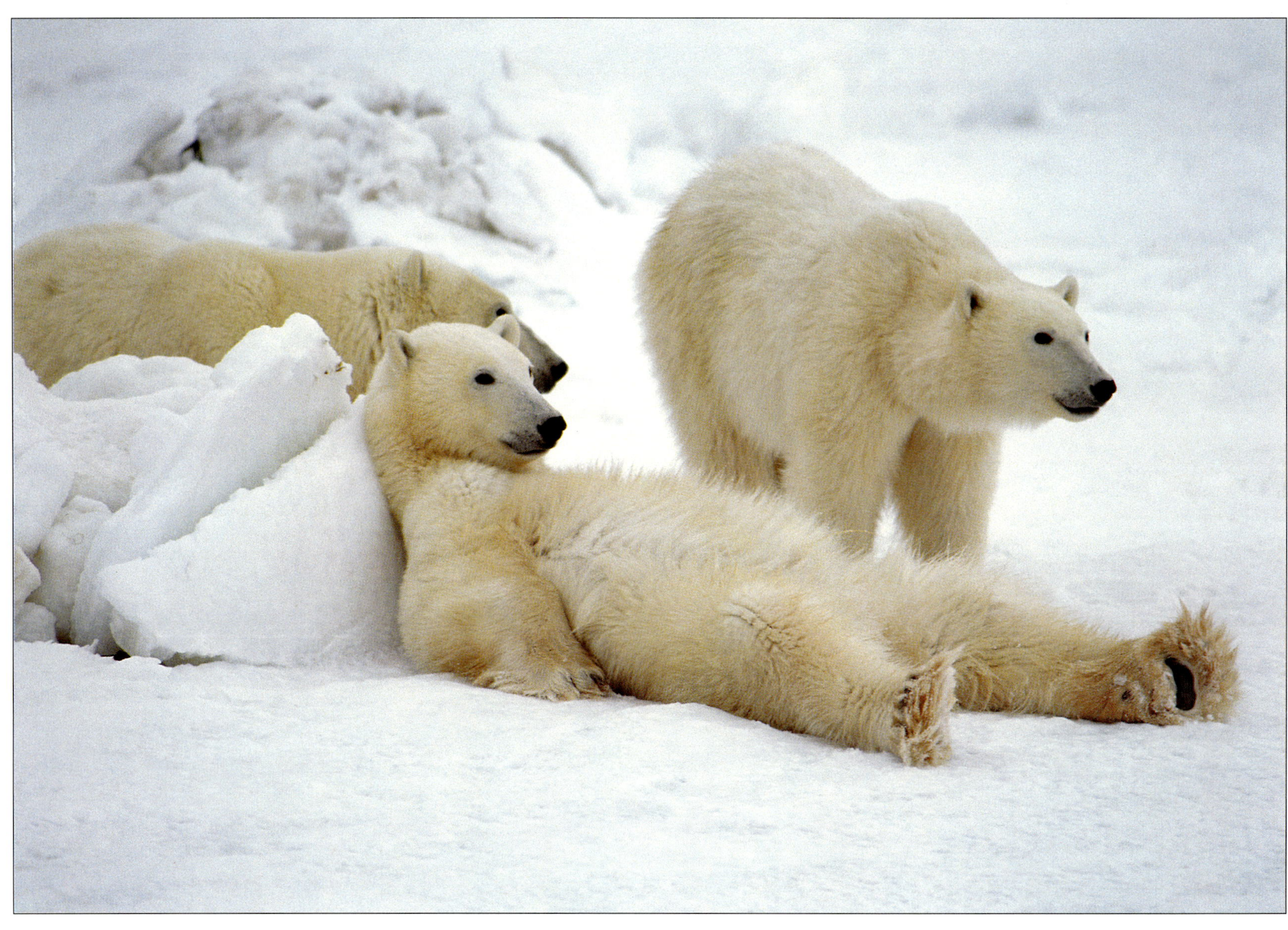

Thomas D Mangelsen
United States of America
HIGHLY COMMENDED

Reclining polar bear

"I have been to Hudson Bay every November for the past seven years to photograph polar bears. This is one of the few times of the year when they socialise. Two or three bears may join together to play-fight or just hang out. Once the bay freezes, the bears separate and go out onto the ice alone to hunt seals."

NIkon F4S with 500mm lens; bean bag; 1/250 sec at f5.6; Fujichrome 100

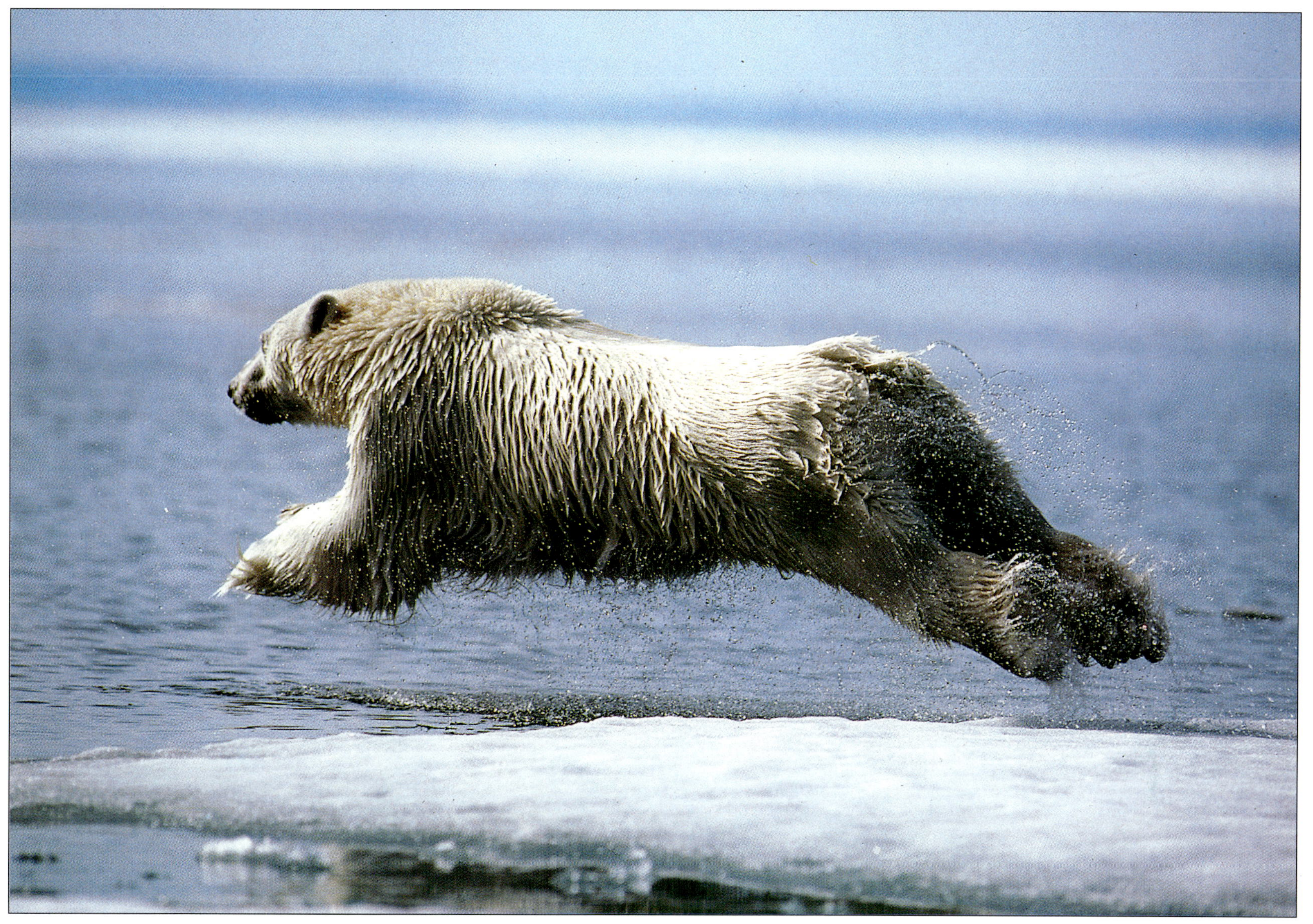

Charles Lindsay
Canada
HIGHLY COMMENDED

Polar bear

"We surprised this young male, as he was feeding on a seal in Wager Bay in the northern part of Hudson Bay, Canada. At the time, I was taking pictures for a story about polar bears at their summer ground for a Japanese magazine."

Nikon F4 with 300mm lens; 1/500 sec at f5.6; Kodachrome 64

Animal Behaviour

- ALL OTHERS -

Photographs entered in this category can show any animal (except birds or mammals) actively doing something. The pictures are judged for their interest as well as aesthetic appeal.

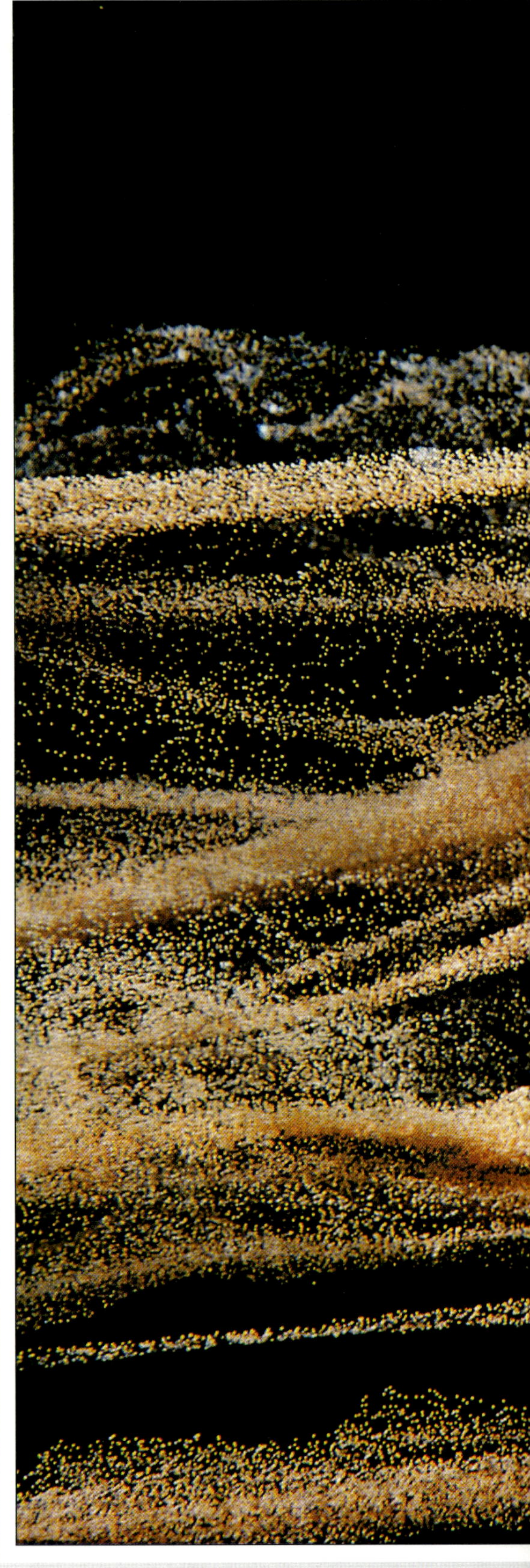

Franklin J Viola
United States of America
WINNER

Tube sponge spawning

"Here a female tube sponge releases thousands of golden eggs into the current of the Caribbean. The eggs are held in sticky strands up to two metres long which prevent the eggs from dispersing immediately and increase the likelihood of them being fertilised by sperm floating in the water. Mass ovulation occurs once a year, in synchrony with sperm production by spawning males."

Nikon F3 with 55mm macro lens and motordrive in underwater housing; strobes; 1/90 sec at f16; Kodachrome 25

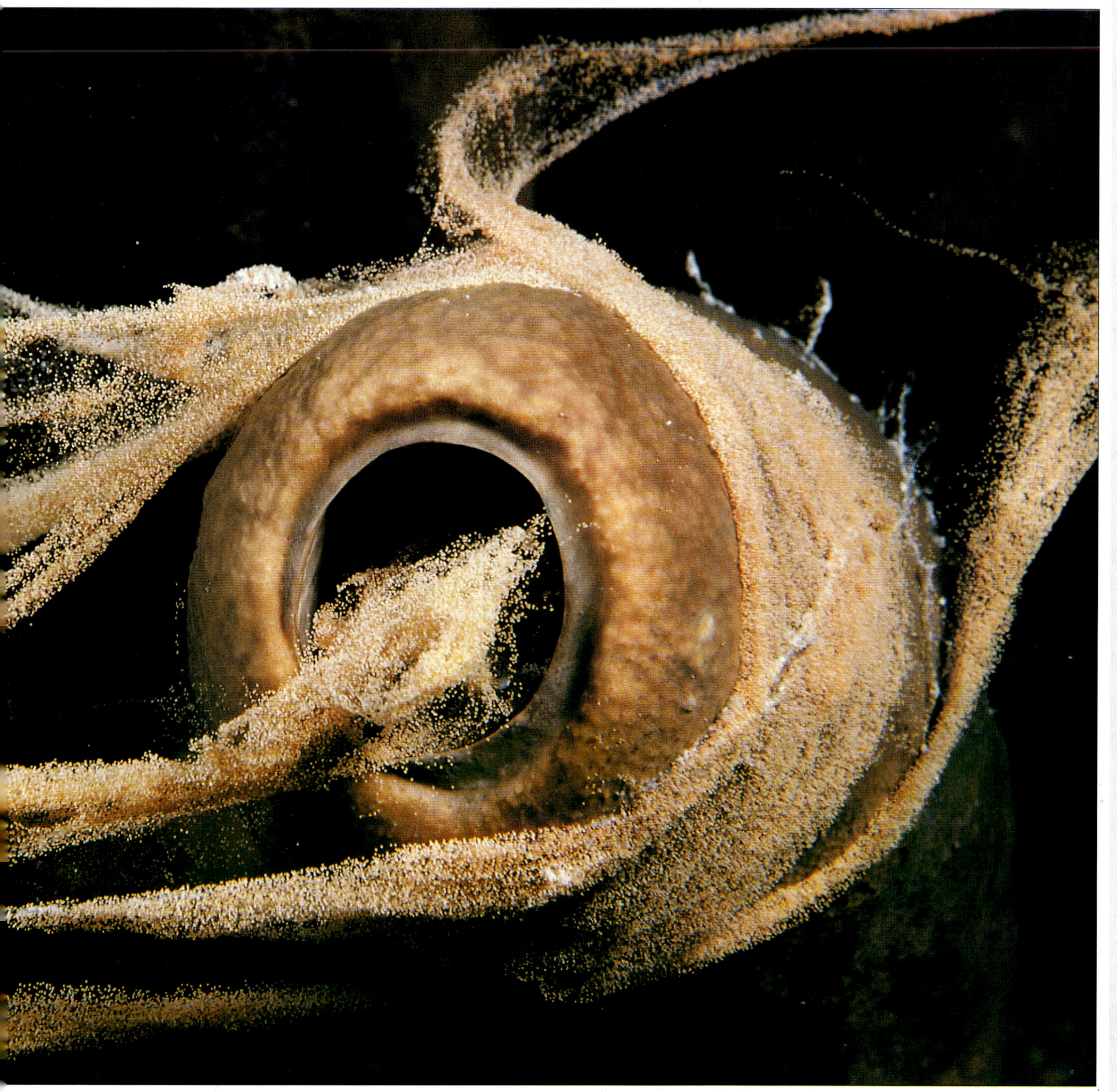

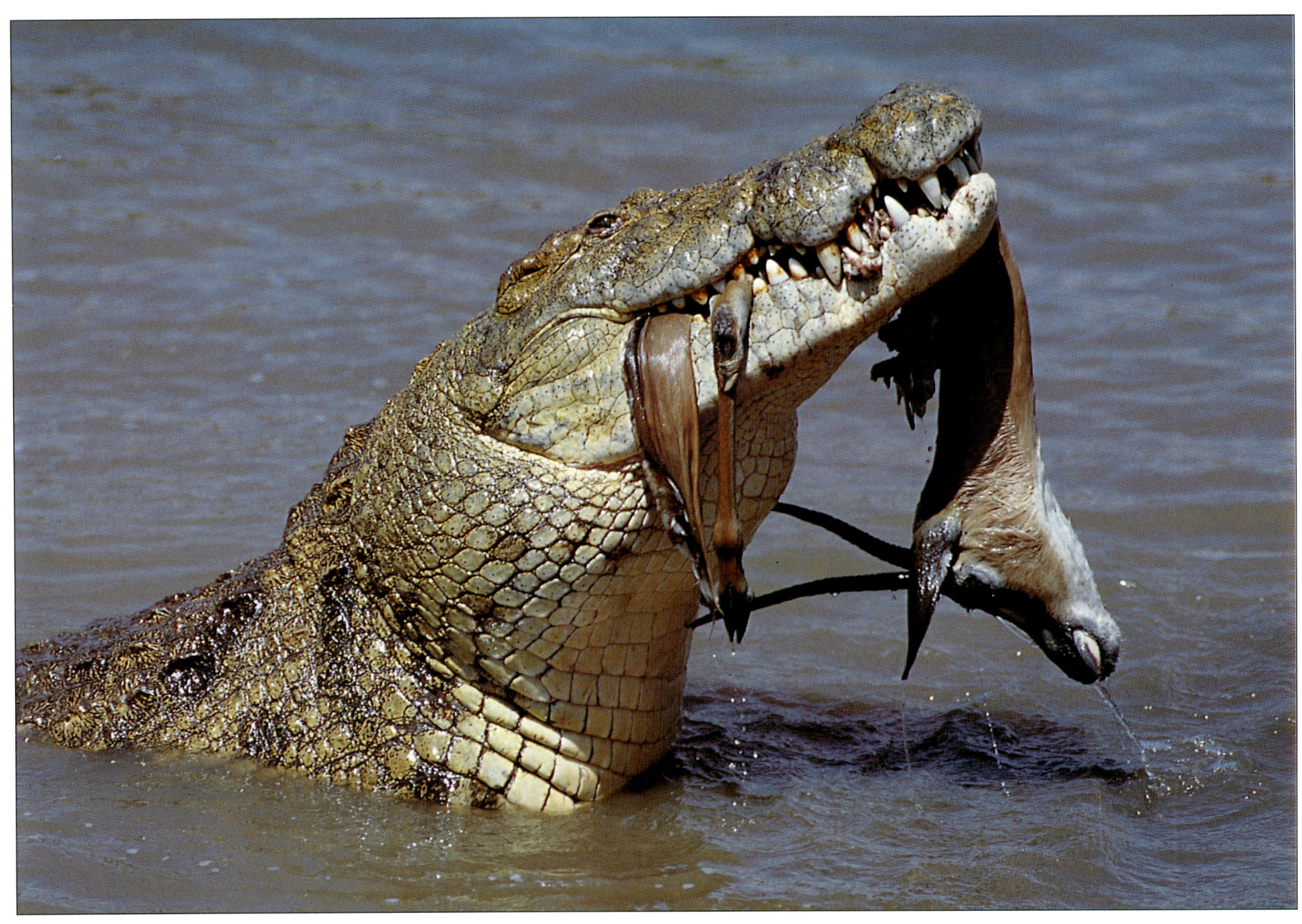

Fritz Pölking
Germany
RUNNER-UP

Dinner-time in the Mara

"I was driving in the Maasai Mara looking for wildebeest crossing the Mara River on migration when I noticed a crocodile in the distance. It was killing a Grant's gazelle but was too far away to photograph. A little later it surfaced much closer with its prey – I always enjoy photographing a great dinner!"

Nikon F4 with 600mm lens; Ektachrome Panther 100

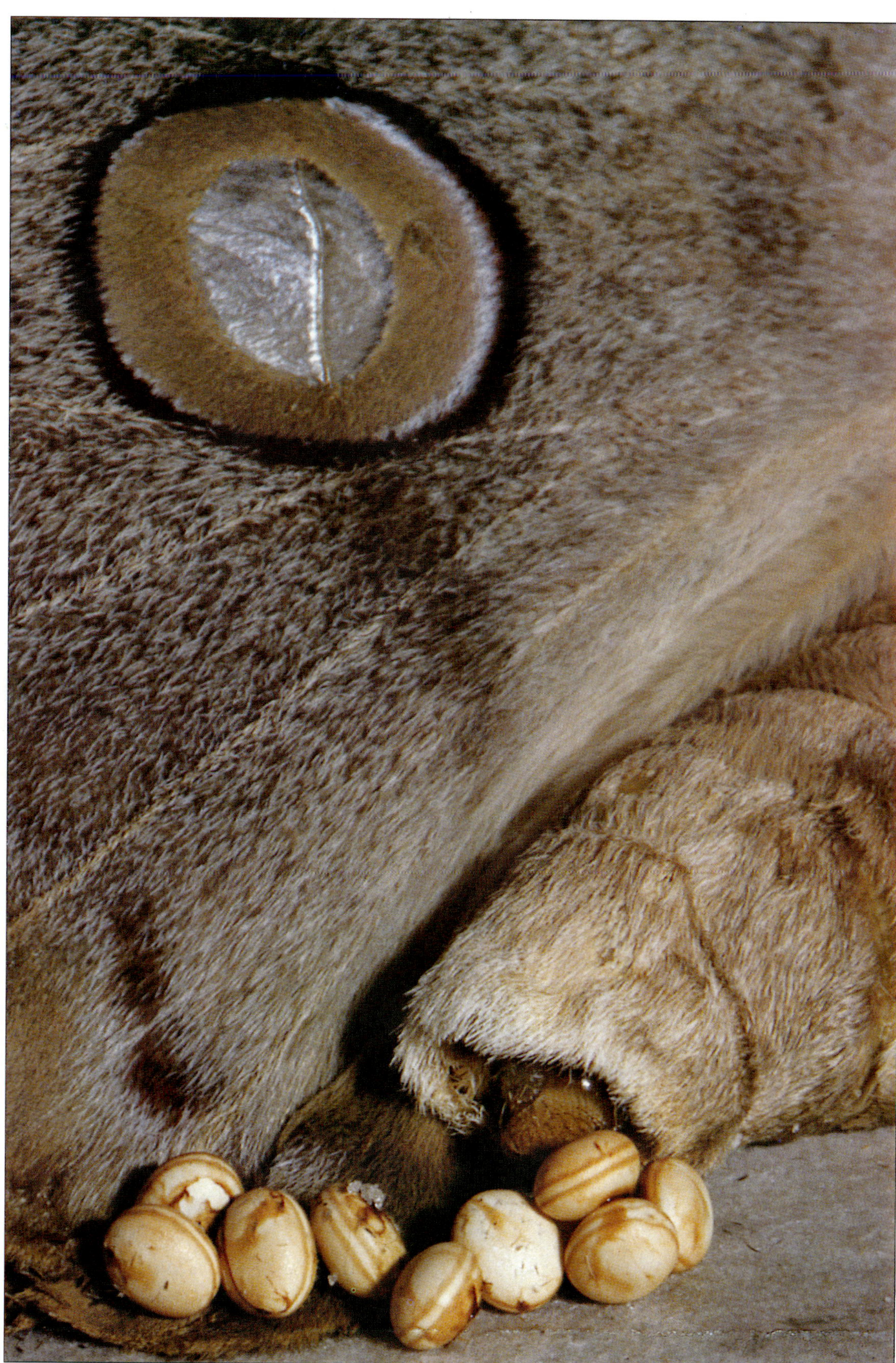

Dr P Kumar
India
HIGHLY COMMENDED

Moth laying eggs

"When I got close to this moth I realised why it hadn't flown away – it was busy laying eggs. At regular intervals it deposited an egg, which was translucent at first but quickly turned opaque. After laying 6-10 eggs, the moth would move forward to find more space. After two and a half hours the entire leaf was speckled with eggs. What a pity that these beautiful giant moths die almost immediately after laying their eggs."

Nikon 801 with 105mm macro lens and extension tubes and extender; flash; 1/250 sec at f16; Fujichrome 100

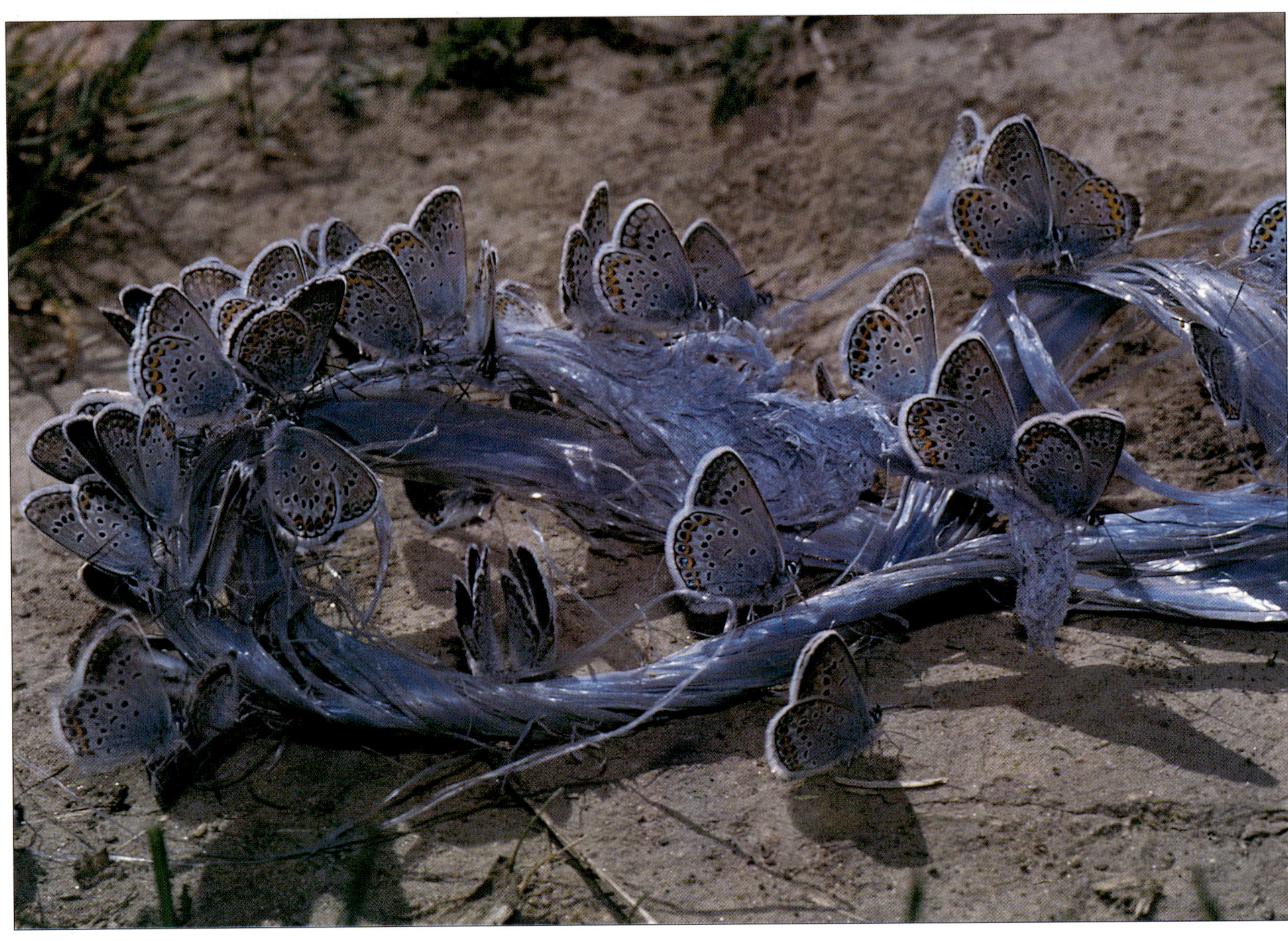

Győző Horváth
Hungary
HIGHLY COMMENDED

Blue butterflies

"On hot summer days, flocks of these blue butterflies congregate at wet places. In this case, a piece of blue plastic rope was the object of their attentions. After taking some photos I decided to experiment and placed some similar, but white-coloured rope nearby. The butterflies continued to favour the blue rope, completely ignoring the white one."

Minolta XD7 with 100mm macro lens; 1/60 sec at f8/11; Fujichrome Velvia

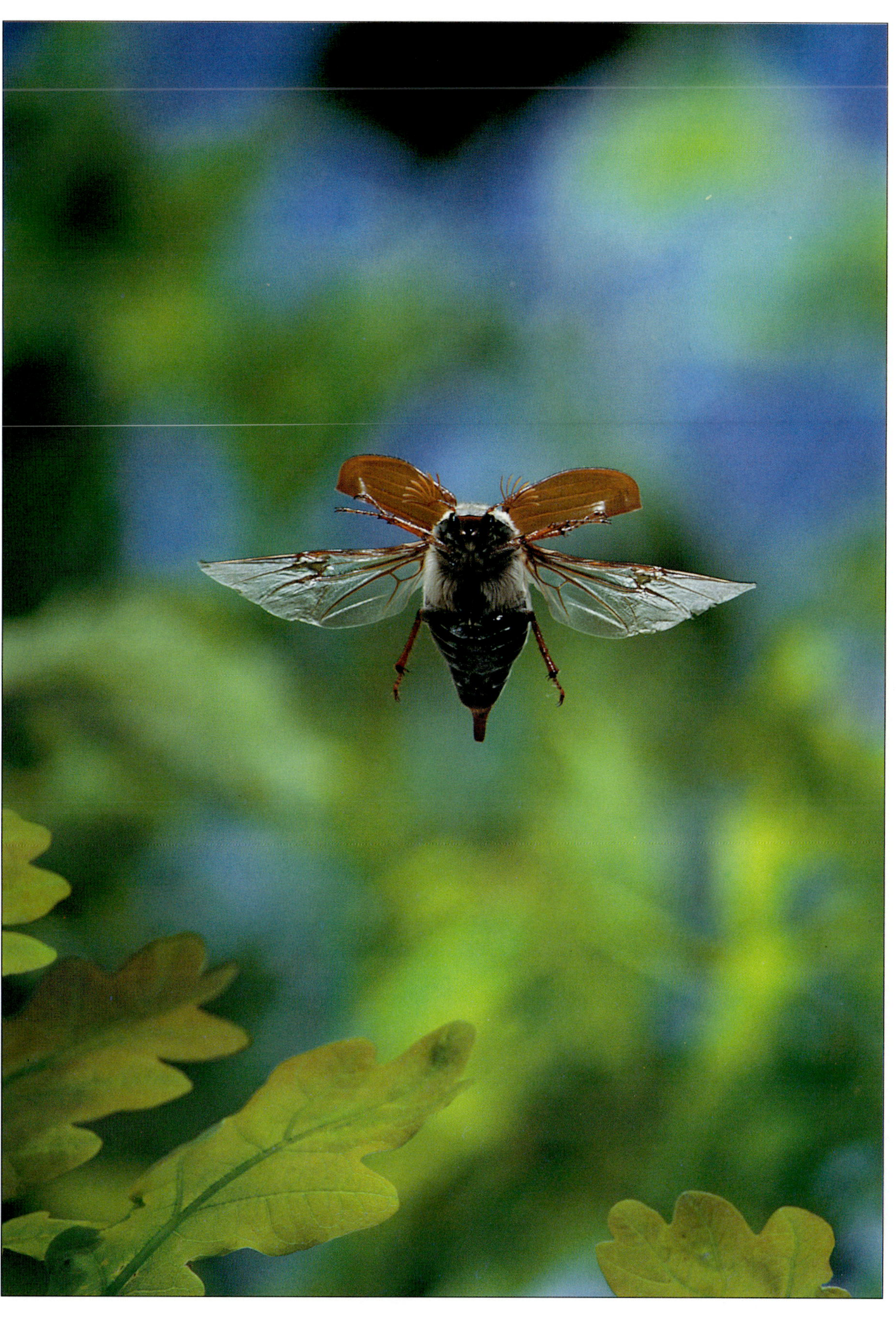

Hans Christoph Kappel
Germany
HIGHLY COMMENDED

Cockchafer

"The cockchafer is one of the best-known insects in Germany and features in popular songs and stories. I concentrate on photographing flying insects and have always wanted to get a shot of a cockchafer in flight. This year, there were an unusually large number of them about and, unusually, they could be seen flying during the day. I got this shot in an old oakwood near my home."

Rollei 6006 with 400mm lens; bellows; flashes; 1/500 sec at f11; Fujichrome Velvia

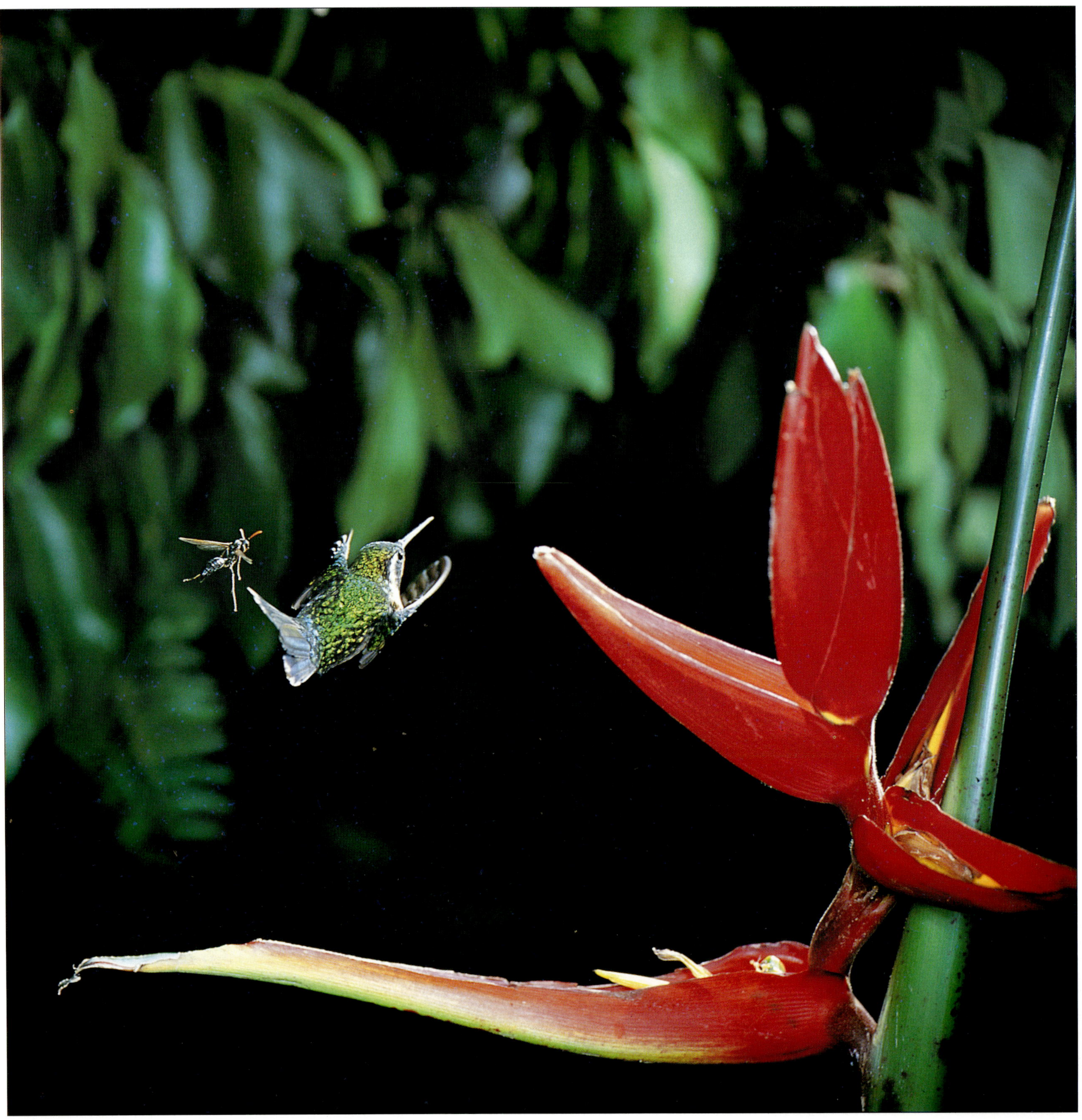

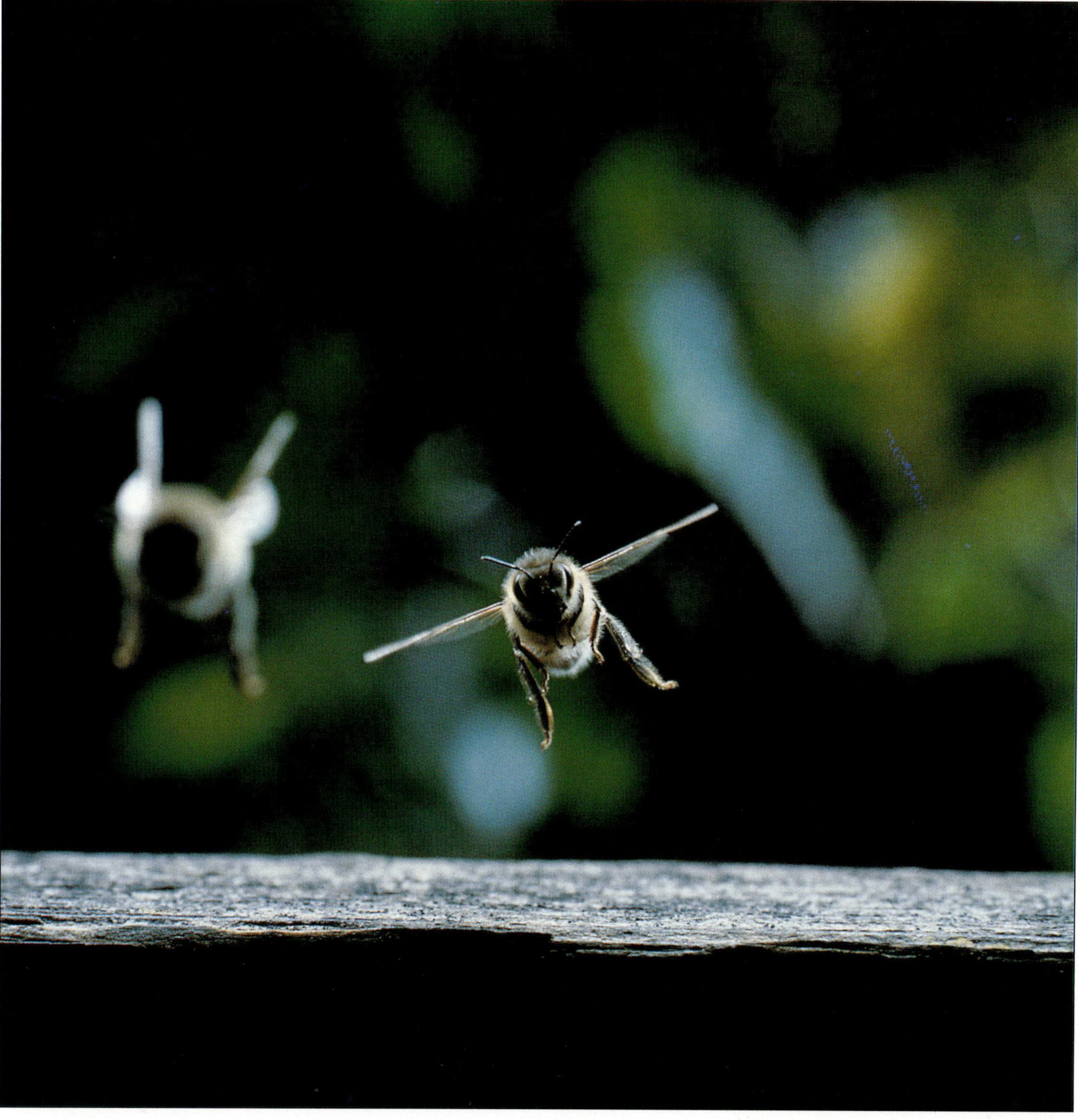

Mitsuhiko Imamori
Japan
HIGHLY COMMENDED

Hummingbird and paper wasp

"While I was in Costa Rica, I often observed wasps and hummingbirds seeming to race to get the best position to suck nectar from flowers. The bird would often flap its wings to ward off the wasp. Here, I used a light sensor to catch the action as a hummingbird and wasp flew towards a heliconia flower."

Pentax 6x7 with 135mm lens; tripod; flash; hand-made shutter; f16; Fujichrome Velvia

Mitsuhiko Imamori
Japan
HIGHLY COMMENDED

Honey bees

"It took two months of preparation to get this shot. I placed a beehive in a tiny room just large enough to take one person. The bees had to come through a window to get to the hive."

Pentax 6x7 with 135mm lens; tripod; flash; hand-made shutter; 1/16 sec at f16; Fujichrome Velvia

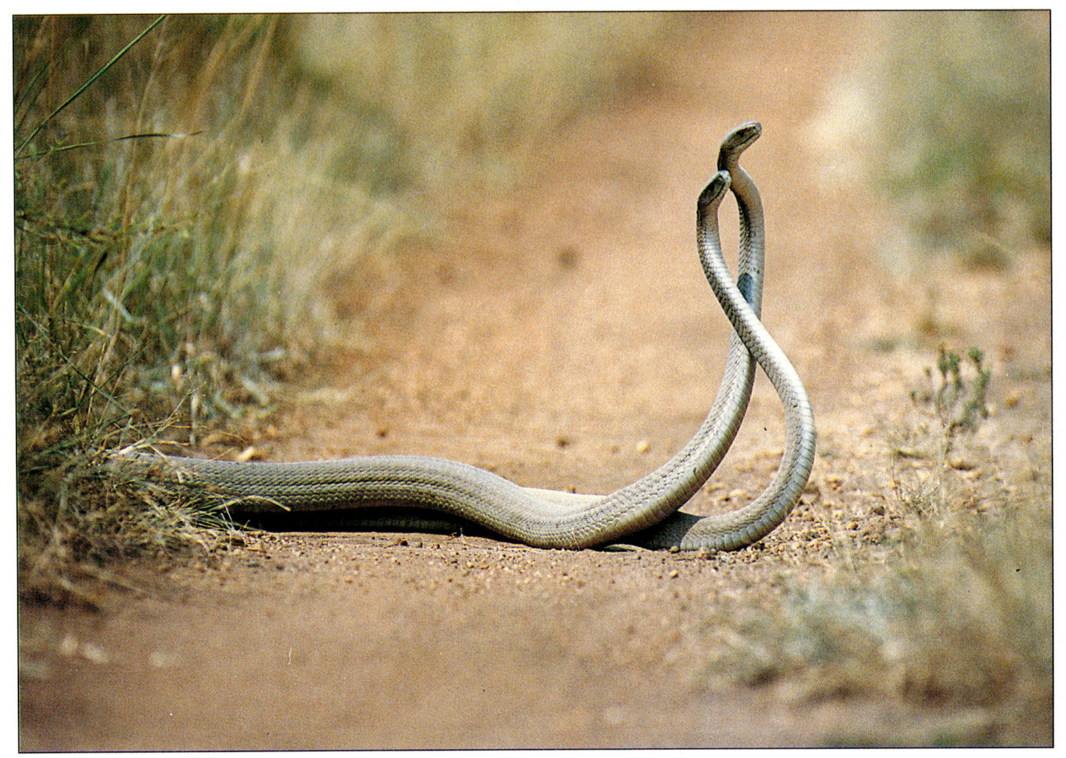

Adrian Warren
United Kingdom
HIGHLY COMMENDED

Black mambas in combat

"This was a surprise encounter while driving in the Akagera National Park, Rwanda. The two male black mambas were fighting, presumably for a female close by, and were so involved that I was able to approach on foot to within 15 metres. I sat on the ground and braced the camera on my knee to take the picture."

Nikon F4 with 300mm lens; 1/500 sec at f2.8; Kodacolour 100

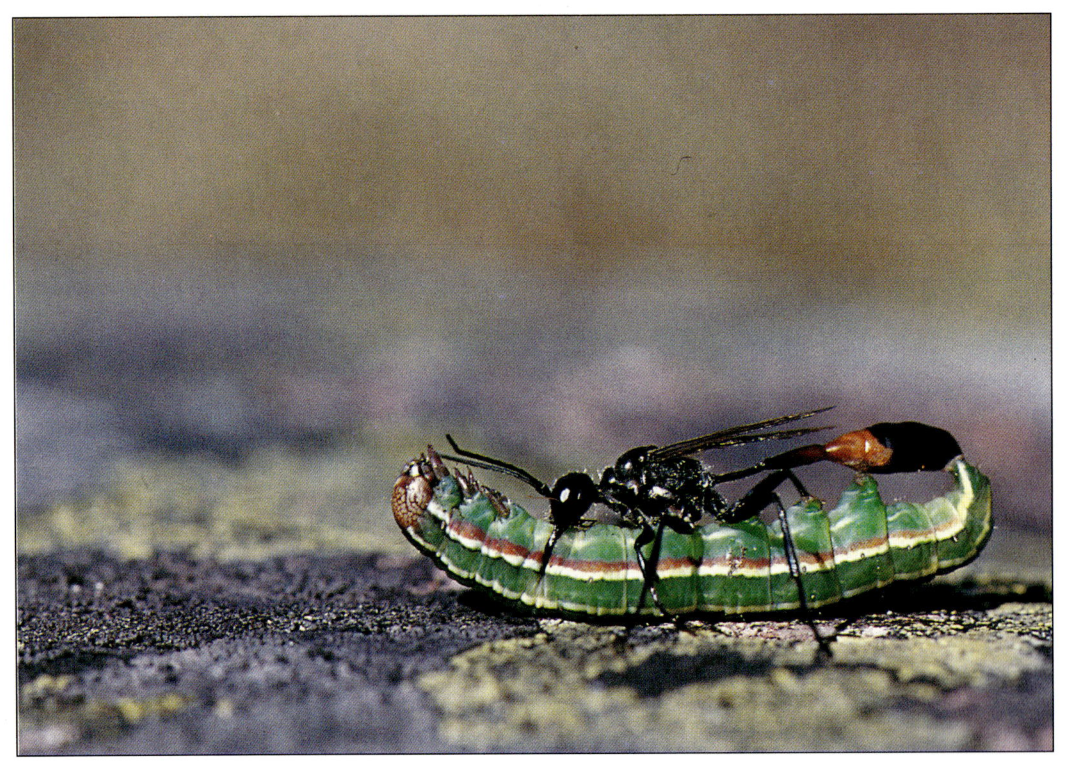

Jussi Murtosaari
Finland
HIGHLY COMMENDED

A *big catch*

"I was on holiday in Aland when my friends spotted this sand wasp, Ammophila sabulosa, *moving a moth caterpillar. The wasp was dragging its huge catch to a specially prepared hole in the sand. The wasp then laid an egg and sealed the hole. When the egg hatched it would have fed on the caterpillar."*

Nikon F3 with 105mm macro lens and extension rings; 1/250 sec at f16; Kodachrome 200

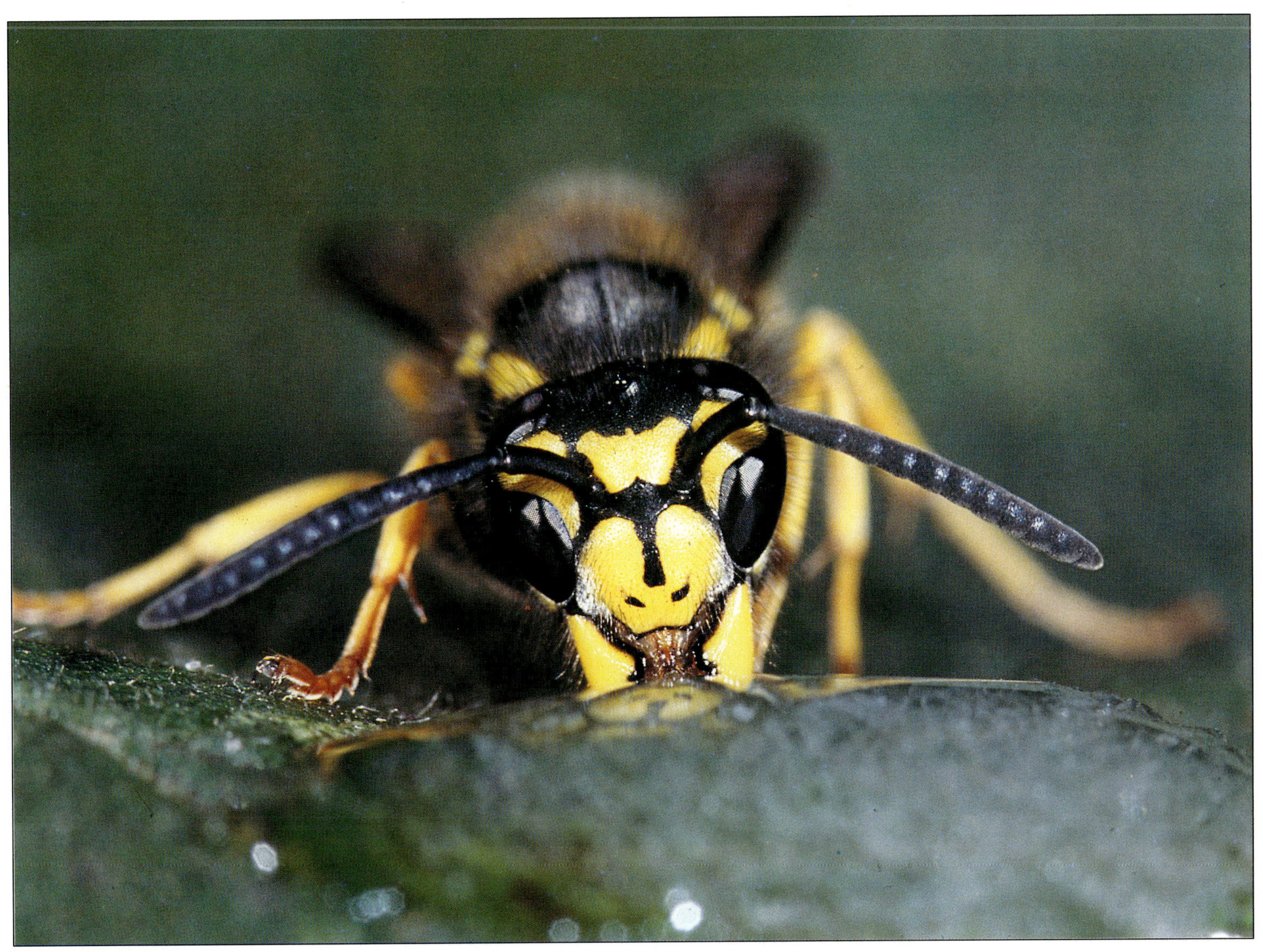

Jürgen Vogt
Germany
HIGHLY COMMENDED

Wasp drinking

"I wanted to get a close-up photograph of the head of a wasp, and so I placed some sugar solution on a leaf in a bush in my garden and set up my equipment."

Nikon F801 with 105mm macro lens; tripod; bellows; flashes; 1/250 sec at f11; Fujichrome 50

Reptiles at Risk

This category was introduced for this year only, to highlight the work of the Reptile Protection Trust. Pictures could feature snakes, lizards, tortoises or turtles, and could show subjects in the wild or illustrate conservation or welfare themes.

The Reptile Protection Trust

The trust was founded in 1989 and became a registered charity in 1990. Its prime objectives are the protection of reptiles and their habitats. It investigates the problems associated with reptile welfare, co-ordinates campaigns, funds research concerned with both wild and captive reptiles, and produces educational publications. The trust specialises in public relations efforts to counter popular fears and misconceptions about reptiles. Currently, it is campaigning to end the reptile pet trade and the exploitation of rattlesnakes in the notorious North American round-ups, and to expose the problems associated with keeping reptiles in artificial conditions.

For more information, contact: Reptile Protection Trust, *College Gates, 2 Deansway, Worcester* WR1 2JD, UK.

Hal Beral

United States of America

WINNER

Green turtle

"All sea turtle populations have declined as the beaches where they breed have been developed, and increasing numbers have been slaughtered for food and caught in fishing nets, especially driftnets. I photographed this green turtle off the coast of Kauai, Hawaii. *A number of diving boats in the area had been feeding the turtles, which had become quite used to the boats and would come right up to them. I had just entered the water when this individual swam by close to the surface."*

Nikonos V with 15mm lens; strobe; Fujichrome

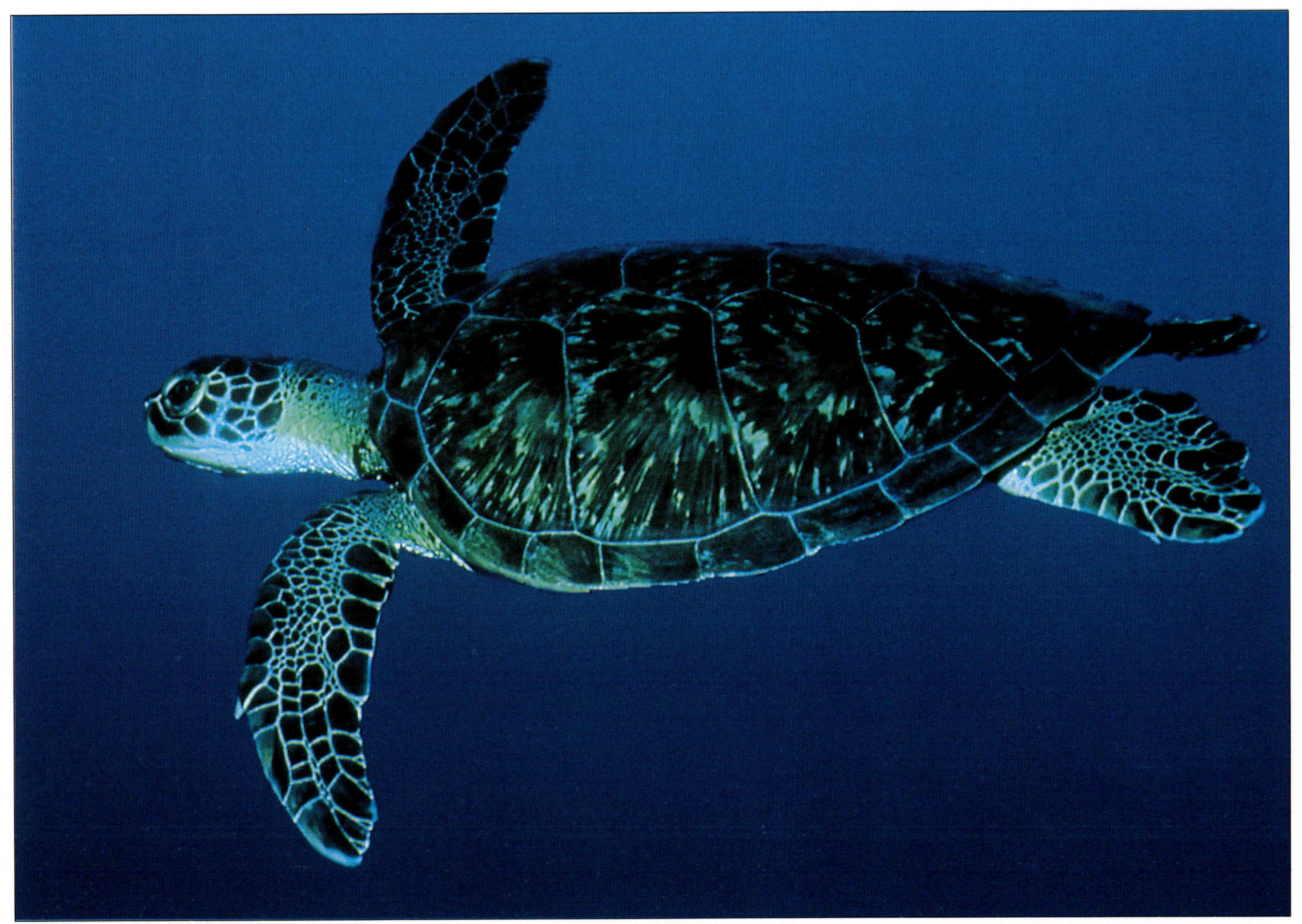

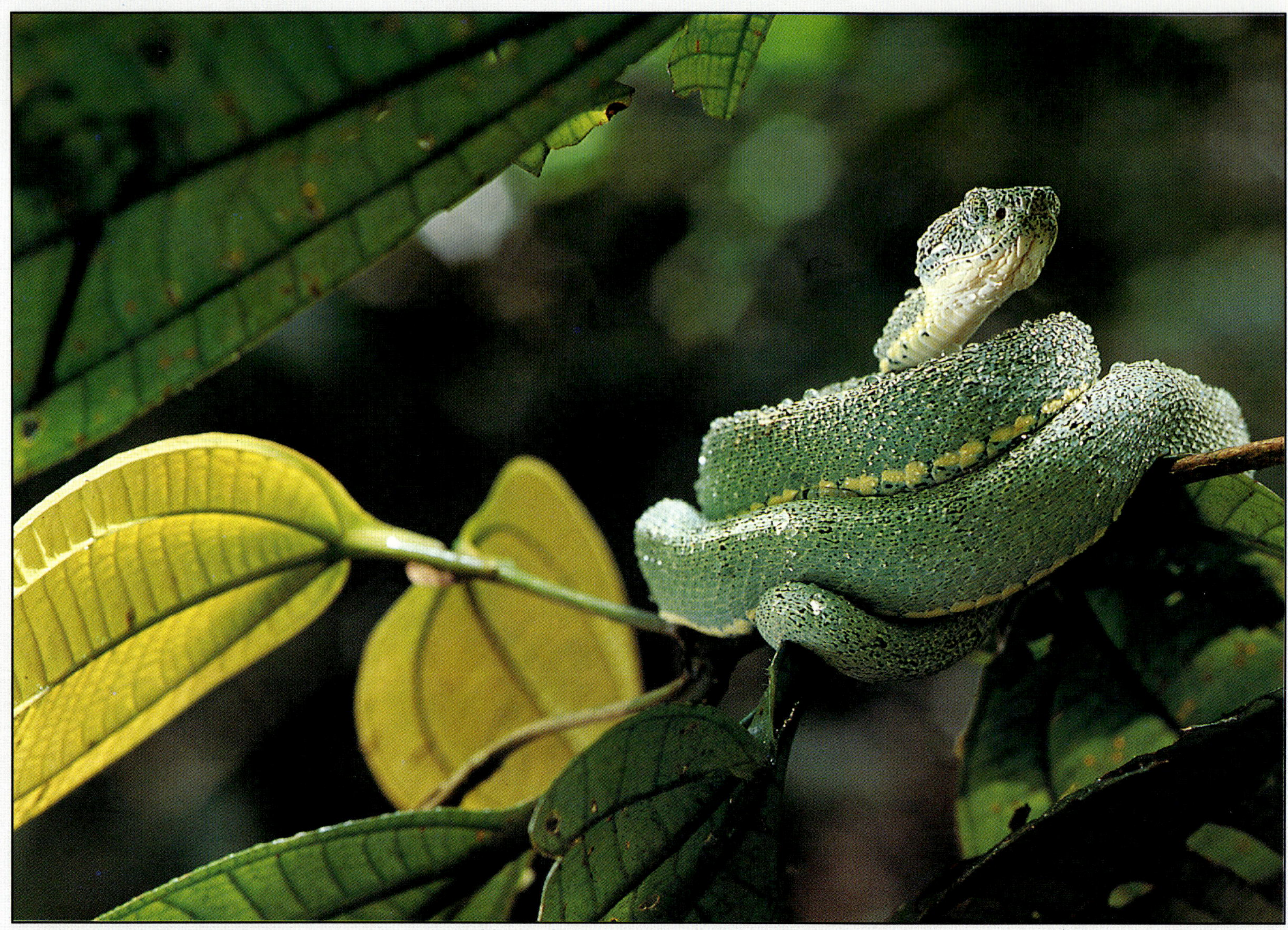

André Bärtschi
Liechtenstein
RUNNER-UP

Emerald forest pit viper

"On my visits to Peru, I have been looking for several years for the beautiful emerald forest pit viper Bothriopsis bilineata smaragdina*. One morning, shortly after dawn, I came across two of these snakes. At first the light was very poor, and so I just watched. After a while conditions improved, and I set up my tripod."*

Nikon FM2 with 105mm macro lens; tripod; reflector; 1/2 sec at f5.6; Fujichrome Velvia

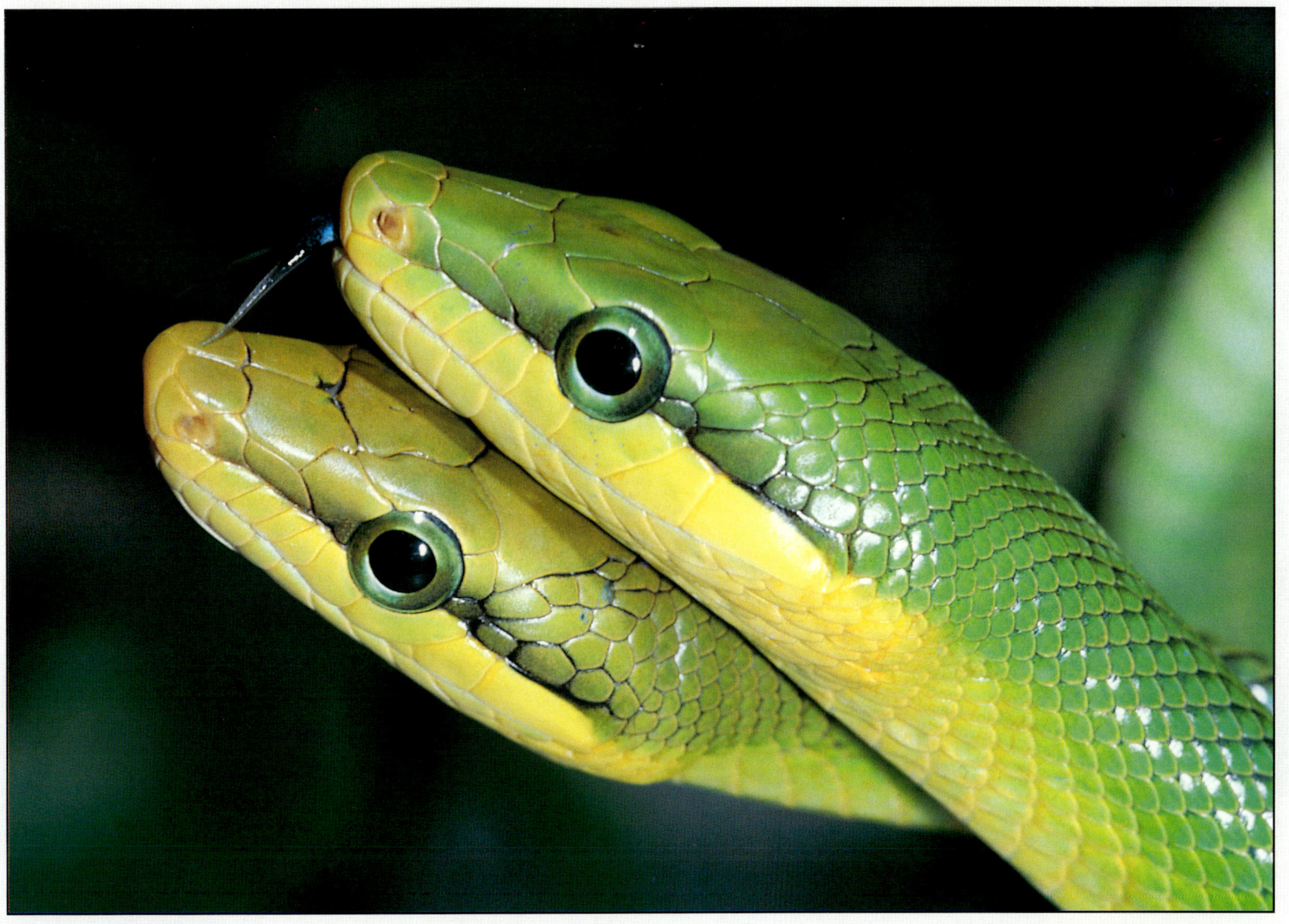

Herbert Kehrer
Germany
HIGHLY COMMENDED

Red-tailed rat snakes

"It took almost a year of visiting the Stuttgart Zoo before I saw these snakes with such vivid coloration. Their colour depends on the time of year and the condition of the skin."

Nikon 801S with 105mm lens; flashes; 1/250 sec at f16; Fujichrome Velvia

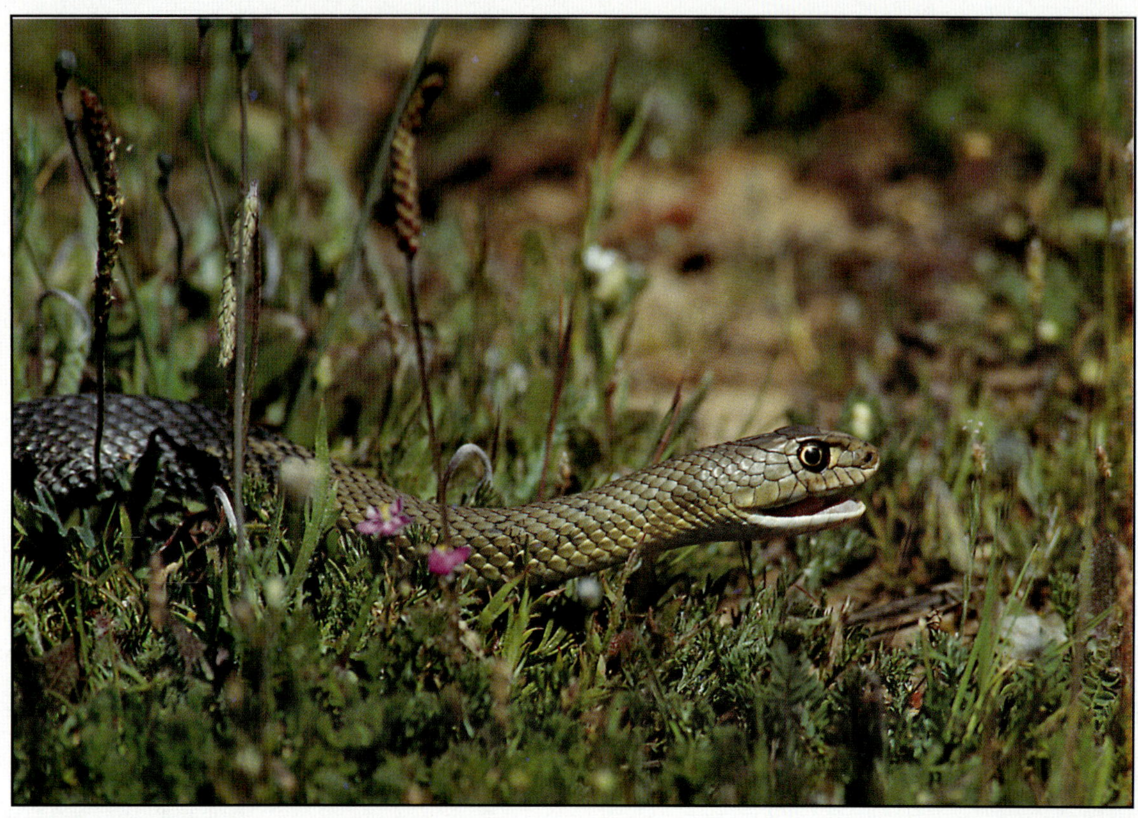

Markus Michael Botzek
Germany
HIGHLY COMMENDED

Montpelier snake

"I found this snake Malpolon monspessulanus *beside a road in* Extremadura, Spain, *where snakes are common road casualties. It was moving slowly in the short grass. I had not taken many pictures before I realised that it had been injured by a car."*

Nikon F801S with 300mm lens; tripod; Kodak Elite 100

Charles Lindsay
Canada
HIGHLY COMMENDED

Green turtle hunter

"Here a green turtle is being captured for live sale in Bali, *for festival sacrifices. Each year, more than* 5,000 *are killed for this reason in* Bali *alone. As they become rarer, turtles become even more valuable as sacrificial offerings. The picture will be included in the book on this subject:* Turtle Islands - Balinese ritual and the green turtle, *by* Lyall Watson."

Nikonos V with 28mm lens; 1/30 sec at f5.6; Kodachrome 200

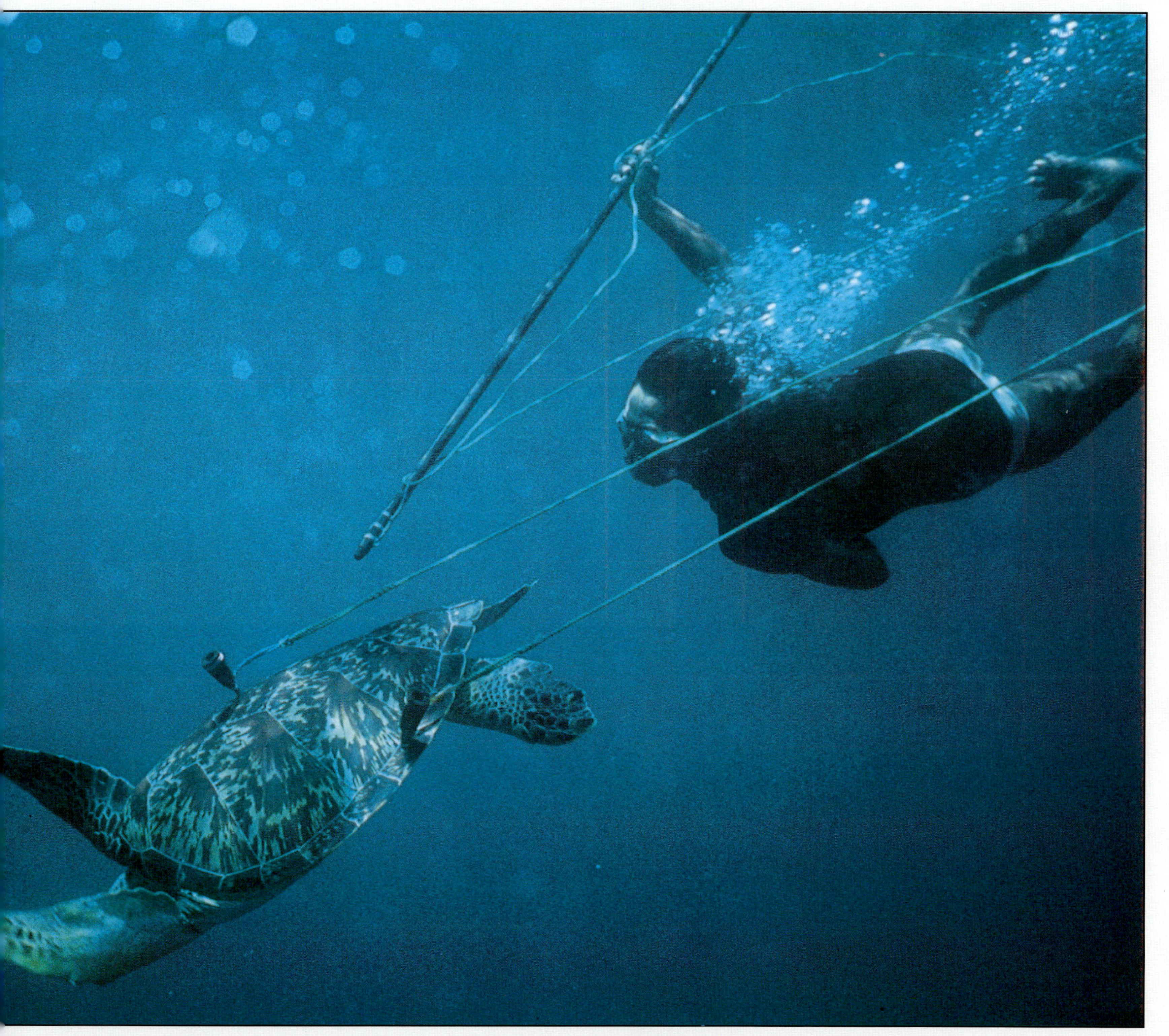

Endangered Wildlife

Photographs entered for this category illustrate species which are officially listed as 'Endangered' at a national or international level.

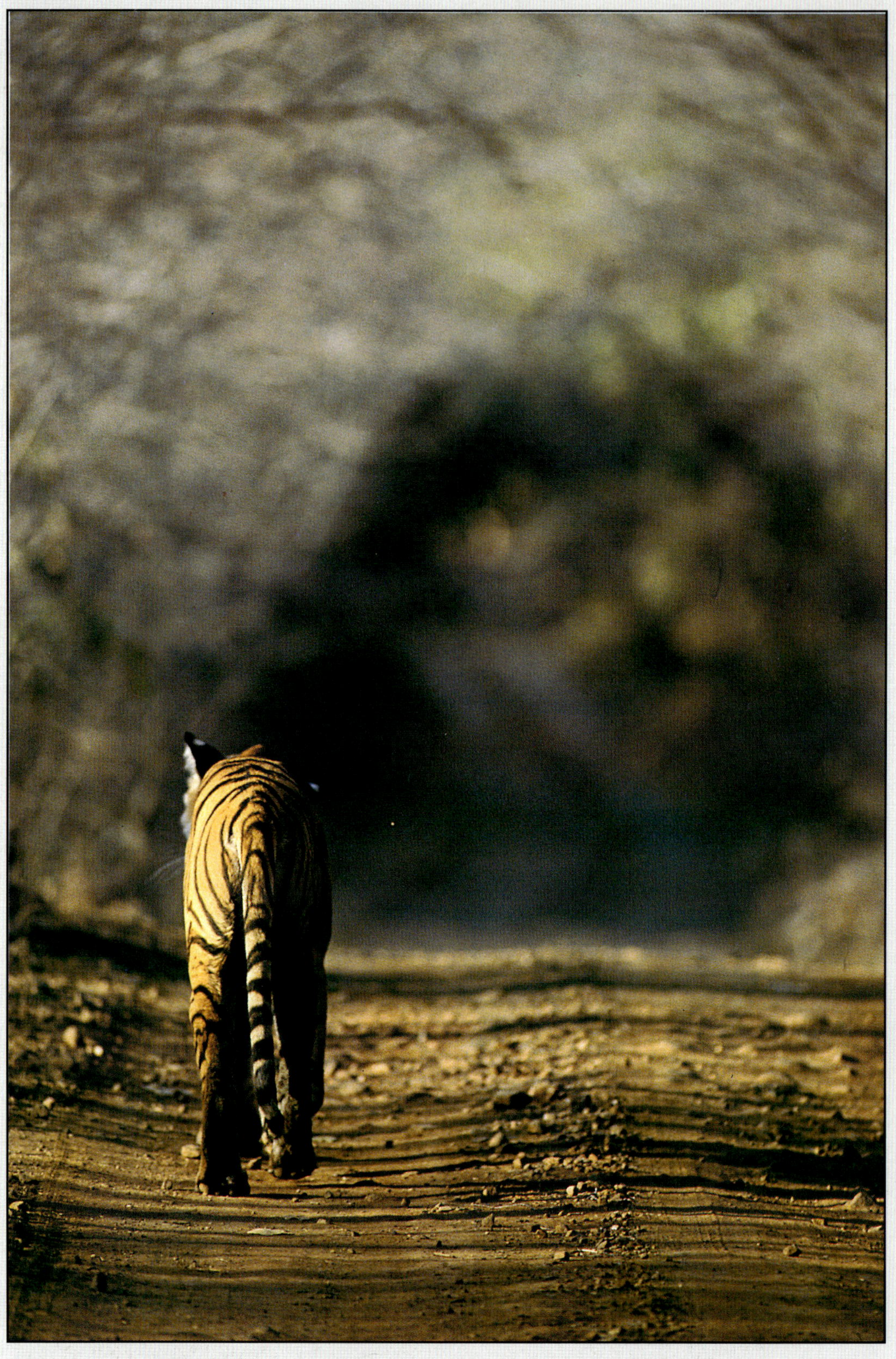

Mary Ann McDonald
United Sates of America
WINNER

Indian tiger

"This picture was taken on a visit to Ranthambore National Park. The tigress, known as Noon, had two cubs, but on this occasion she was walking her territory alone, scent marking as she went. Unfortunately, because of an increase in poaching in the park, the tiger population there has been halved, and we don't know if Noon has survived."

Nikon F3 with 300mm lens; bean bag; 1/250 sec at f5.6; Fujichrome 100 rated at 200

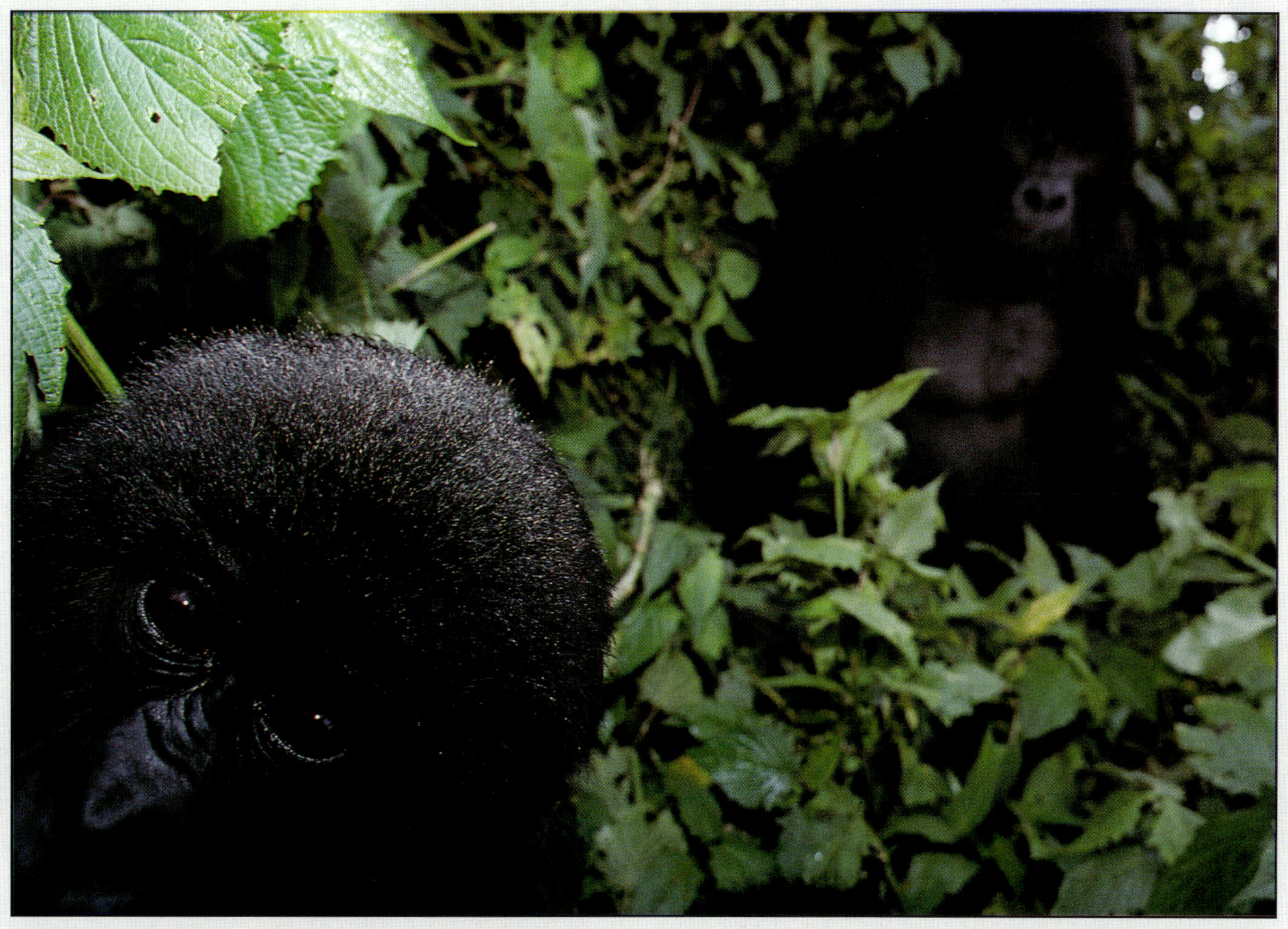

Bruce Davidson
Kenya
JOINT RUNNER-UP

Young mountain gorilla

"The working distance for a wildlife photographer from his or her subject is very much determined by the species and how familiar the individuals may be with humans. I always try to work as unobtrusively as possible. I photographed this inquisitive young mountain gorilla on a visit to the Virunga National Park, Zaire. The gorillas were used to visitors and tolerated me at a close distance, allowing the luxury of using a wide-angle lens."

Minolta 9000 with 24mm lens; Kodachrome 64

Konrad Wothe
Germany
JOINT RUNNER-UP

Black rhino

"I watched black rhino in the Ngorongoro Crater and noticed that they had particular places where they defecated. Afterwards, they frequently kicked it with their hind feet. Presumably, this behaviour is part of territory marking - the population of rhinos in the crater is quite high."

Canon EOS1 with 600mm lens; auto at f4.5; Fujichrome 50

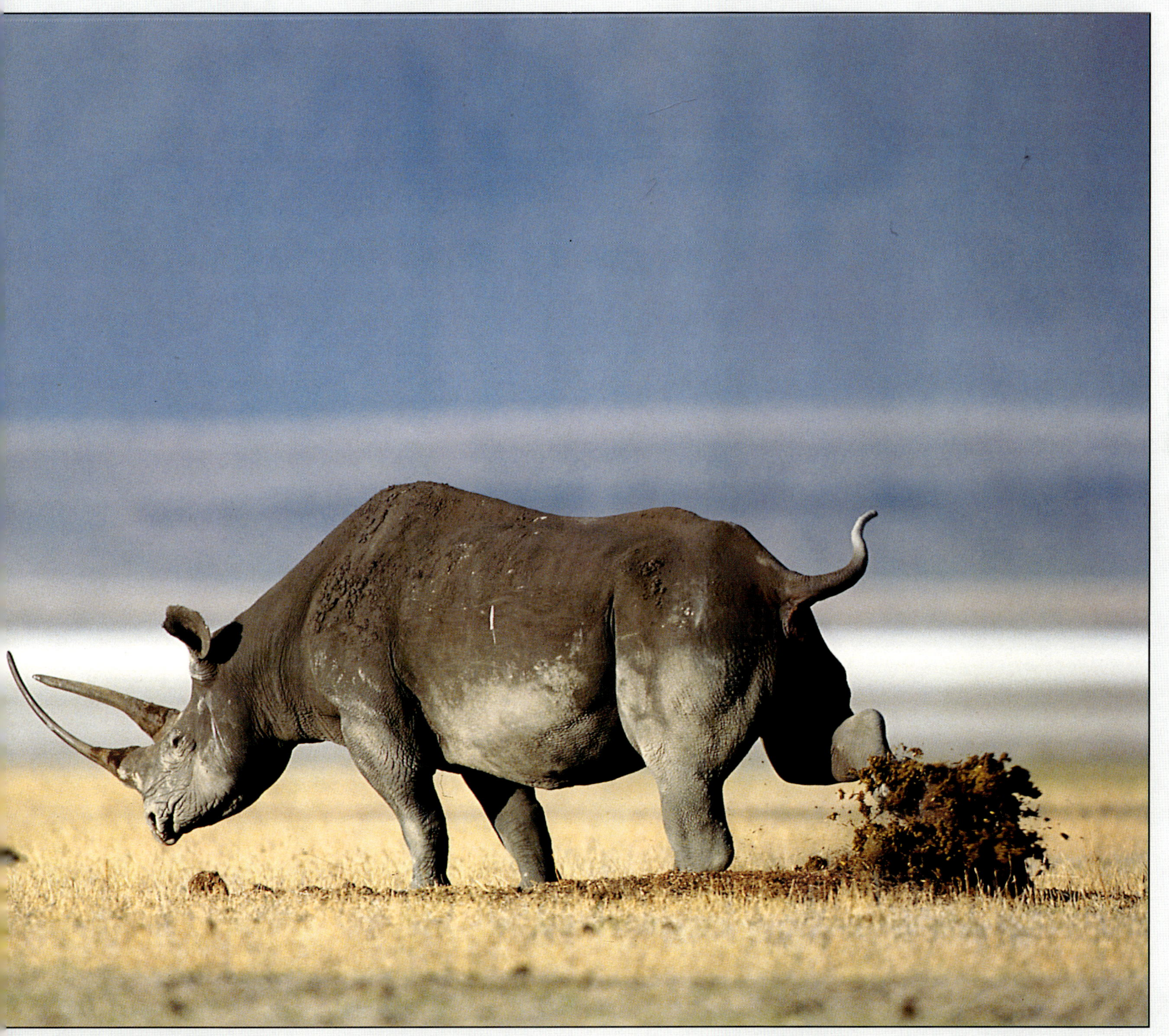

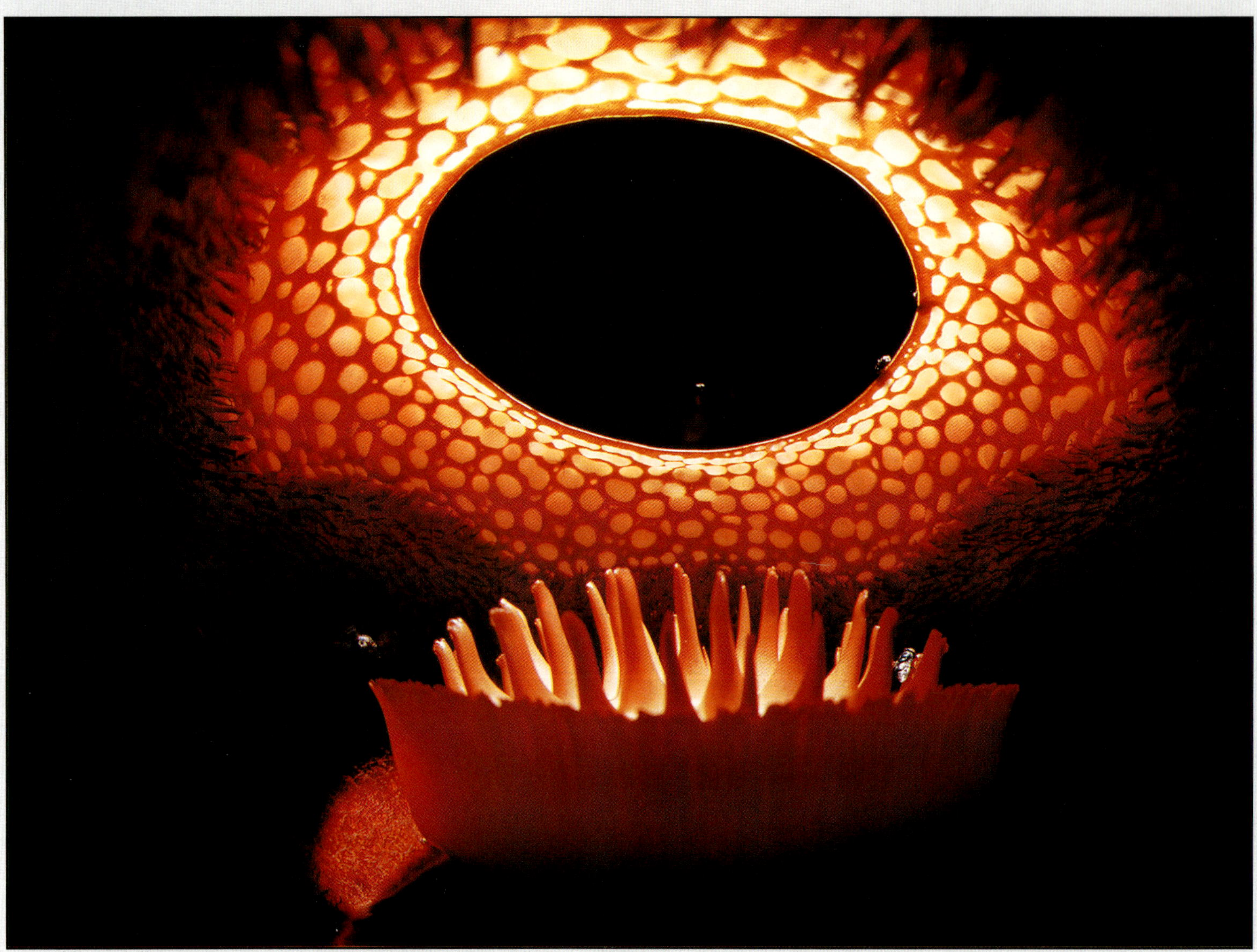

Mitsuhiko Imamori

Japan

HIGHLY COMMENDED

Rafflesia

"I lived in the Indonesian rainforest for about two months in order to photograph the huge rafflesia flower. Rafflesia is pollinated by flies which are attracted by its strong smell of ammonia. The flowers are very difficult to find. To take a fly's eye view of the inside of the flower, I inserted my camera lens through a crack in its side."

Nikon F4 with 16mm lens; tripod; flash; 1/60 sec at f11; Kodachrome

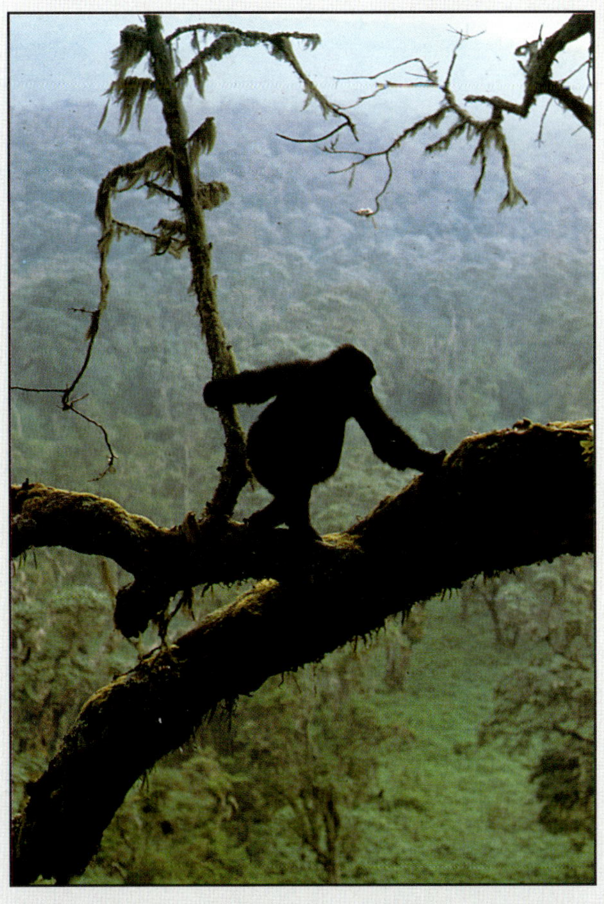

Adrian Warren
United Kingdom
HIGHLY COMMENDED

Mountain gorilla

"This young male was one of a group playing on the branches of a great hagenia tree overhanging a valley in the Virunga Volcanoes on the border of Rwanda and Zaire. At the time, I was researching and observing the gorillas for a BBC film."

Nikon F4 with 200mm lens; 1/125 sec at f4; Kodachrome 200

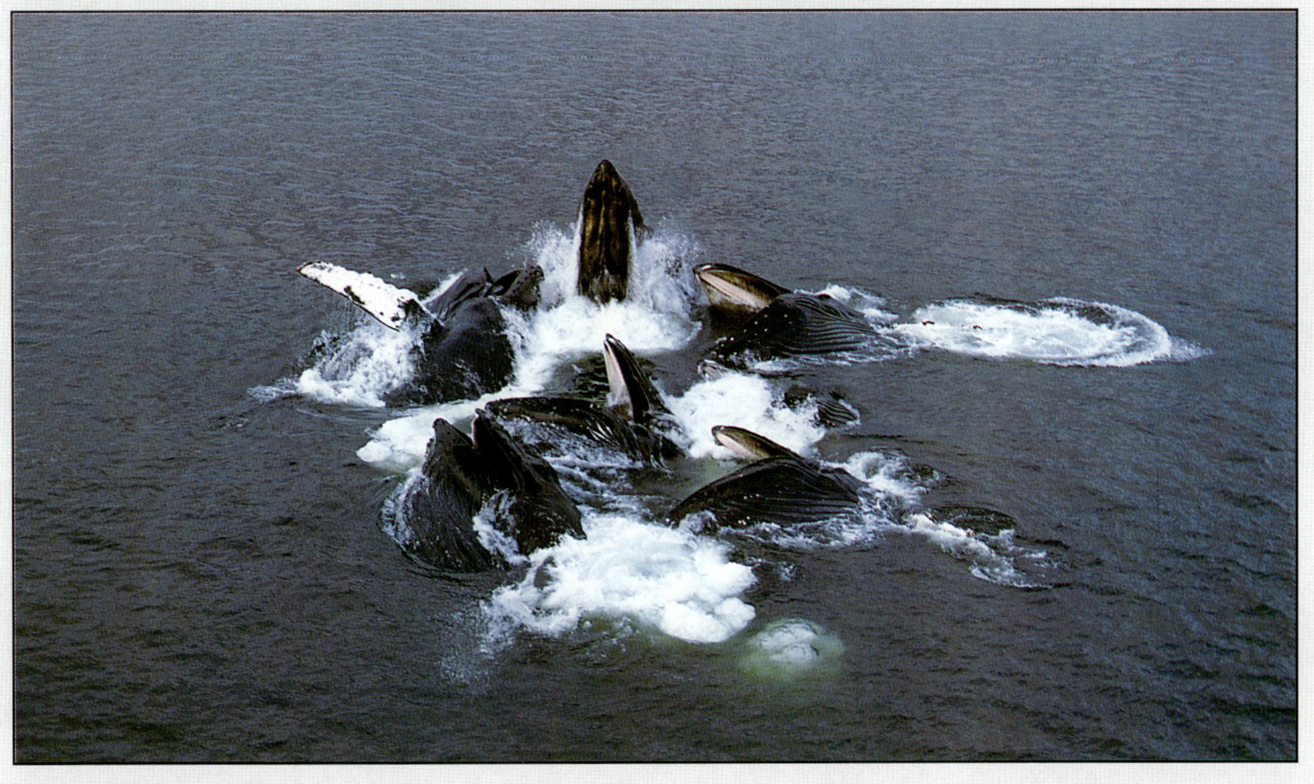

Kennan Ward
United states of America
HIGHLY COMMENDED

Humpback whales feeding

"I was on board a boat off the coast of Alaska, documenting whale behaviour when we came across these humpbacks. They were feeding co-operatively, driving a school of fish into an ever-decreasing circle."

Nikon F4 with 80-200mm lens; Kodachrome 64

The Underwater World

The photographs entered in this category must be taken under water and can show marine or freshwater subjects.

Kelvin Aitken
New Zealand
WINNER

Spotted dolphins

"Spotted dolphins gather in the shallows on the Bahama Banks off Grand Bahama to rest and play after feeding and have become used to human visitors. On this occasion I was fortunate enough to see this mother and calf split from the main group and play together. Body contact is very important to dolphins, especially in the mother-calf relationship. The caressing and rubbing between them reminded me of a mother soothing a hyper-active child."

Nikonos V with 15mm lens; 1/250 sec at f4.5; Kodachrome 64

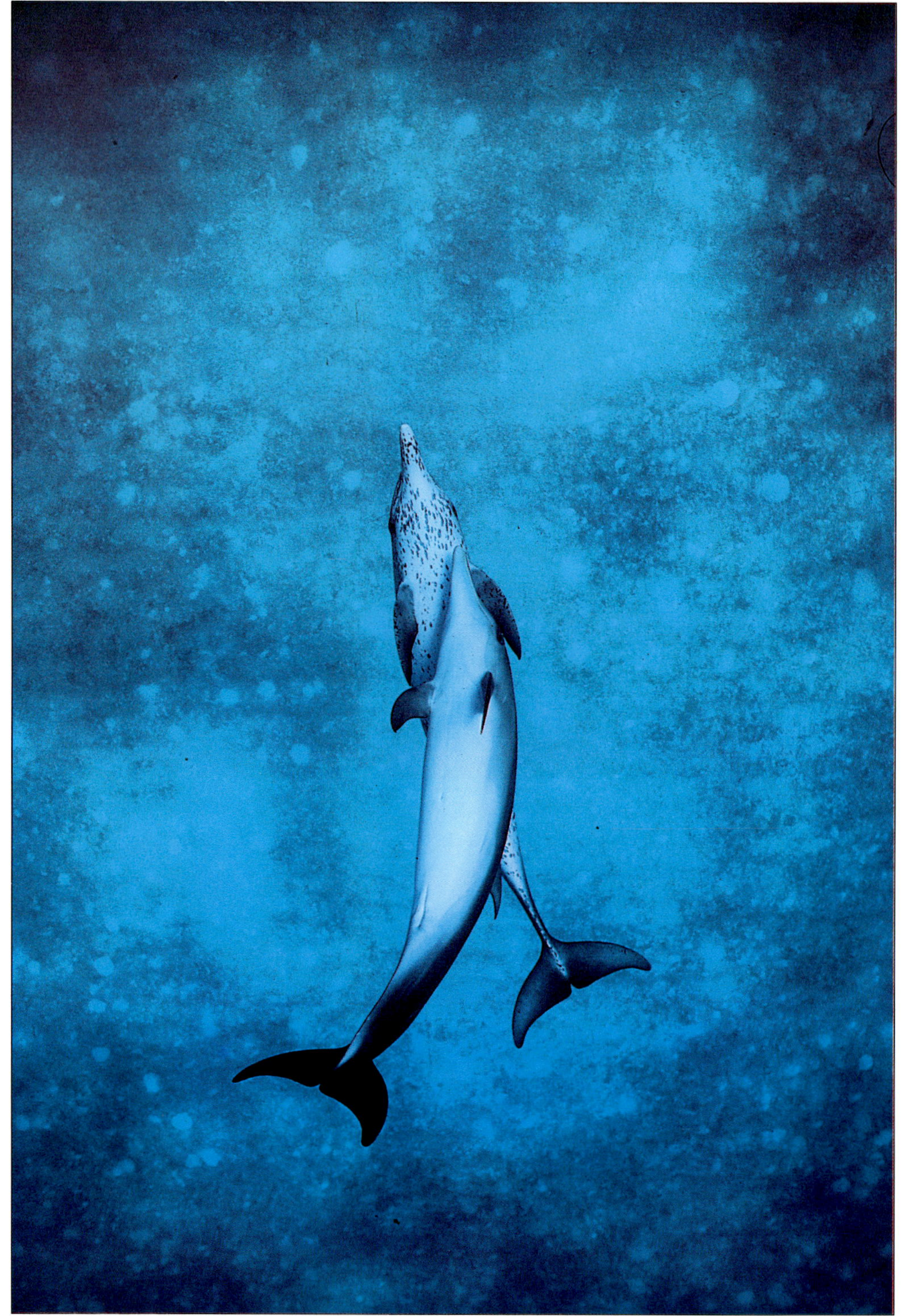

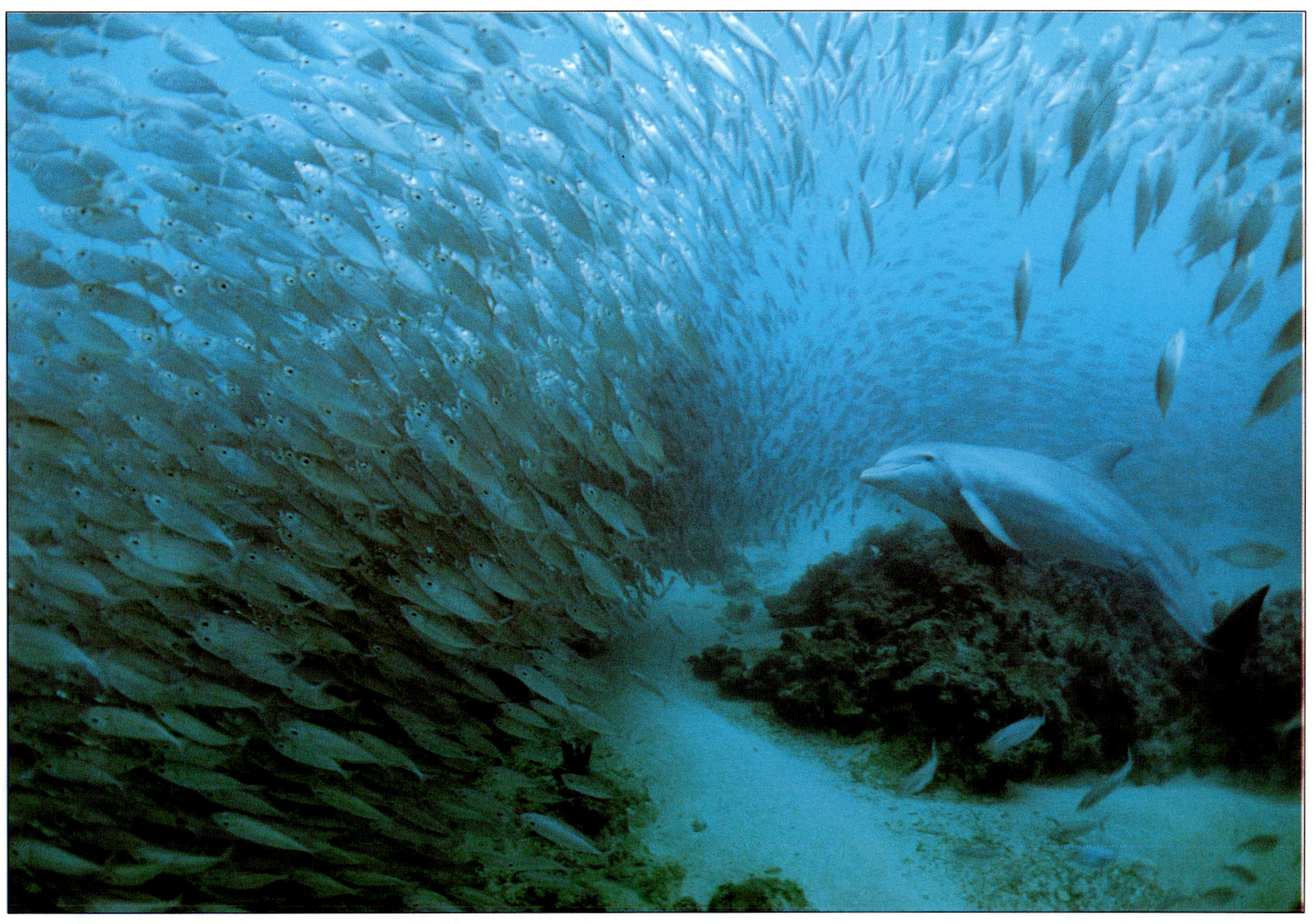

Norbert Wu
United States of America
HIGHLY COMMENDED

Bottle-nosed dolphin and school of fish

"I am not keen on dolphins being held in captivity, but the Institute of Marine Sciences in Roatan, Honduras, is one of the best and most humane captive facilities I have seen. The one-acre holding encompasses a small beach, eel grass and coral reef, and schools of fish are free to come and go through the holding net."

Nikon F4 with 16mm lens in underwater housing; 1/125 sec at f4; Kodachrome 64

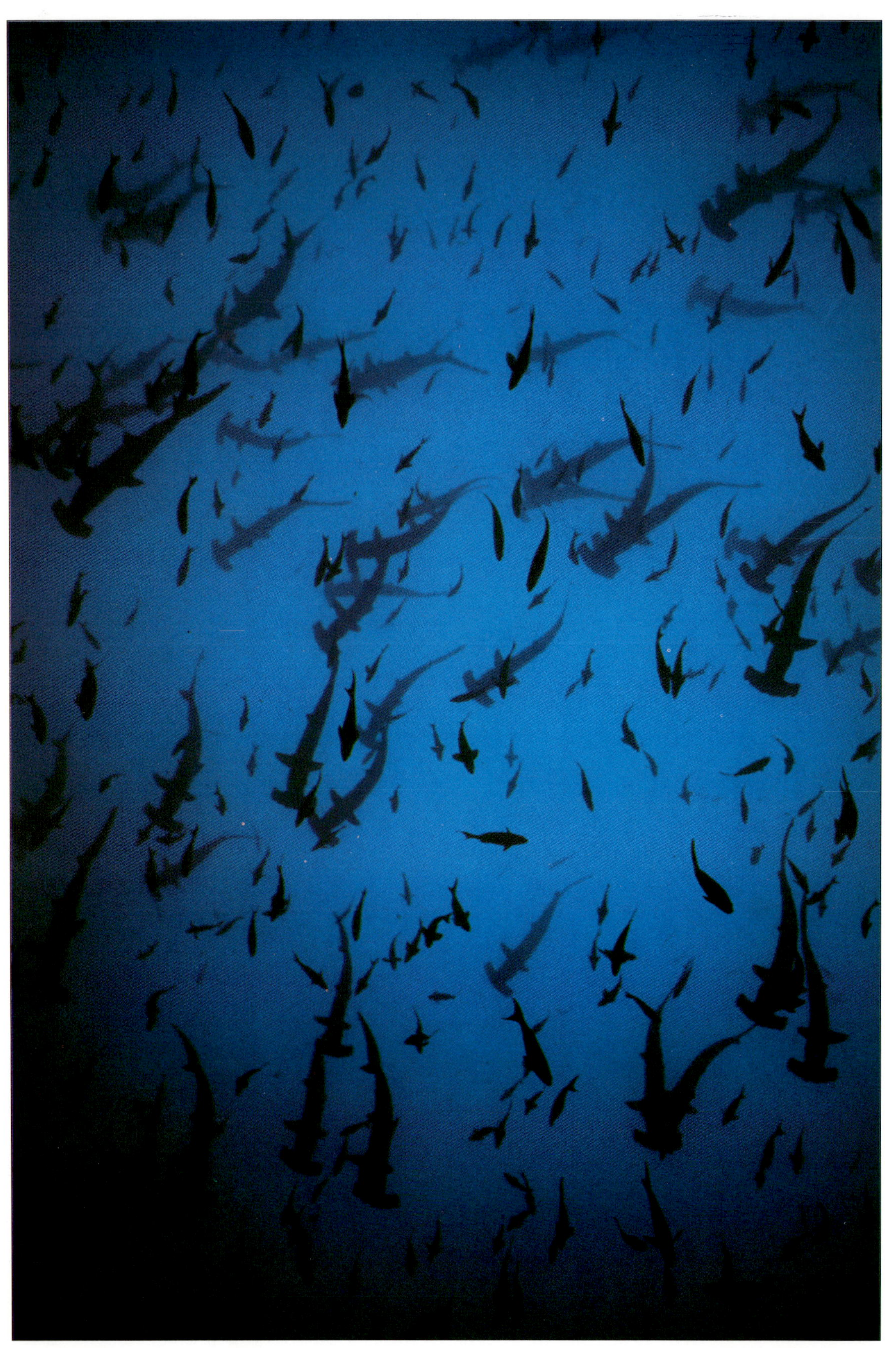

Norbert Wu

United States of America

RUNNER-UP

Hammerhead sharks

"I photographed this school of scalloped hammerhead sharks Sphyrna lewini *off Cocos Island, west of Costa Rica, at a seamount. Seamounts are underwater pinnacles that attract large gatherings of marine life. In the foreground are several creolefish, about 30 centimetres long; the sharks are about two metres long. No one knows why hammerheads gather like this, but they have never been known to attack divers while in schools. In fact, they actively avoid them, and to get close, a diver must hold his breath."*

Nikon F4 with 18mm lens in underwater housing; 1/125sec at f8; Kodak Lumiere 100

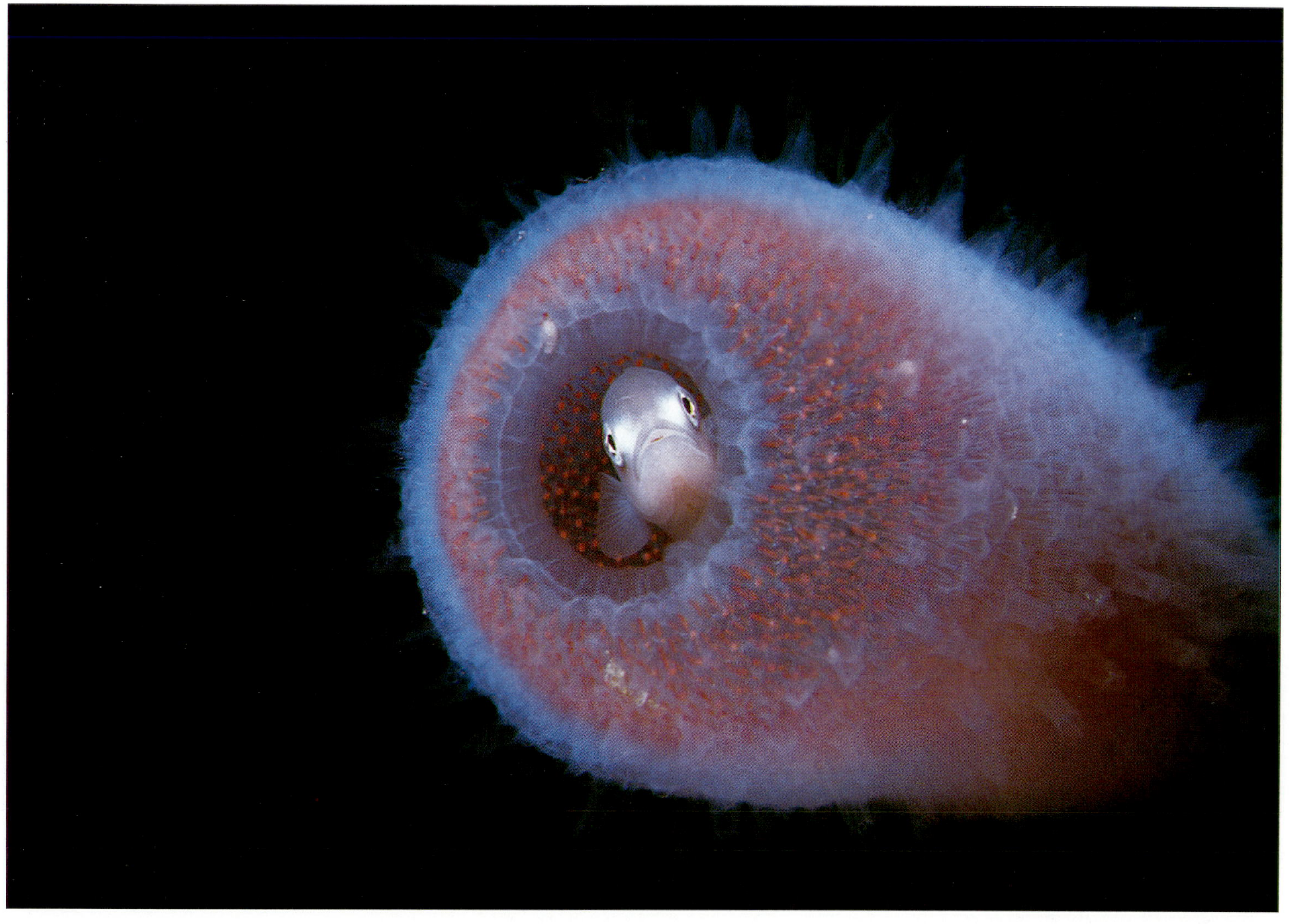

Mike Johnson
United States of America
HIGHLY COMMENDED

Comensal fish and salp

"Small fish in the open sea will often adopt any object larger than themselves for cover from predators: flotsam, kelp, and, in this case, another animal, the salp Pyrosoma tuberculata. *I came across this fish on a night dive 15 miles west of San Diego in late summer. At this time, the warm offshore waters of southern California are rich in zooplankton."*

Nikon F2 with 55m lens in underwater housing; flash 1/90 sec at f16; Kodak Elite 100

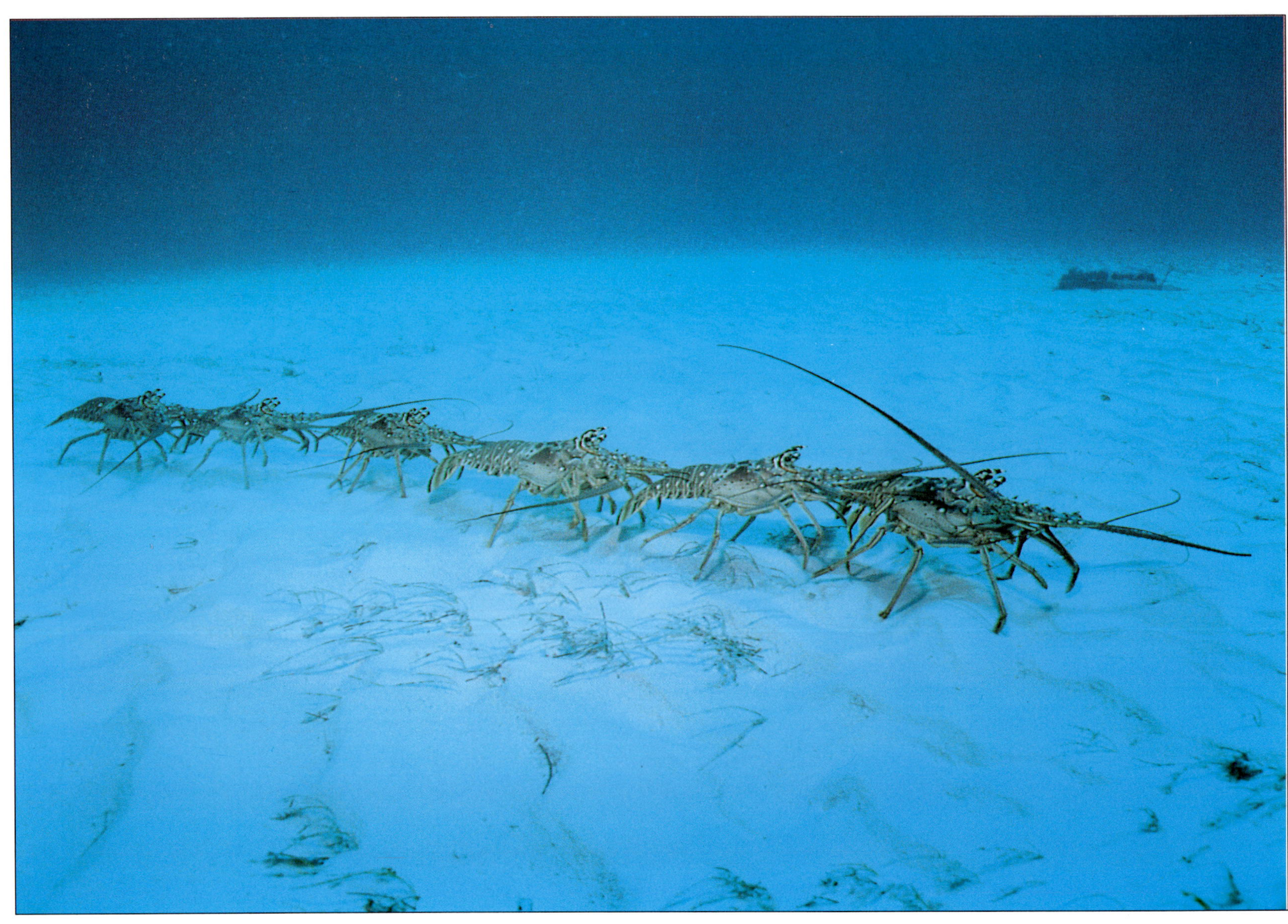

Howard Hall

United States of America

HIGHLY COMMENDED

Spiny lobsters migrating

"I photographed these Caribbean spiny lobsters in the Bahamas. They were migrating from the shallow waters of the Bahama Banks to deeper water and reefs, after the first storm of the season."

Nikon 8008 with 24mm lens in underwater housing; strobe; 1/60 sec at f11; Kodachrome 64

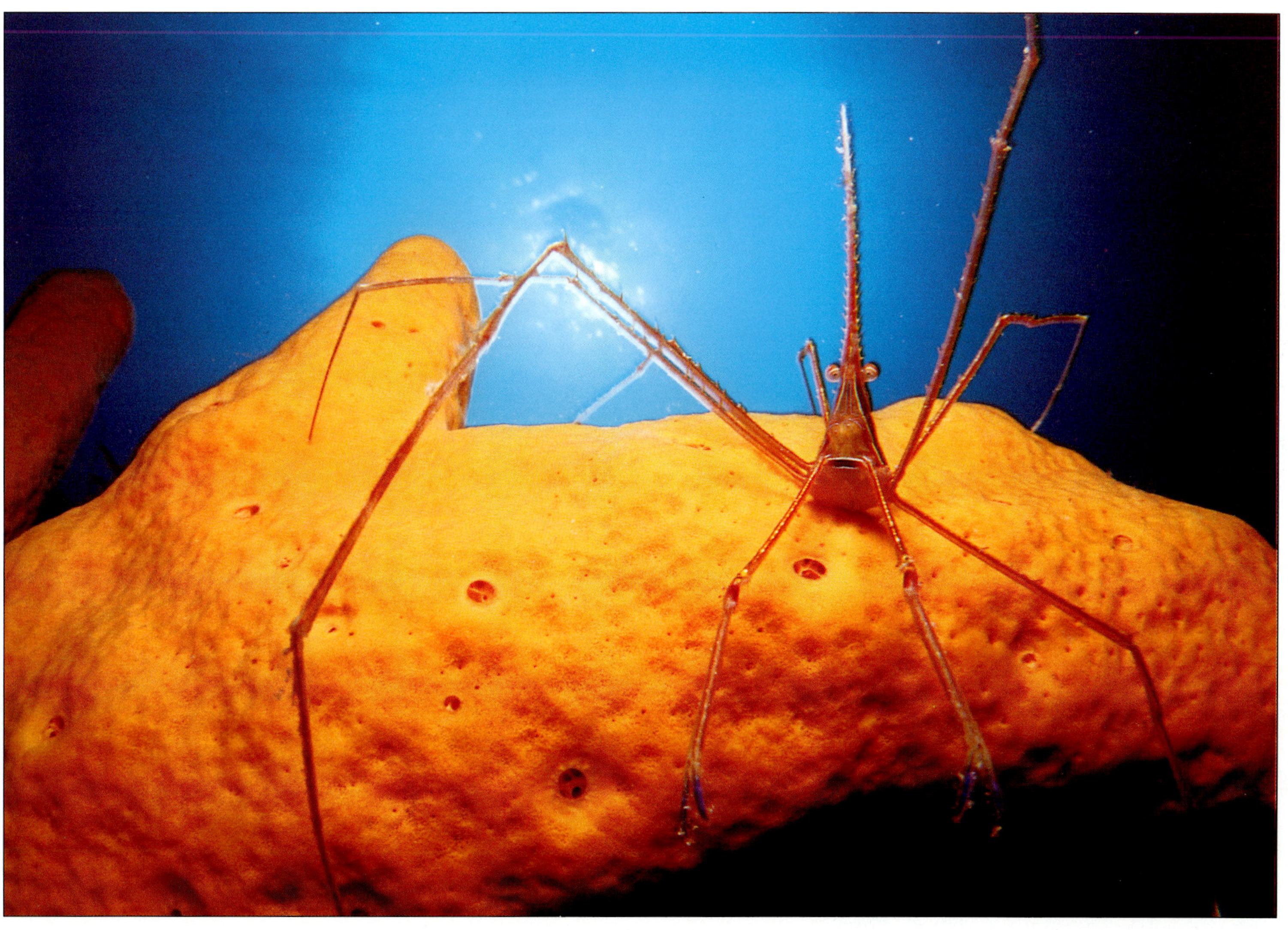

Jürgen Freund
Germany
HIGHLY COMMENDED

Arrowcrab

"While on a dive off the Isla de la Juventad, Cuba, I came across an arrowcrab sitting in the open on a sponge. This bold creature with its rolling eyes was not put out when I moved in closer and even tried to crawl onto the camera. I used a specially designed lens, which has a greater depth of field than an ordinary macro lens."

Nikonos III with macro lens; 1/15 sec at f32; Fujichrome 100

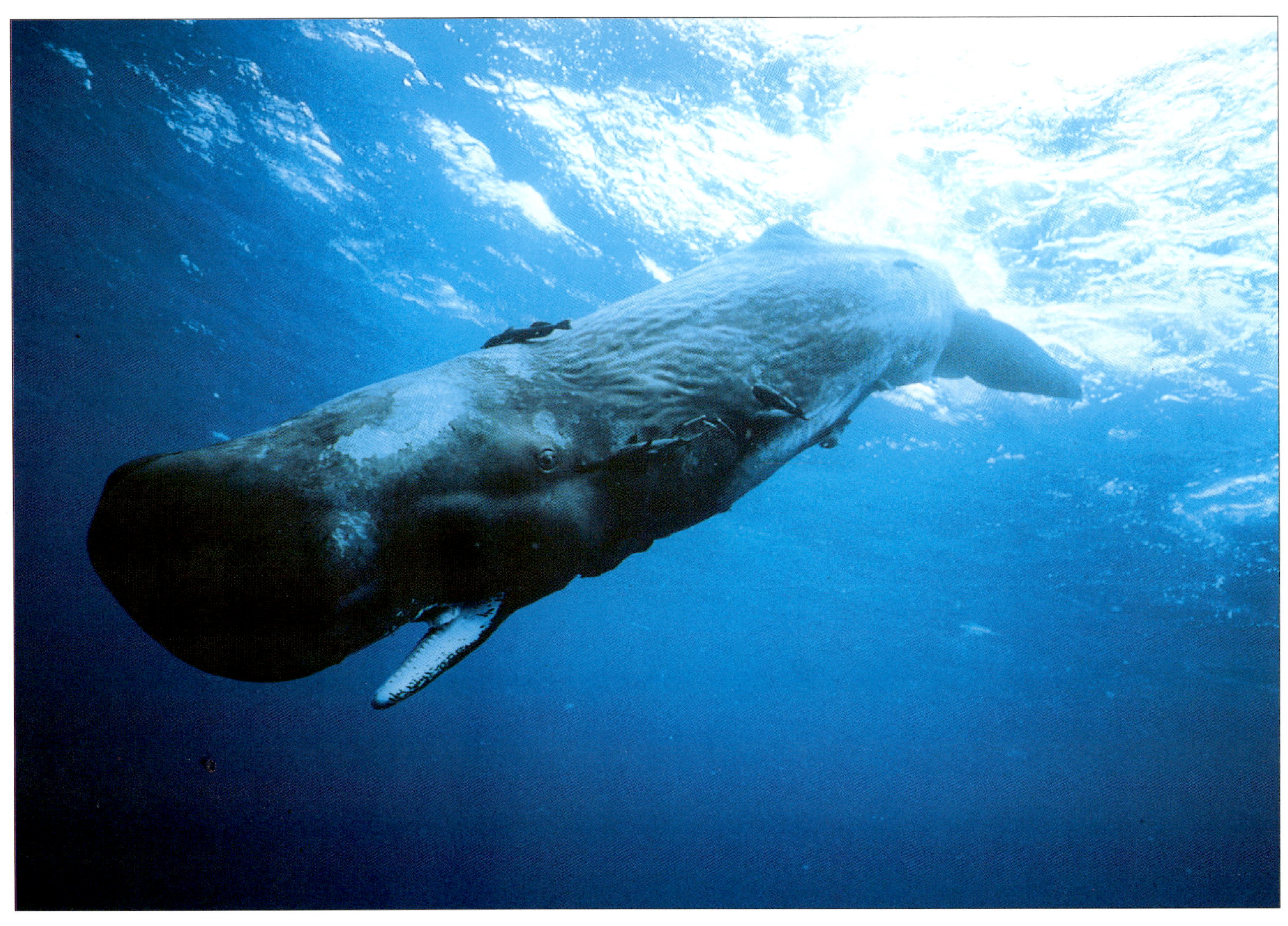

Howard Hall
United States of America
HIGHLY COMMENDED

Sperm whale

"This baby sperm whale, photographed off Dominica in the Caribbean, was waiting at the ocean surface for its mother to return from the deep, where she was probably feeding."

Nikonos III with 15mm lens; 1/60 sec at f8; Kodachrome 64

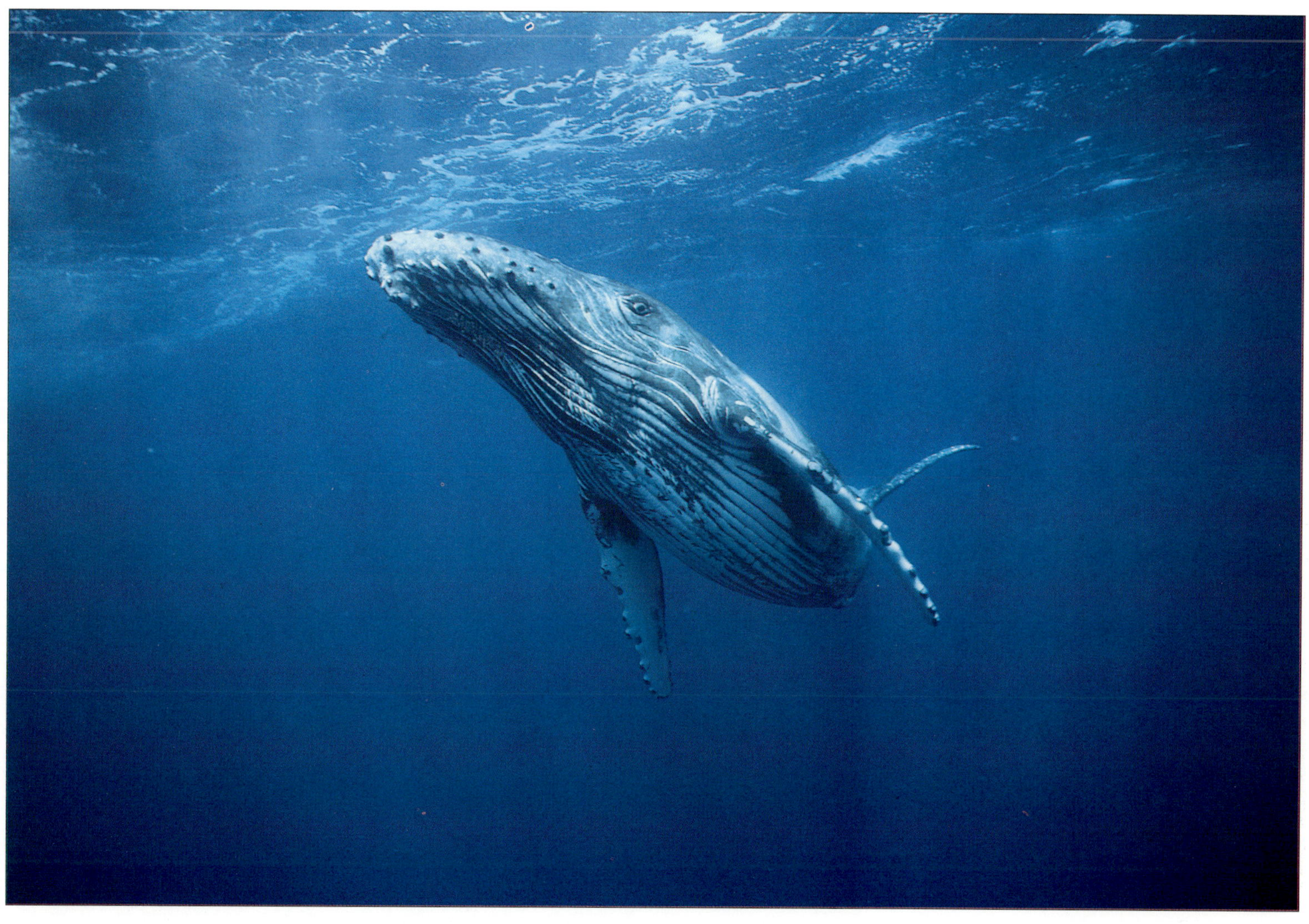

Kelvin Aitken
New Zealand
HIGHLY COMMENDED

Humpback whale calf

"While working on an article about the marine life north of Tonga, we followed this calf with its mother and made several unsuccessful attempts to photograph them. Once, when I saw the calf dive in our direction, I jumped into the water, swam to about eight metres from it and managed to take almost a complete roll of film as it swam past me, never once taking its enquiring eye off me."

Nikonos V with 15mm lens; 1/250 sec at f4; Kodachrome 64

Animal Portraits

Photographs entered for this category must show animal subjects in close-up.

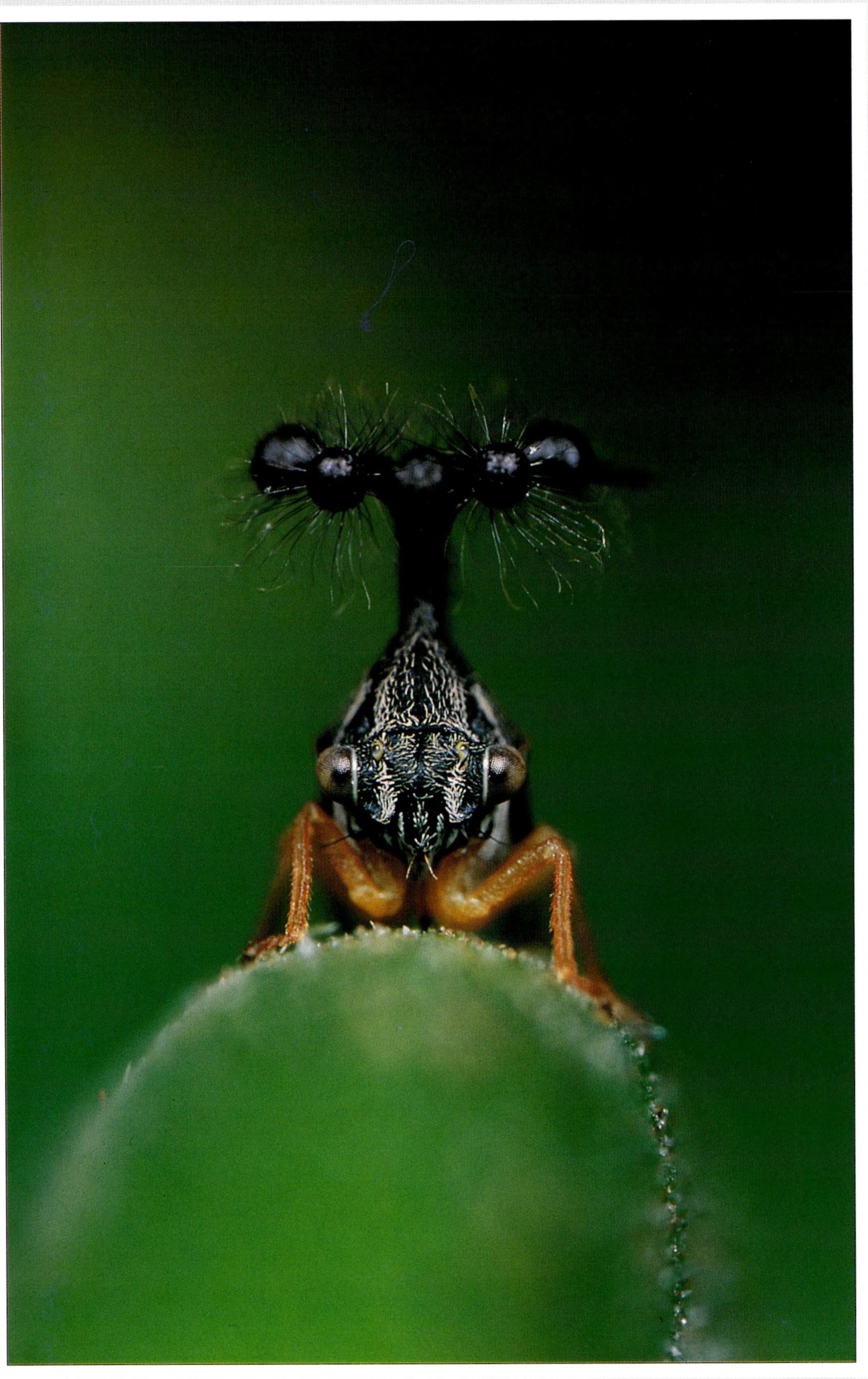

Mitsuhiko Imamori
Japan
WINNER

Four-humped treehopper

"The four-humped treehopper Bocydium globulare *lives in light, open areas of forest and is often found sucking sap from young leaves. When it is surprised, for example by a photographer approaching, it jumps. It jumps so fast and is so tiny – about six millimetres – that the human eye cannot follow its movement.*
I photographed this insect in Brazil using some specially made bellows to magnify the creature."

Pentax 6x7 with 50mm lens; bellows; tripod; flash; 1/30 sec at f16; Fujichrome Velvia

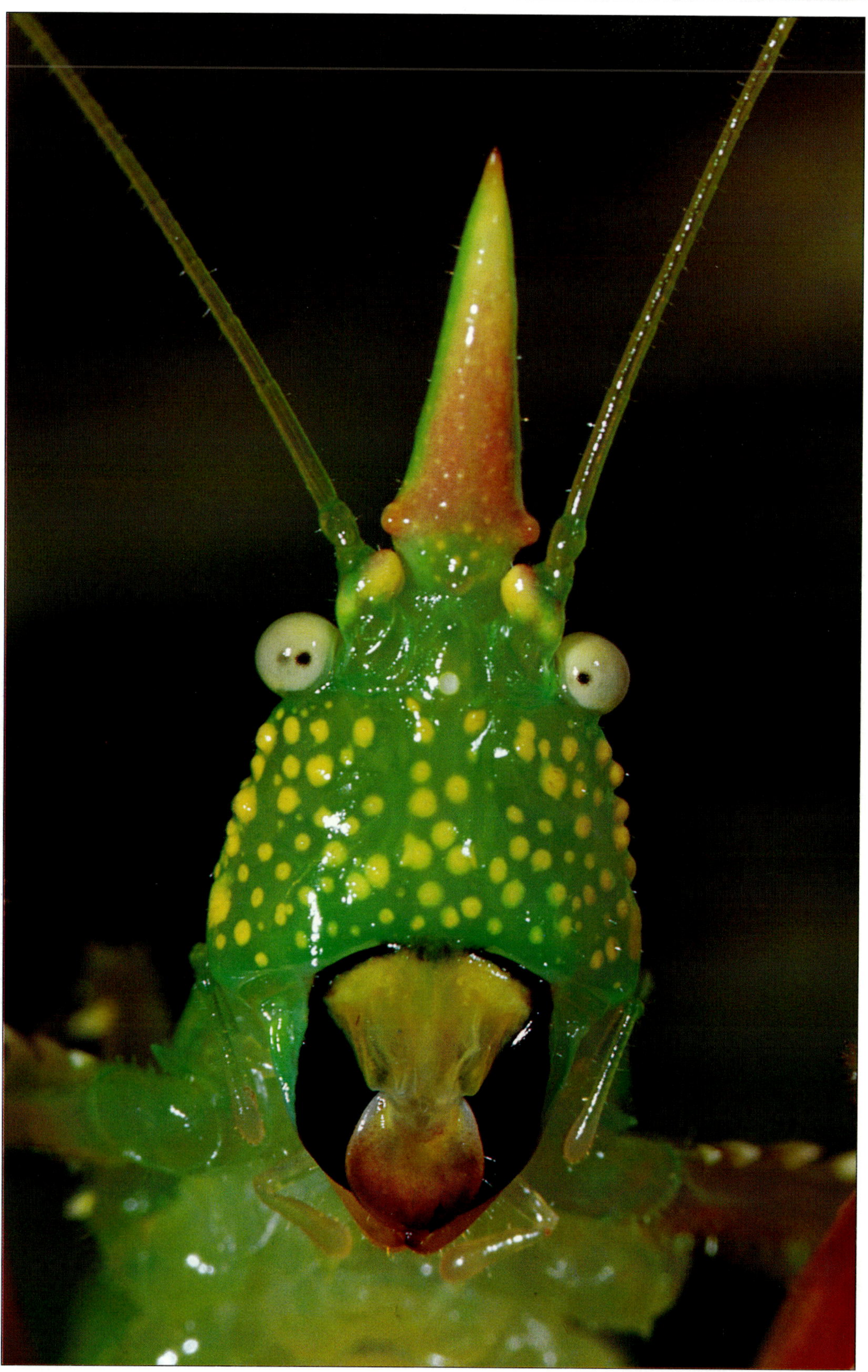

Brian Kenney
United States of America
RUNNER-UP

Young horned katydid

"I found this horned katydid one night in the rainforest in Costa Rica. From the side, this insect seems to be a simple leaf imitator. Its bizarre appearance only becomes clear on close examination. I didn't have enough light to take a close-up, and so I caught the katydid and photographed it the next morning and then released it back into the wild."

Nikon 8008s with 105mm macro lens and extension tubes; flash; 1/250 sec at f16; Fujichrome Velvia rated at 40ASA

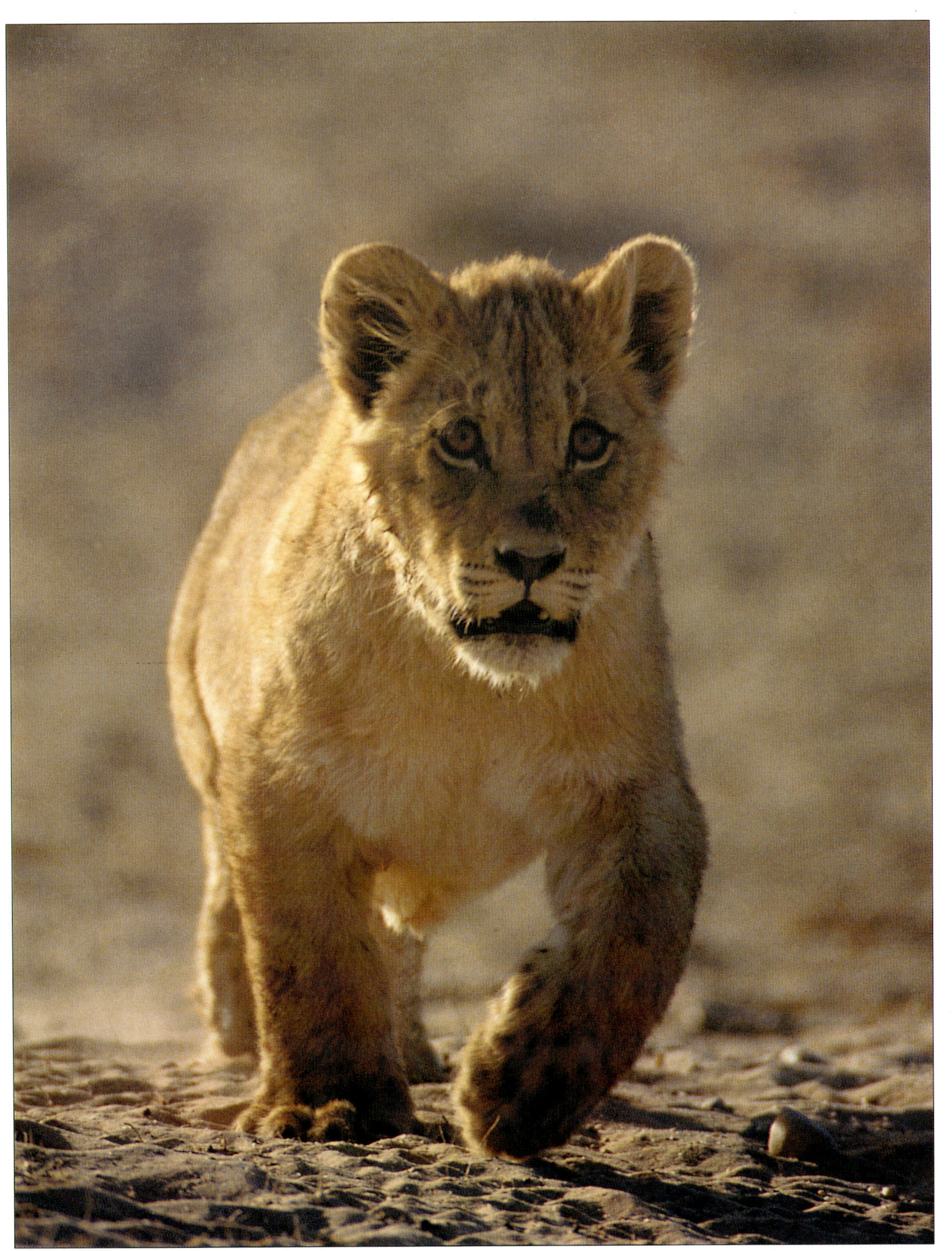

Tim Jackson
United Kingdom
HIGHLY COMMENDED

Young lion cub

"When I first saw this lion cub he was as wide as he was tall as he was long. He is the only surviving cub of a litter, and rather spoilt because of it. I watched him chase nine elands, each of which can weigh up to 900kg, and took this picture just as he was strutting back to the pride. He then proceeded to annoy the big pride male by chewing on various parts of his body."

Nikon F801S with 400mm lens; bean bag; 1/250 sec at f5.6; Fujichrome 100

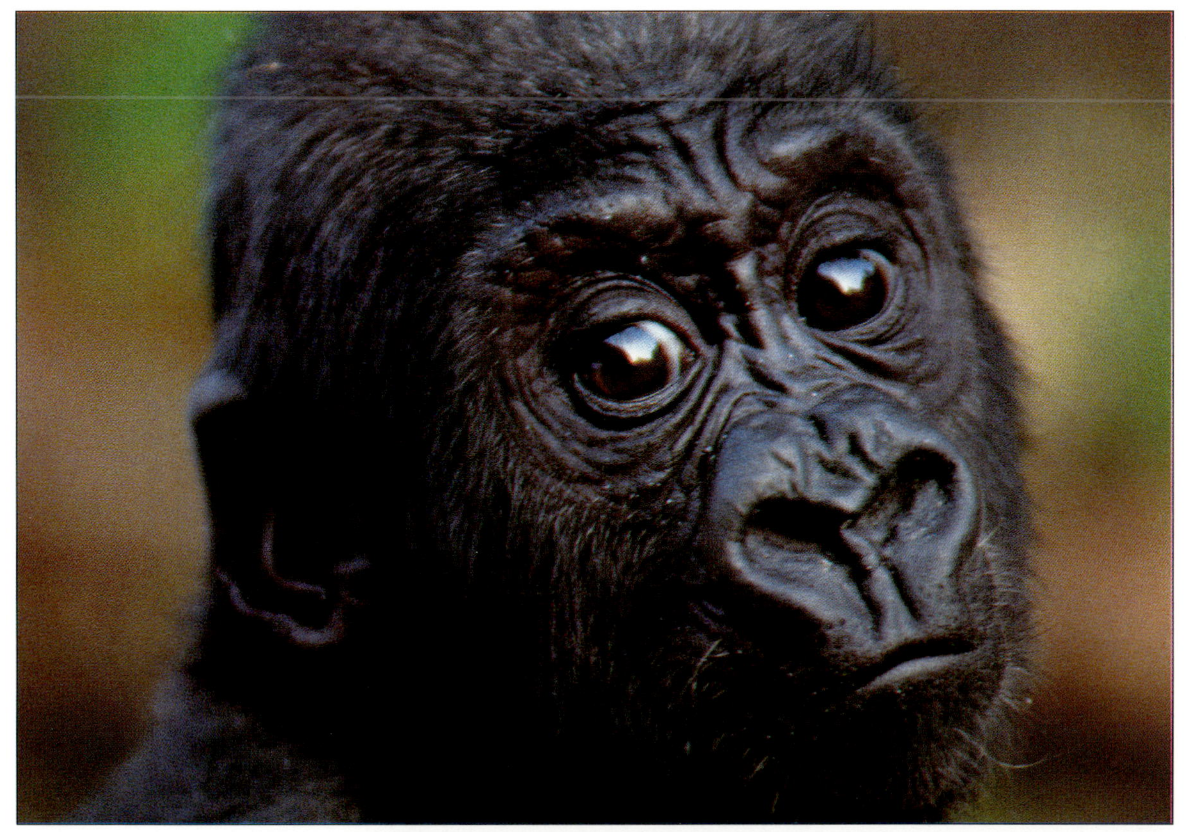

Jan Vermeer
The Netherlands
HIGHLY COMMENDED

Baby gorilla

"Kukuma was born at Apenheul Zoo and is about seven months old in this photograph. The zoo has excellent facilities for primates, and I took the picture as part of a project to illustrate a book about the zoo. Kukuma now lives in Belfast Zoo."

Nikon 801S with 80-200mm lens; 1/60 sec at f5.6;

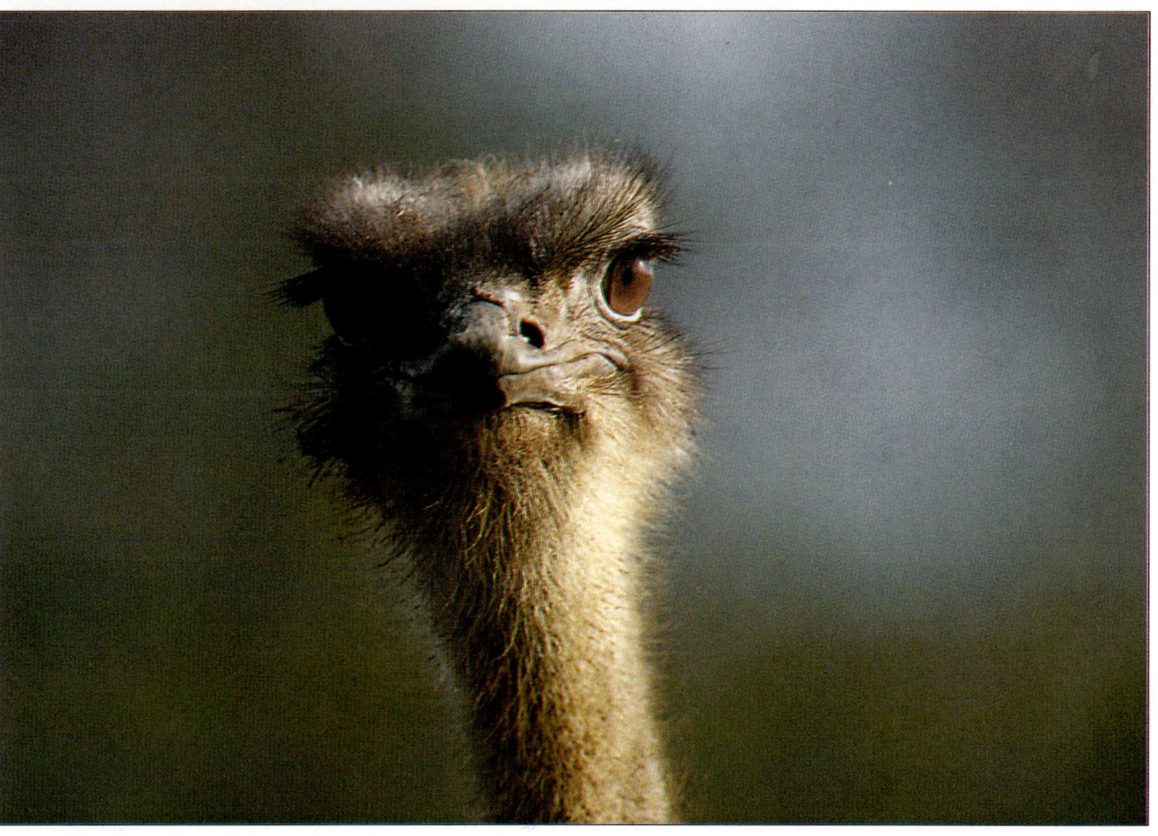

Tony Hamblin
United Kingdom
HIGHLY COMMENDED

Rhea

"I made a special trip to the Cotswold Wildlife Park to take portraits of more unusual subjects for my entry for this competition. Despite being captive, this rhea was surprisingly difficult to photograph as it was constantly on the move in its large enclosure."

Canon T90 with 500mm lens and x1.4 extender; tripod; 1/60 sec at f8; Kodachrome 64

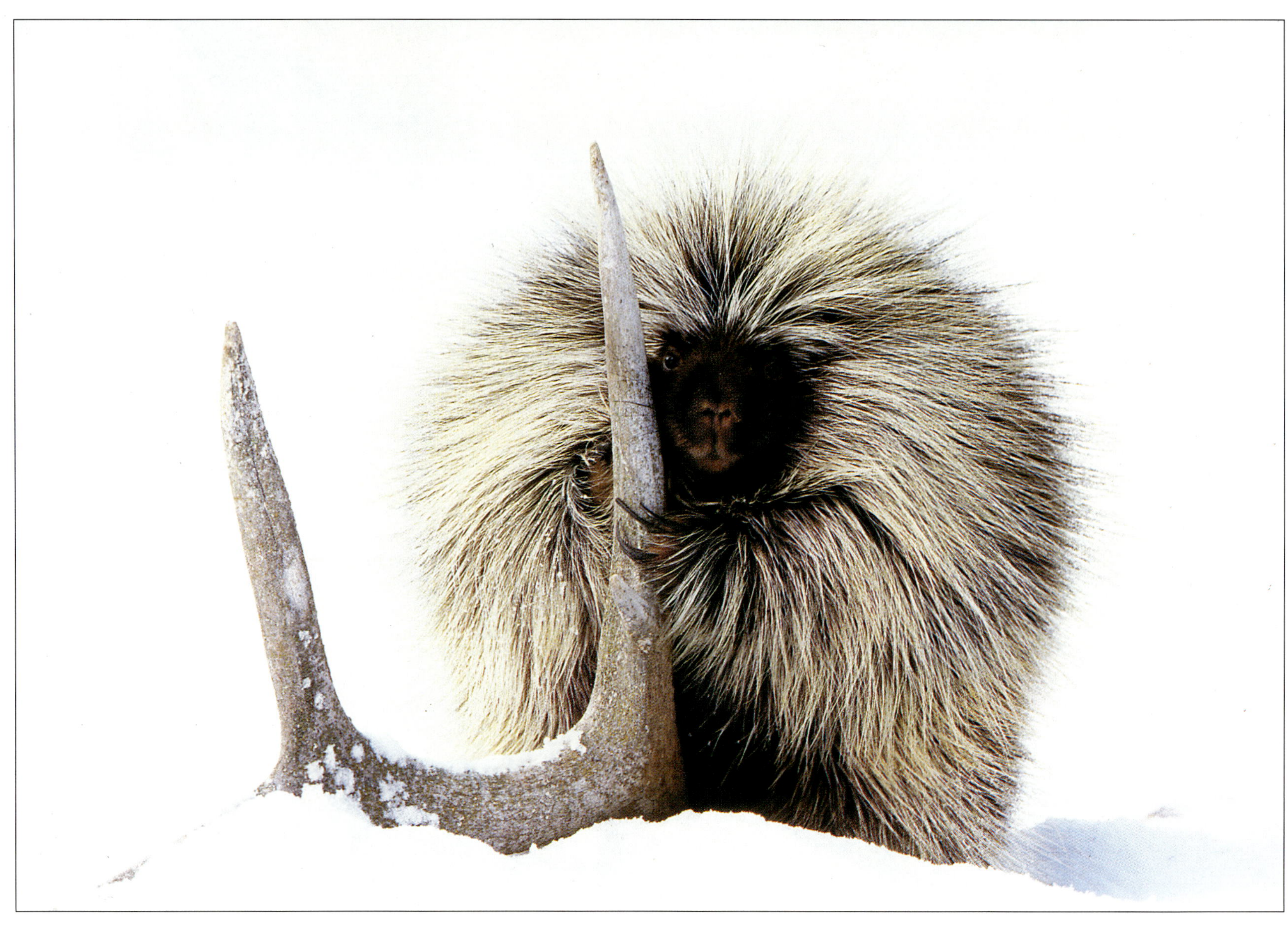

Carl R Sams II
United States of America
HIGHLY COMMENDED

Porcupine and elk antler

"I came upon this porcupine in the Glacier National Park after the sun had already dropped behind the mountain. Usually they run away, but shed elk antler is an important food because of the salts and minerals it contains, and so the porcupine stayed and posed for a short time."

Nikon F4 with 80-200mm lens; 1/8 sec at f5.6; Fujichrome 100

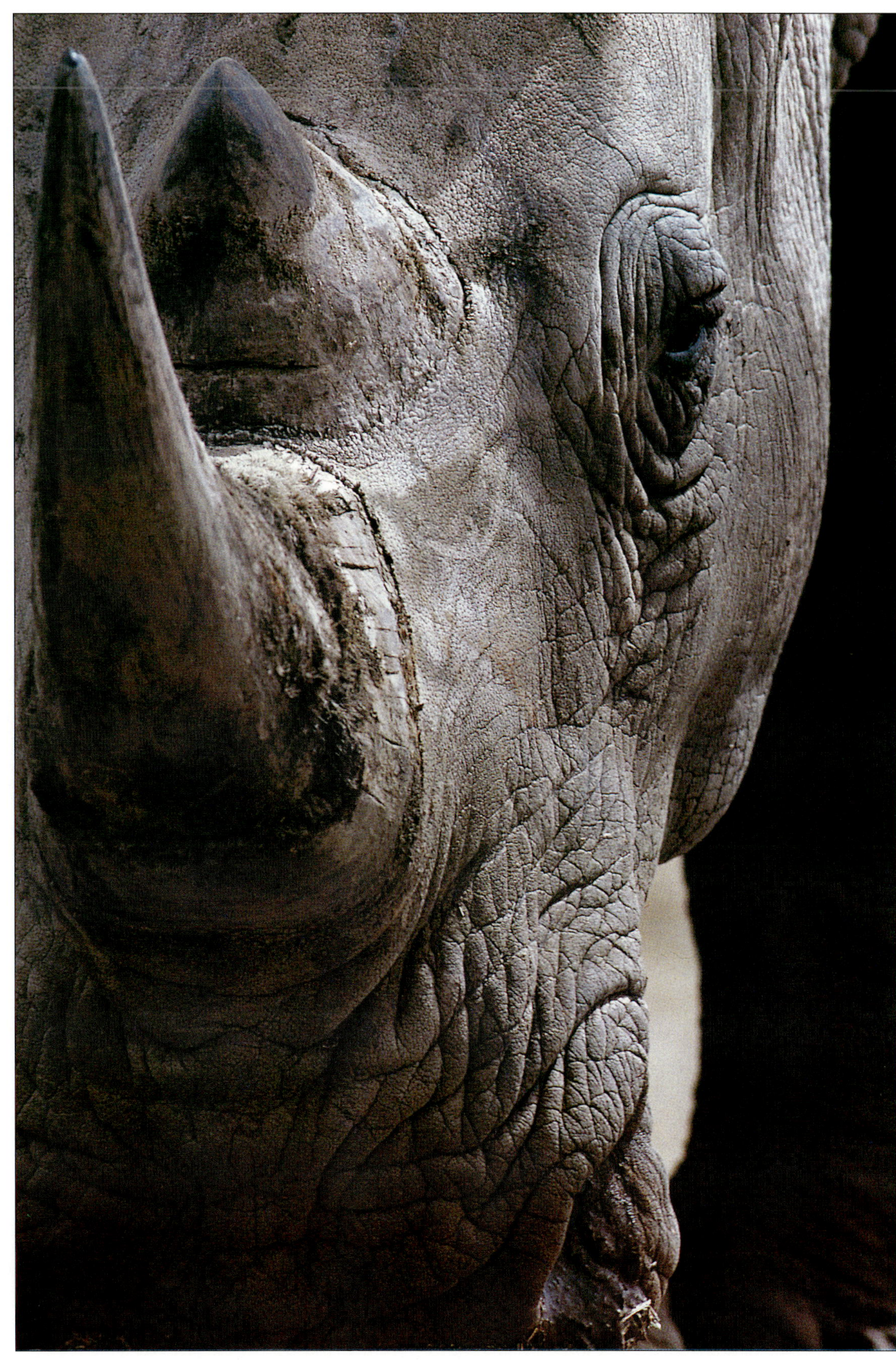

Karl Ammann
Switzerland
HIGHLY COMMENDED

White rhino

"Several Laikipia ranches have southern white rhinos. They are much more approachable than the black rhinos. In this case, the rhino was accompanied by a herdsman, and I was able to lie on the ground and get this low-level shot with side lighting to create a half face portrait."

Nikon 8008S with 80-200mm lens; 1/125 sec at f8; Kodachrome 200

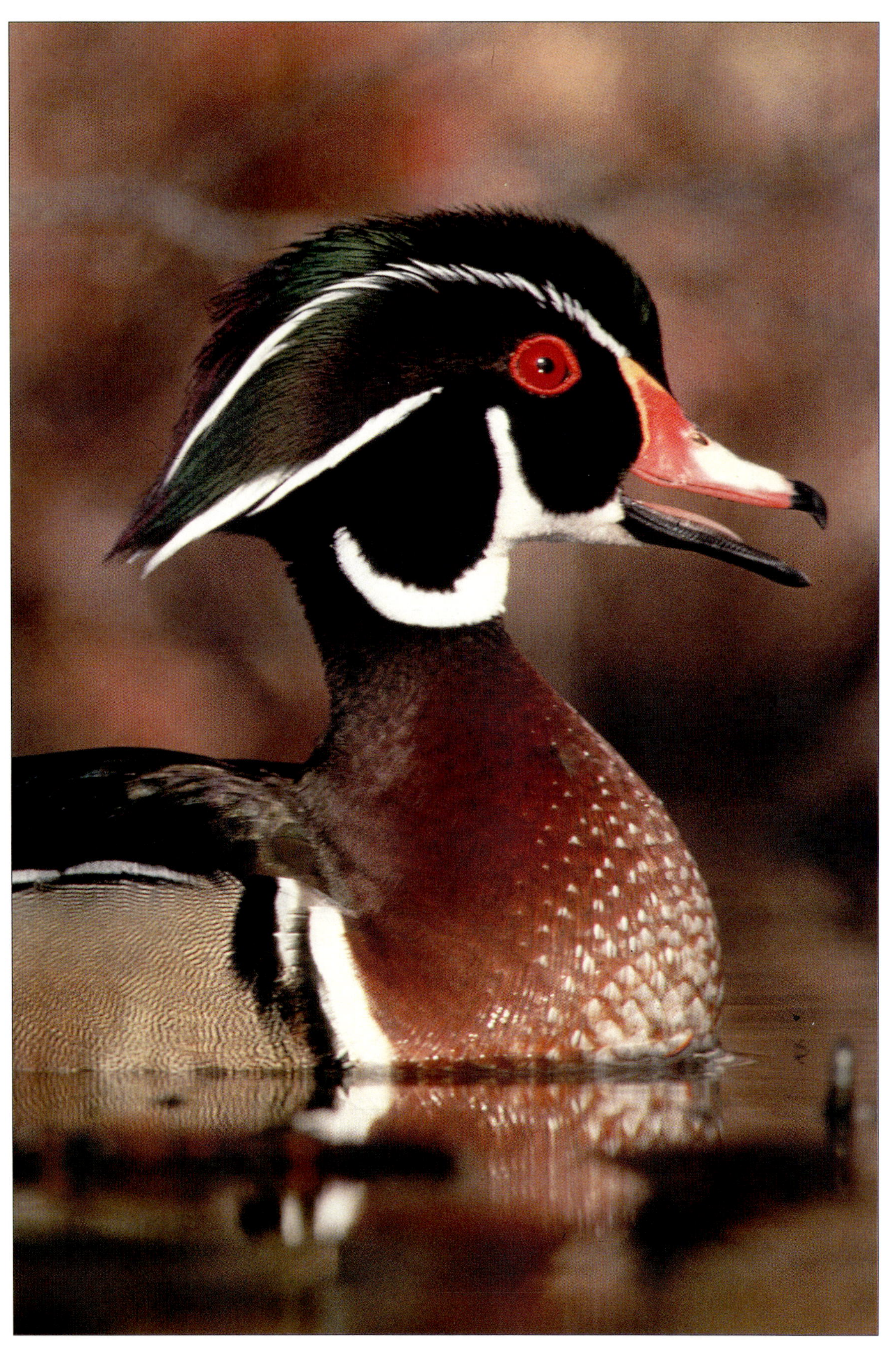

Scott Nielsen
United States of America
HIGHLY COMMENDED

Wood duck drake

"I came across a pair of wood duck looking for a nest site in a tree cavity and set up a hide. Only the hen goes into the potential nest hole while the male stays on the water calling and raising his brilliantly coloured crest so that she can easily find him again. This is often the best time to get close-up photographs."

Nikon F4 with 300mm lens and x2 extender; 1/250sec at f8; Fujichrome 100

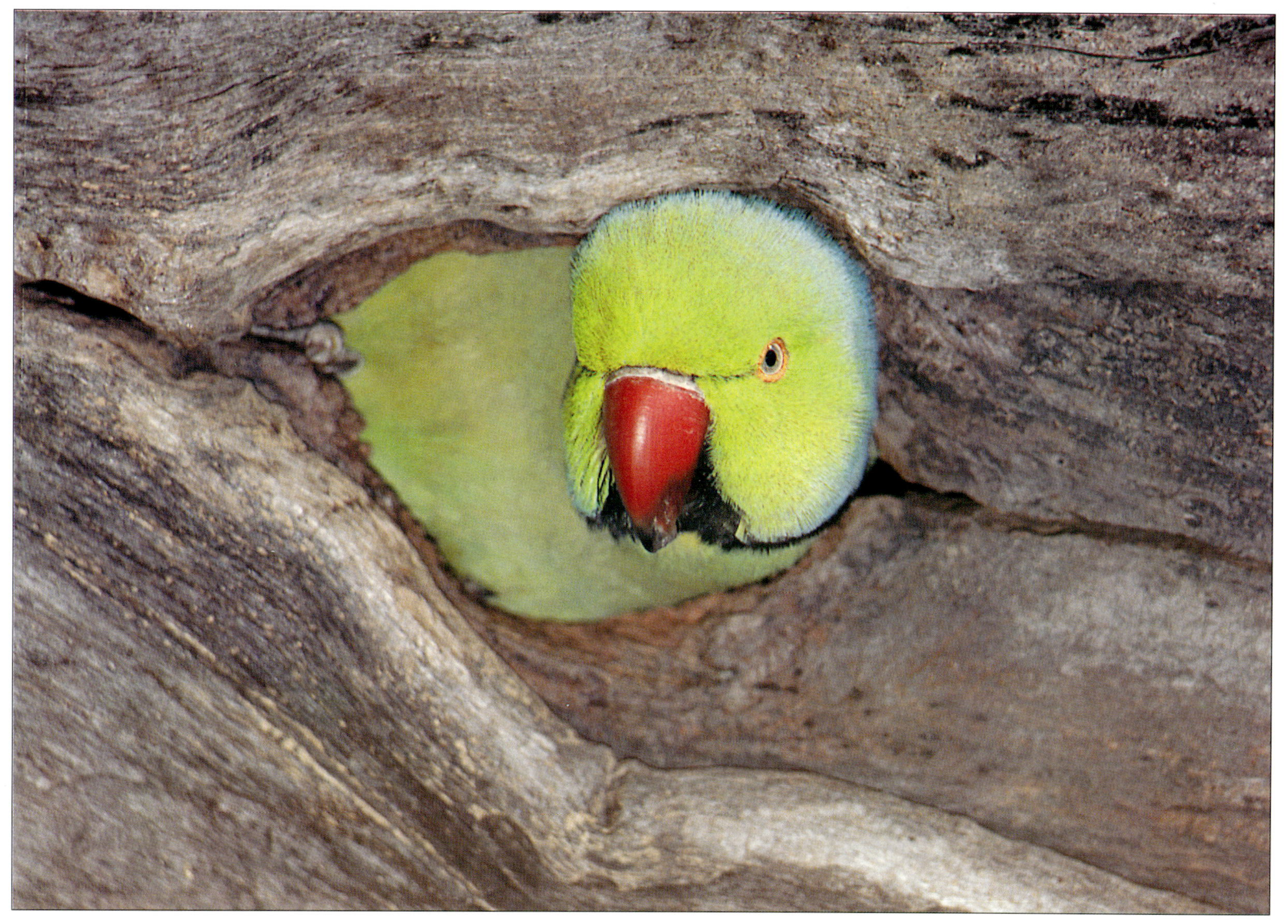

Dr P Kumar
India
HIGHLY COMMENDED

Rose-ringed parakeet

"Rose-ringed parakeets are common in Keoladeo Ghana National Park, Bharatpur. During February and March they start to select suitable tree holes for nesting. As we passed this tree, the parrot inside popped its head out. We enjoyed watching it surveying its surroundings, rotating its head almost 360° as it did so."

Nikon 801 with 300mm lens and extension tube; flash; 1/250 sec at f11; Fujichrome 100

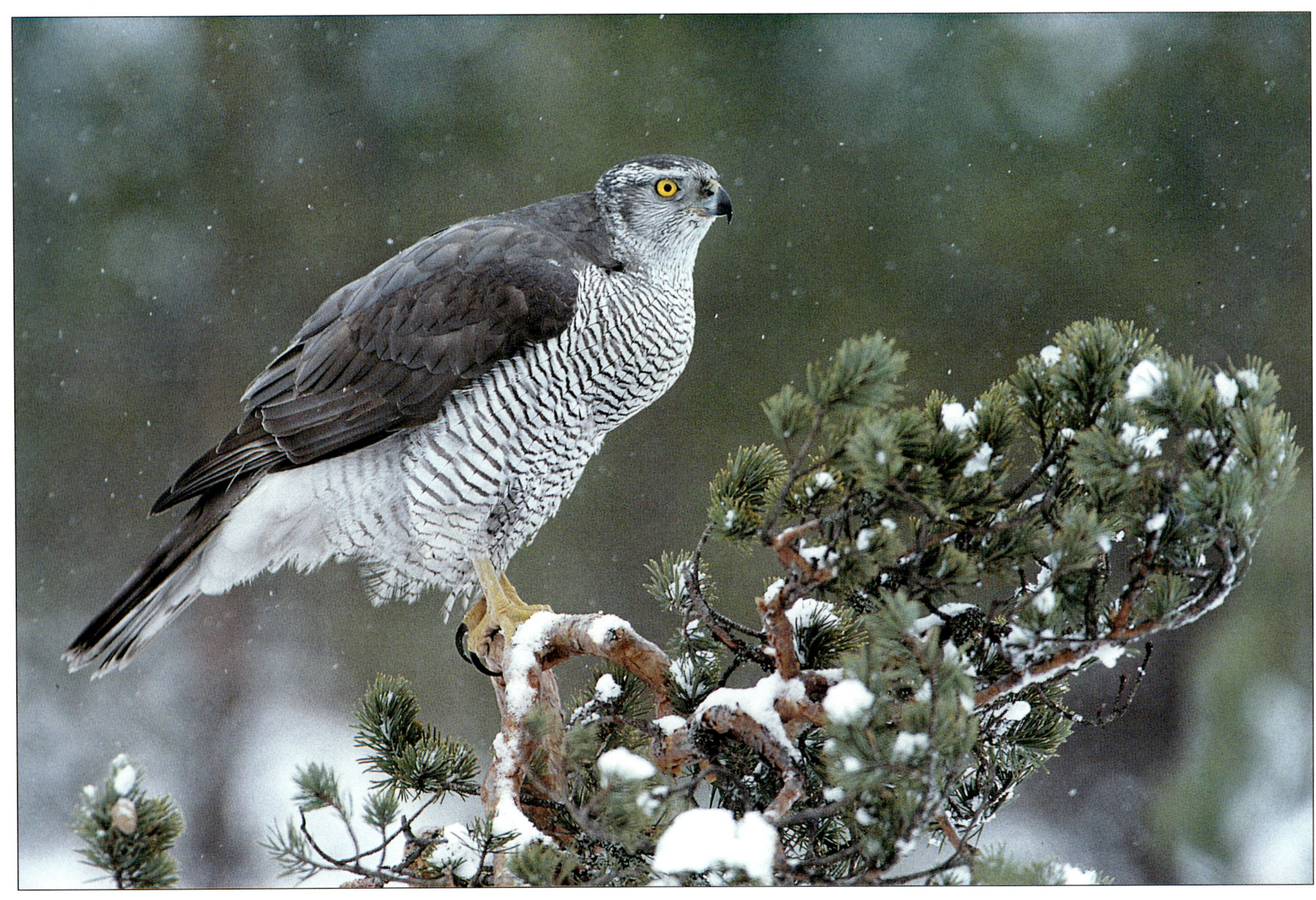

Tapani Räsänen
Finland
HIGHLY COMMENDED

Goshawk

"The goshawk is one of Finland's most handsome birds, and for several years I have dreamt of taking a photograph of one in the snow. I know from experience that, after eating, the goshawk flies to the nearest tree staying there for just a short time. I have managed to take many pictures of the goshawk, but only one when it was snowing."

Canon EOS10 with 300mm lens; tripod1/250 sec at f4.5; Kodachrome 200

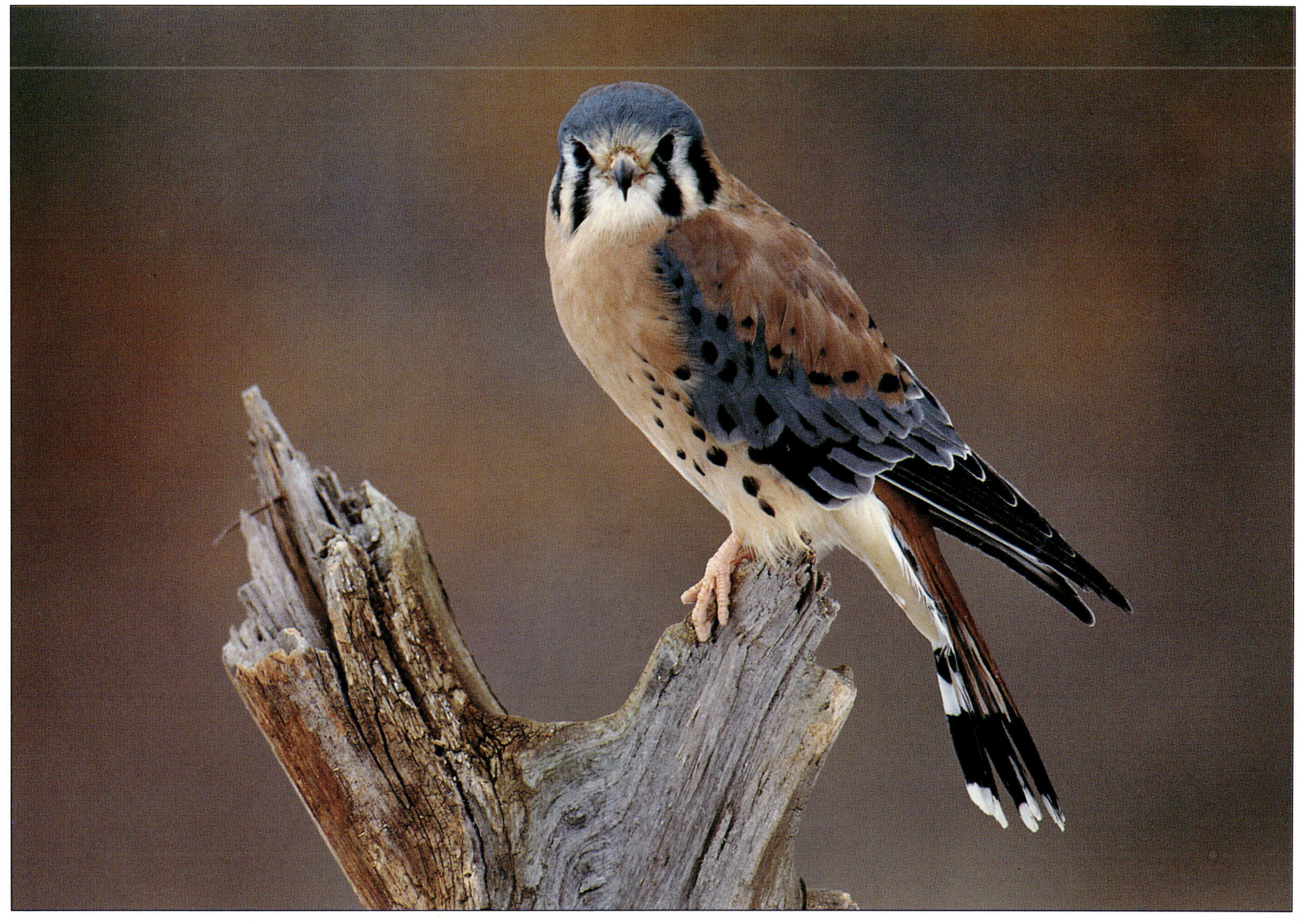

Doug Locke
United States of America
HIGHLY COMMENDED

American kestrel

"The American kestrel is one of the smallest and most common falcons in North America. I took this photo during the Fall at a Raptor Rehabilitation Center in Michigan."

Nikon 8008 with 300mm lens; tripod; Fujichrome Velvia

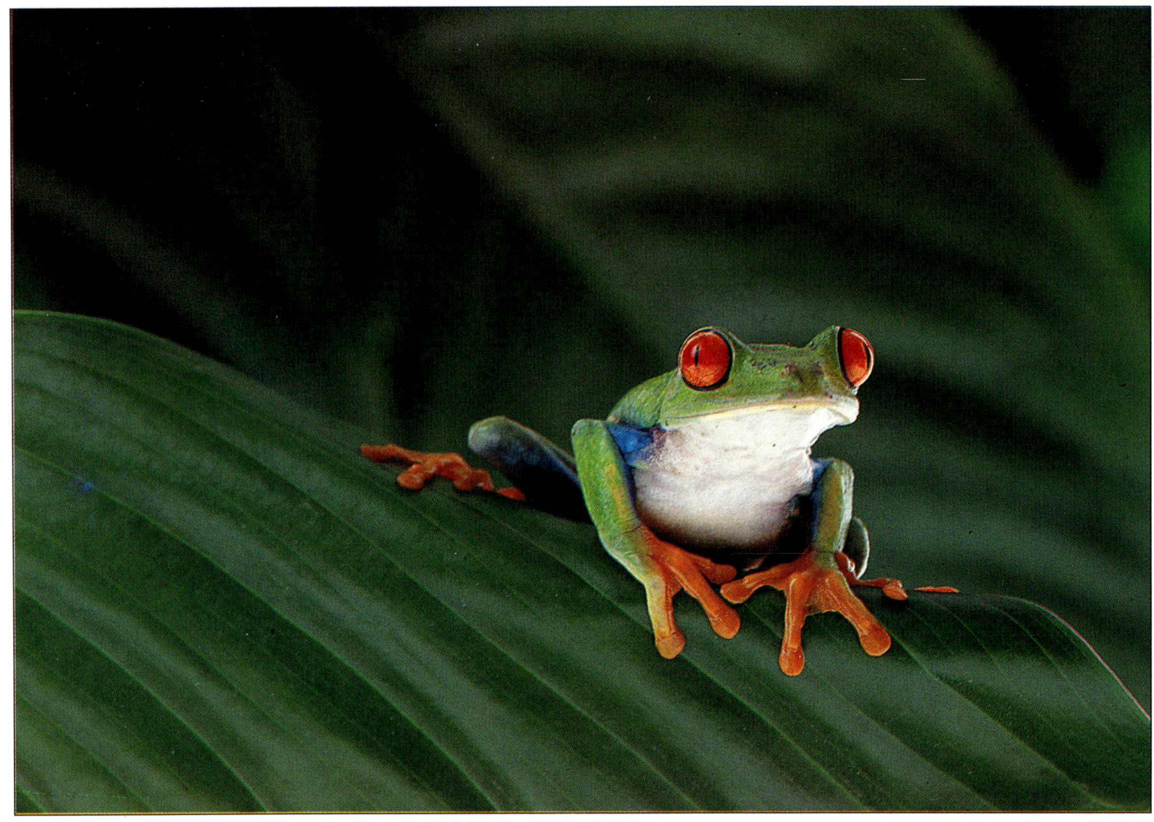

Renee Lynn
United States of America
HIGHLY COMMENDED

Red-eyed tree frog

"The red-eyed tree frog Agalychnis callidryas is native to the rainforests of Central and South America. This individual was born in captivity, and I photographed it on a Spathiphyllum, a South American plant."

Nikon F4 with 105mm lens; flash; Fujichrome Velvia

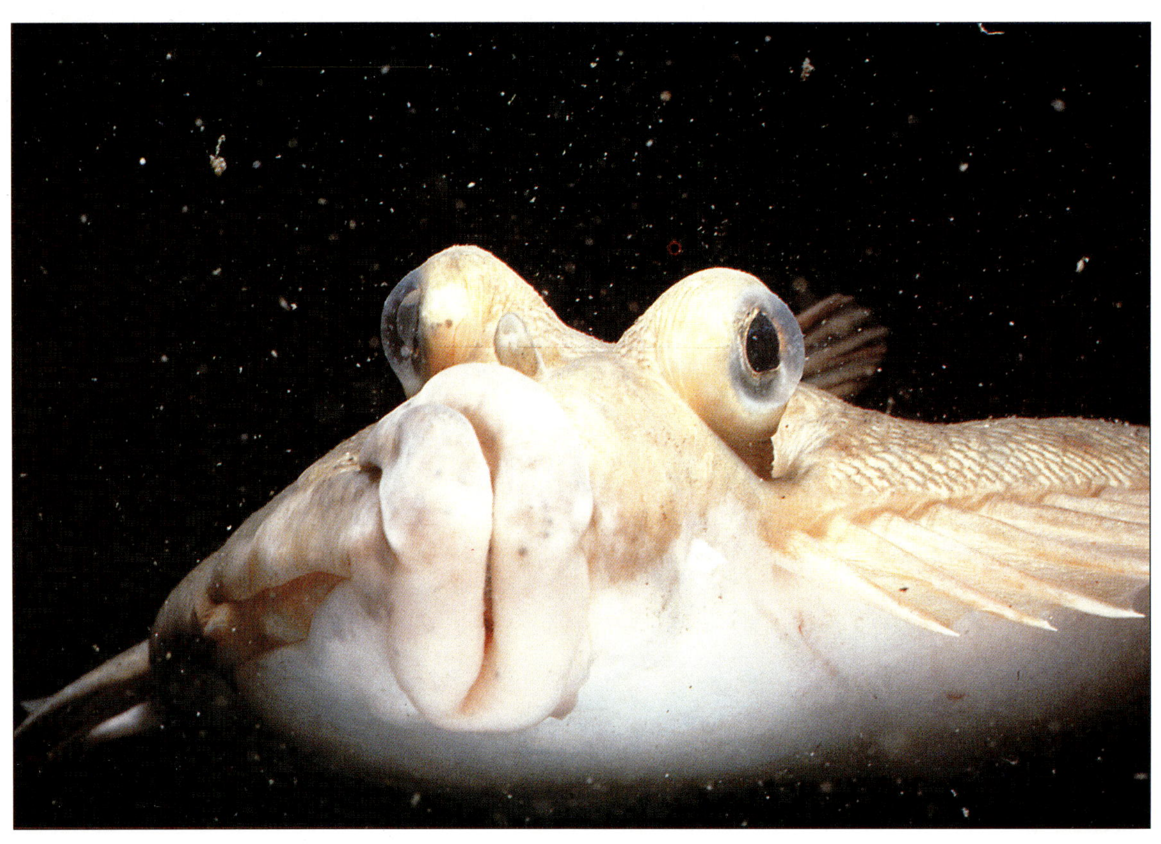

Jeffrey L Rotman
United States of America
HIGHLY COMMENDED

Windowpane flounder

"This close-up was taken to illustrate the eye migration which occurs during the first six months of the flounder's life. The eye on the right side migrates all the way to the left side, and the fish spends the rest of its life lying on its side. I took the picture off the coast of Massachussetts. "

Nikon F3 with 55mm lens; flash; f16; Kodachrome 64

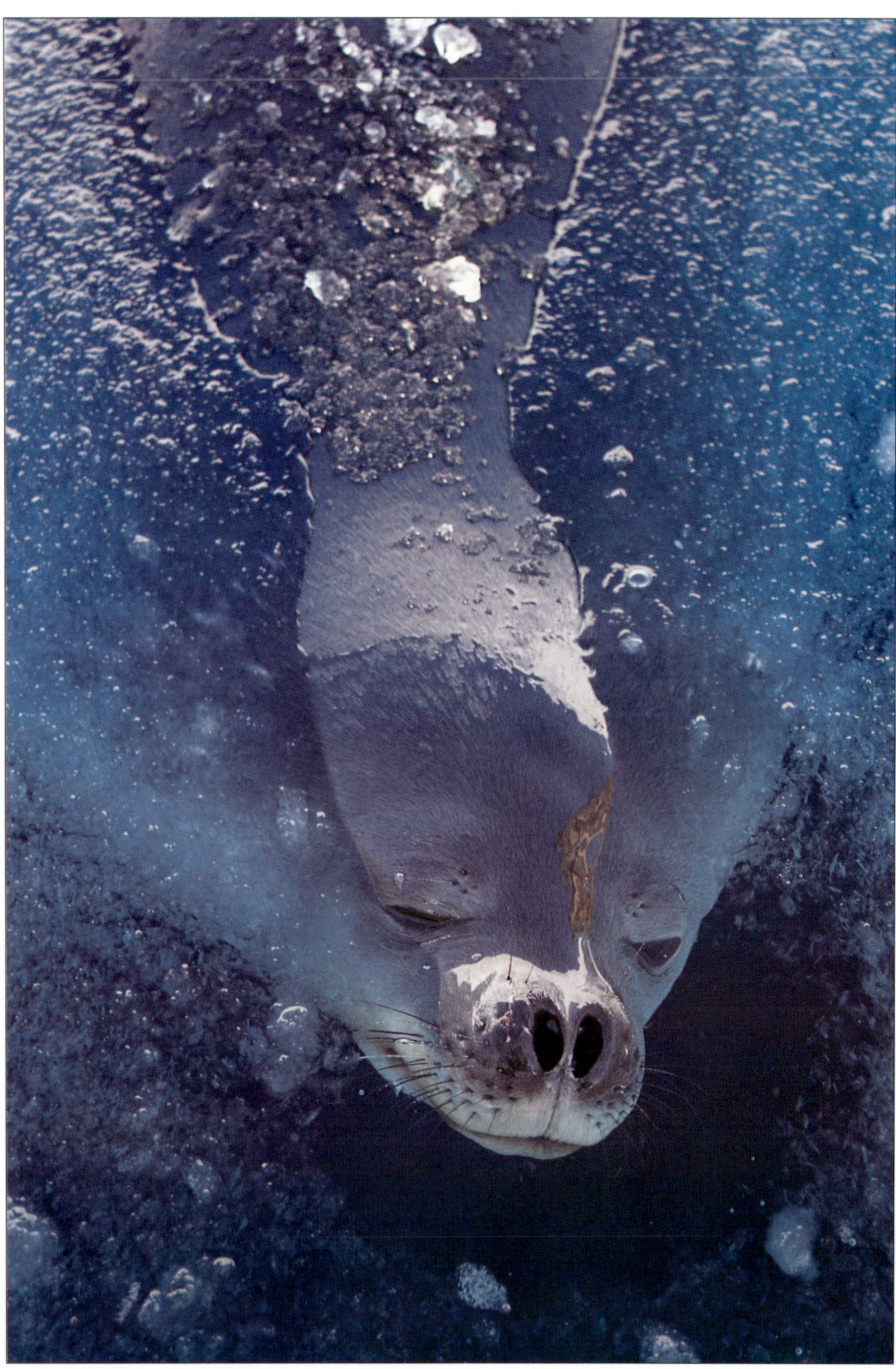

Kim Westerskov
New Zealand
HIGHLY COMMENDED

Weddell seal

"Weddell seals can dive to a depth of 600 metres and stay under water for up to an hour at a time. I photographed this individual as it surfaced to a breathing hole in the ice. At the time, I was on assignment in Antarctica taking photographs for the Antarctic Visitor Centre in Christchurch."

Canon F1 with 28-85mm lens; Fujichrome 100

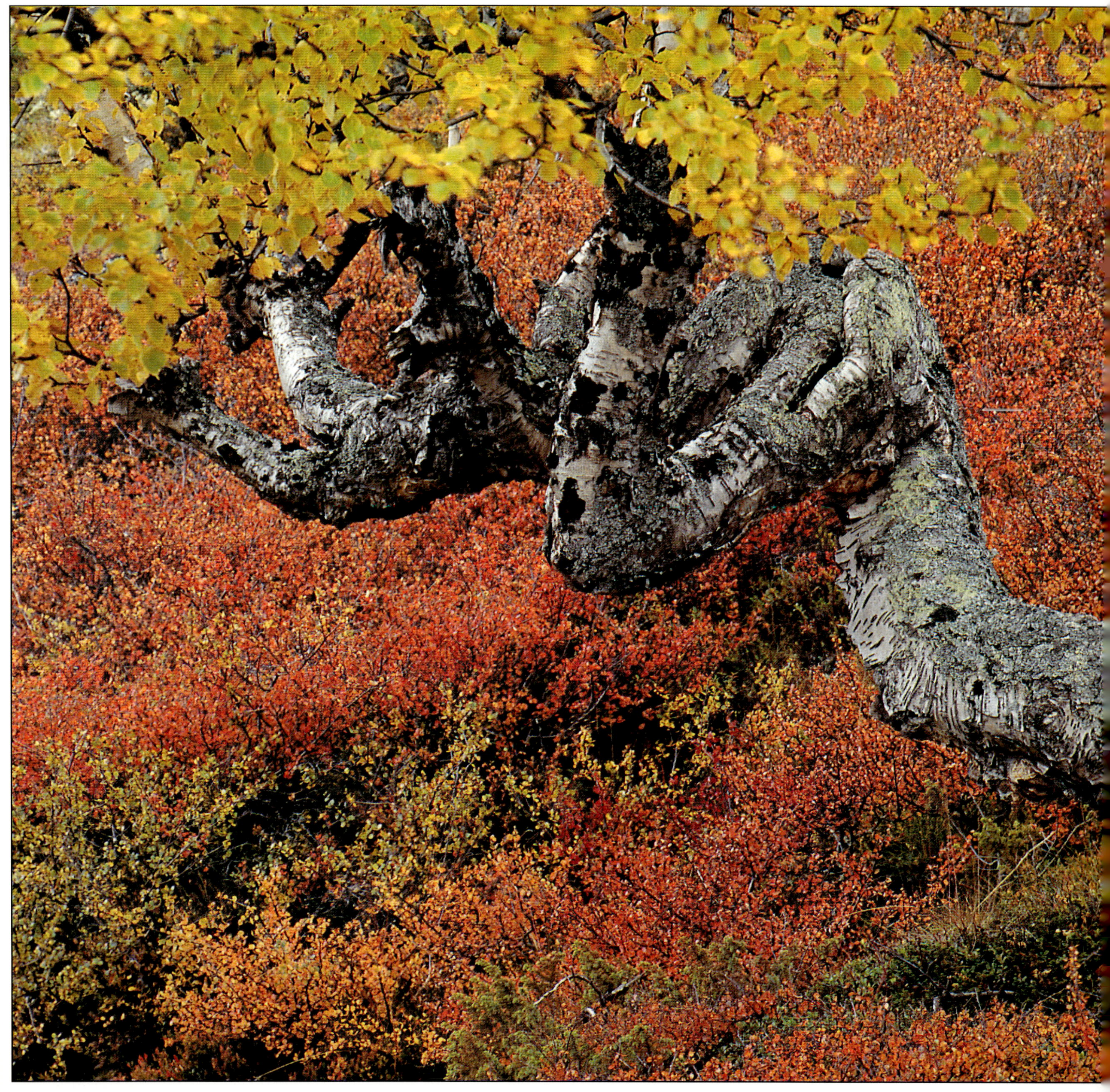

In Praise of Plants

Photographs entered in this category can illustrate flowering or non-flowering plants, and should highlight their beauty and/or importance.

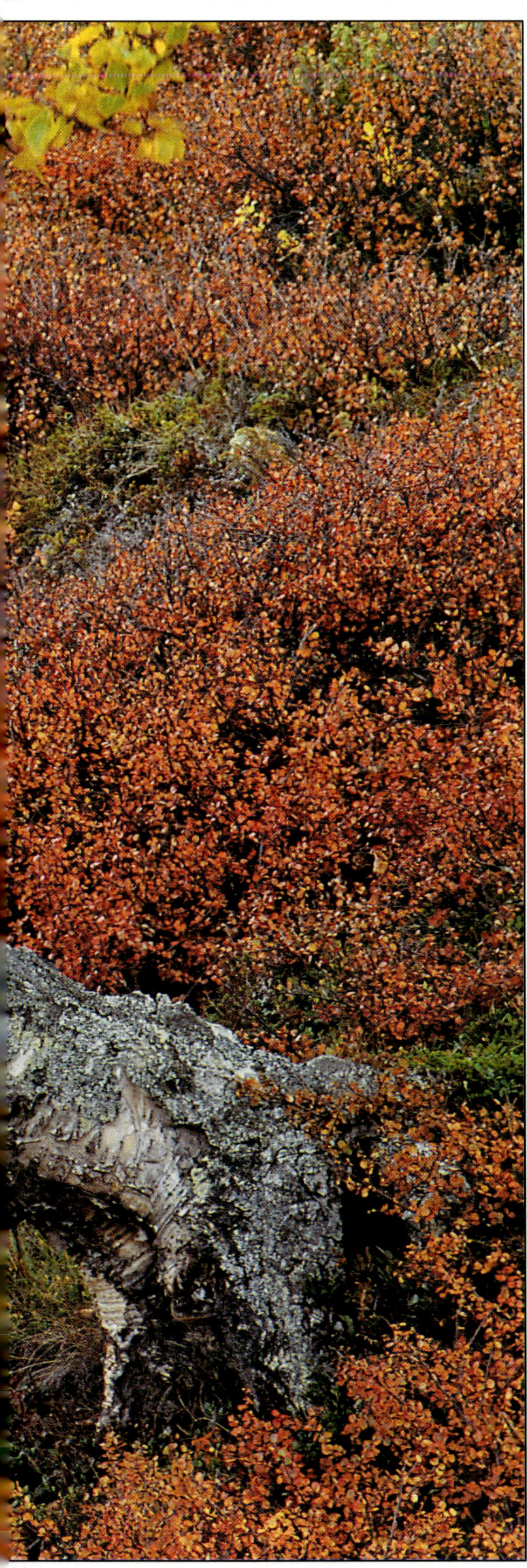

Asle Hjellbrekke
Norway
WINNER

Mountain birch

"I photographed this birch tree in the Leirdalen Valley, near the Jotunheimen National Park, which is more than 1,000 metres above sea level. It was a grey, overcast day, with soft light enhancing colour, perfect for capturing details."

Nikon F4E with 80-200mm lens; tripod; 2 secs at f22; Fujichrome Velvia

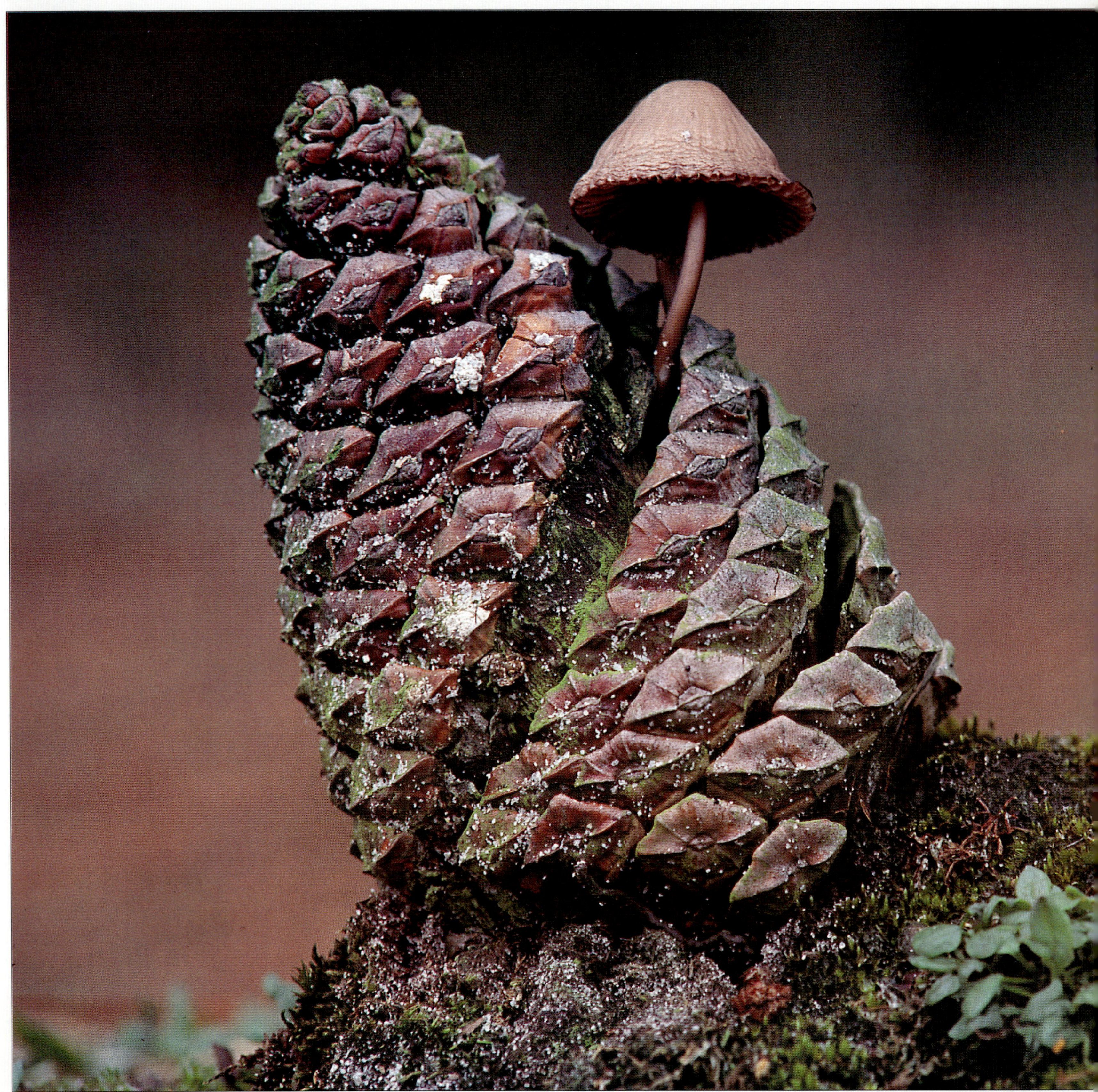

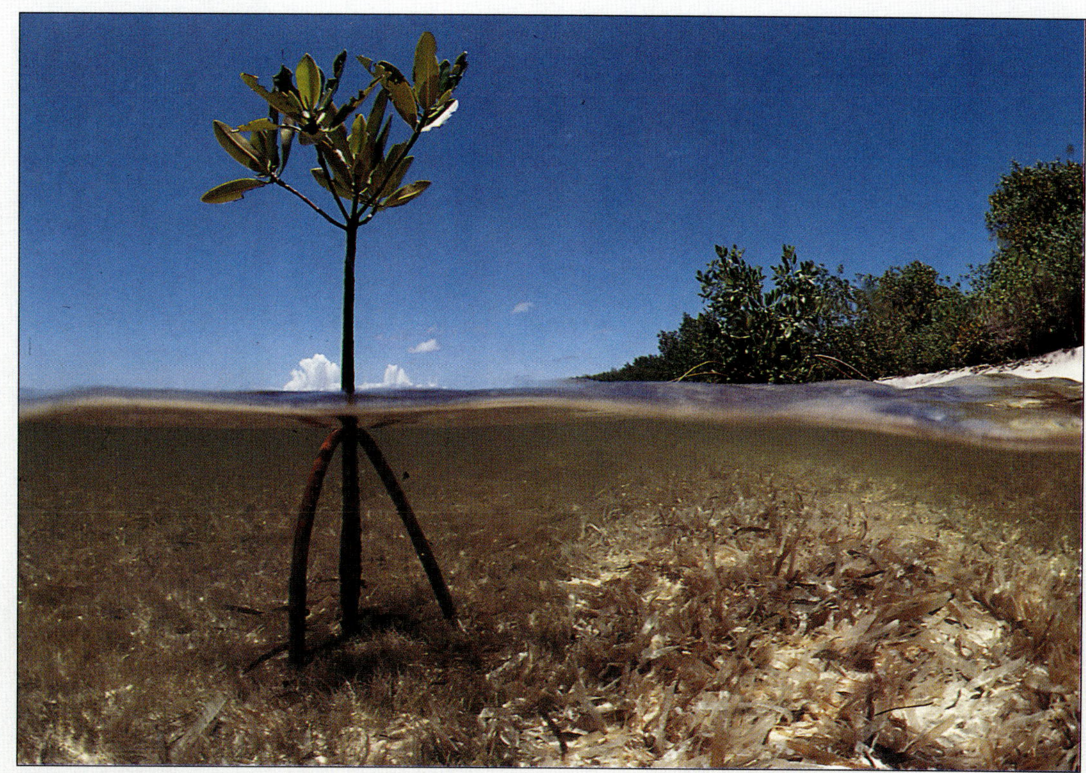

Bernard Castelein
Belgium
RUNNER-UP

Toadstool and fir cone

"This was a lucky find after a long walk in Kalmthoutse Heide, a moorland nature reserve in North Belgium, looking for subjects to photograph. The soft light was perfect for the Velvia film I had in my camera."

Nikon F3 with 200mm lens; tripod; 1/8 sec at f8; Fujichrome Velvia

Jürgen Freund
Germany
SPECIALLY COMMENDED

Mangrove tree

"The massive root systems of mangrove trees are home to extremely rich communities of animal life. I wanted to show a mangrove as it lives – above and below water. To take this type of split-level picture, you have to use an underwater housing that has a big front port, shaped like half a ball. At the time, I was on a diving holiday in Cuba."

Nikon F4 with 16mm lens in underwater housing; 1/60 sec at f16; Fujichrome 100

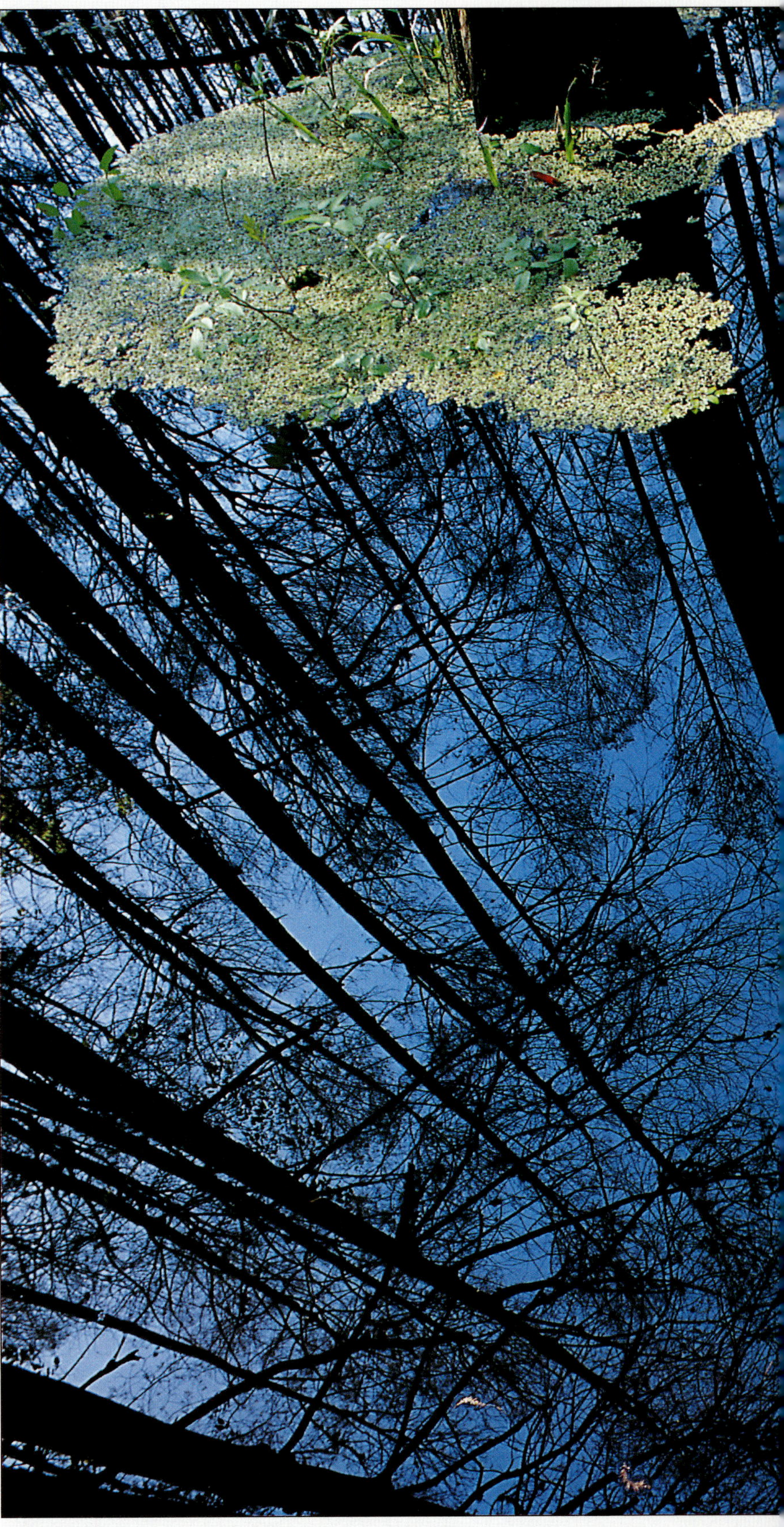

Gary Braasch
United States of America
HIGHLY COMMENDED

Forest pond

"Cypress trees are reflected in this pond of waterlilies and duckweeds, creating a three-dimensional effect which forces the viewer's eye to move into the reflection. I came across this pond in the Highlands Hammock State Park in Florida."

Nikon camera with 24mm lens;
Fujichrome Velvia

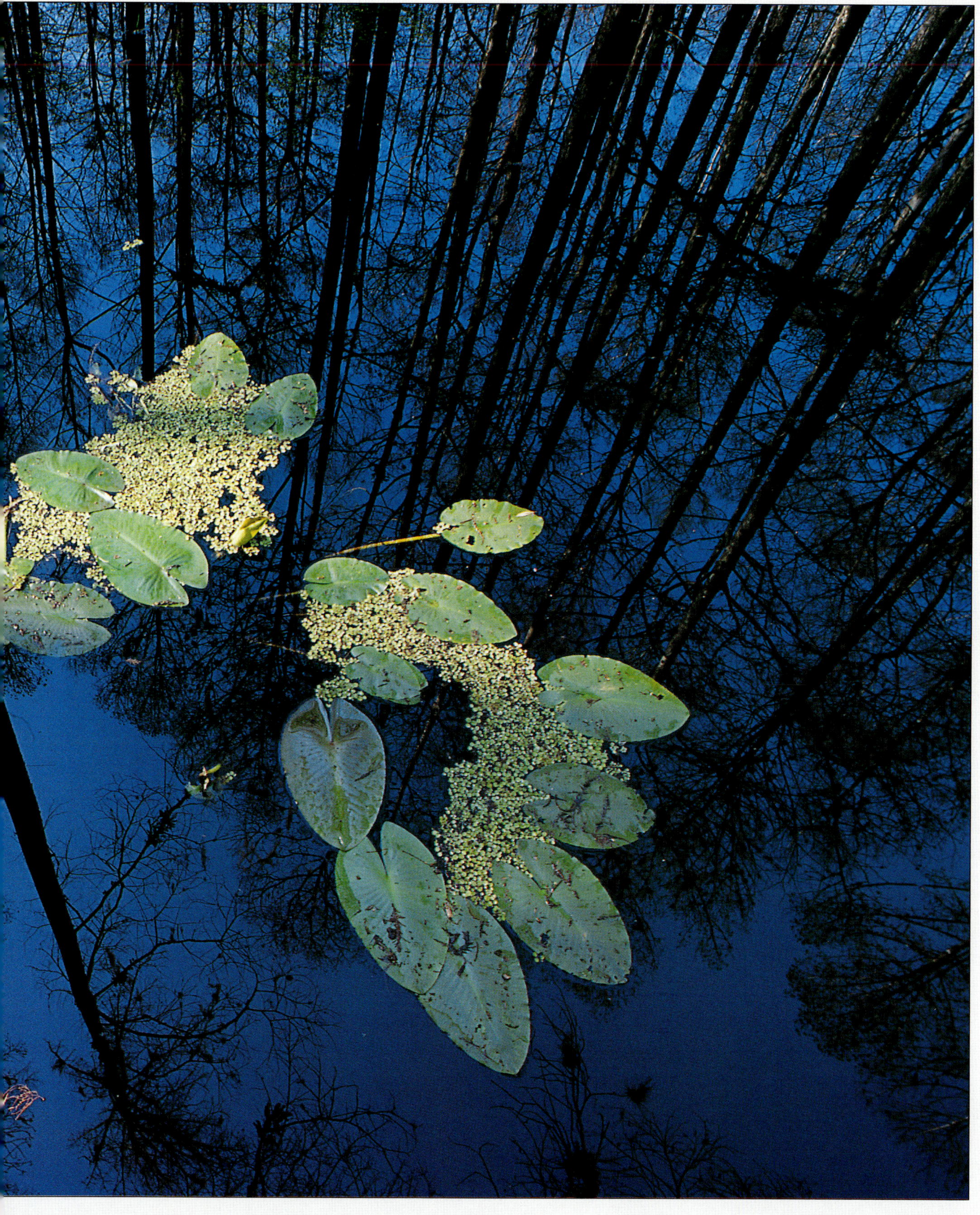

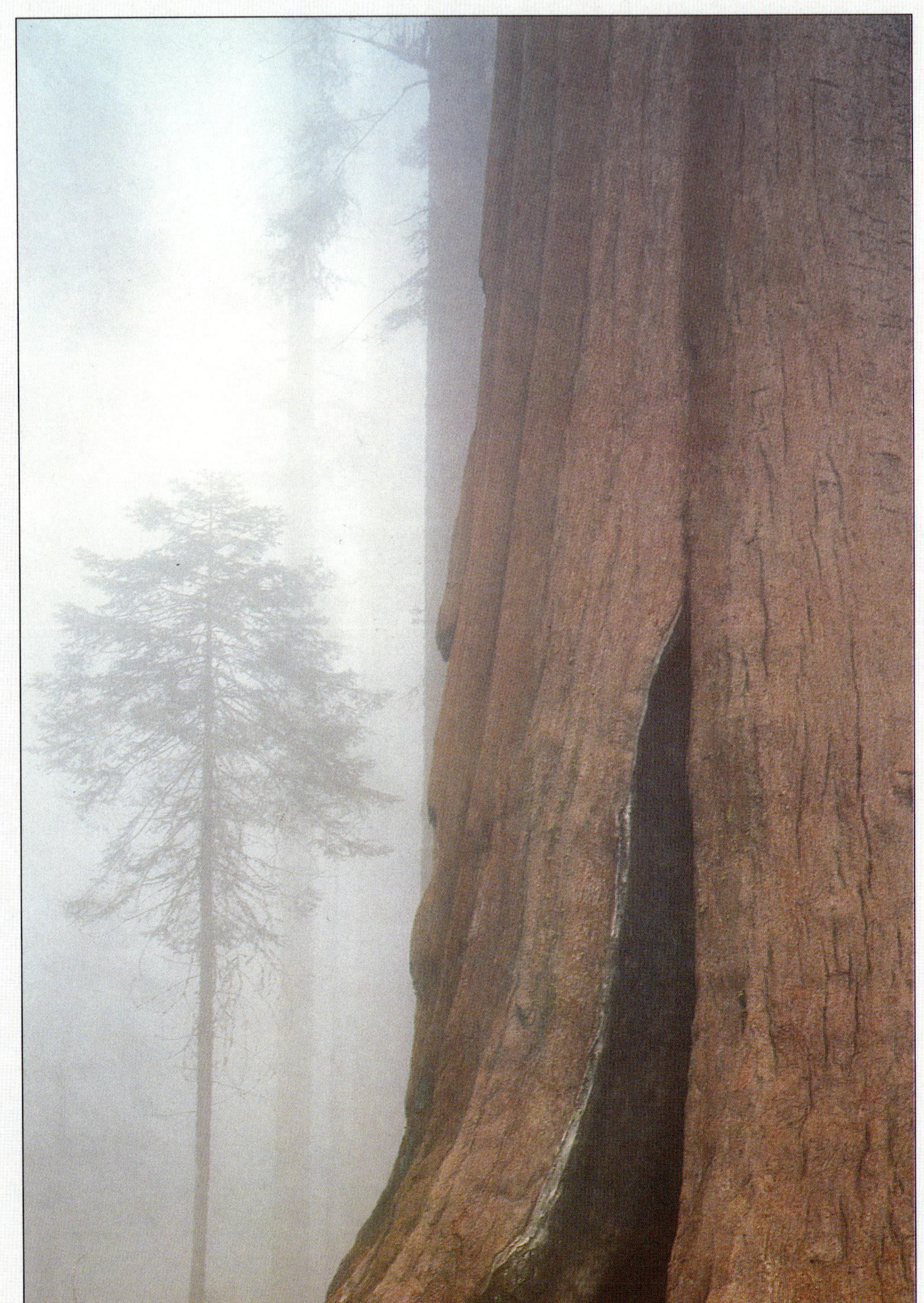

William Neill
United States of America
HIGHLY COMMENDED

Giant sequoia tree

"I photographed this giant sequoia next to a fir tree to show the huge contrast in size, making the most of the foggy conditions, which are quite rare in the Sequoia National Park, California."

Wista 4x5 with 210mm lens; tripod; 10 secs at f45; Fujichrome Velvia

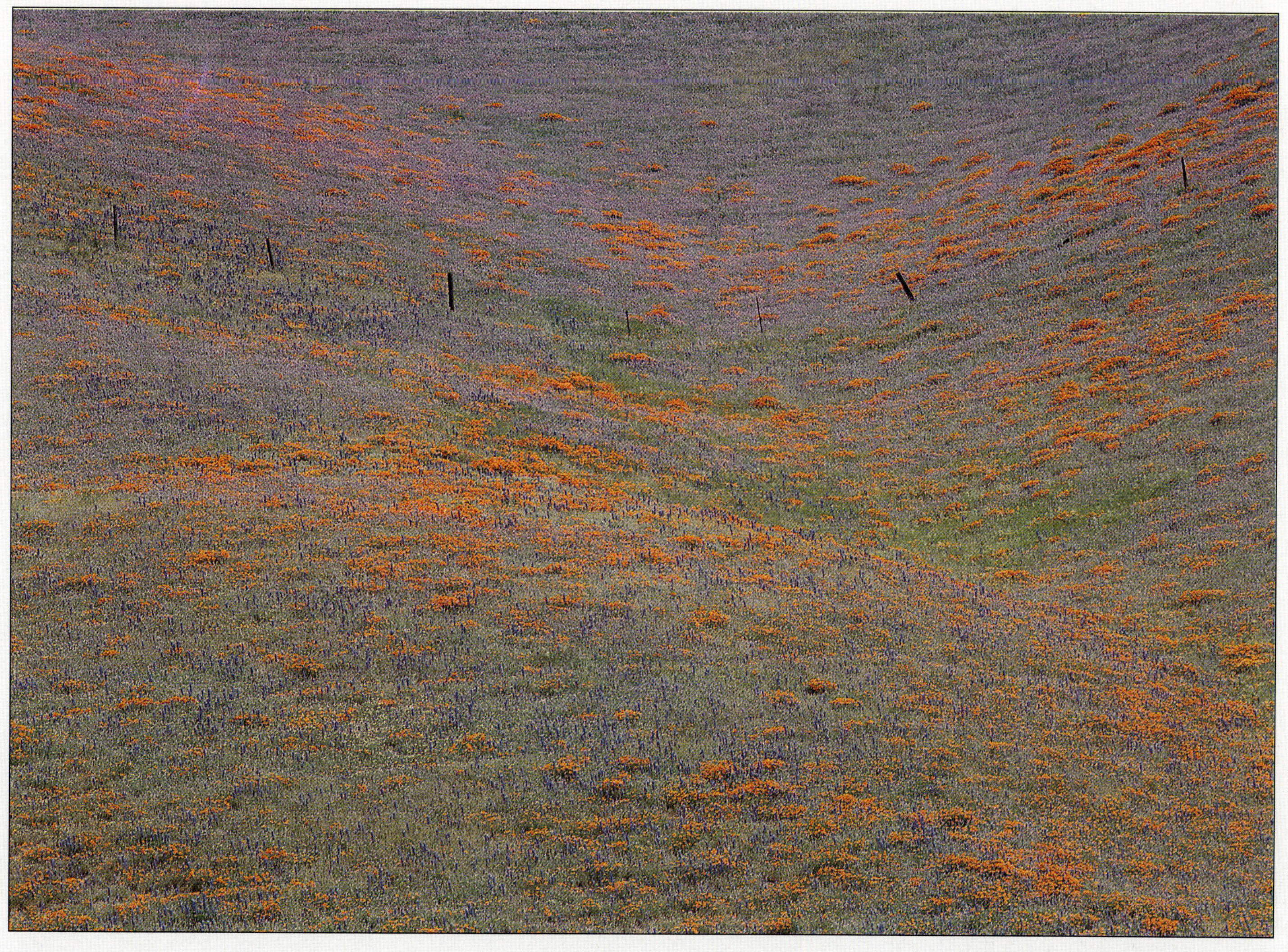

Thomas D Mangelsen
United States of America
HIGHLY COMMENDED

Poppies and lupines

"Wildflower cycles in the western desert areas are unpredictable and depend on the amount and timing of the winter rainfall. When conditions are optimal, entire hillsides are covered in early spring with colourful flowers of the California poppy and miniature lupine as well as numerous other species. In early morning light, the beautiful patterns of colour on this hillside in the Tehachapi Mountains in California made for an abstract and somewhat impressionistic image."

Pentax 645 with 600mm lens; tripod; 1/15 sec at f16; Fujichrome Velvia

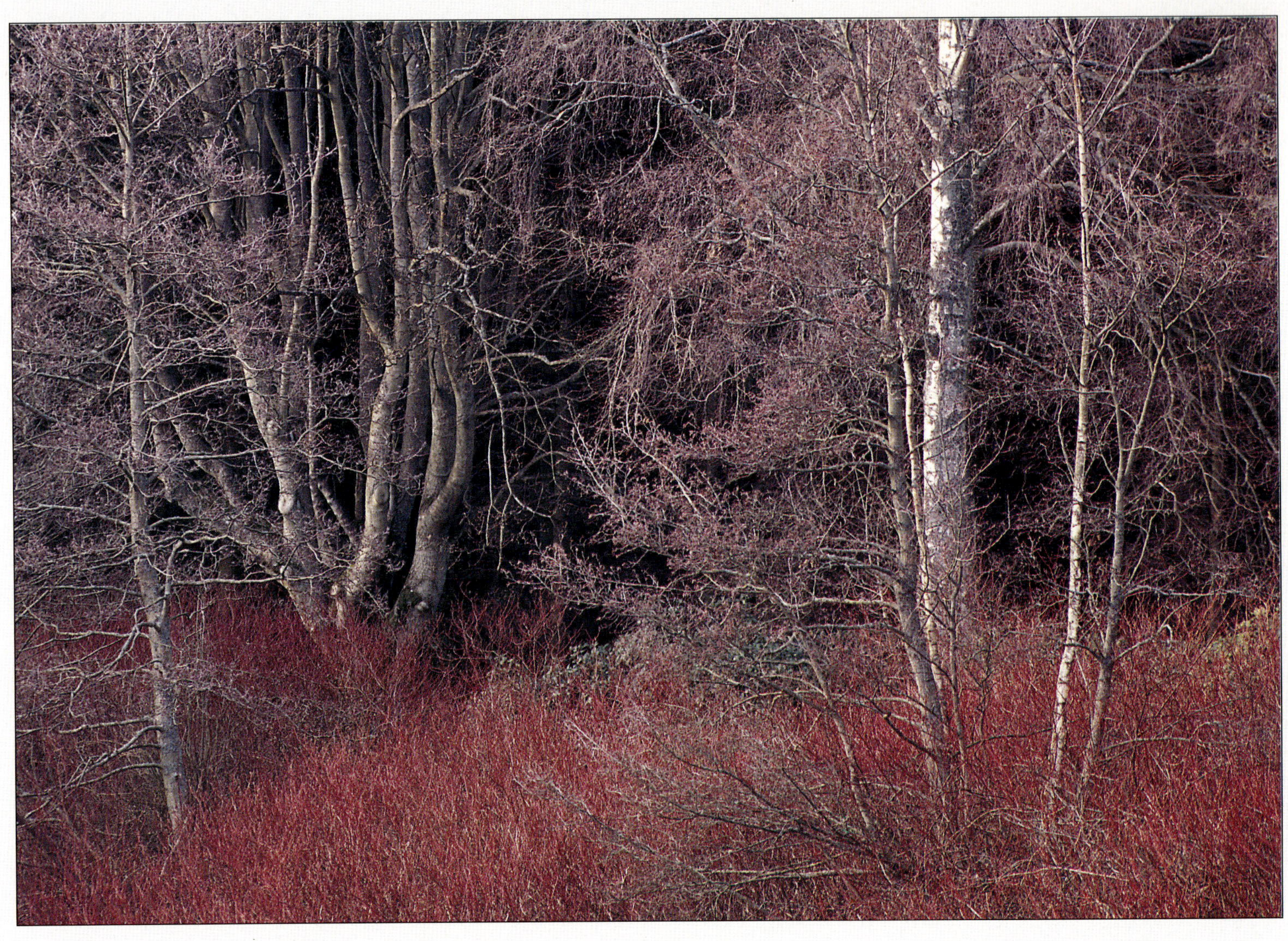

Niall Benvie
United Kingdom
HIGHLY COMMENDED

Loch-side woodland

"This photograph of a mixed grove of alder, beech, birch and dogwood was taken in Guthrie, Angus, in March for my stock files."

Nikon F4S with 300mm lens; Ben-v bean bag; 1/15 sec at f8; Ektachrome Panther 100X

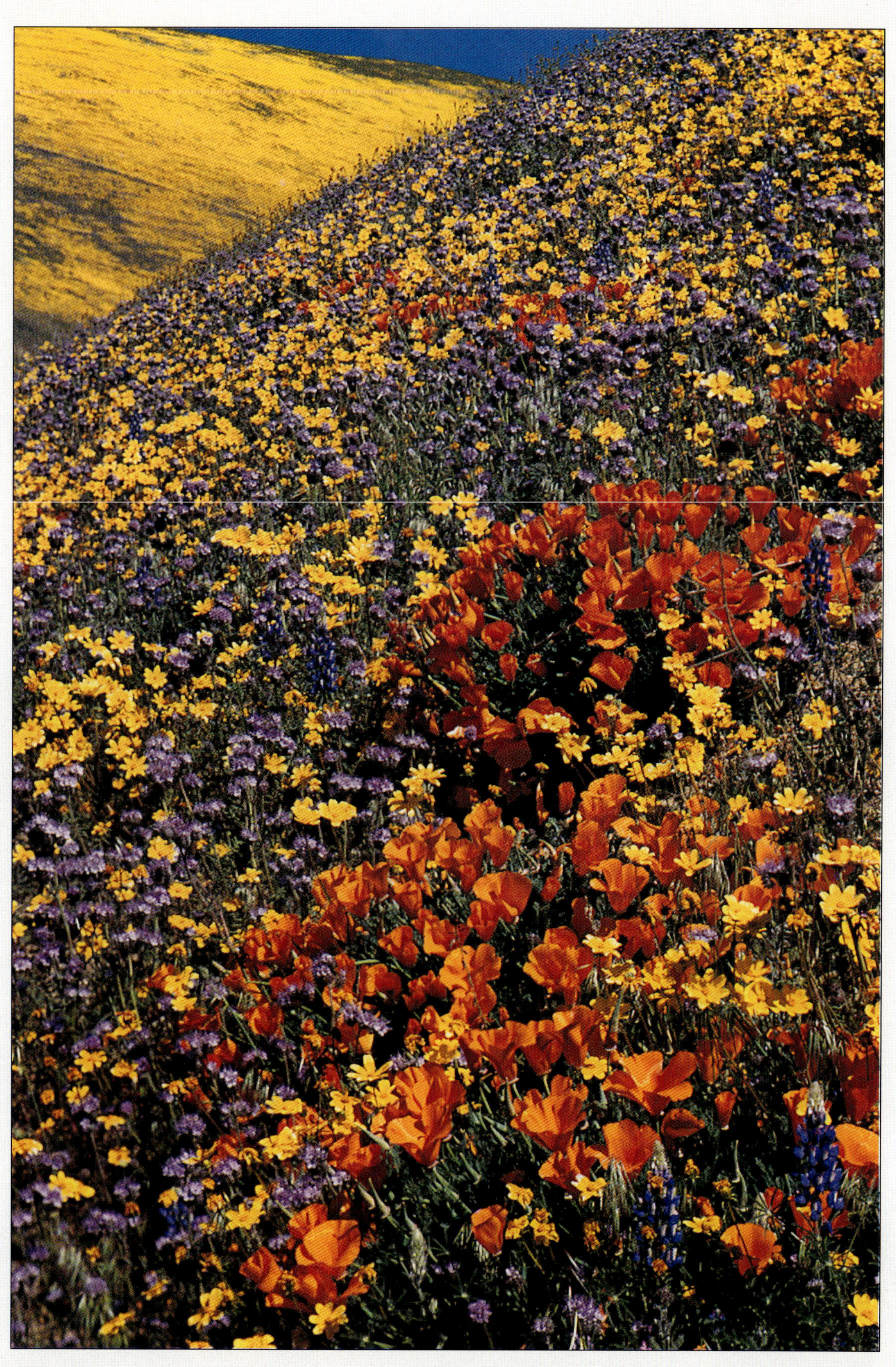

Wendy Shattil
& Bob Rozinski
United States of America
HIGHLY COMMENDED

Poppies and coreopsis

"A very dry year made this area of central California in Kern County virtually the only place where this spectacular blooming occurred. A strong wind blew constantly, but it was worth spending the time necessary to take pictures."

Canon A2E with 90mm lens; tripod; f11; Fujichrome Velvia

Urban and Garden Wildlife

Pictures entered for this category must show animals or plants in an obviously urban or suburban setting.

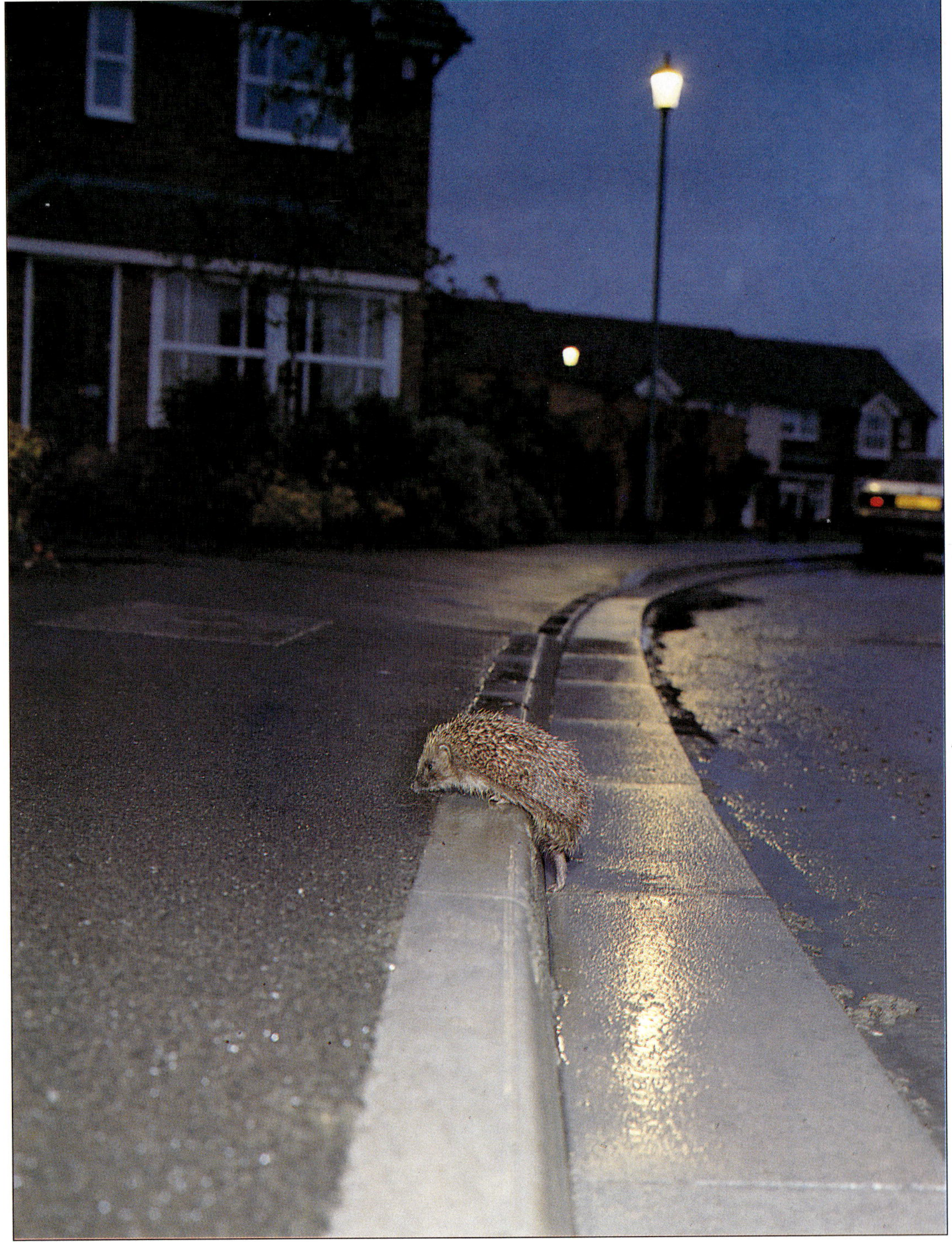

Jason Venus
United Kingdom
WINNER

Hedgehog

"Hedgehogs are seen more on the road than anywhere else - unfortunately, often as casualties. I wanted to show one which had successfully crossed a road. I chose a quiet location and a wet evening, which added colour to the otherwise dull road. The hedgehog was a patient at a local wildlife care unit and was used to being handled. It was released into the wild a few months later when the weather was warmer."

Bronica ETRS with 70mm lens; tripod; fill in flash for hedgehog; 1 sec at f11; Fujichrome Velvia

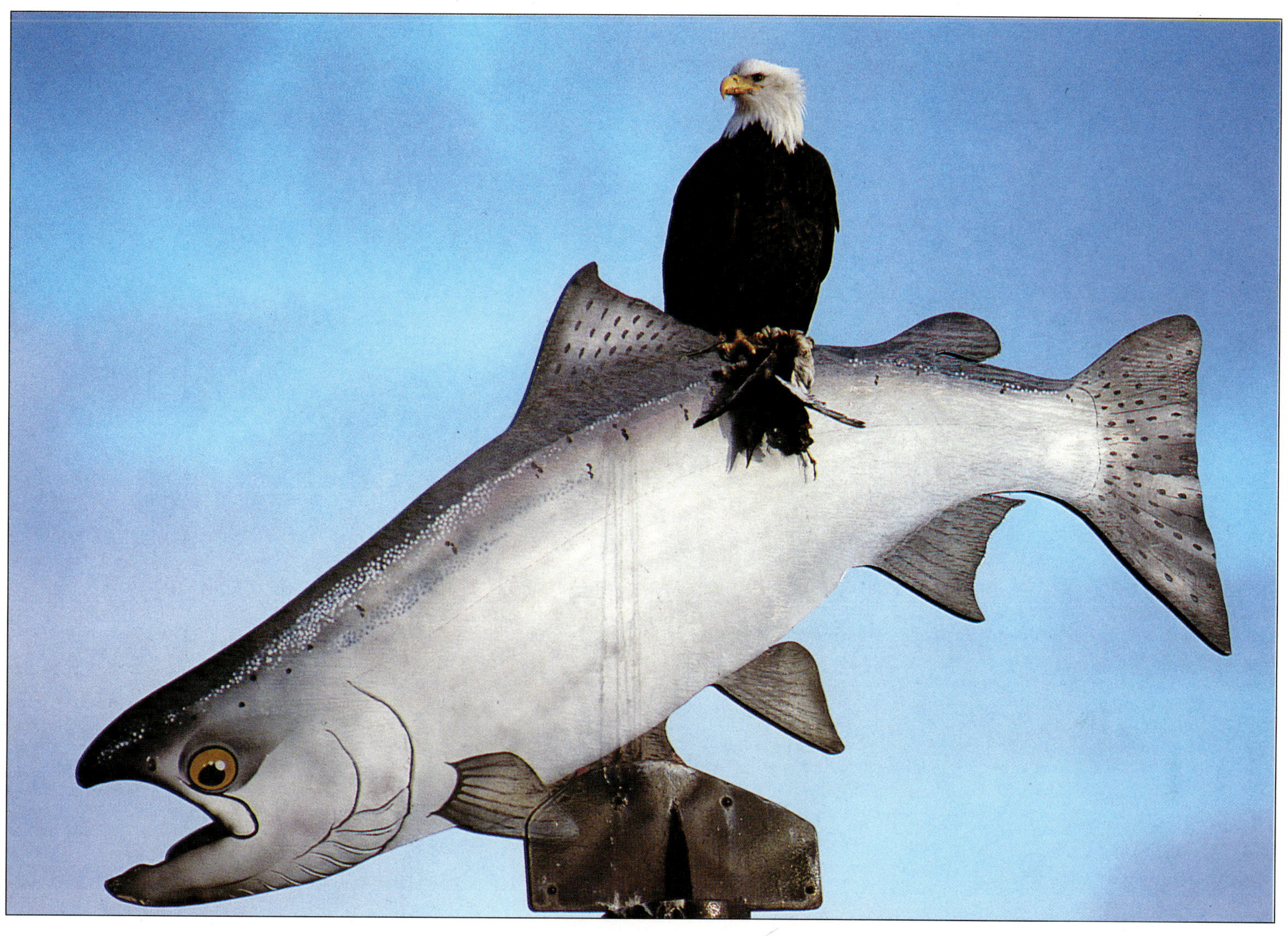

Thomas D Mangelsen
United States of America
RUNNER-UP

Eagle on salmon sign

"This bald eagle had either killed or scavenged a murre in nearby Kachemak Bay and was using the salmon sign as a perch while it fed. The sign advertised a fish market on the Homer spit in Alaska."

Nikon F4S with 300mm lens; 1/250 sec at f2.8; Fujichrome Velvia

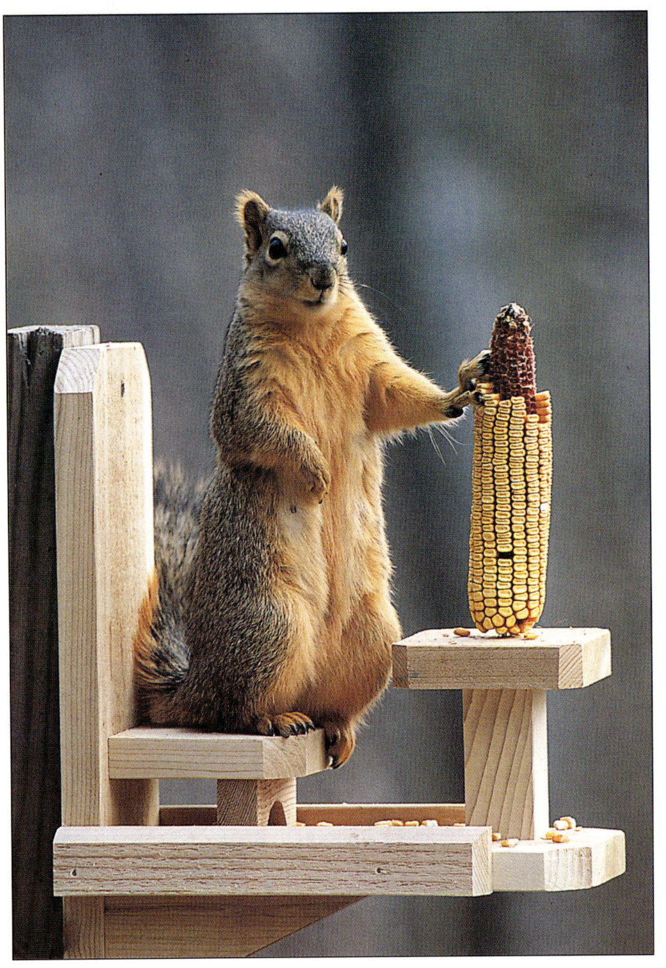

Doug Locke
United States of America
HIGHLY COMMENDED

Fox squirrel at feeder

"I put up this feeder specially for the fox squirrels, to keep them off the bird feeders in my backyard. This was the first of many squirrels to come to the table and dine on a feast of corn."

Nikon 8008s with 300mm lens; tripod; Fujichrome Velvia

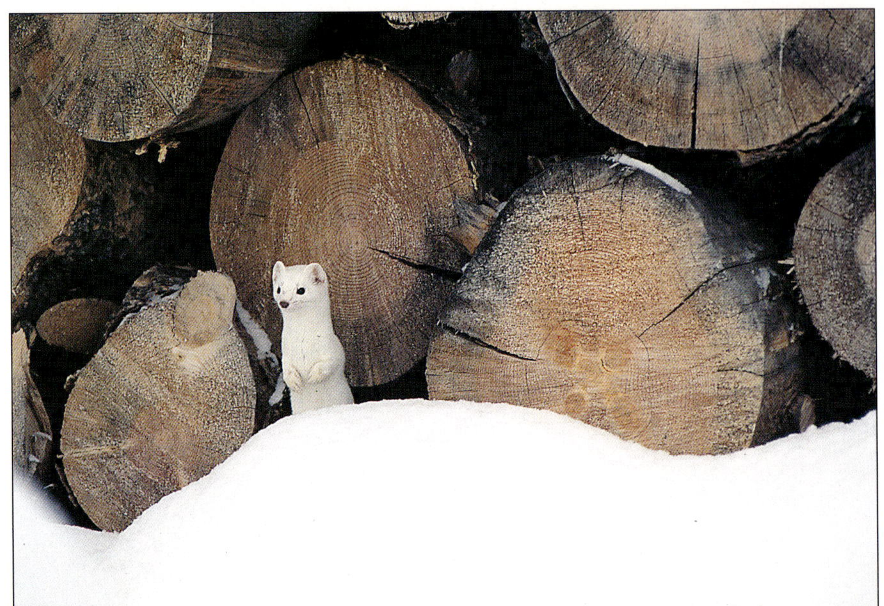

Thomas D Mangelsen
United States of America
HIGHLY COMMENDED

Ermine in woodpile

"I photographed this ermine in the woodpile in my yard where it hunts for mice". The ermine spends nights under my cabin and keeps my home free from mice. By day, it hunts for hibernating ground squirrels and for mice in the woodpile."

Nikon F4 with 80-200mm lens; 1/250 sec at f5.6; Fujichrome Velvia

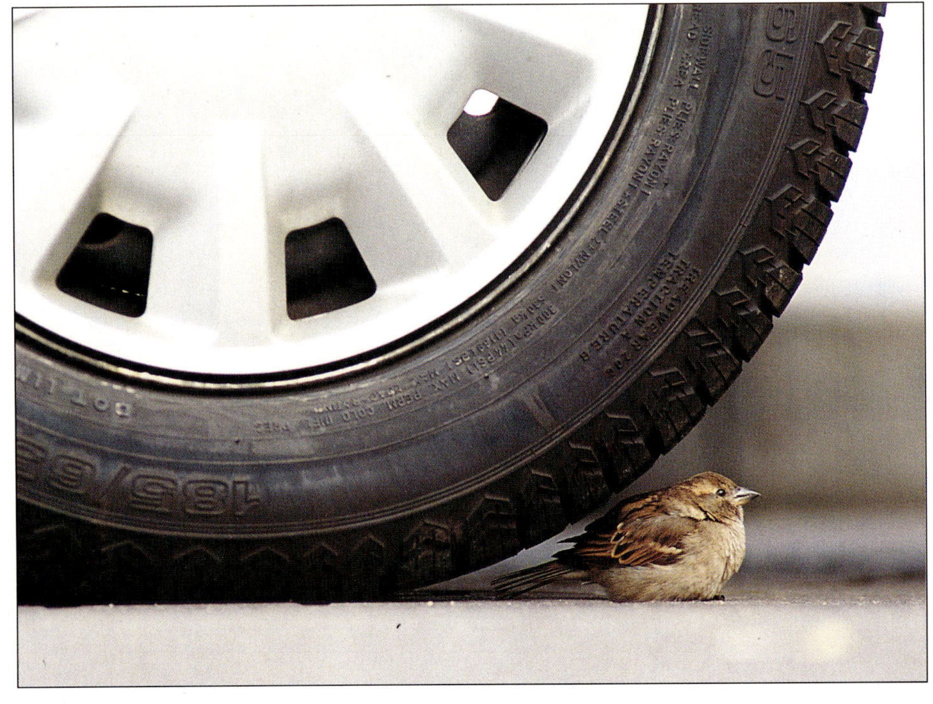

Niall Benvie
United Kingdom
HIGHLY COMMENDED

House sparrow

"I photographed this female house sparrow one Sunday morning in Montrose's central carpark. It was quite early, around 8.30am - about the only time I would consider lying prone in the carpark!"

Nikon F4 with 300mm lens and x1.4 extender; Ben-v bean bag; 1/30 sec at f5.6; Ektachrome Panther 100X

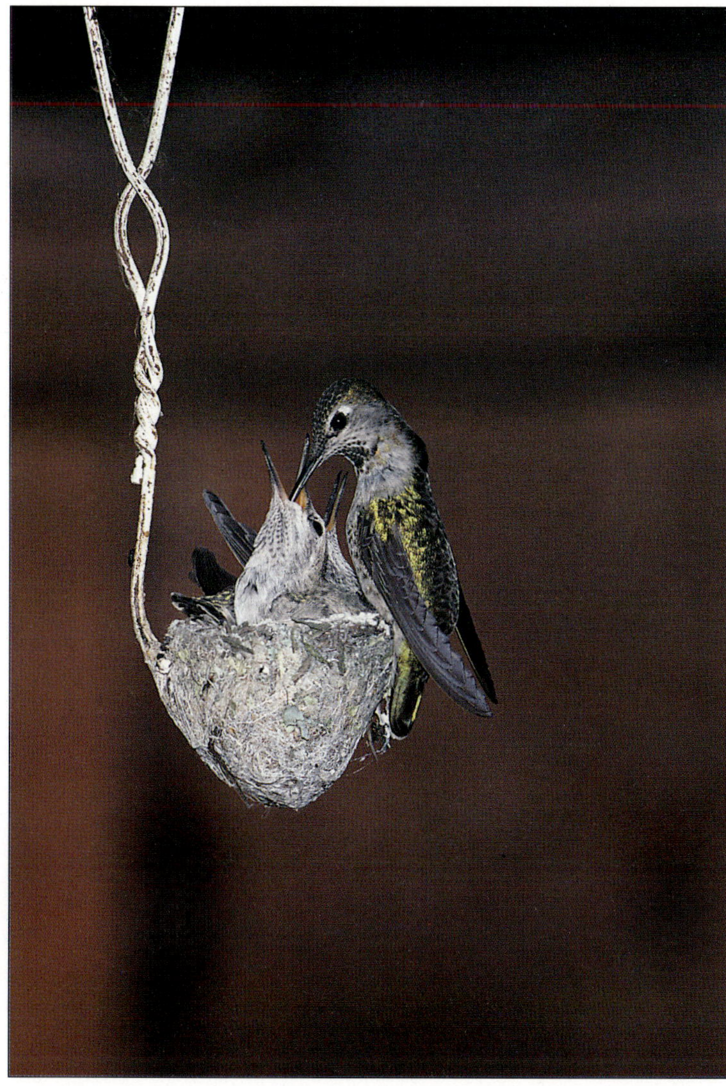

George D Lepp

United States of America

HIGHLY COMMENDED

Hummingbird feeding young

"I photographed this Anna's hummingbird locally, in a carport. The bird had chosen the hook of a clothes hanger to build her nest on."

Canon EOS1 with 100-300mm lens; flash; Kodachrome 64

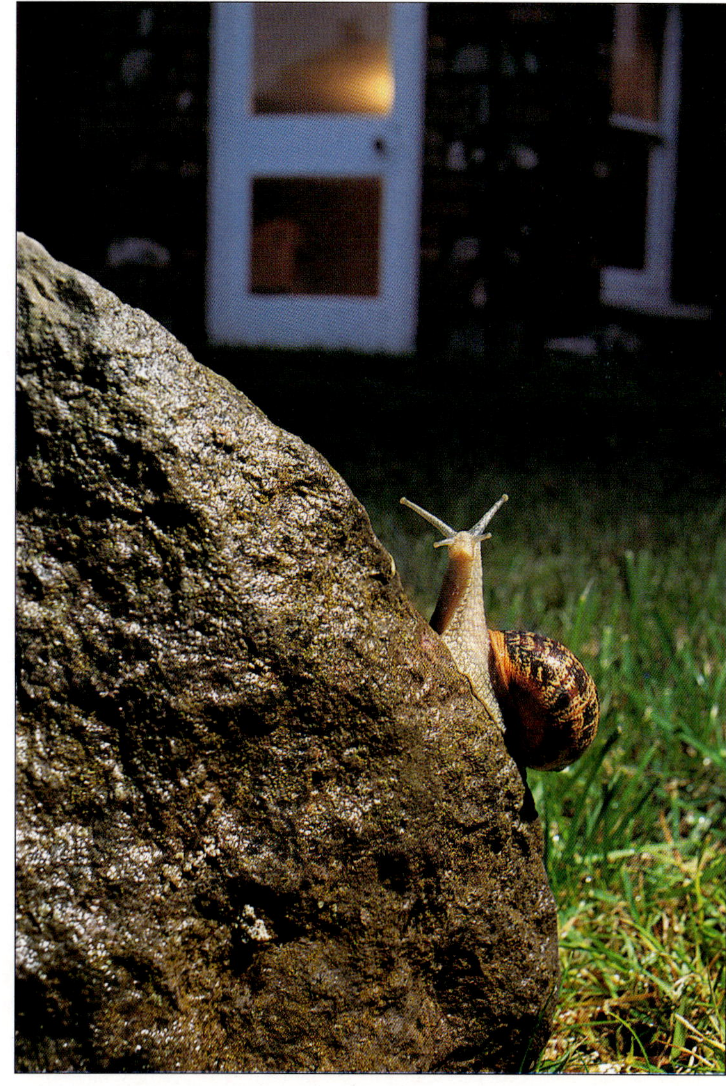

Warwick J Sloss

United Kingdom

HIGHLY COMMENDED

Common garden snail

"This picture, as with all my most successful images, started as an idea which developed further in its execution. Inspired by the healthy snail population in my parents' garden, I set out to photograph a snail at dusk against an obviously urban setting. This picture actually turned out pretty close to what I had planned."

Nikon FE with 24mm lens; tripod; flash; Fujichrome Velvia

From Dusk to Dawn

Pictures entered in this category have to be taken between sunset and sunrise and must feature animals. The sun may be on but not above the horizon.

Antti Leinonen
Finland
WINNER

Brown bear after sunset

"In April, when old male bears, such as this one, start to come out of their winter dens, the snow is still deep and they prefer to travel at night, when walking is easier. I have been taking pictures of bears for several years, and this particular individual is an old friend - I have been photographing him since 1986. This picture was taken just an hour after sunset."

Canon T90 with 200mm lens; f2.8; Fujichrome 400

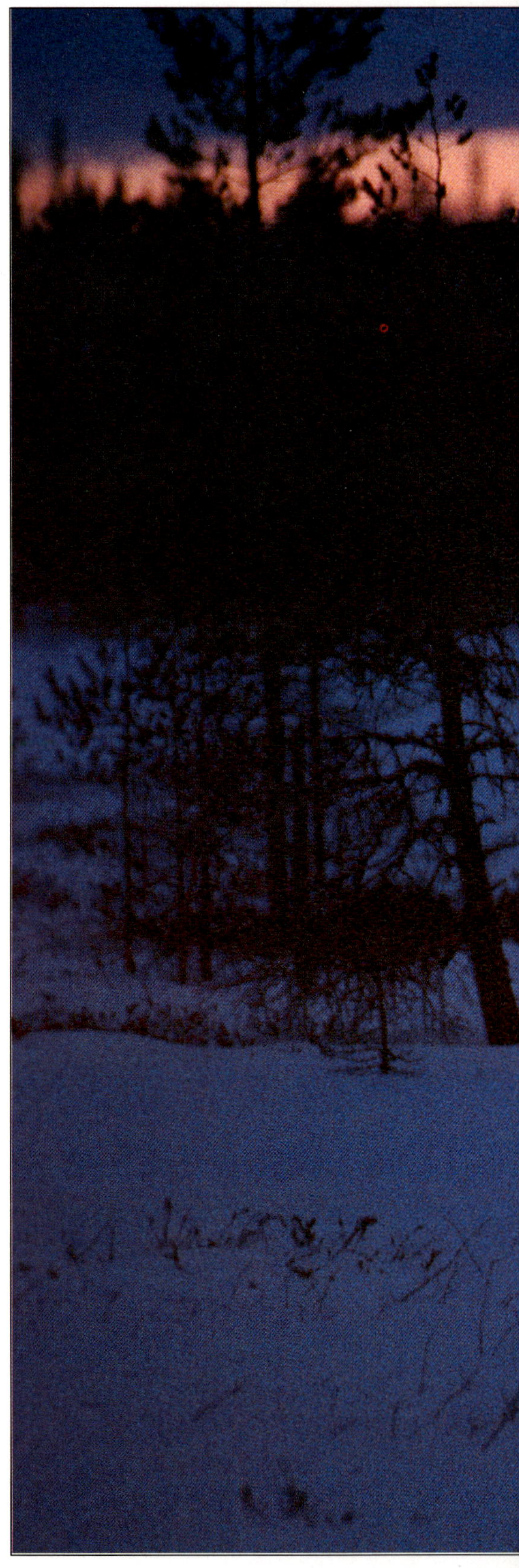

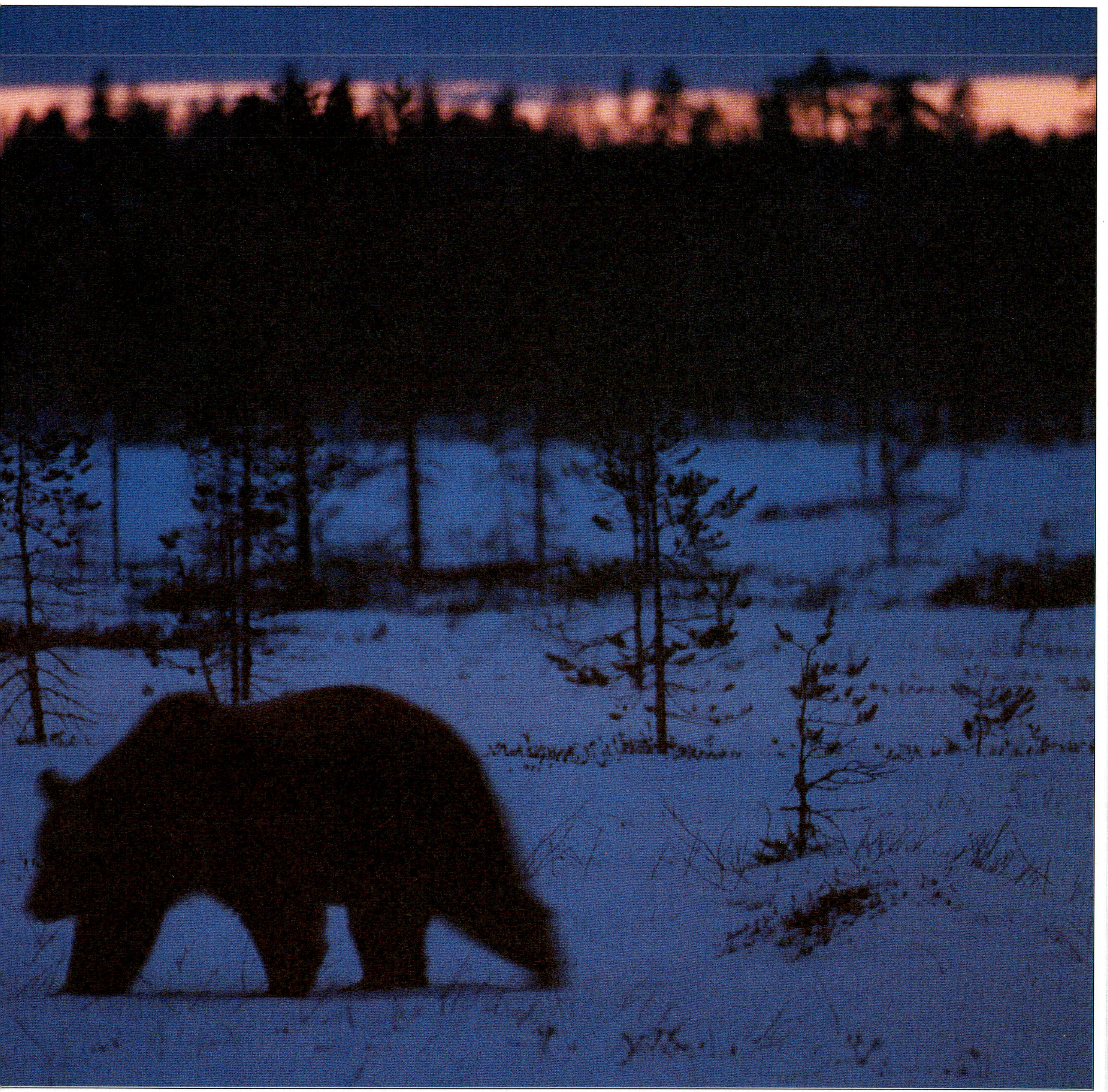

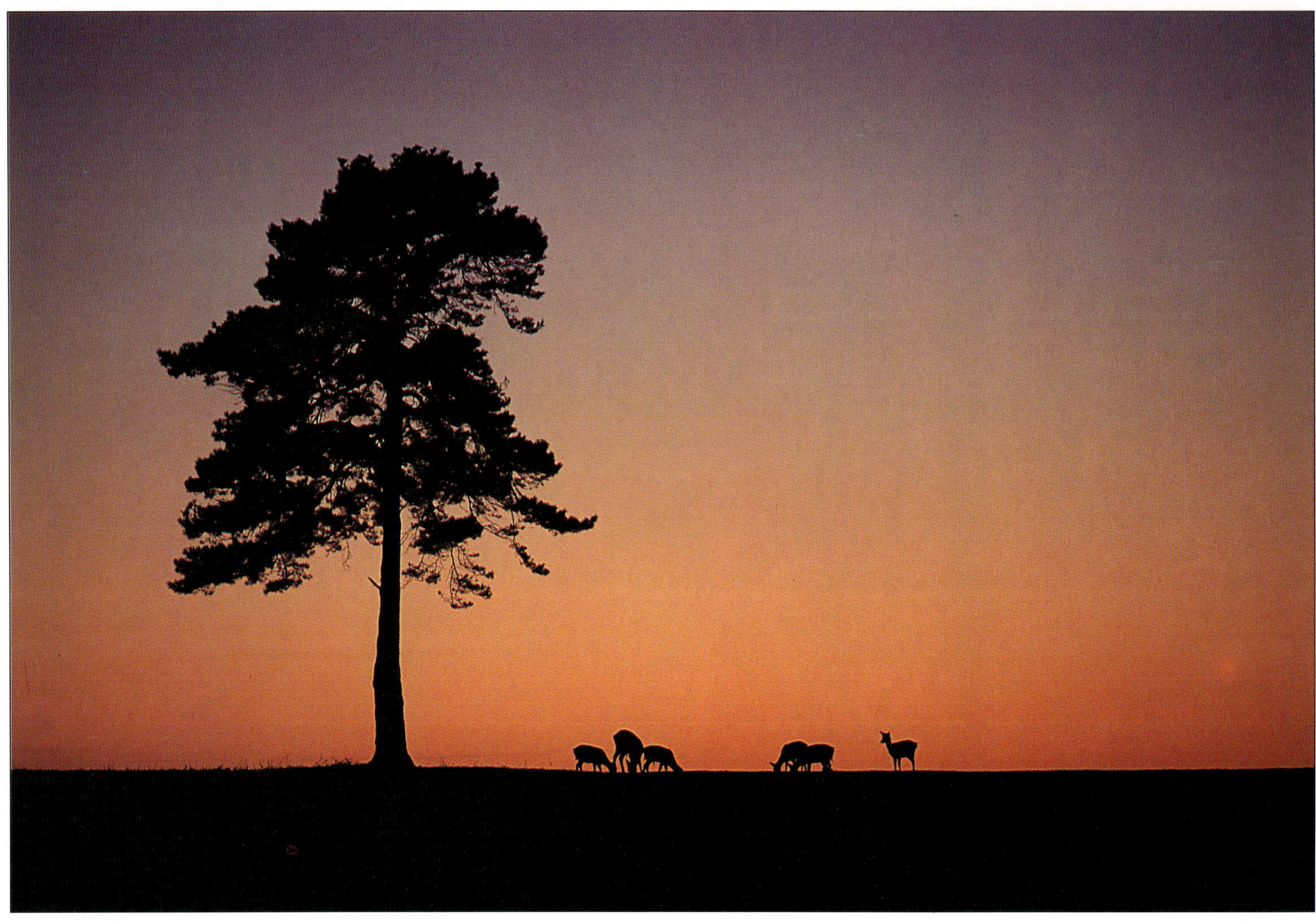

Geoff Doré
United Kingdom
JOINT RUNNER-UP

Fallow deer at dusk

"I have visited this part of the New Forest frequently to photograph deer, ponies and trees at sunset. On this occasion, in February, the deer I was hoping to photograph were frightened away by walkers, but the colour of the sky was so special that, despite plummetting temperatures, I stayed to photograph the Scots pine tree against the dusk sky. Fifteen minutes later, the deer reappeared on the skyline, and I was able to take several photos before the colours faded."

Nikon FE2 with 80-200mm lens; tripod; 1/8 sec at f4; Fujichrome Velvia

Mitsuhiko Imamori
Japan
JOINT RUNNER-UP

Madagascan bull's-eye silkmoth

"The bull's-eye silkmoth occurs only in Madagascar. At rest, its wings look like leaves, but when threatened, it opens its wings to show its eye-spots. At night, these moths often fly into people's houses near the forest. I took this photograph in the cottage I was staying in, using an infra-red sensor and high-speed flashlights."

Pentax 6x7 with 135mm lens; tripod; flash; 1/30 sec at f16; Kodachrome 64

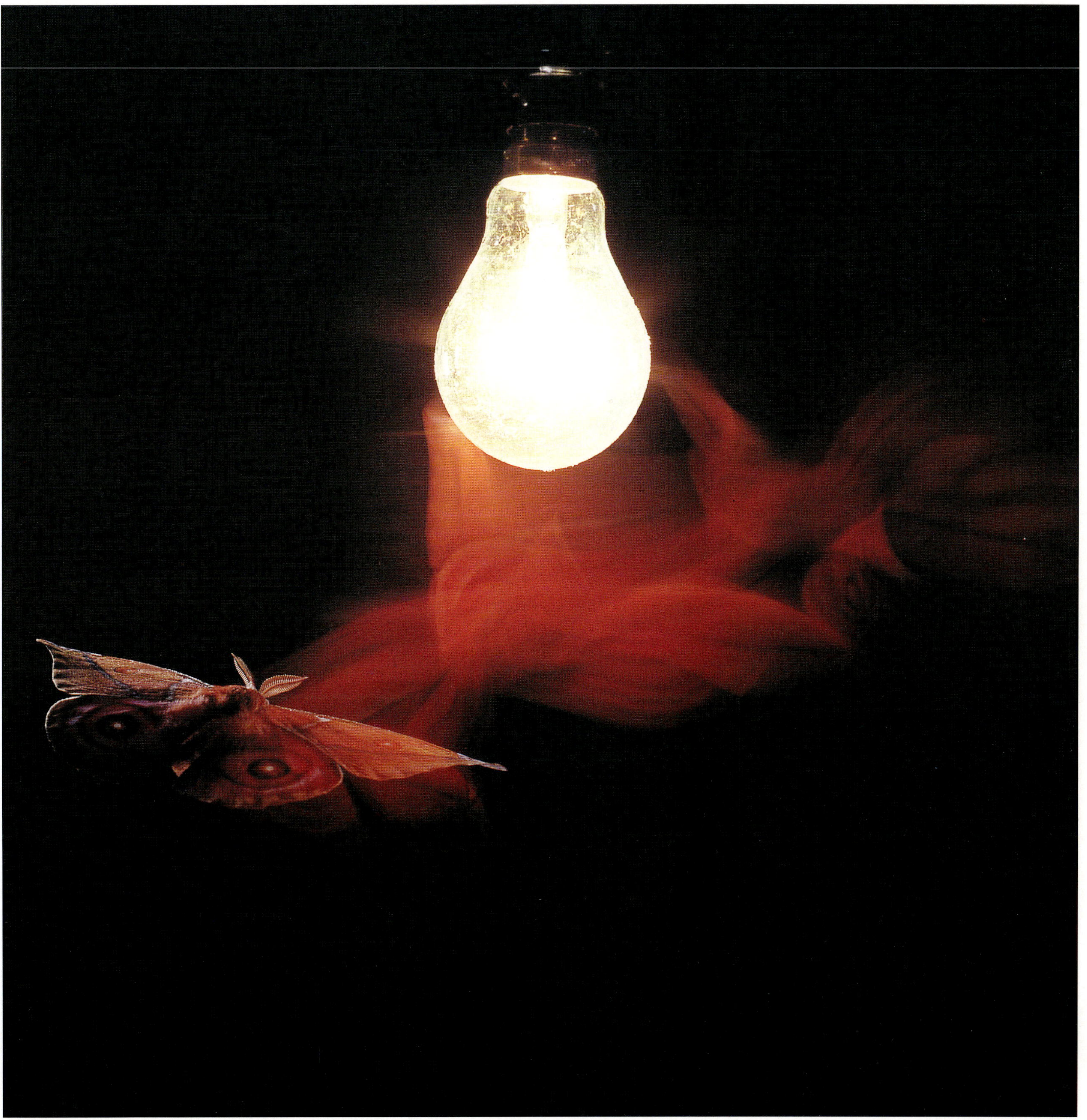

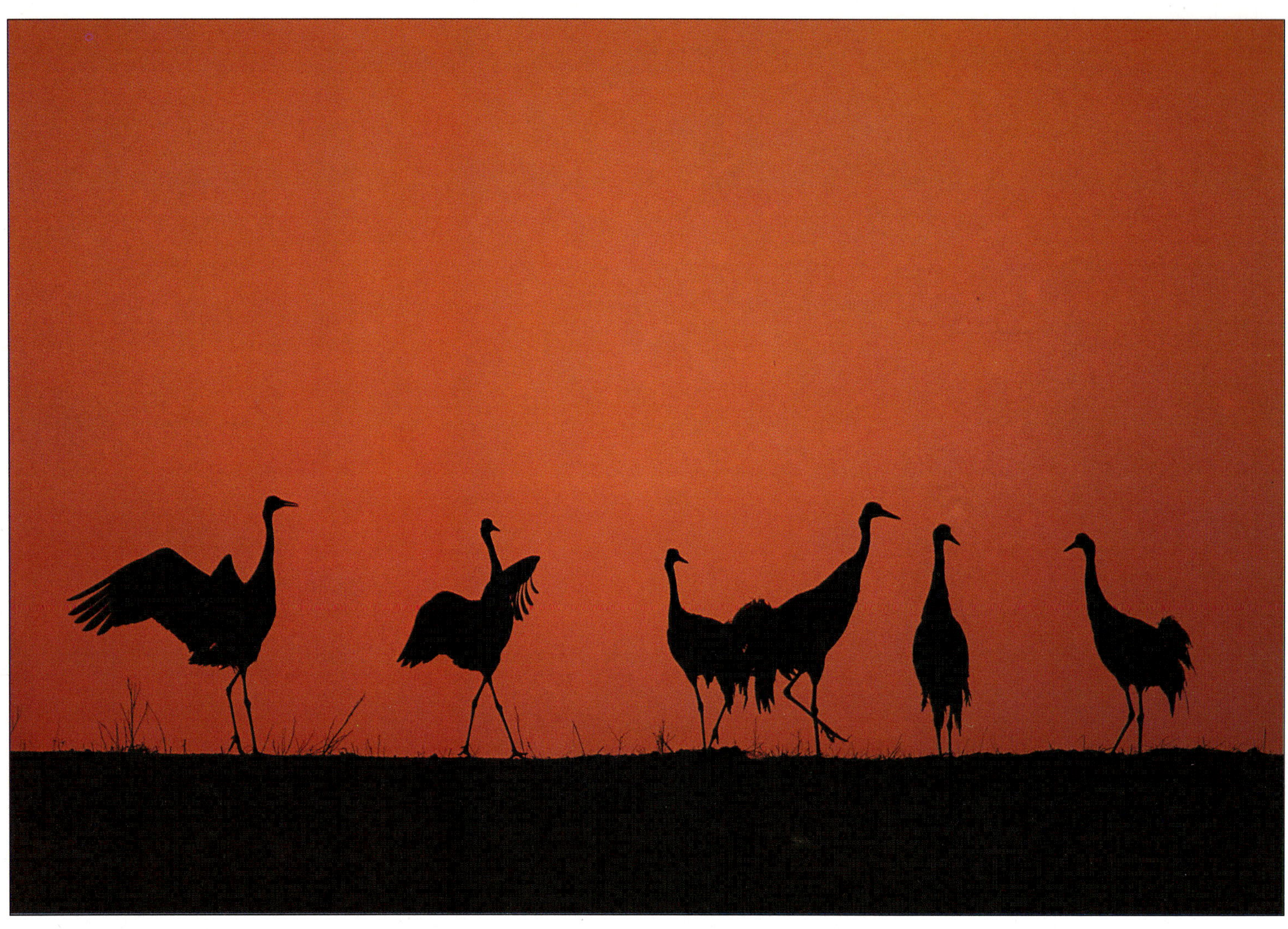

Francisco Márquez
Spain
HIGHLY COMMENDED

Cranes at dawn

"I am working on a book about cranes and have photographed them at their wintering grounds in Spain and in Scandanavia where they breed. This picture was taken from a hide very early one April morning in Hornborgasjõn when the birds were starting to search for food."

Nikon F4S with 80-200mm lens; 1/30sec at f11; Kodak Panther 100

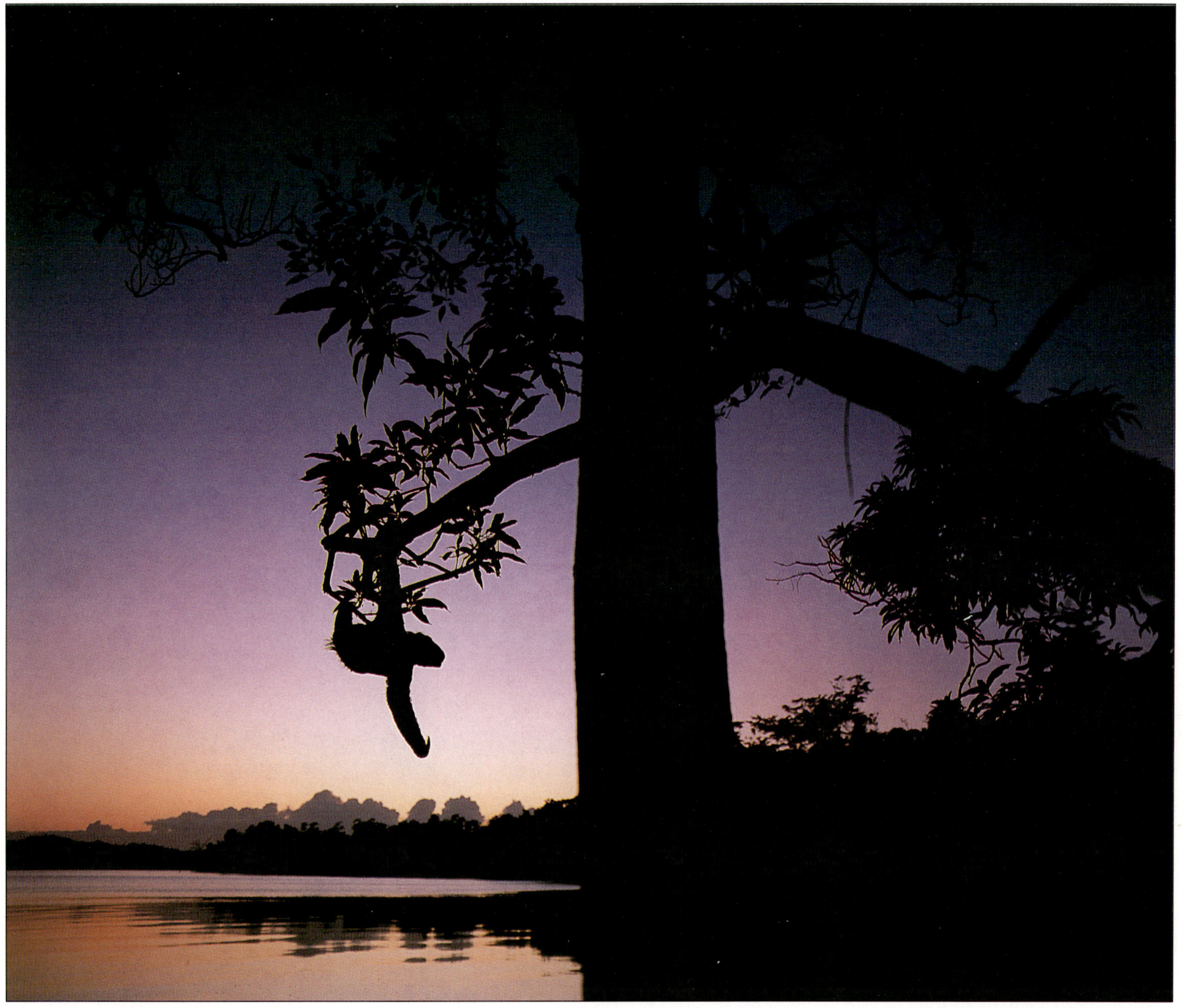

Mitsuhiko Imamori
Japan
HIGHLY COMMENDED

Three-toed sloth

"The three-toed sloth is nocturnal and spends most of the day in a tree without moving. Here, at dusk, one has just started to become active. While taking this picture I was attacked by a swarm of mosquitoes."

Pentax 6x7 with 45mm lens; tripod; 1/125sec at f8; Fujichrome Velvia

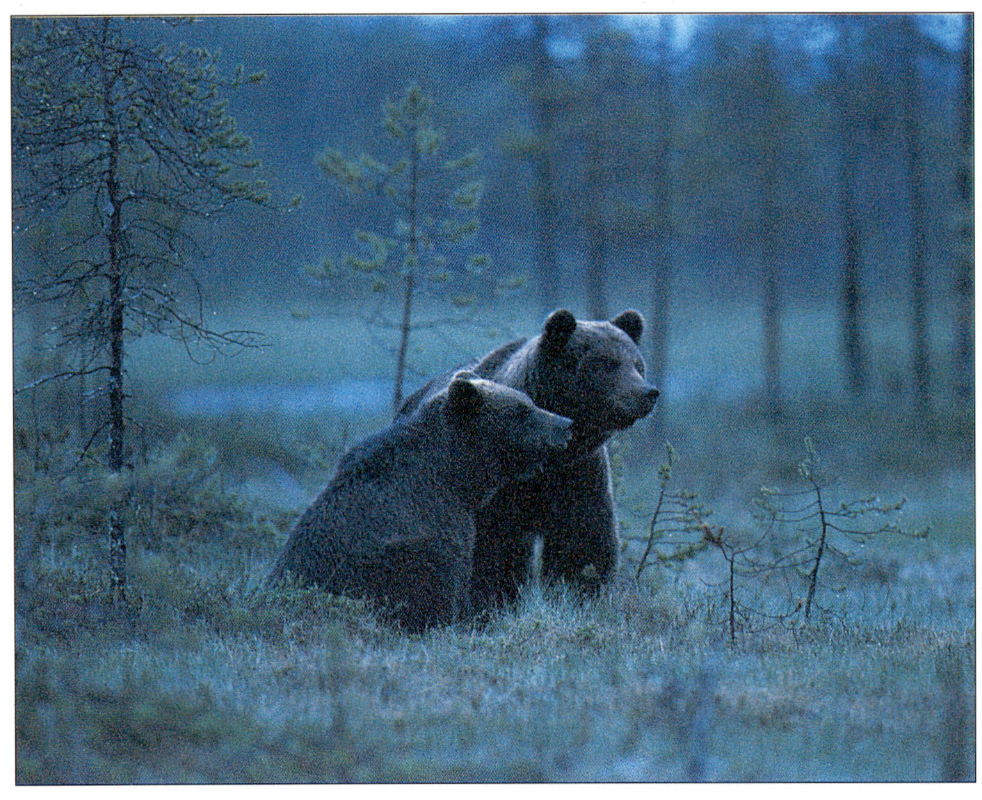

Philippe Henry

France

HIGHLY COMMENDED

Brown bears

"It is very rare to see a pair of bears. When you do, normally the male is chasing after the female, but on this occasion the pair stayed together like this for about half an hour before disappearing into the forest. I had set up a hide in North-east Finland, close to the Russian border, specially to watch bears. These two were dominant and would always come first to the bait I put out. Others followed later. During this night, the light was a particular blue which gave a mysterious effect to the photos I took."

Pentax Z1 with 600mm lens; tripod; 1/15 sec at f4; Kodachrome 200

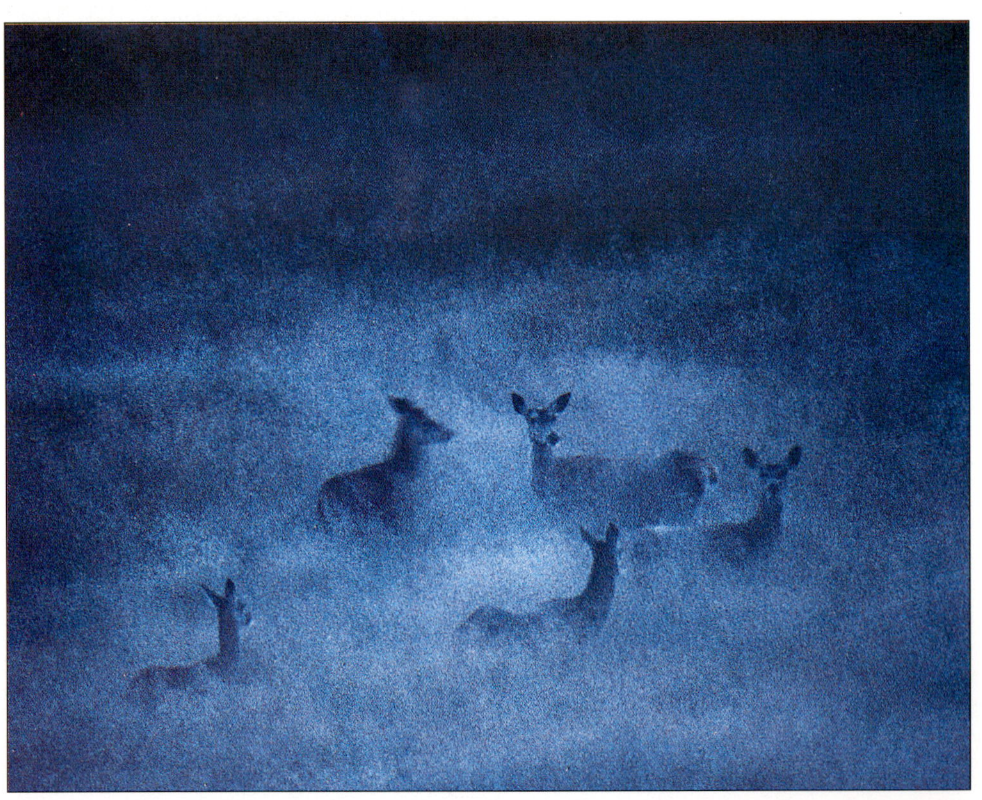

Pål Hermansen

Norway

HIGHLY COMMENDED

Deer at night

"This picture was taken in the middle of the night, in July, in a meadow not far from the coast. The field was full of deer and covered with mist. I wanted to create a graphic effect by using a fast film to give a colourless, grainy image."

Nikon F4S with 600mm lens; 1/8 sec at f4; Fujichrome 1600

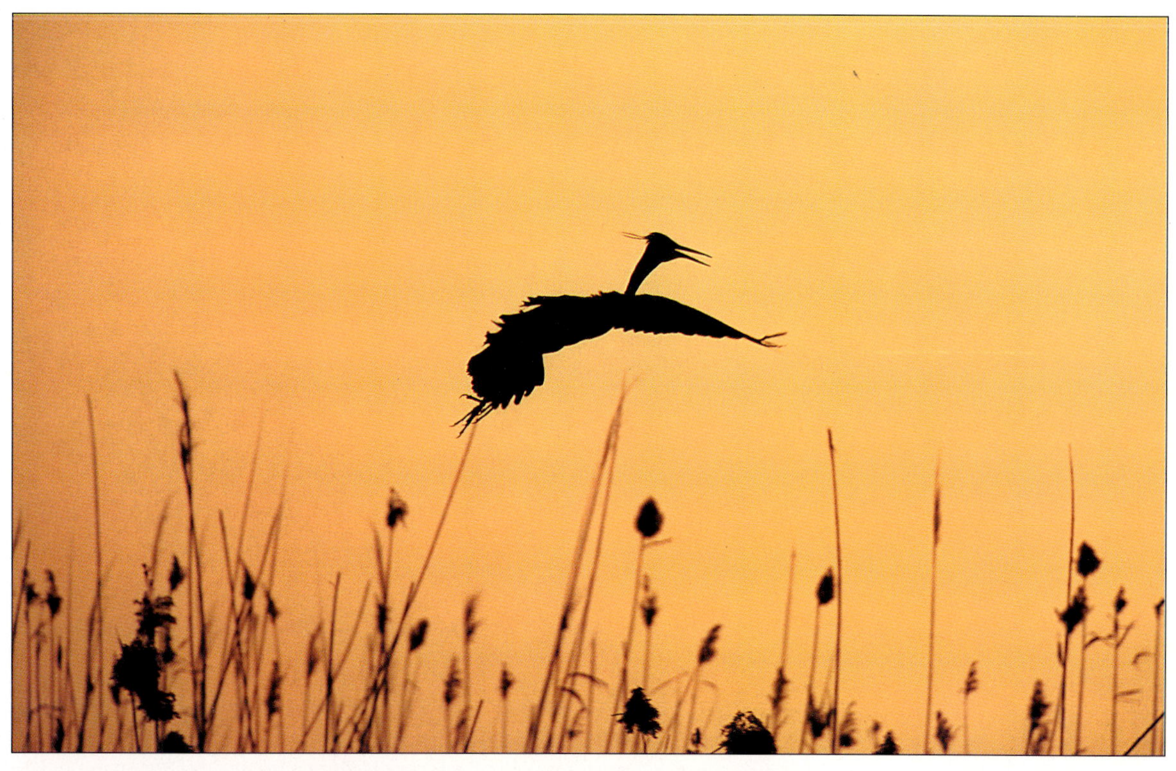

Antonio Sabater Artús
Spain
HIGHLY COMMENDED

Purple heron

"I photographed this purple heron in the Guadalquivir marshes, near the Coto Doñana National Park. I am currently working on a book about Andalusia's wetlands, and I might use this image on the cover."

Canon EOS1 with 300mm lens; tripod; Fujichrome Velvia

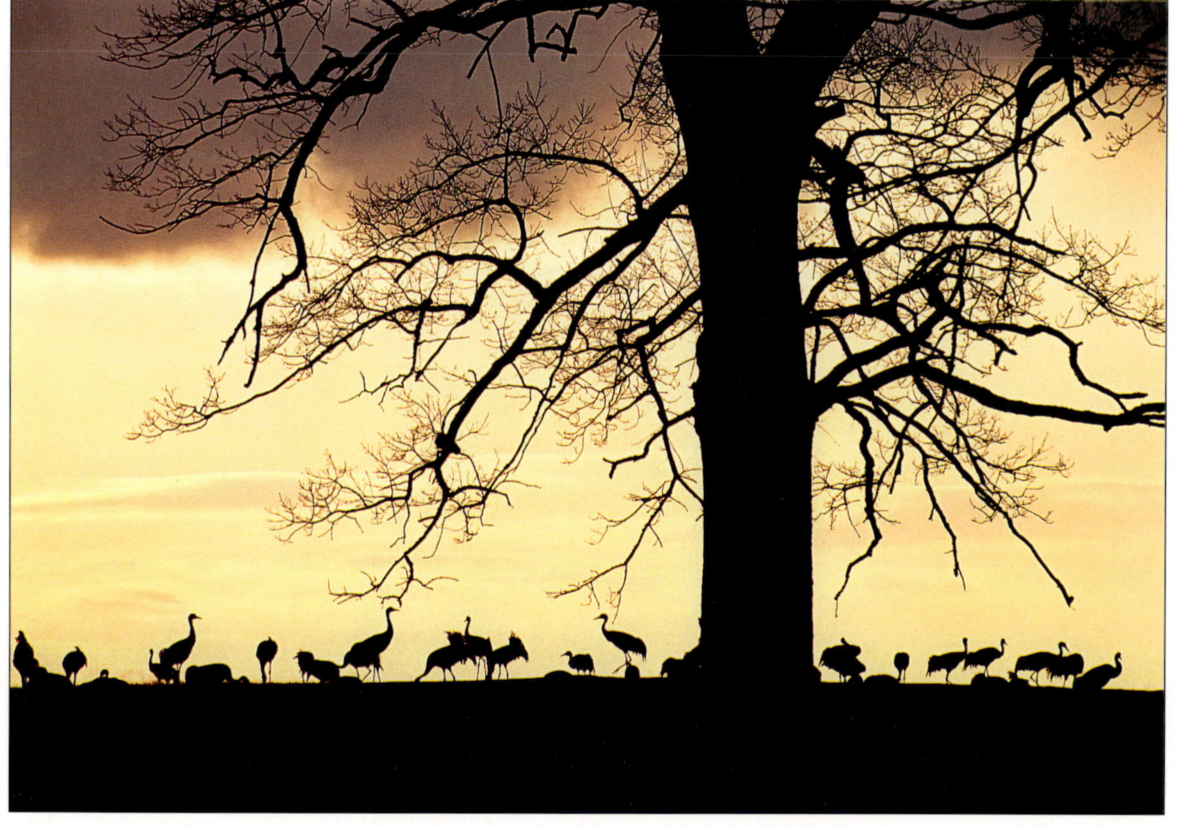

Bernard Castelein
Belgium
HIGHLY COMMENDED

Common cranes dancing

"These cranes had just landed at their feeding grounds on Lake Hornborga in Sweden, when they immediately started to dance. I hoped there was enough light to capture the cranes against the wonderful dawn sky."

Nikon F4 with 400mm lens; tripod; hide; 1/125 sec at f3.5; Fujichrome Velvia

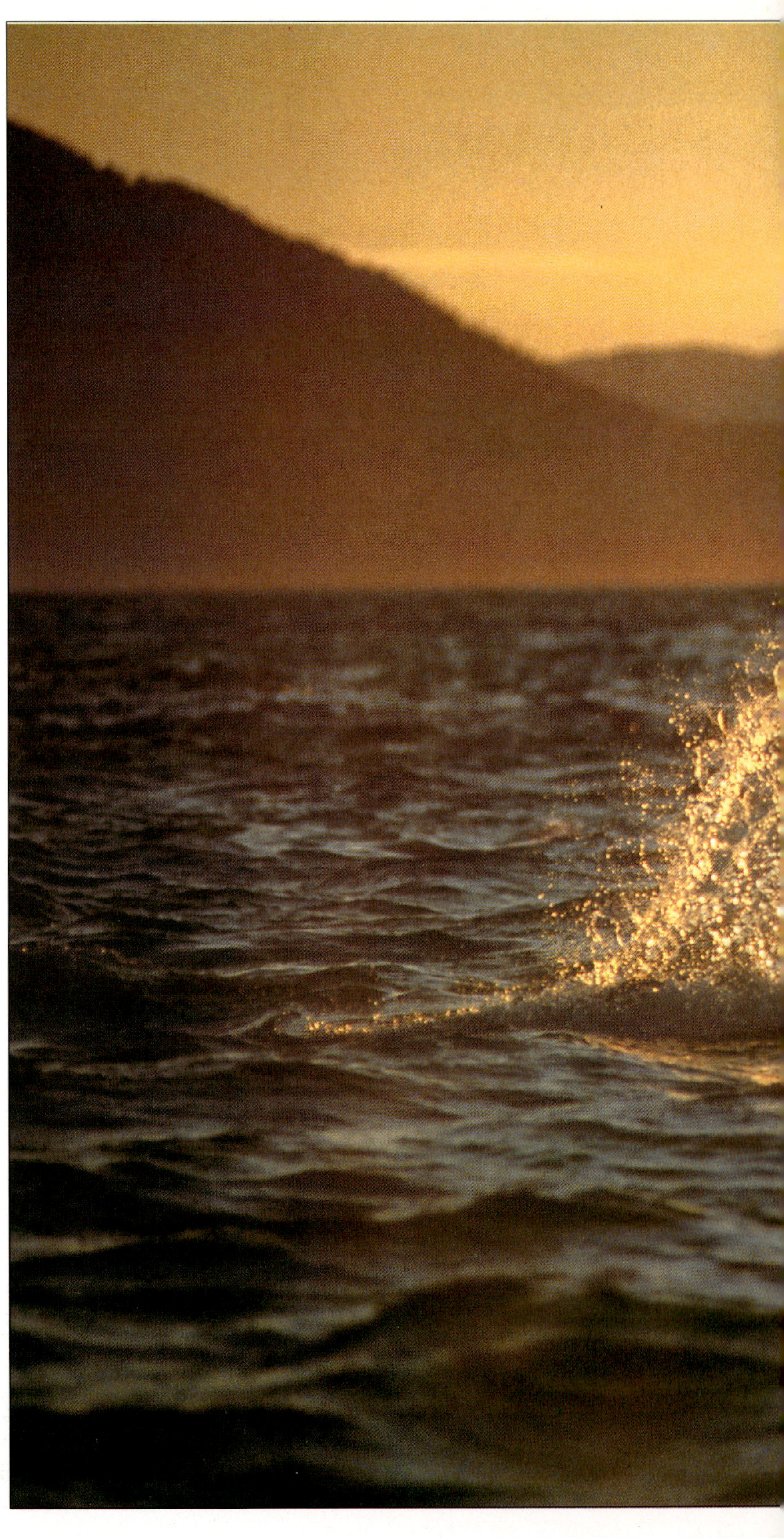

Art Wolfe
United States of America
HIGHLY COMMENDED

Humpback whale

"I photographed this humpback whale at Point Adolphus, South-east Alaska, for my book The Kingdom, a study of North American wildlife."

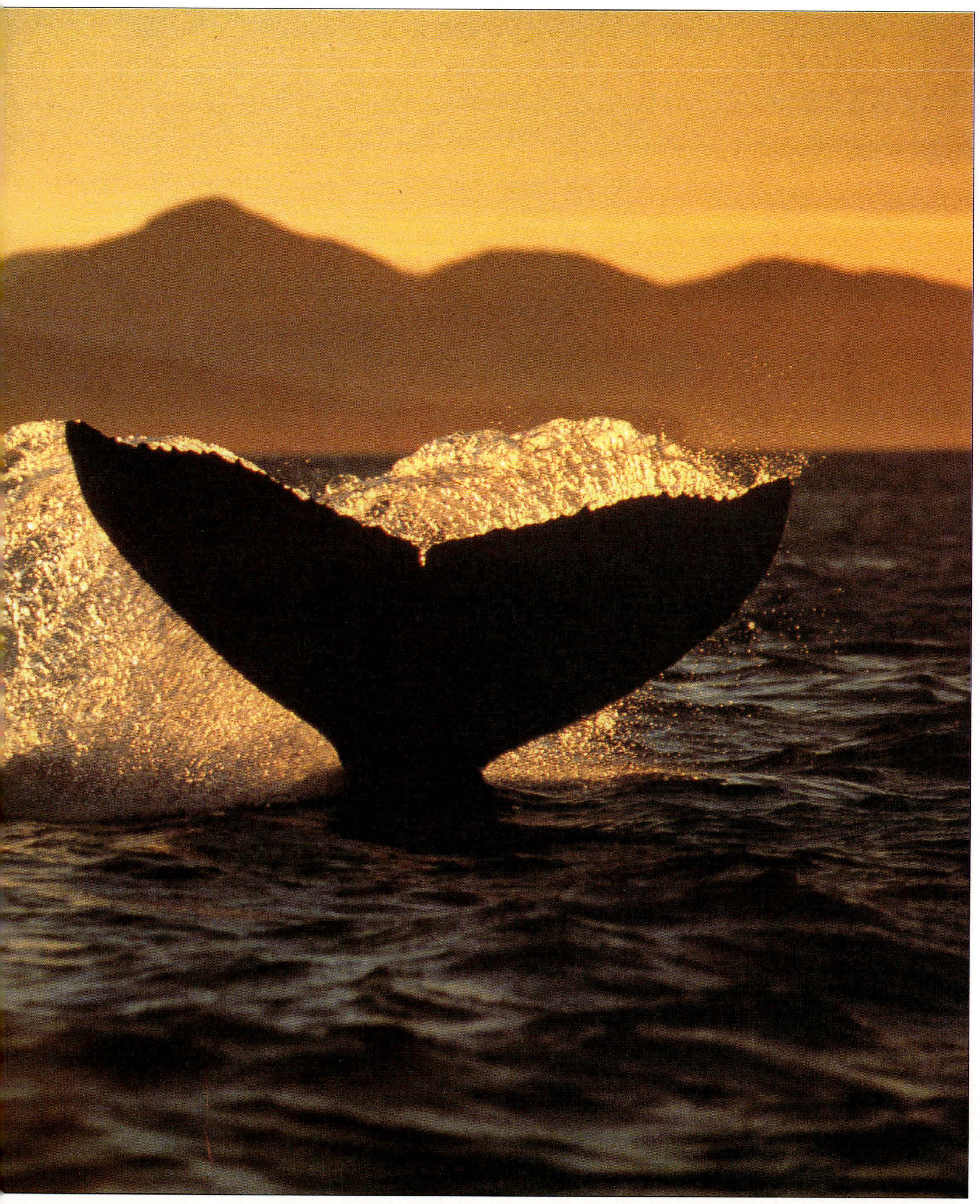

Composition and Form

This category is for abstract pictures of natural subjects. The entries are judged for their aesthetic values.

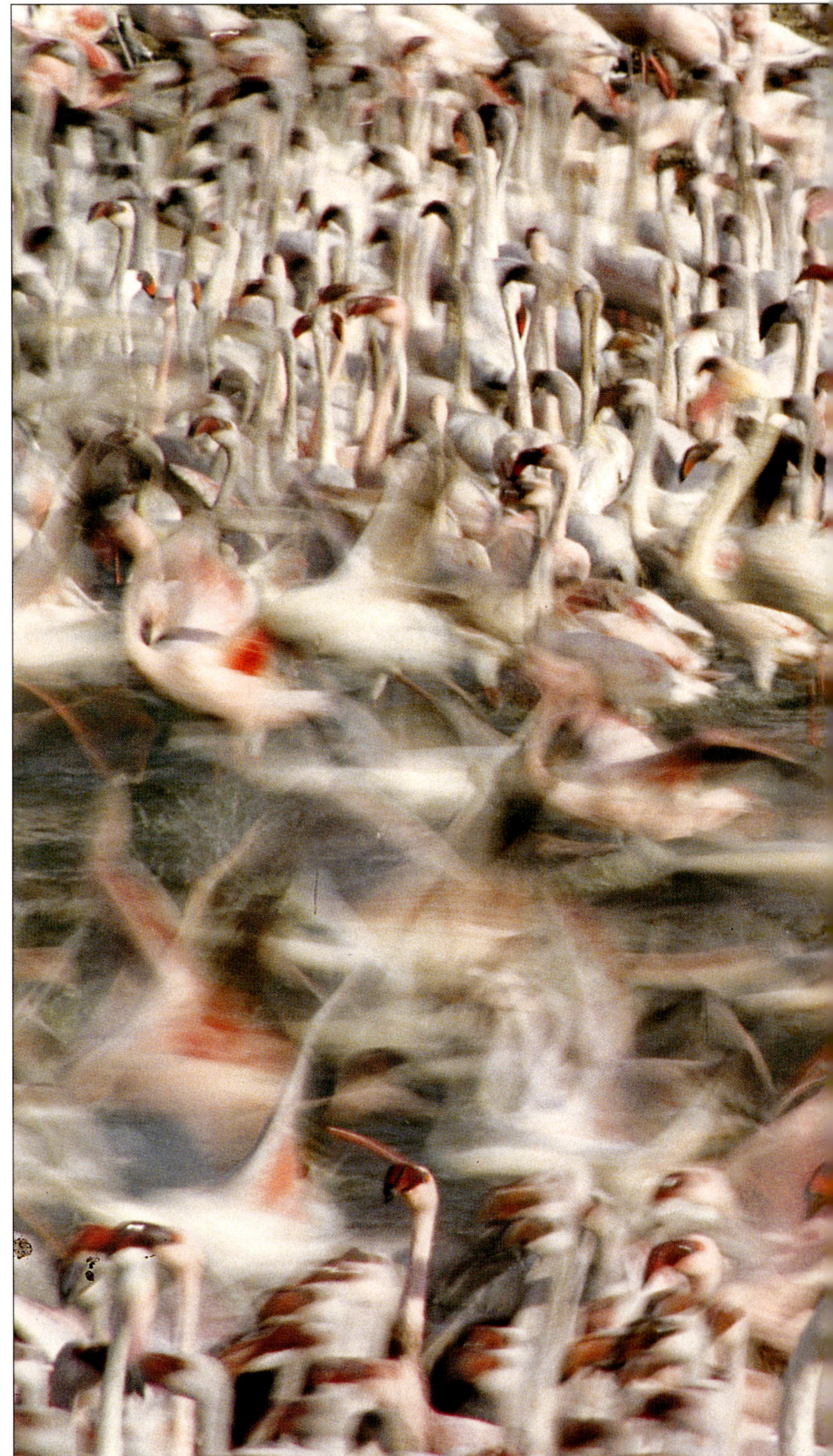

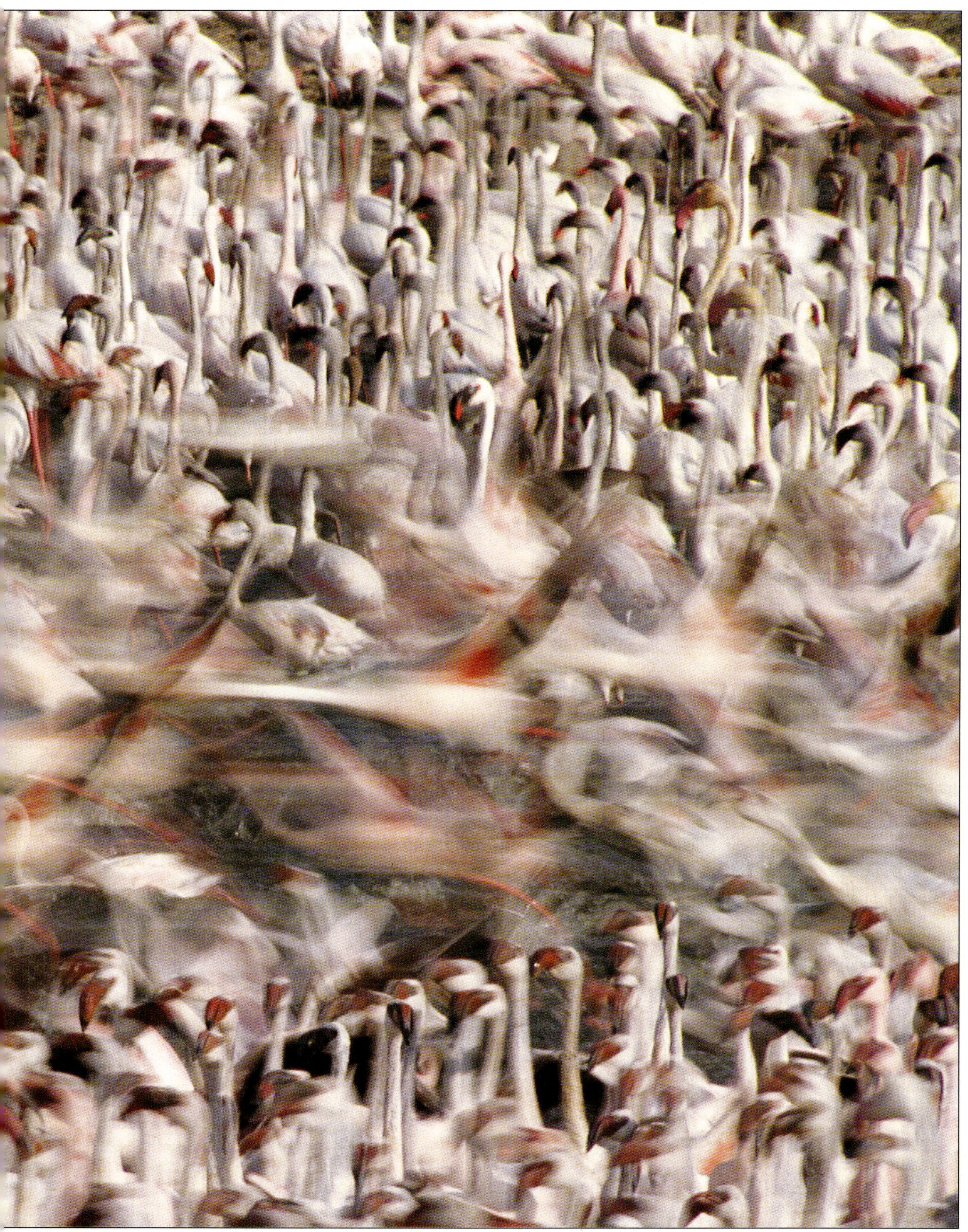

Mike Hill
United Kingdom
JOINT WINNER

Lesser flamingos

"While on holiday in Kenya, I spent three days on Lake Bogoria to photograph flamingos. Large numbers gathered to drink at freshwater sources along the shores. Normally they would drink and turn back into the lake in an orderly fashion, but on this occasion a family of greater kudu appeared from the bush. A few flamigos took fright and flew off. I chose a slow shutter speed to blur the movement of the flying birds through the middle of the frame."

Nikon F4 with 600mm lens; bean bag; 1/15 sec at f16/22; Fujichrome Velvia

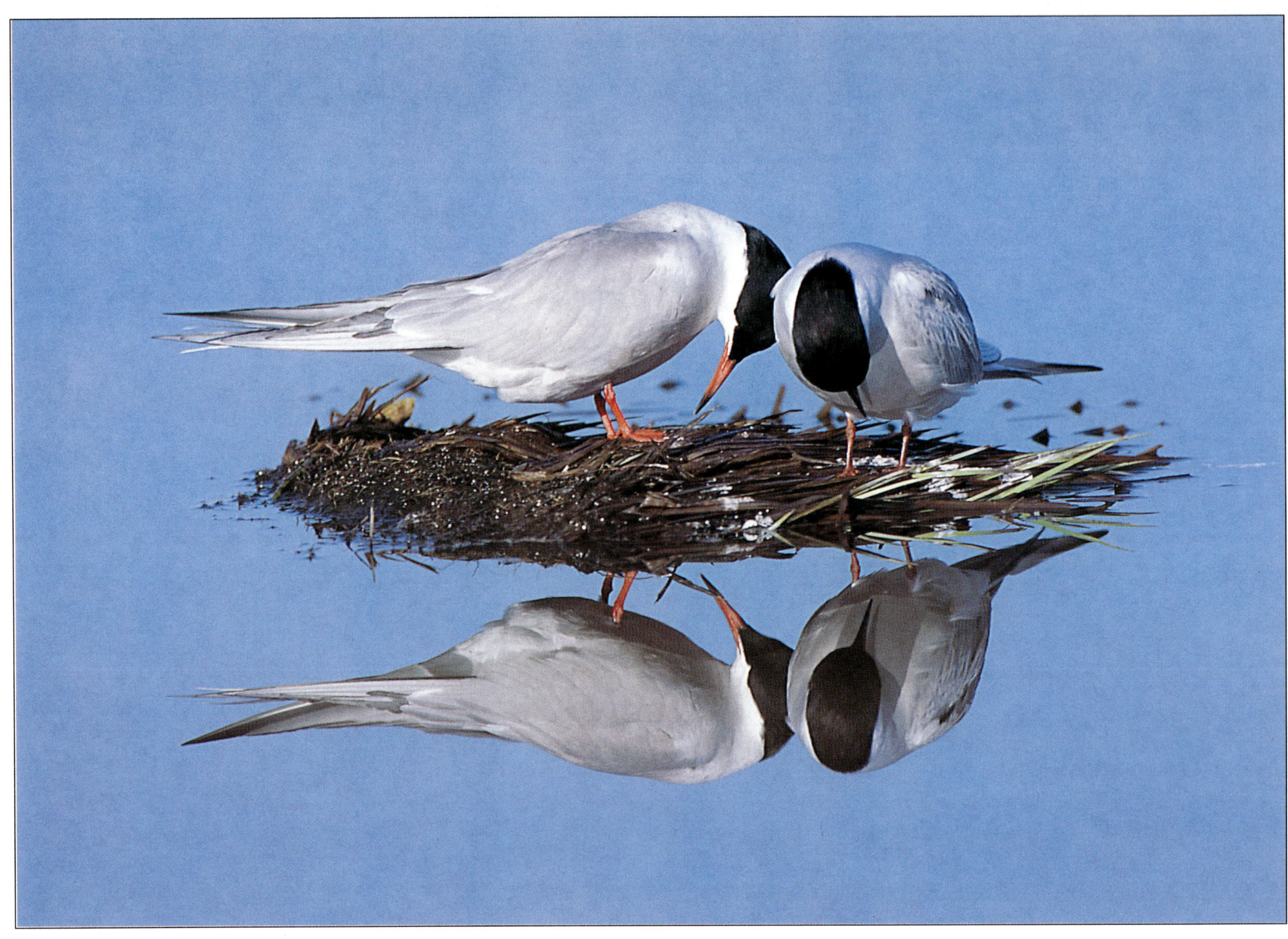

Asko Hämäläinen
Finland
JOINT WINNER

Common terns reflected

"Lake Junkkarinjärvi, where I photographed these terns, is one of my favourite bird- photography venues. I had photographed the male tern, courting the female with freshly caught fish offerings. Finally, the birds stopped moving and I managed to capture this image of them with their reflections in the calm water.

Canon EOS1 with 300mm lens; tripod; 1/250 sec at f2.8; Fujichrome Velvia

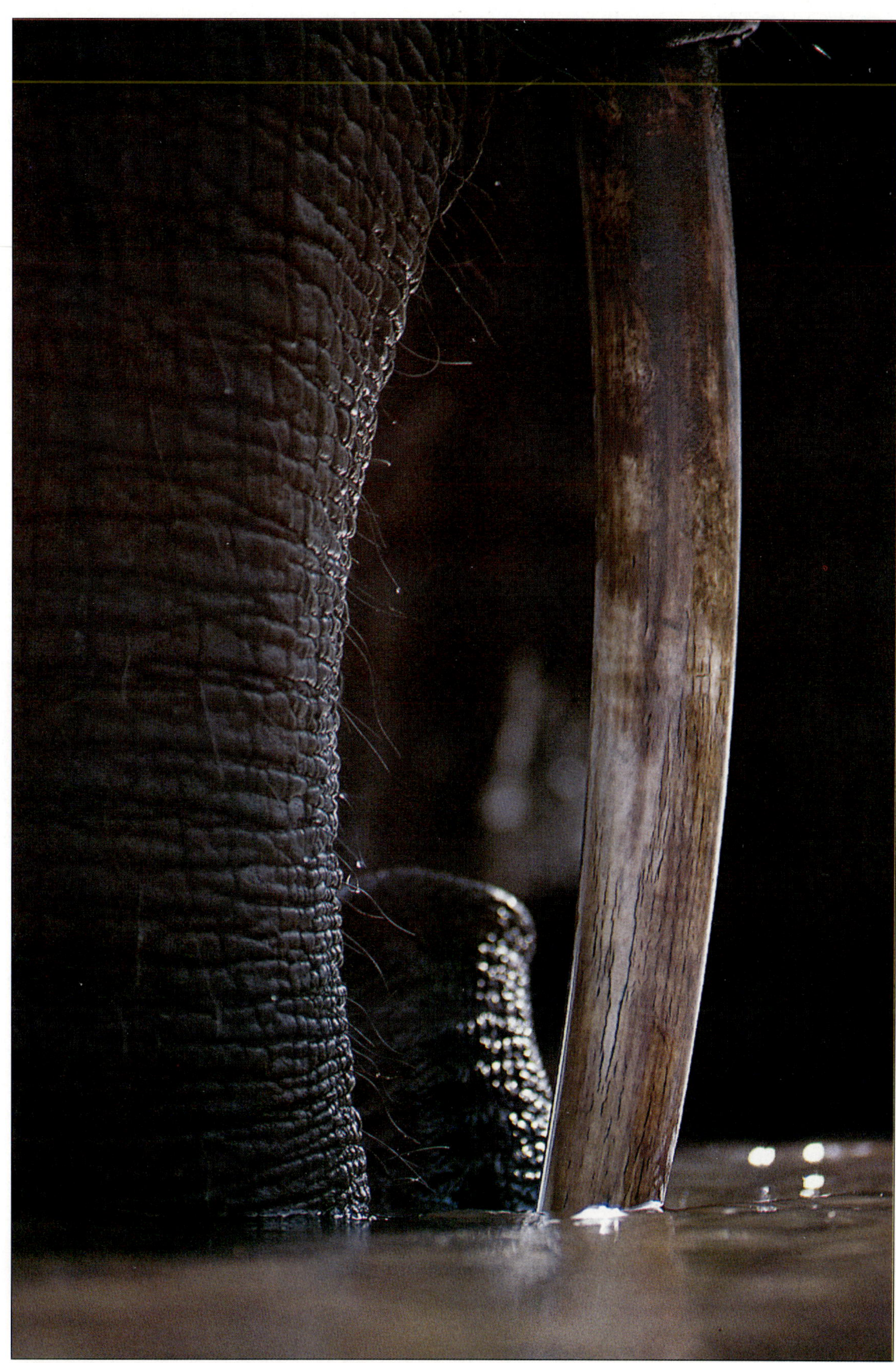

Bruce Davidson
Kenya
SPECIALLY COMMENDED

Tusk and trunk

"I came across this elephant drinking in the Virunga National Park, Zaire, and decided to focus close in on the elephant's distinctive features - its trunk and tusk."

Minolta 9000 with 600mm lens; tripod; Kodachrome 64

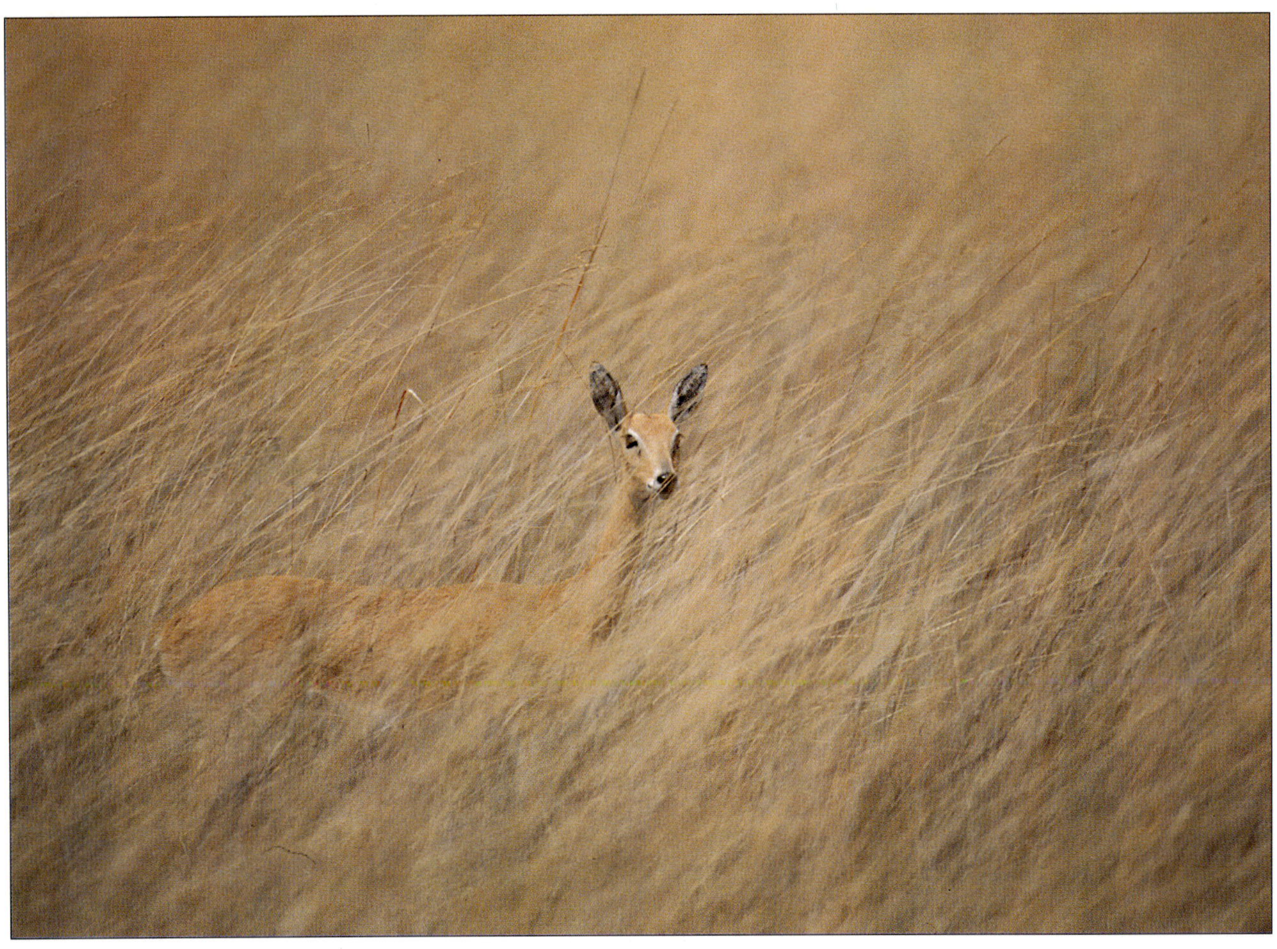

Ralph Snook
United Kingdom
HIGHLY COMMENDED

Oribi

"The Liuwa Plains is a remote area of Zambia, rarely visited by tourists. It has a variety of short and long grass plains, and oribi use the long grass to good effect as camouflage. I wanted to capture the beauty and fragility of the subject, as well as to show how effectively camouflaged it was in the grass."

Minolta 7000i with 75-300 lens; bean bag; 1/250 sec at f5.6; Kodachrome 200

Dr Hermann Brehm
Germany
HIGHLY COMMENDED

Gemsbok

"On holiday in Namibia, we walked for four or five hours into the sand dunes. The complete harmony of the dunes was reason enough to take photographs, but the appearance of two gemsbok made it even more impressive."

Canon T90 with 150-600mm lens; tripod; auto at f5.6; Fujichrome Velvia

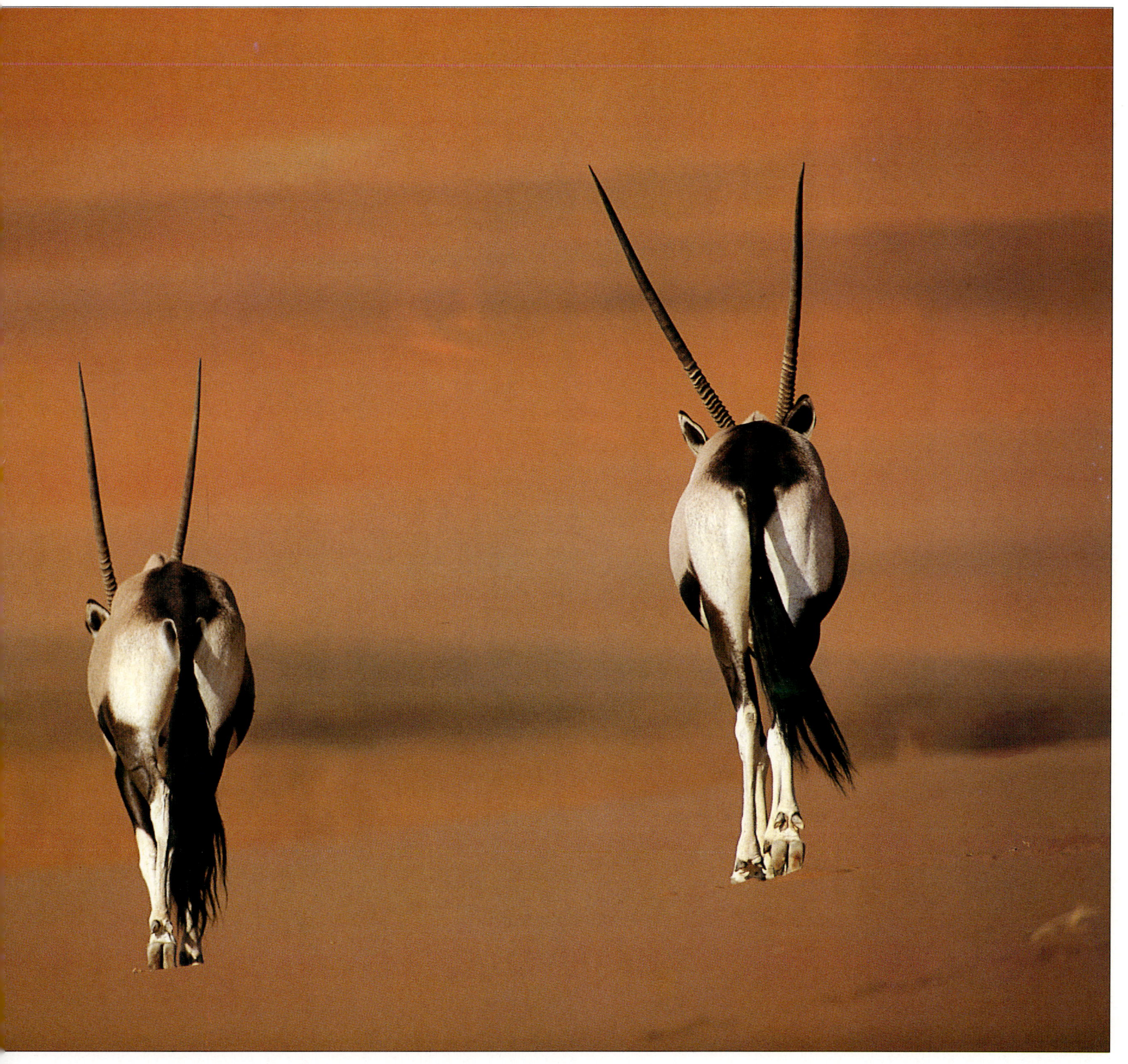

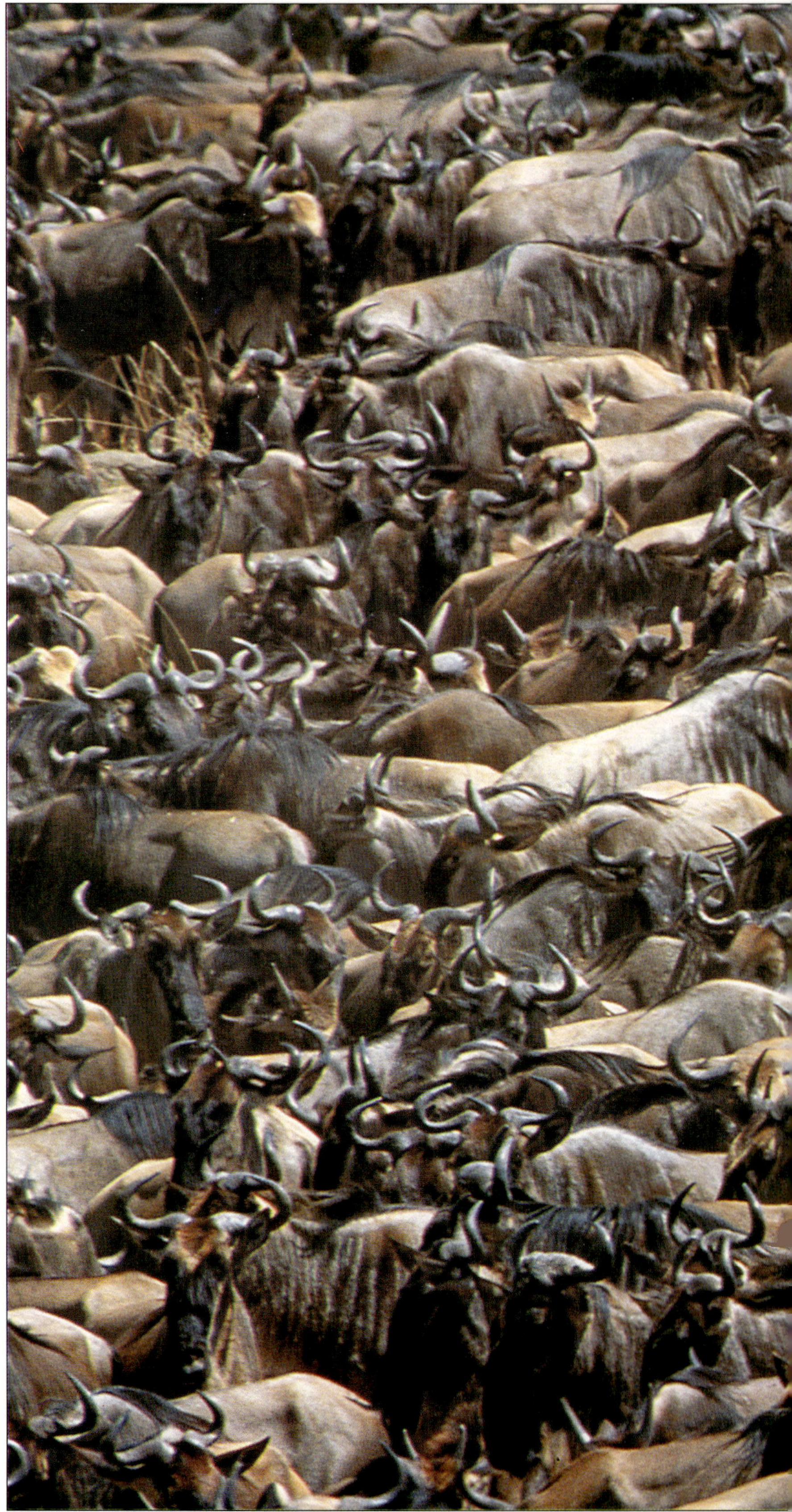

Art Wolfe

United States of America

HIGHLY COMMENDED

Wildebeest and Grant's zebra

"This picture was shot during the annual wildebeest migration in the Maasai Mara Game Reserve, Kenya. A lone Grant's zebra was separated from its herd and swept into the milling mass of wildebeest. I was photographing from a vehicle and the zebra was on a mound, which made it stand out so well. At the time I was taking pictures for my book Migrations.*"*

Nikon F4 with 600mm lens; 1/30 sec at f16; Fujichrome Velvia

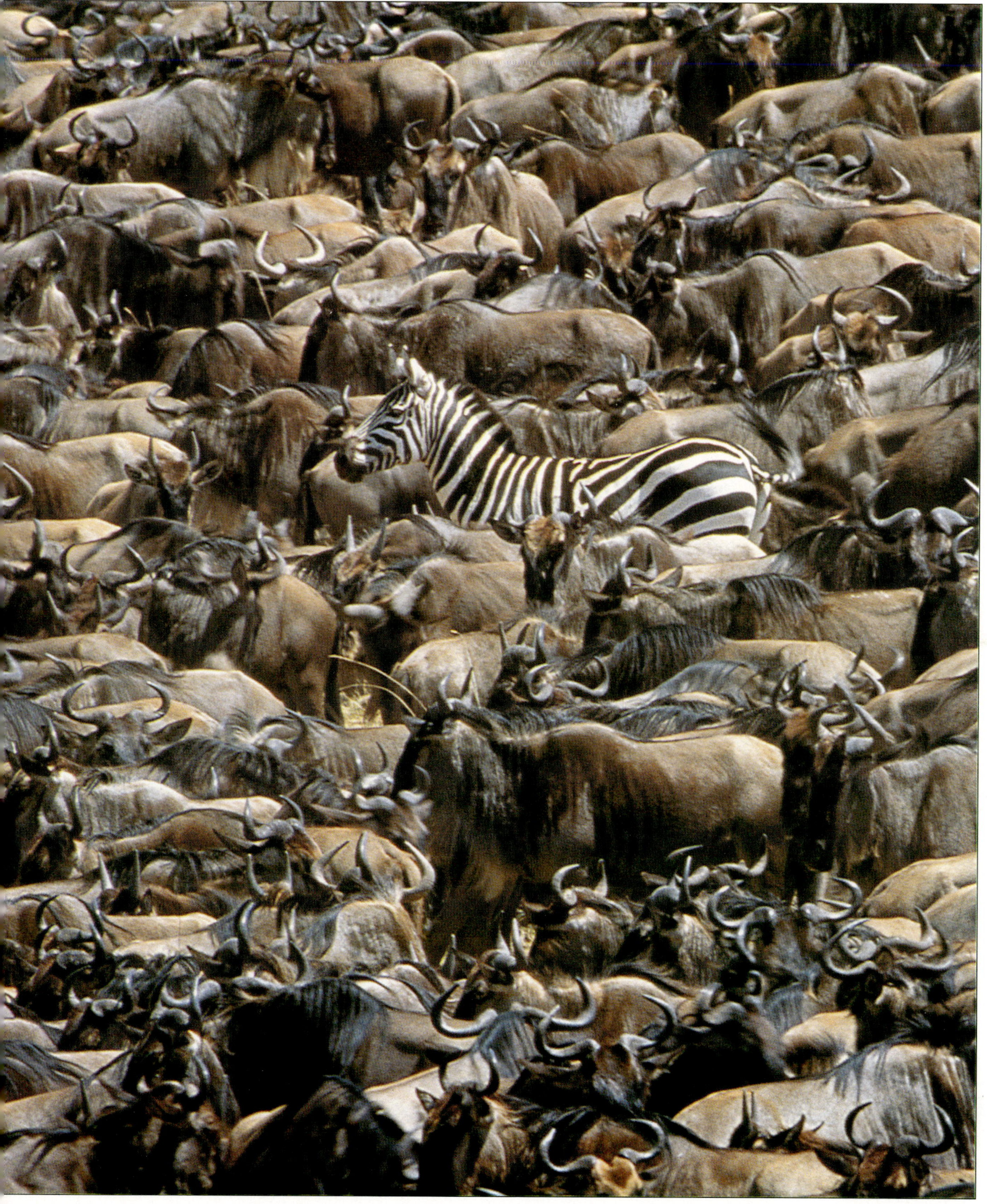

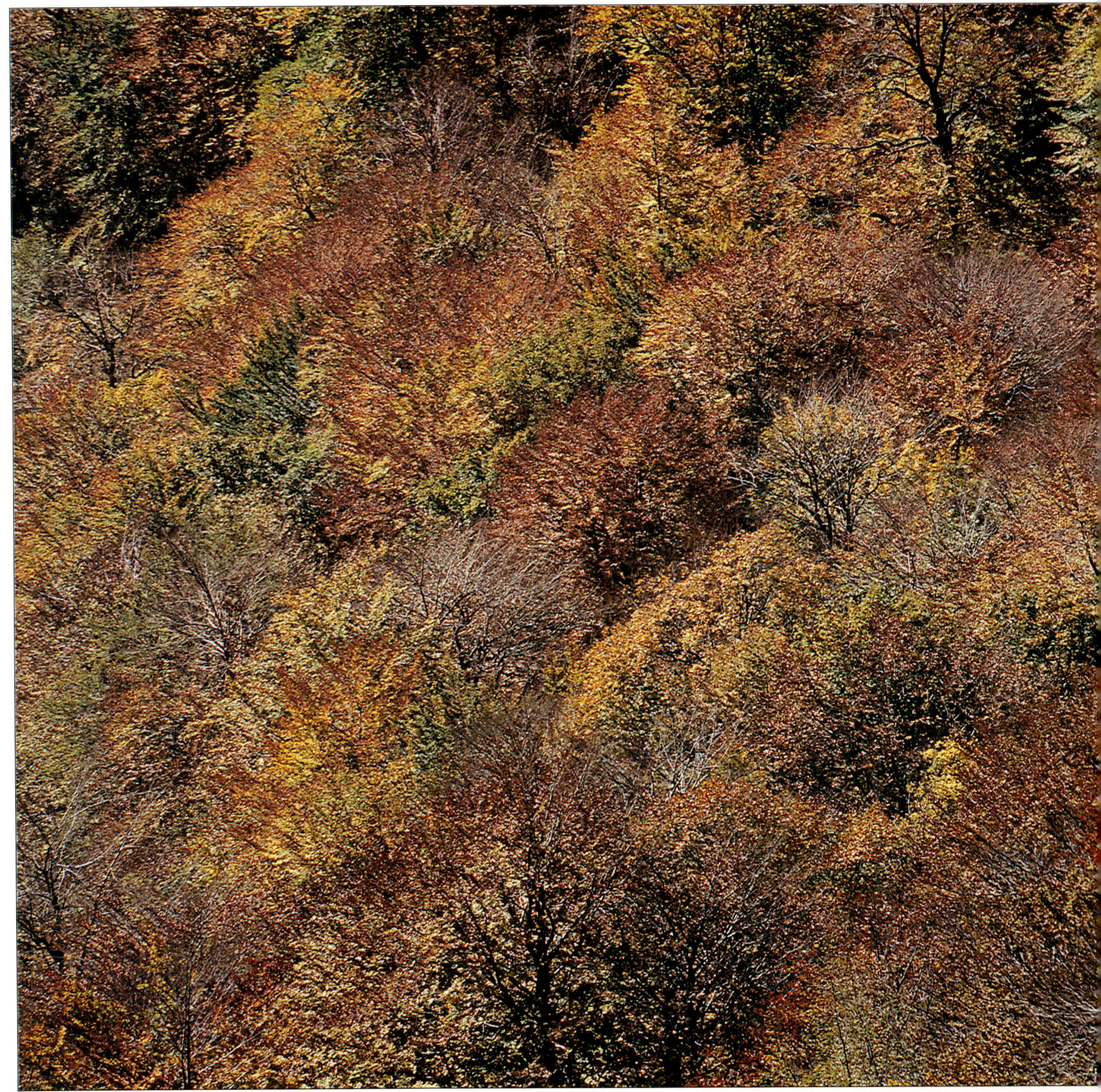

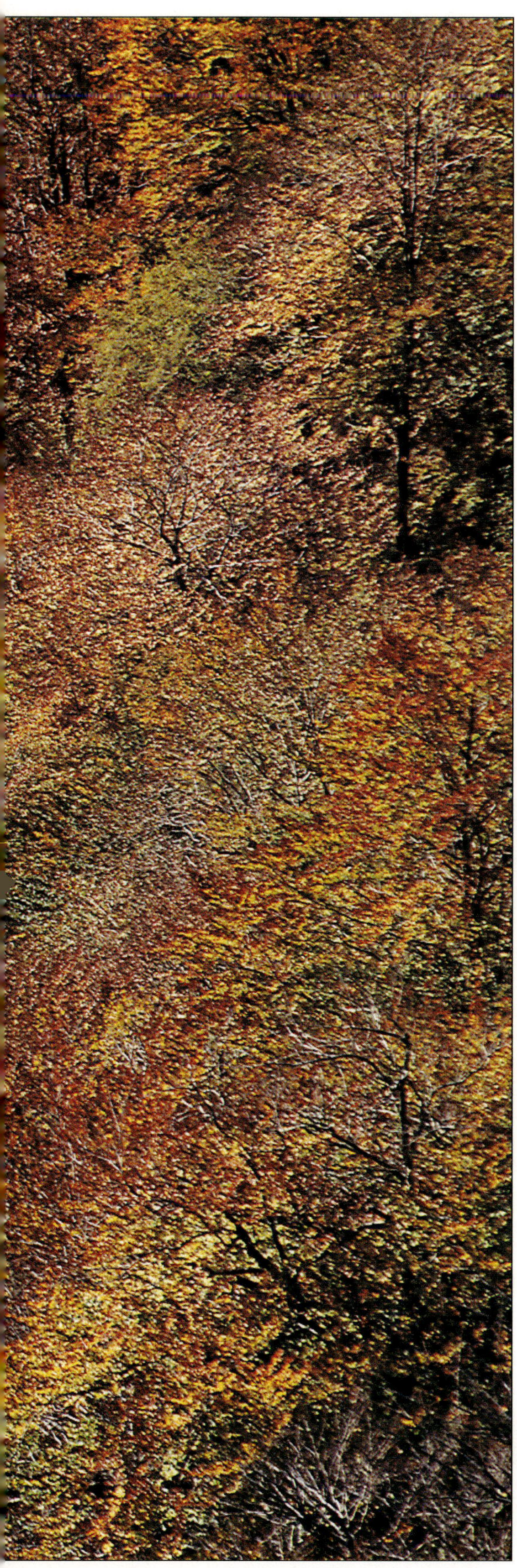

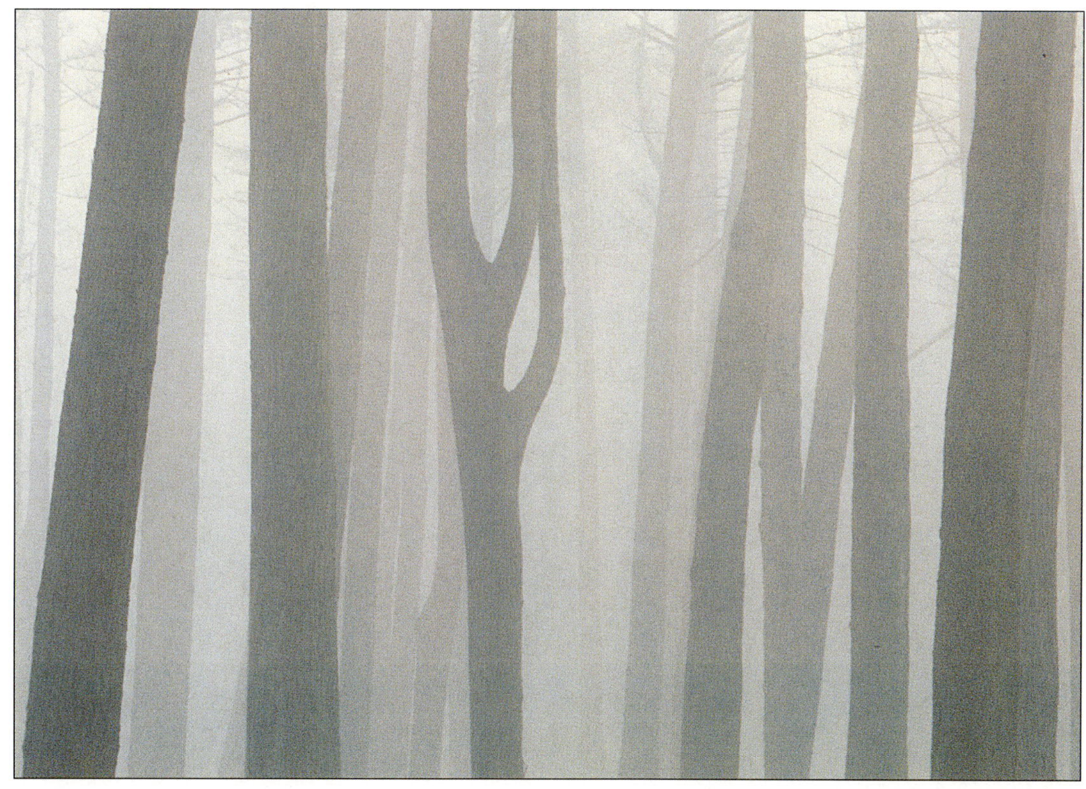

Marko Masterl
Slovenia
HIGHLY COMMENDED

Autumn colours

"I wanted to catch this special moment when the autumn colours are at their best in the Borovska Gora. This area, near Kocevje, was closed during the Communist regime and is quite untouched."

Nikon F801 with 80-200mm lens; Ektachrome Elite 100

Brenda Tharp
United States of America
HIGHLY COMMENDED

Cypress trees in fog

"I waited for a year for the right weather conditions to take this photograph in the Golden Gate Natural Recreation Area, California. I wanted to achieve a graphic pattern of the trunks of isolated trees within the forest, and I needed low-altitude fog to render the effect."

Canon EOS2 with 80-200mm lens; tripod; 2 secs at f22; Fujichrome 100

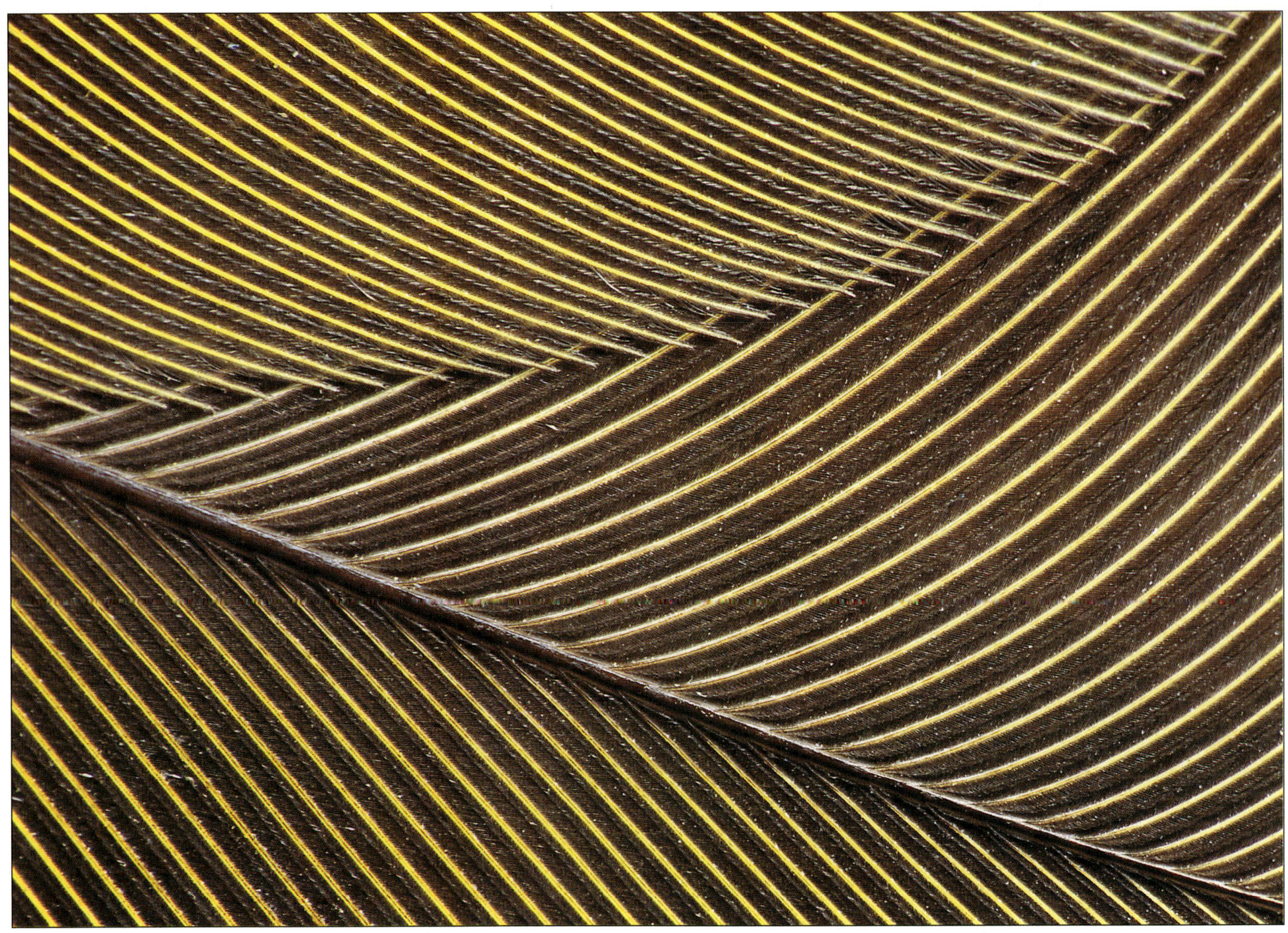

Martin van Lokven
The Netherlands
HIGHLY COMMENDED

Feather detail

"I had at home a wing of a dead green woodpecker and decided last winter to photograph the feathers in close-up."

Nikon FE2 with 105mm macro lens with extender; tripod; 8 secs at f22; Fujichrome Velvia

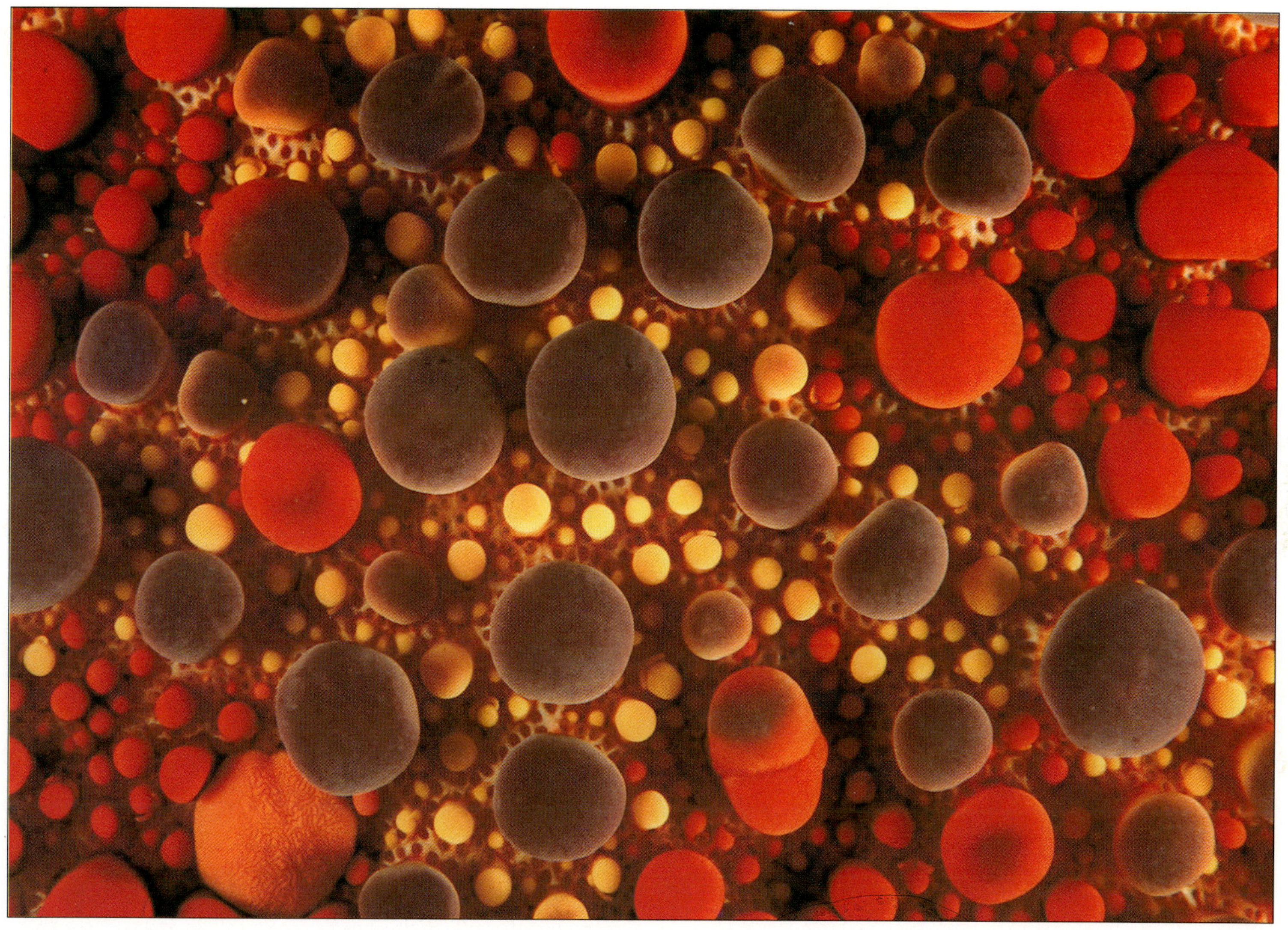

Andrew N Drake
United States of America
HIGHLY COMMENDED

Starfish detail

"This is a close-up of a starfish that I found on a dive in Jervis Bay, New South Wales, Australia. I took the picture as part of an on-going study of colour, pattern and form in starfish around the world."

Nikon F4 with 60mm macro lens in underwater housing; strobes; 1/125 sec at f22; Fujichrome Velvia

Wild Places

This category is for pictures of landscapes which convey a feeling of wildness and/or create a feeling of wonder and awe.
No prizes were awarded this year.

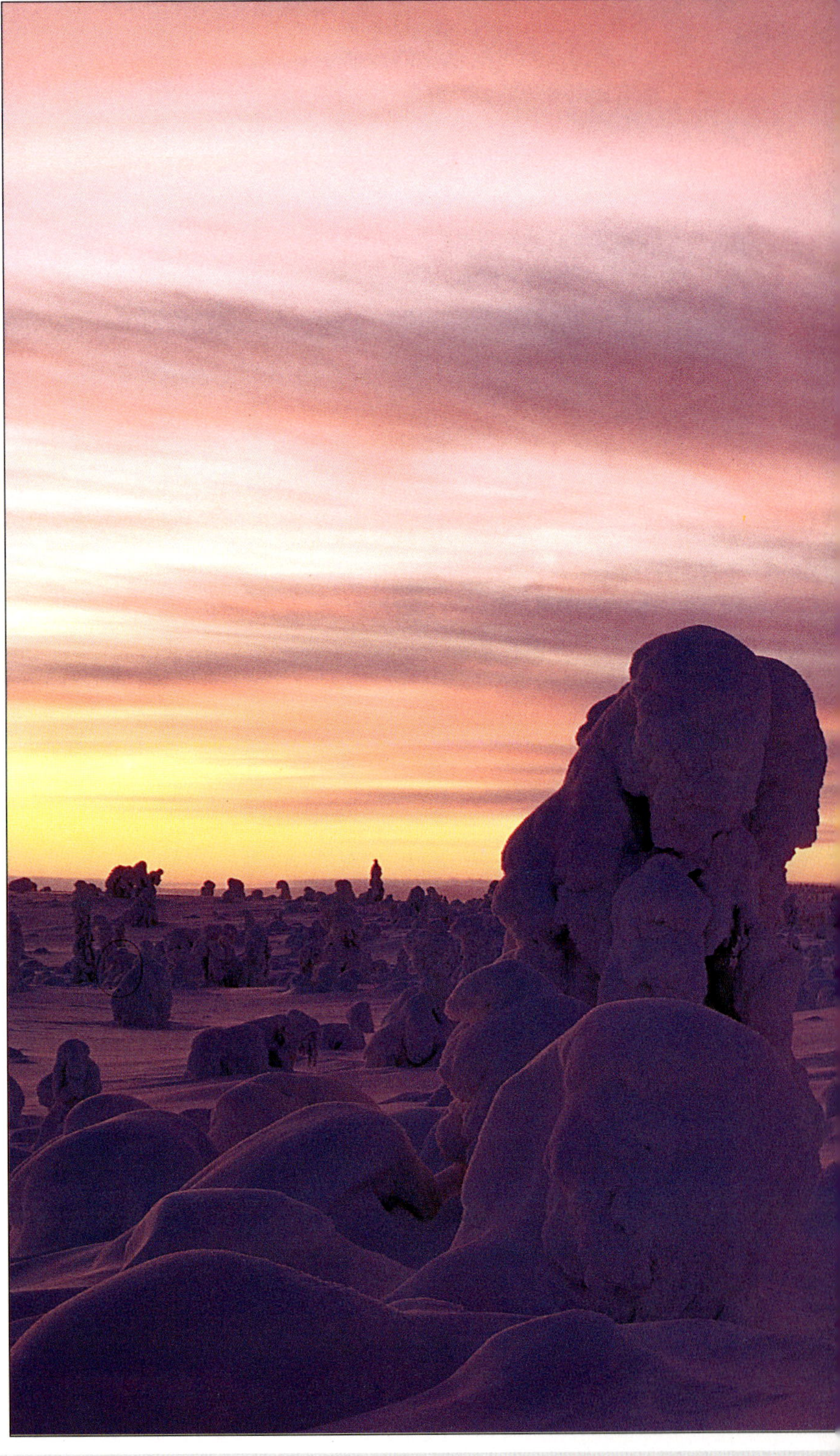

Markku K Aikioniemi
Finland
HIGHLY COMMENDED

Winter in Lapland

"The winter of 1994 was splendid in intensity and unusually rich in snow. This photograph, taken 70 miles north of the Arctic Circle at Mount Vasatunturi, draws on the special light effect known to Finns as 'Kaamos'. Although the sun does not appear over the horizon, a blue twilight envelops the landscape, creating a unique atmosphere of tranquil beauty. I dedicated my 1994 winter photography to exploring different aspects of this blue light."

Pentax Z1 with 28-80mm lens; tripod; Fujichrome Velvia

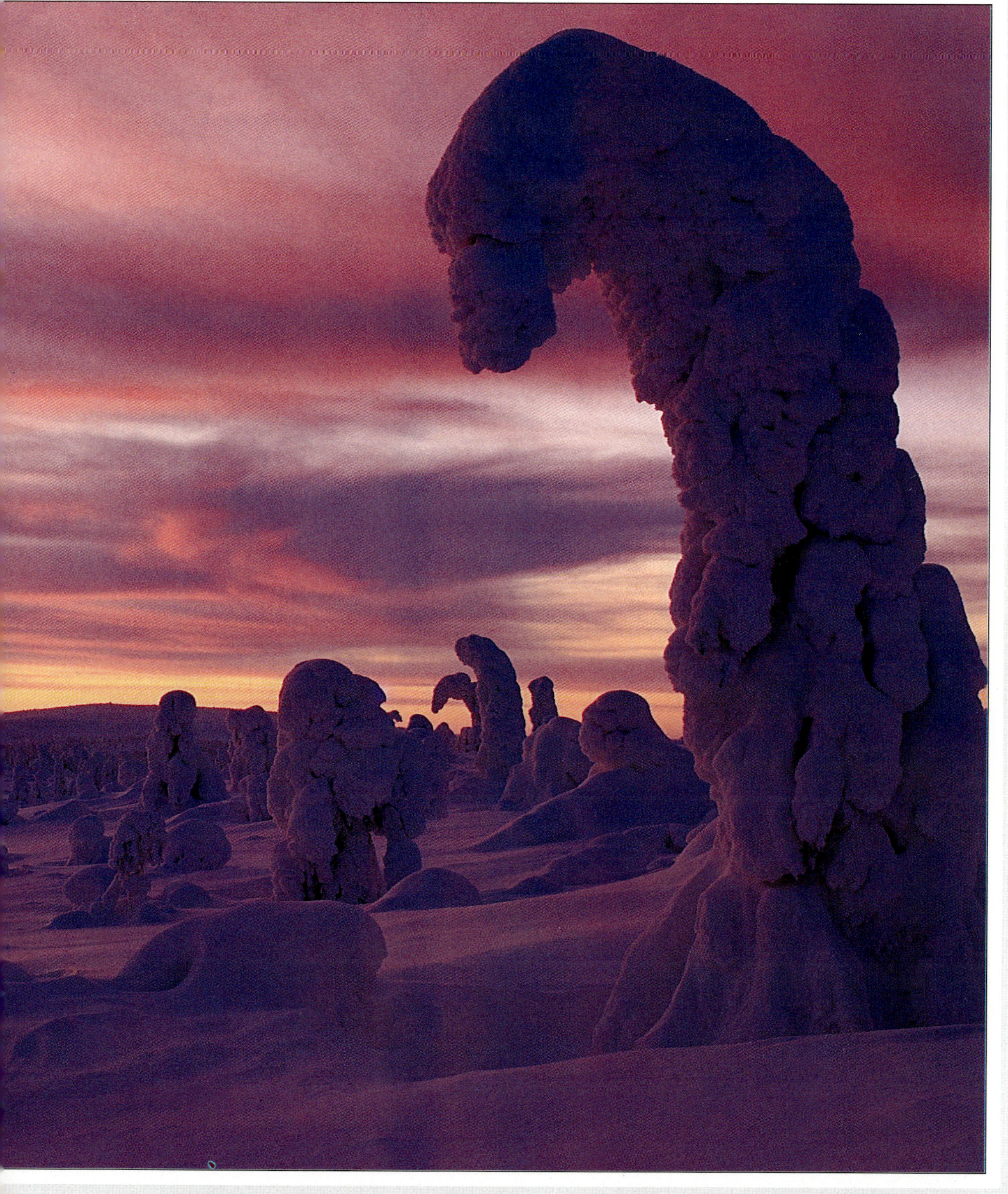

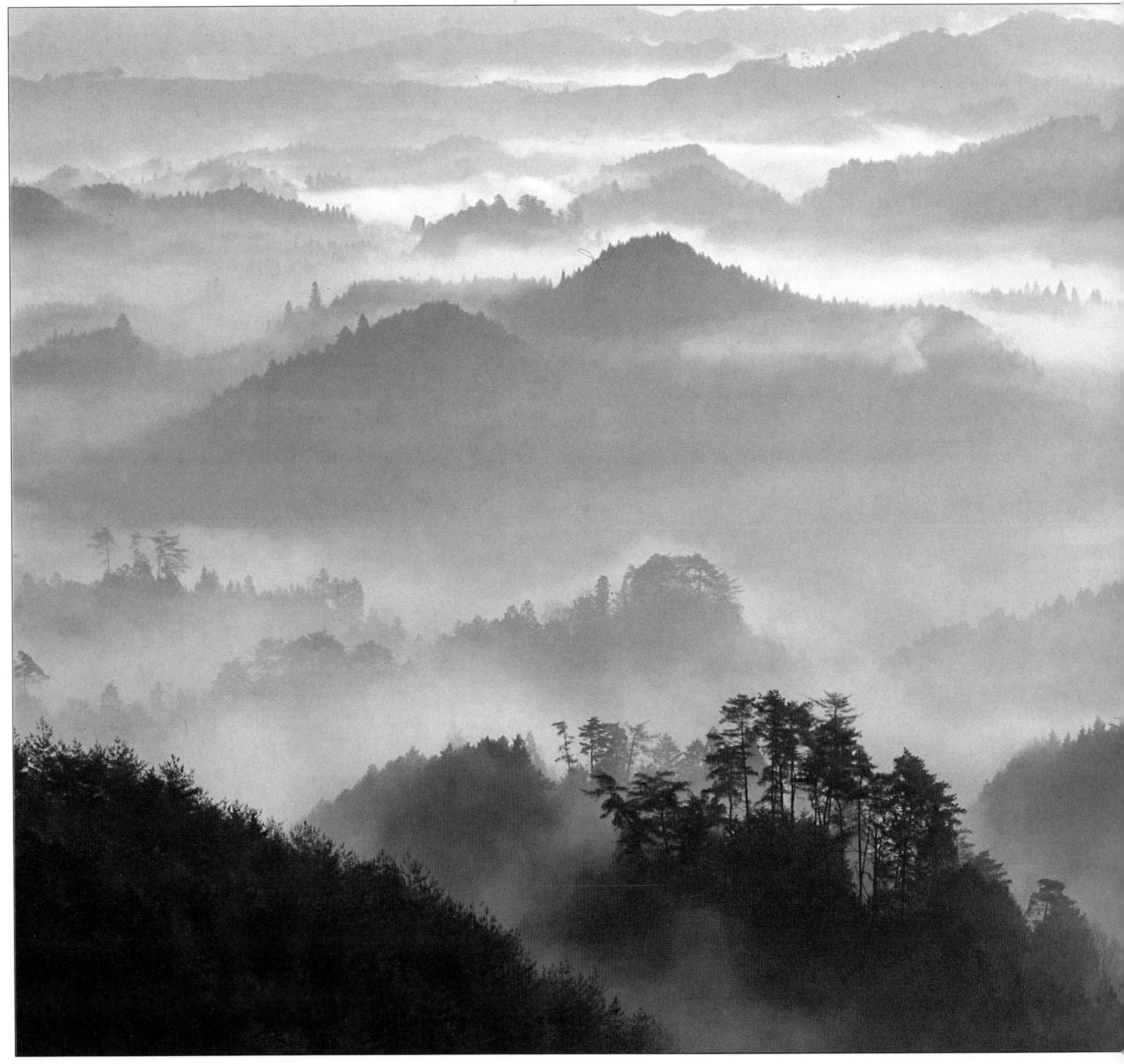

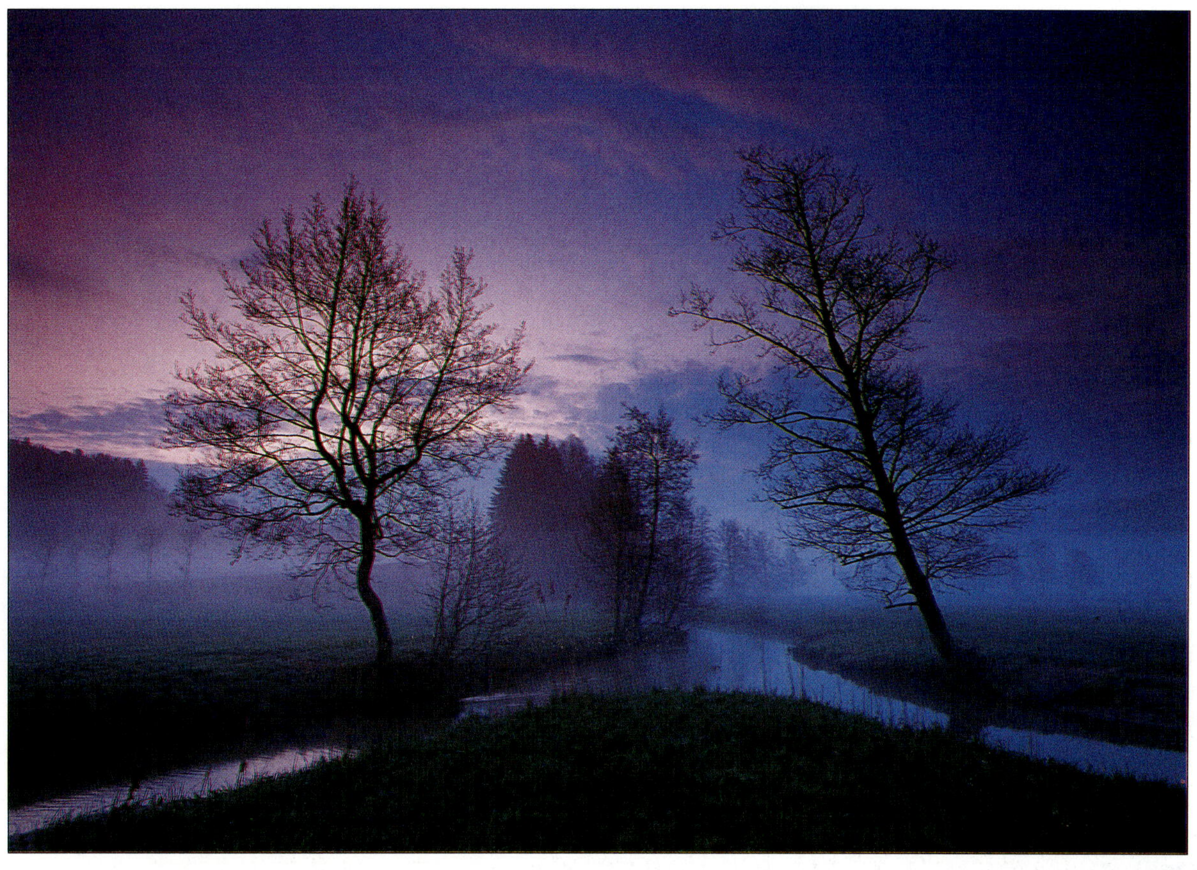

Hijiri Okamoto
Japan
HIGHLY COMMENDED

Morning mist

"This mist occurs only in autumn and winter. To take this picture, I left home at 4am one November morning and took up position on a small mountain overlooking the valley. It was so cold that my hands froze to the tripod."

Canon T60 with 80-200mm lens; tripod; auto at f16; Fujichrome 100

Herbert Kehrer
Germany
HIGHLY COMMENDED

River at dawn

"It took three years of visiting Swabia, an hour's travel from my home, before I was able to photograph this river in these perfect conditions. Morning mist and the rising sun combined to create a special atmosphere."

Nikon F3 with 24mm lens; tripod; 1/15 sec at f11; Fujichrome Velvia

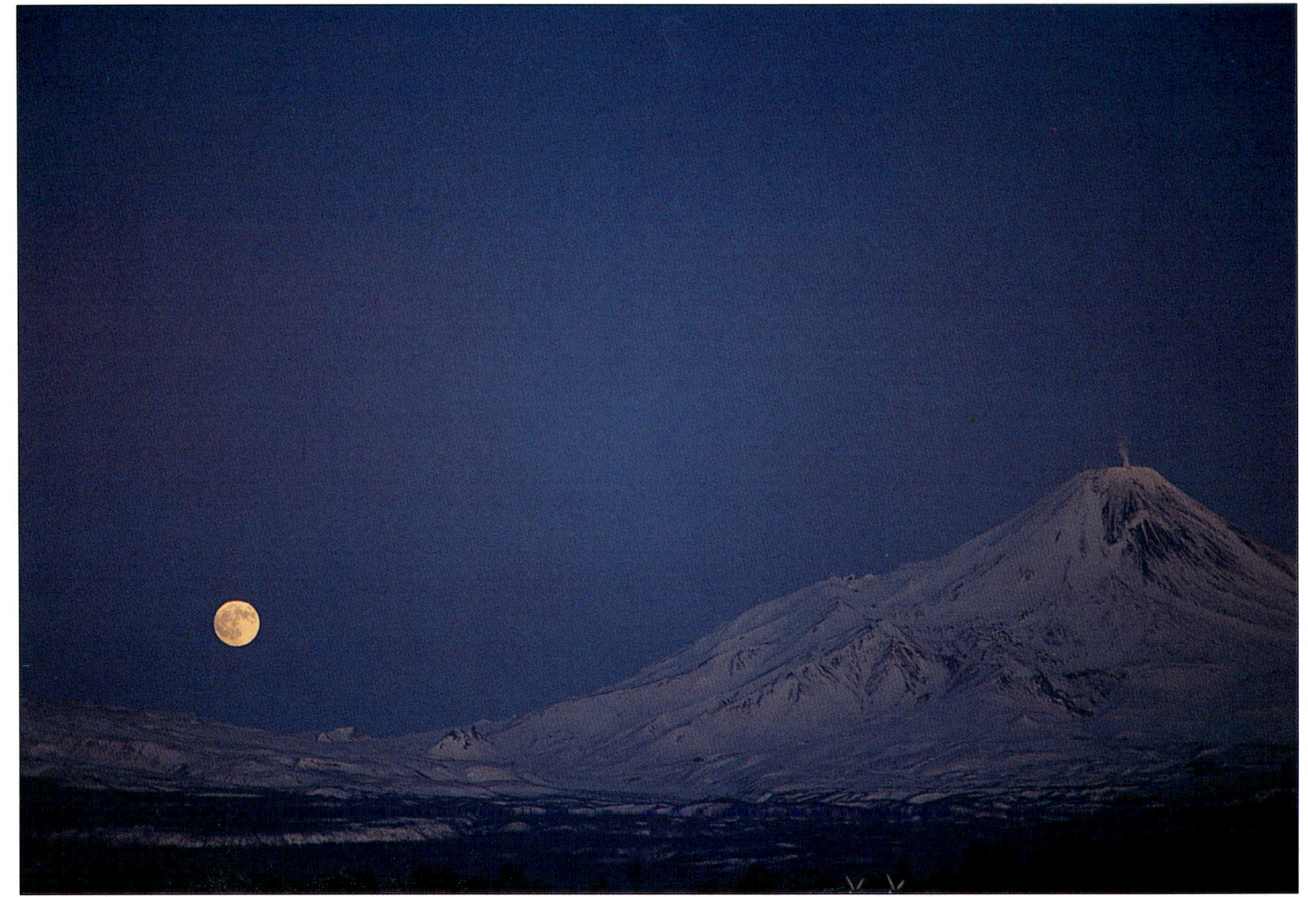

Klaus Nigge
Germany
HIGHLY COMMENDED

Volcano with moon

"On a trip to photograph the wildlife and landscapes of Kamchatka, Russia, I decided to photograph this active volcano by moonlight."

Nikon F801; Kodachrome 64

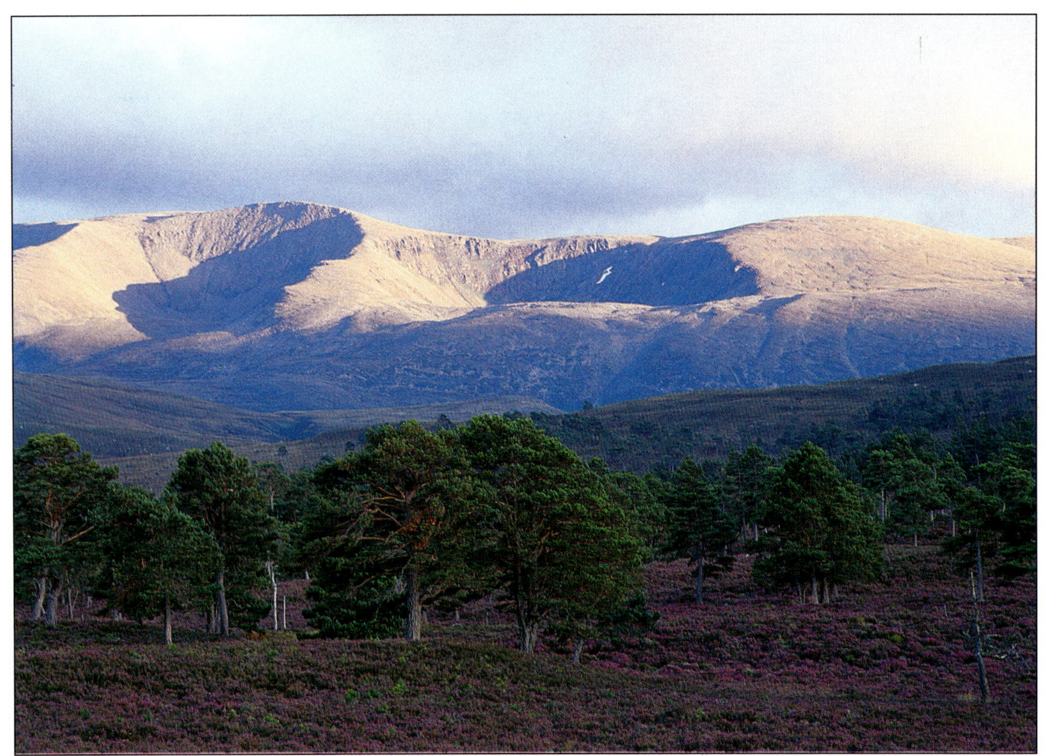

Neil McIntyre
United Kingdom
HIGHLY COMMENDED

Cairngorm mountains and Rothiemurchus forest

"I took this picture at around 8pm one August evening, while returning from a trip on the high tops. The view at this point revealed the beauty of the Cairngorm mountains, where I had just been, as well as the Rothiemurchus ancient pine forest."

Canon T90 with 50-135 zoom lens; tripod; 1/30sec at f11; Fujichrome Velvia

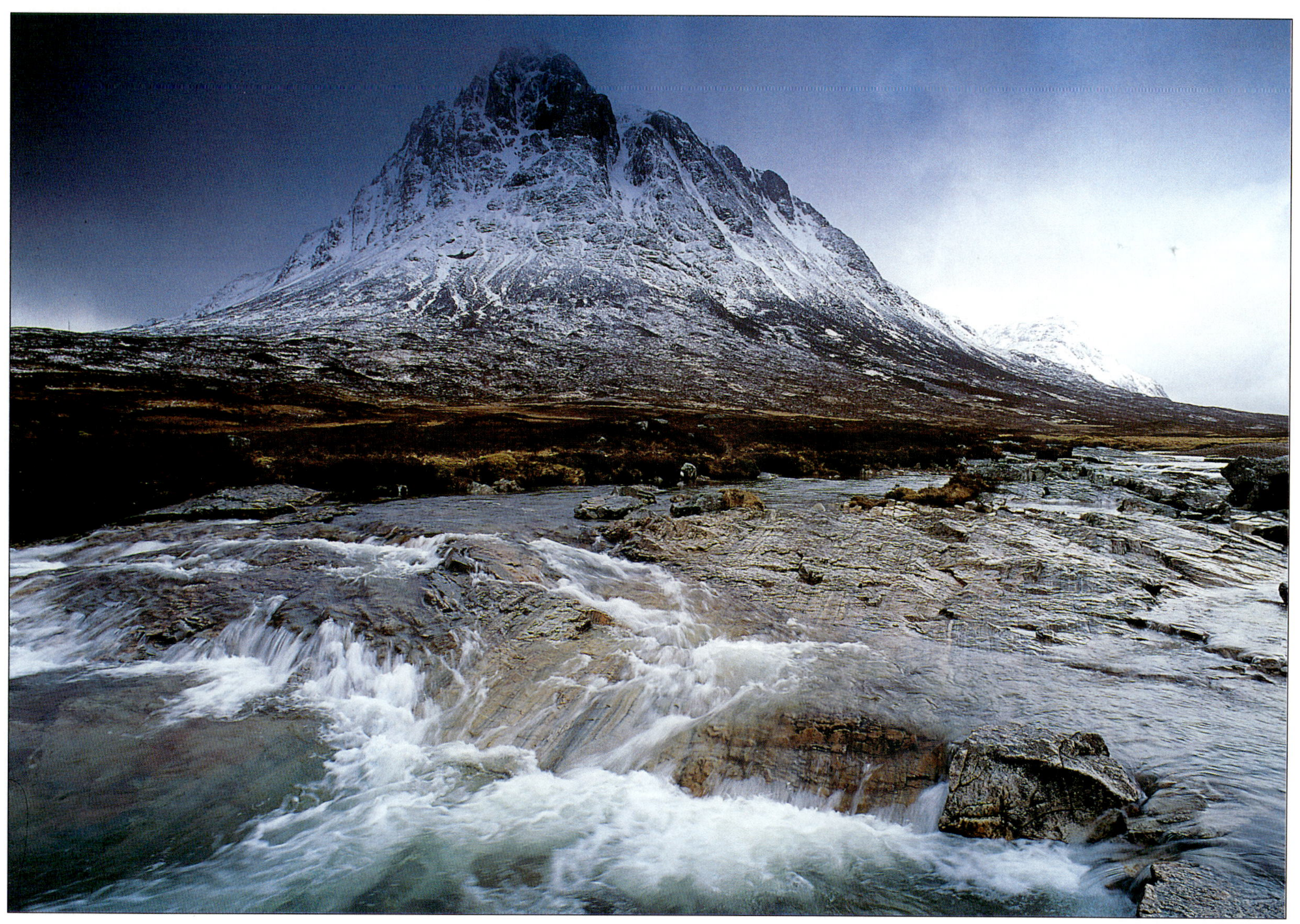

Laurie Campbell

United Kingdom

HIGHLY COMMENDED

Buachaille Etive Mór

"This mountain, by Glen Coe, is probably one of the most photographed in Scotland. I'd always intended to take a picture of it, but only got round to doing so on a day when I had some time to kill. As in many of my landscape pictures, I think that the adverse conditions at the time - rain after snow - actually added atmosphere to the scene."

Nikon F4 with 24mm lens; tripod; 1/8 sec at f16; Fujichrome Velvia

The World In Our Hands

This category is for pictures which illustrate in a realistic or symbolic way our dependence on the natural world or our capability of inflicting harm on it. No runner-up prize was awarded.

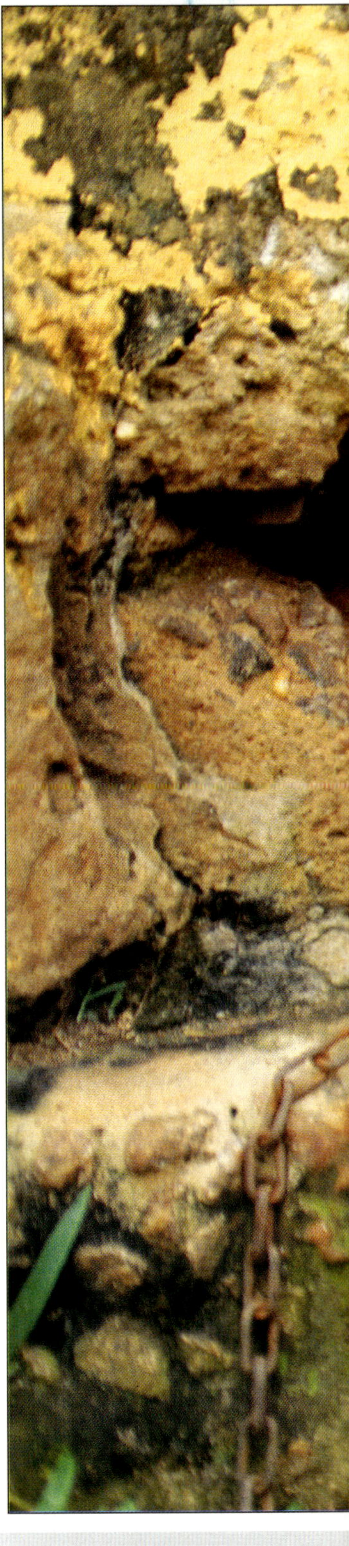

Karl Ammann
Switzerland
WINNER

The prisoner

"I took this picture as part of a project to document the plight of our closest relative, the chimpanzee. Two of the four chimps held at Yaoundé Zoo, Cameroon, the worst I have ever seen, were chained in a broken-down cage. Most of their food is provided by visitors, and so they have learnt to beg through a hole at the base of their cage."

Nikon F4 with 80-200mm lens; 1/125 sec at f8; Kodachrome 200

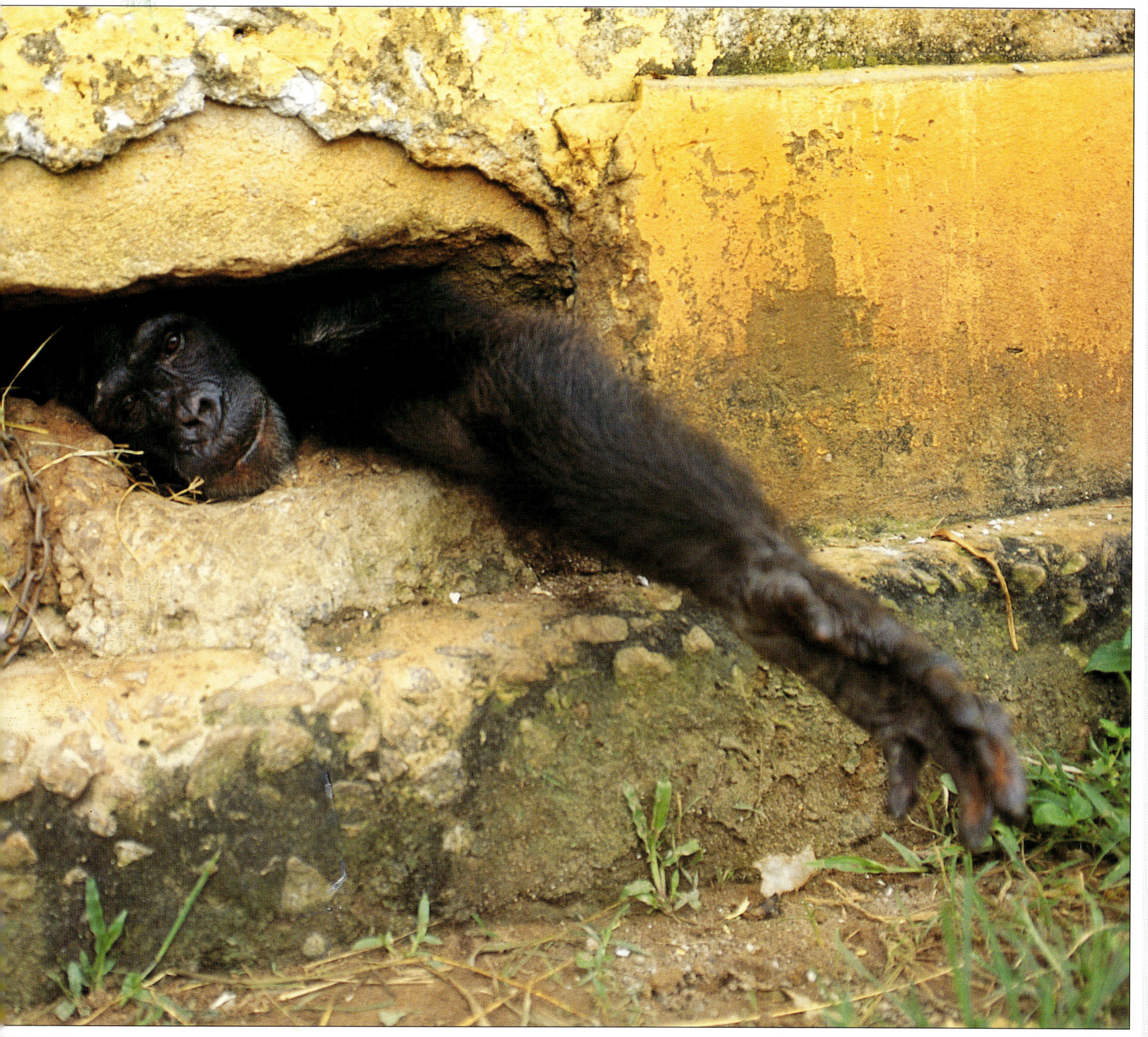

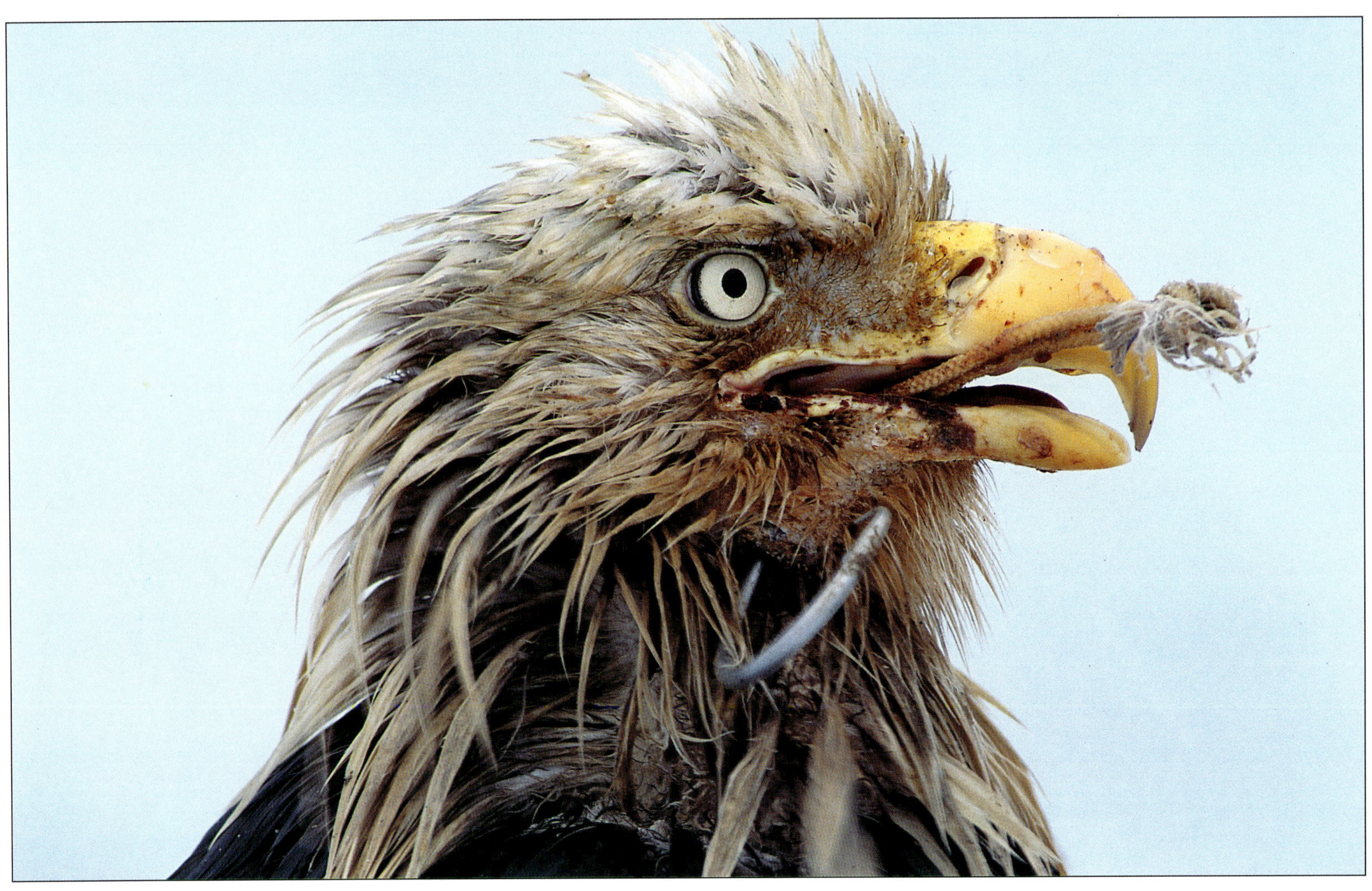

Thomas D Mangelsen
United States of America
HIGHLY COMMENDED

Bald eagle hooked

"This eagle had apparently eaten a halibut head discarded by a fisherman with the hook intact. The bird was unable to preen itself and so its feathers had become dirty and waterlogged. The dreary winter light emphasised the sad plight of the eagle. Later it was captured and the hook removed. Fortunately it had only suffered a puncture wound. A leg band identified the bird as one that had been caught in a muskrat trap four years earlier."

Nikon F4 with 300mm lens; tripod; 1/15sec at f2.8; Fujichrome Velvia

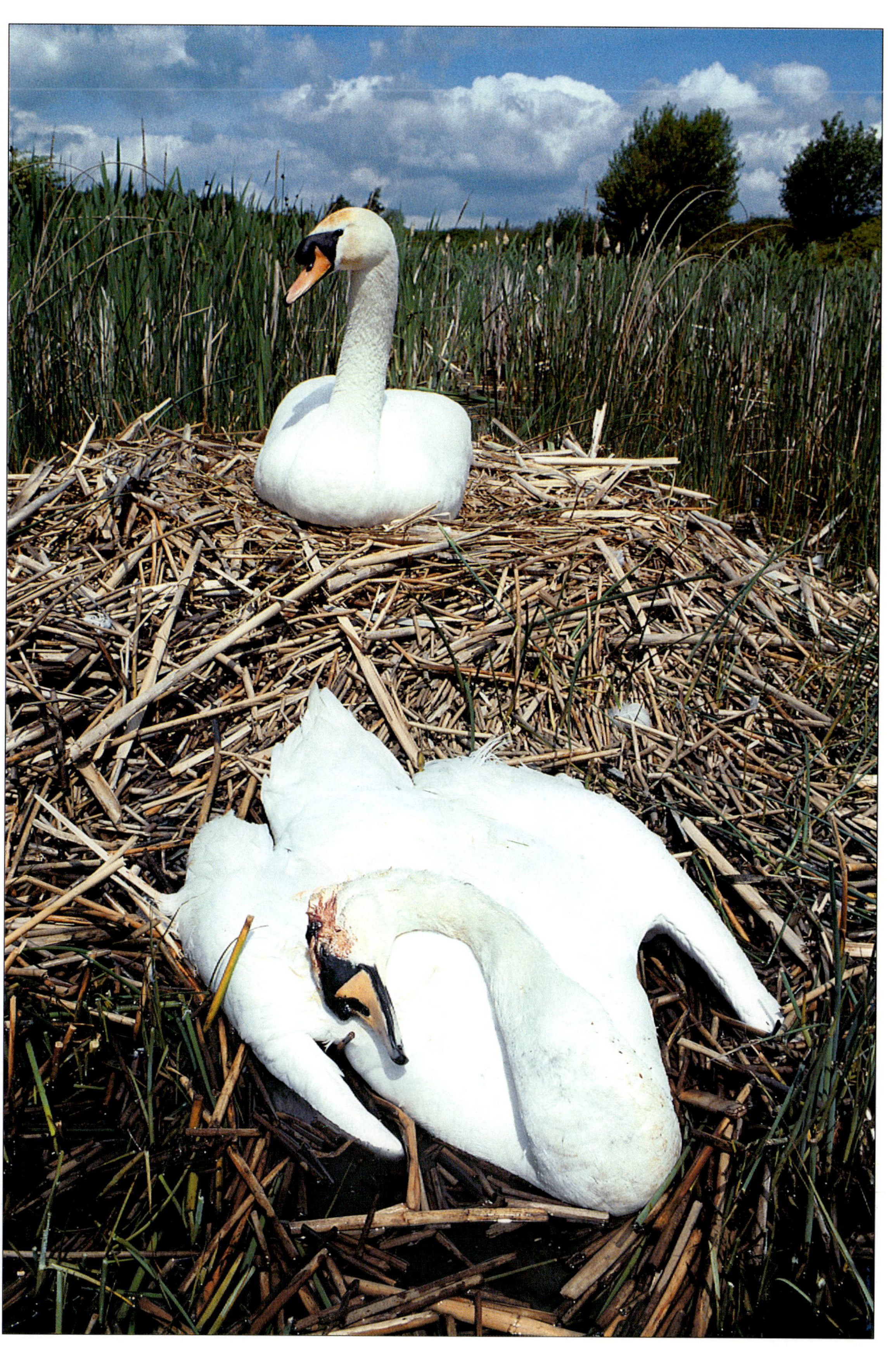

Mark Hamblin
United Kingdom
HIGHLY COMMENDED

Mute swans

"I came across this sad scene in Steetley Quarry in Derbyshire. The female swan had been shot through the head, presumably with an air rifle and probably by local youths, who use the quarry as a 'wild' playground. The male continued to incubate the eggs for some time before leaving the area altogether. I had been following the progress of these swans, because none had nested at the quarry since 1990 when a similar incident occurred."

Olympus OM2 with 28mm lens; 1/60sec at f11; Kodachrome 64

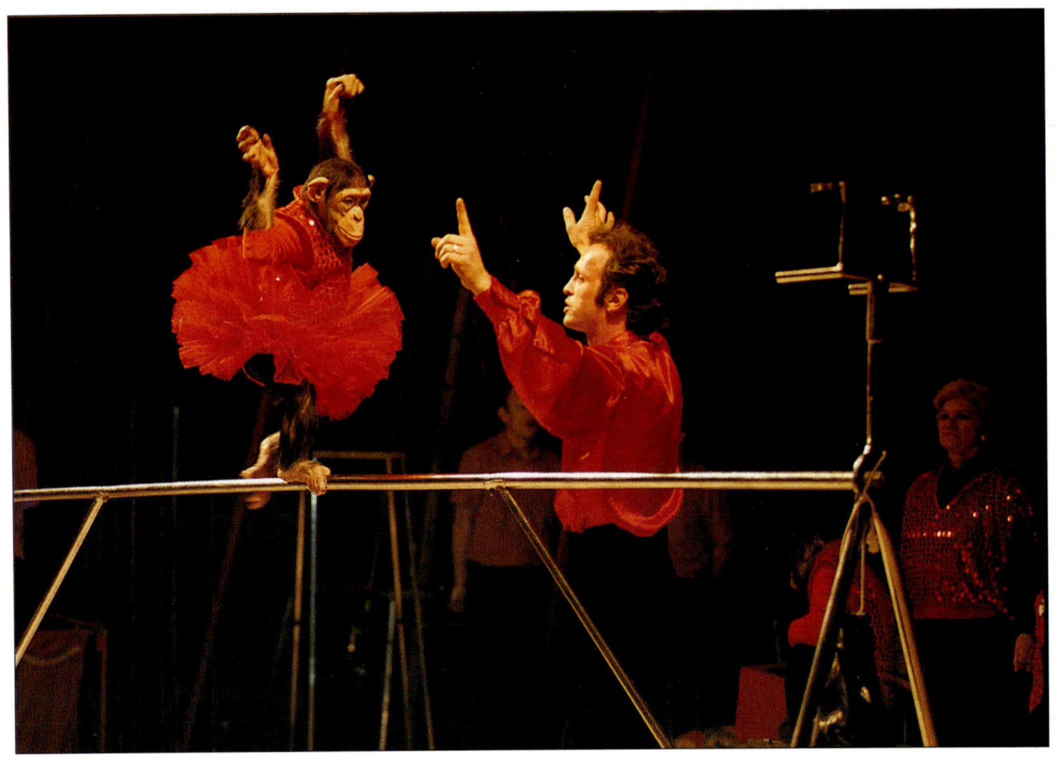

Luis Miguel Ruiz Gordon
Spain
HIGHLY COMMENDED

Chimpanzee tightrope-walking

"I wanted to show the absurdity of the ordeal to which primates are subjected in travelling circuses such as this one in Pinto, Madrid."

Nikon 4S with 80-200mm lens; 1/250 sec at f2.8; Kodak Panther 100

Karl Ammann
Switzerland
HIGHLY COMMENDED

Orphan chimpanzees

"Bush meat is a traditional source of protein in most countries in West and Central Africa. In many regions, gorilla and chimpanzee meat is considered a special delicacy. When a chimp or a gorilla mother is shot, the hunters often take the babies back to their villages where most end up as playthings for the children until they die of malnutrition and disease. Some are taken to the cities to be sold. A few lucky ones - like the baby chimps in this picture - are rescued and cared for in a couple of sanctuaries that have been set up recently in the Congo."

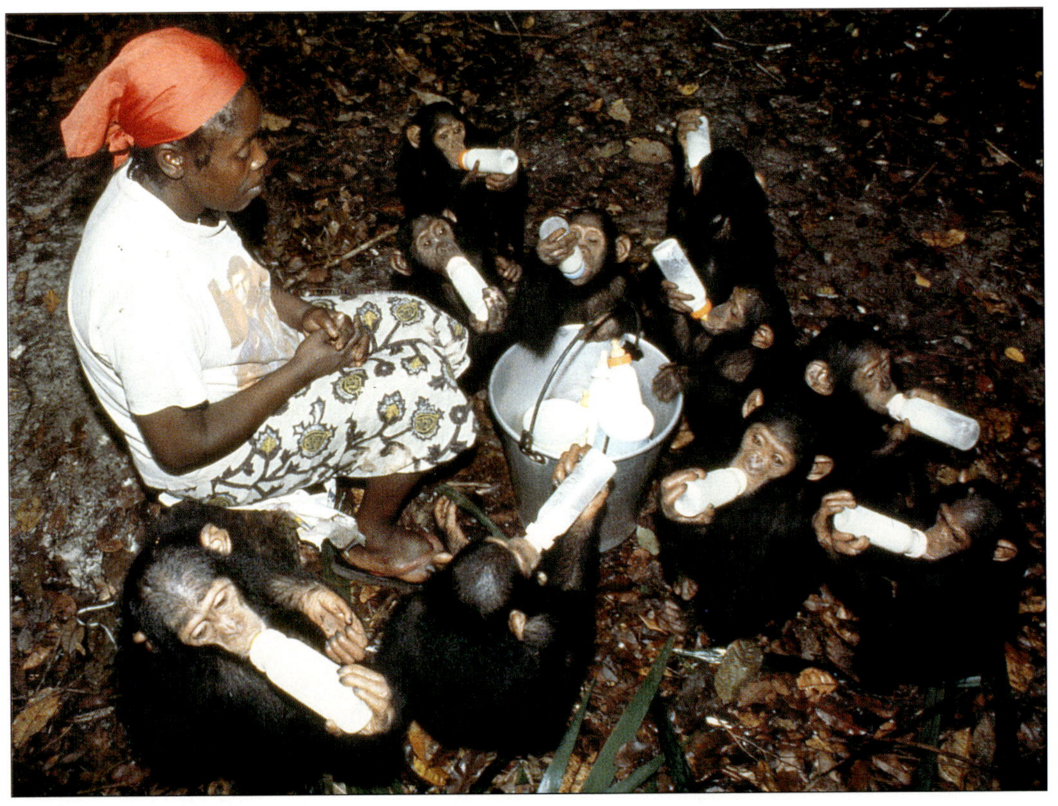

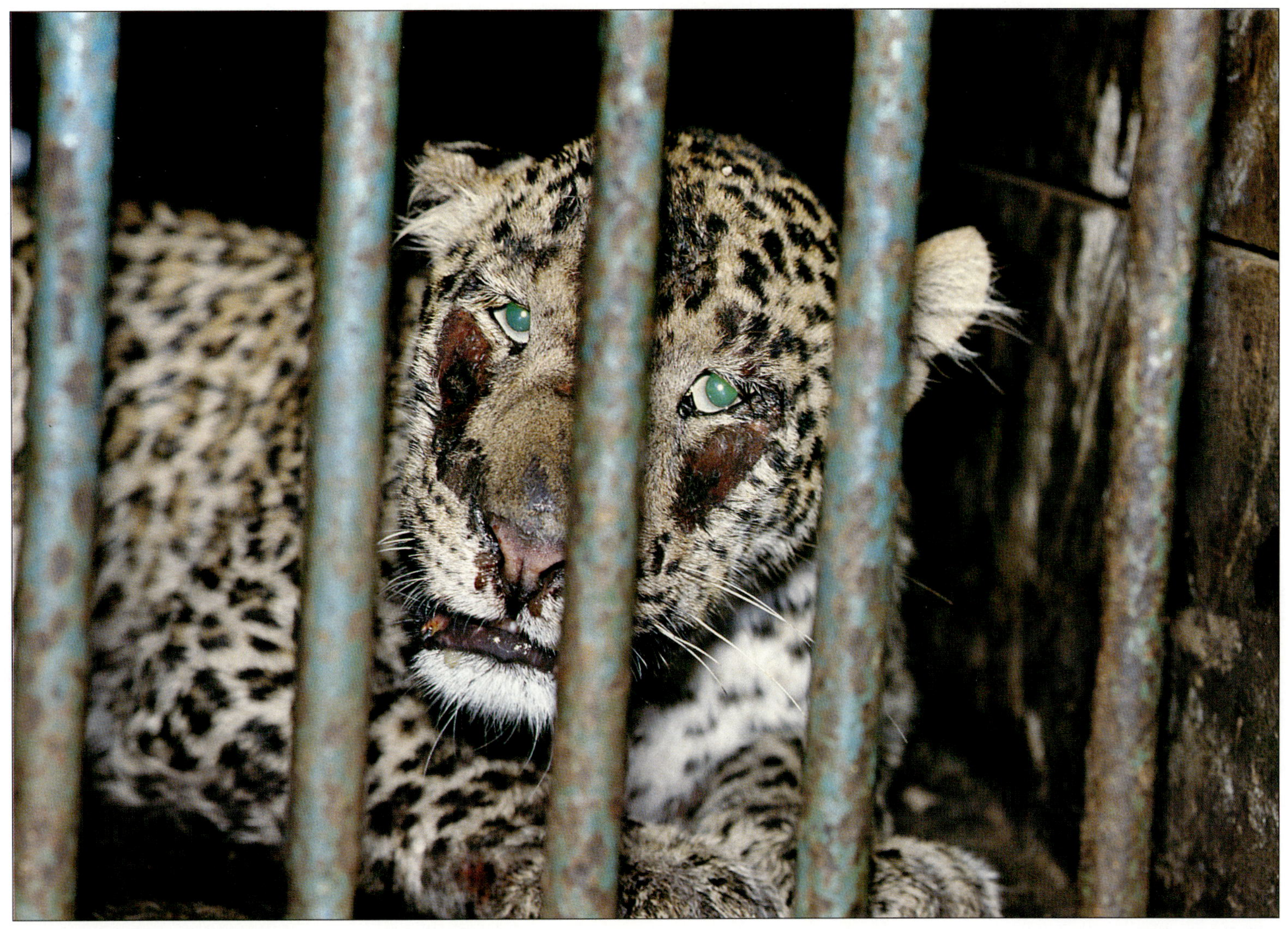

Sunjoy Monga
India
HIGHLY COMMENDED

Injured leopard

"This leopard was caught in the suburbs of Bombay and put in this cage, where it fought against the bars so much it injured itself badly."

Nikon FE with 105mm lens; flash; 1/125 sec at f5.6

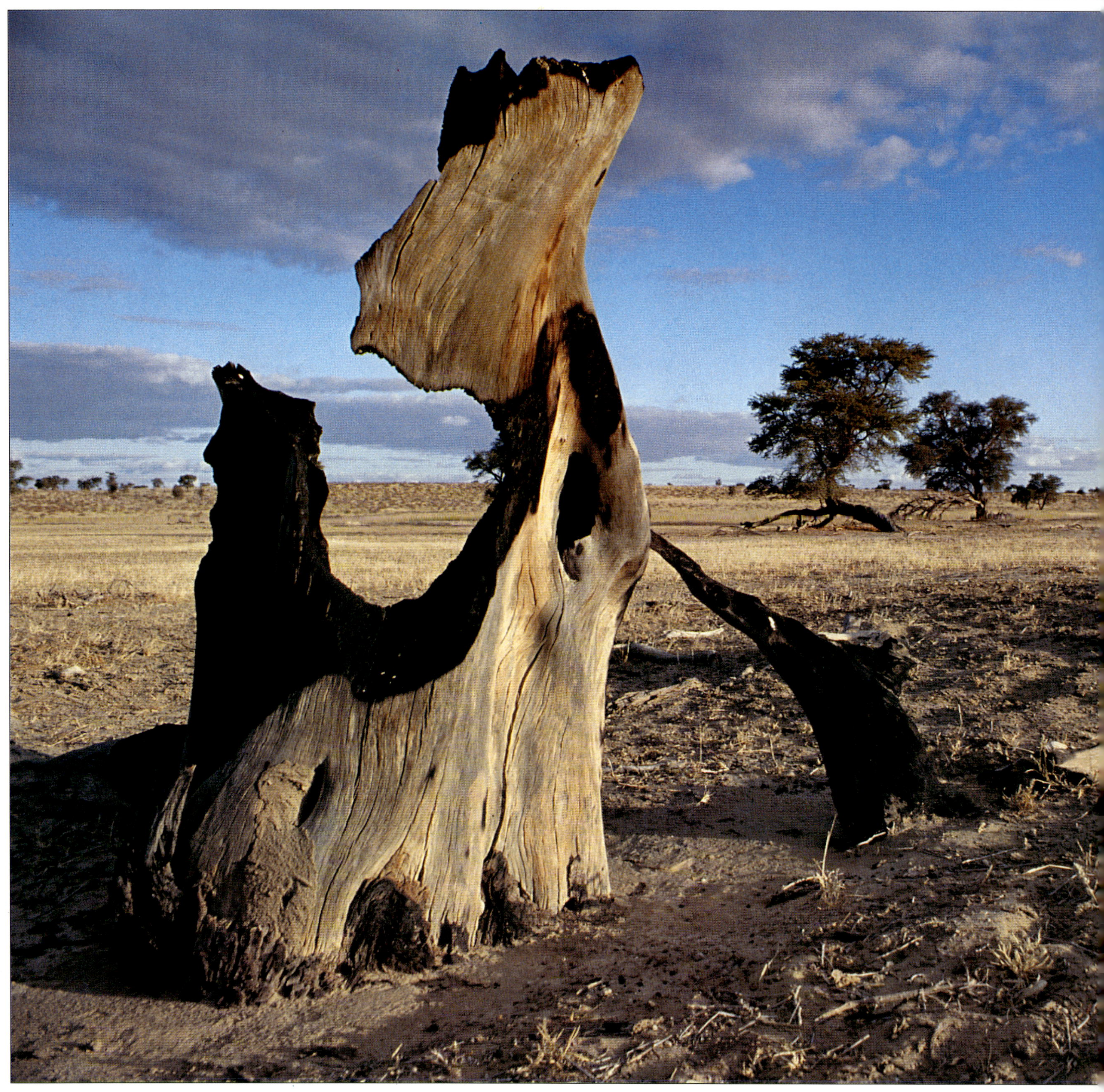

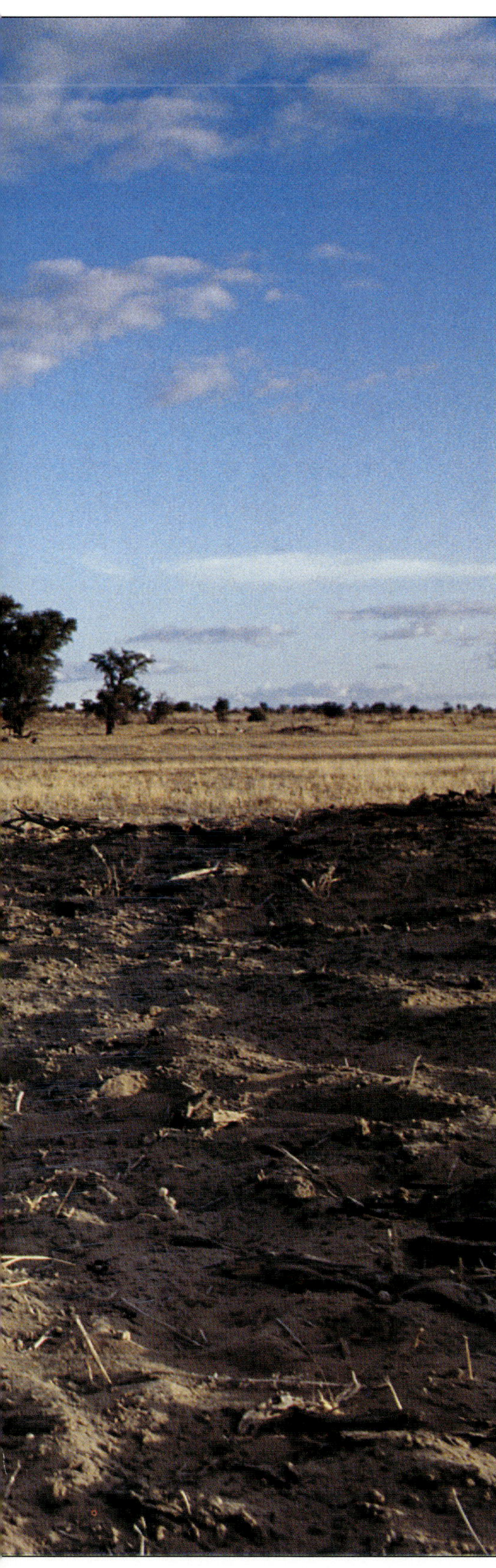

The Eric Hosking Award

This award is given for the best portfolio of six pictures submitted by a photographer aged 26 years or under. The award was introduced in 1991 in memory of Eric Hosking - probably Britain's most famous wildlife photographer. Eric was a supporter of this competition from its earliest days. He presented the prizes for the Dusk to Dawn category, and before 1983 the judging sessions were often held in his house in north London.

The 1994 winner, Peter Chadwick, from South Africa, started taking photographs when he was 12. After leaving school, he embarked on a career in conservation. He finds photography a useful tool for his work and believes it has made him much more observant. Recently, Peter acquired better photographic equipment and has been working with suricates, or meerkats, in the Kalahari Gemsbok Park, where all the pictures in his winning portfolio were taken. He finds the Kalahari an ideal place for photography because of the amazingly clear light, open spaces and diversity of wildlife.

Peter has won a holiday for two to Tasmania, a cheque for £1,000 and a specially commissioned carving of an owl – the bird perhaps most associated with Eric Hosking.

Peter Chadwick
South Africa
WINNER

Burnt tree stump

"The Kalahari landscape is often thought to be uninteresting and barren, but in reality it is full of fascinating shapes, such as this burnt-out tree trunk ."

Canon FTB with 28mm lens; 1/60 sec at f22; Fujichrome 100 rated at 125

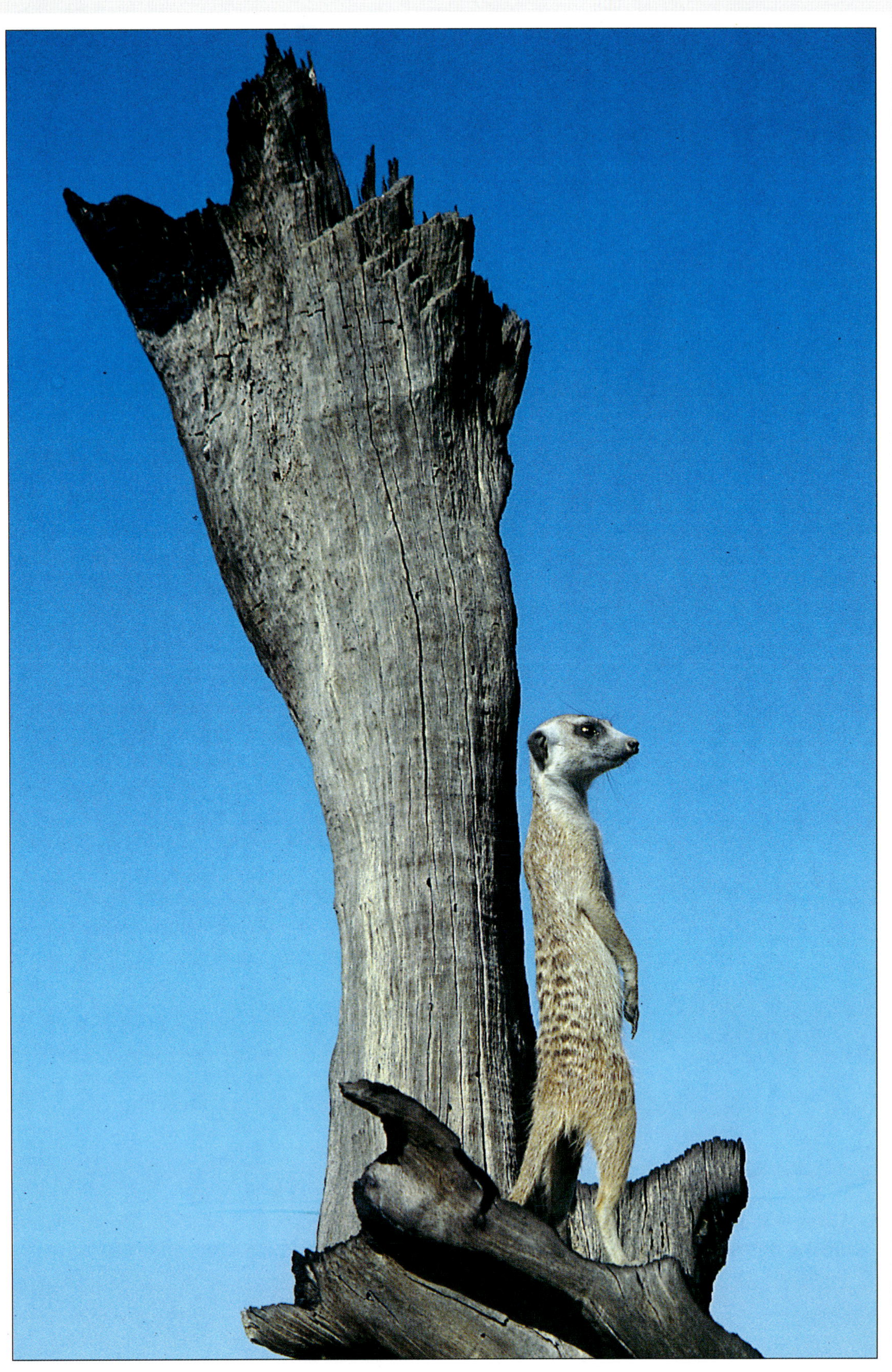

Suricate sentinel

"While the rest of the group were foraging nearby, this suricate was on guard duty, using the highest spot he could find to get a better view of approaching predators."

Canon FTB with 135mm lens; 1/125 sec at f11; Fujichrome 100 rated at 125

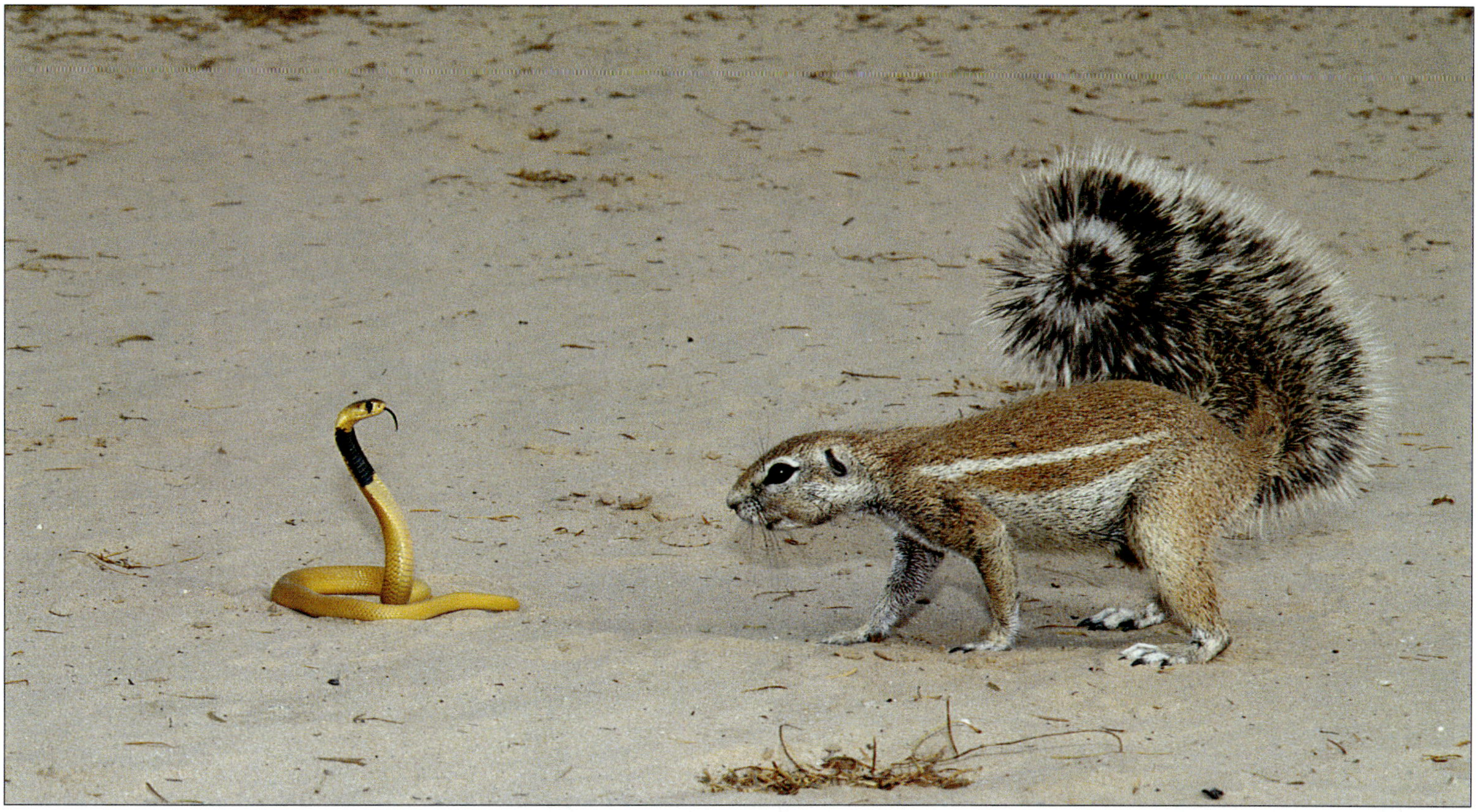

Ground squirrel and Cape cobra

"When the ground squirrel saw a juvenile Cape cobra emerging from one of its burrows, it became very agitated and tried to drive it off. As it approached, the cobra would strike at its tail. The ground squirrel continued to attack, until the snake managed to retreat down another burrow, where it did not follow. The day was very overcast and I had to use flash."

Nikon 801S with 70-210mm lens; flash; 1/125 sec at f5.6; Fujichrome 100 rated at 125

Brown hyaena

"I found this hyaena patrolling its territory one evening. The sun behind it was at a low angle, throwing the animal into silhouette, in contrast to the golden grass."

Nikon 801S with 400mm lens; 1/60 sec at f5.6; Fujichrome 100 rated at 125

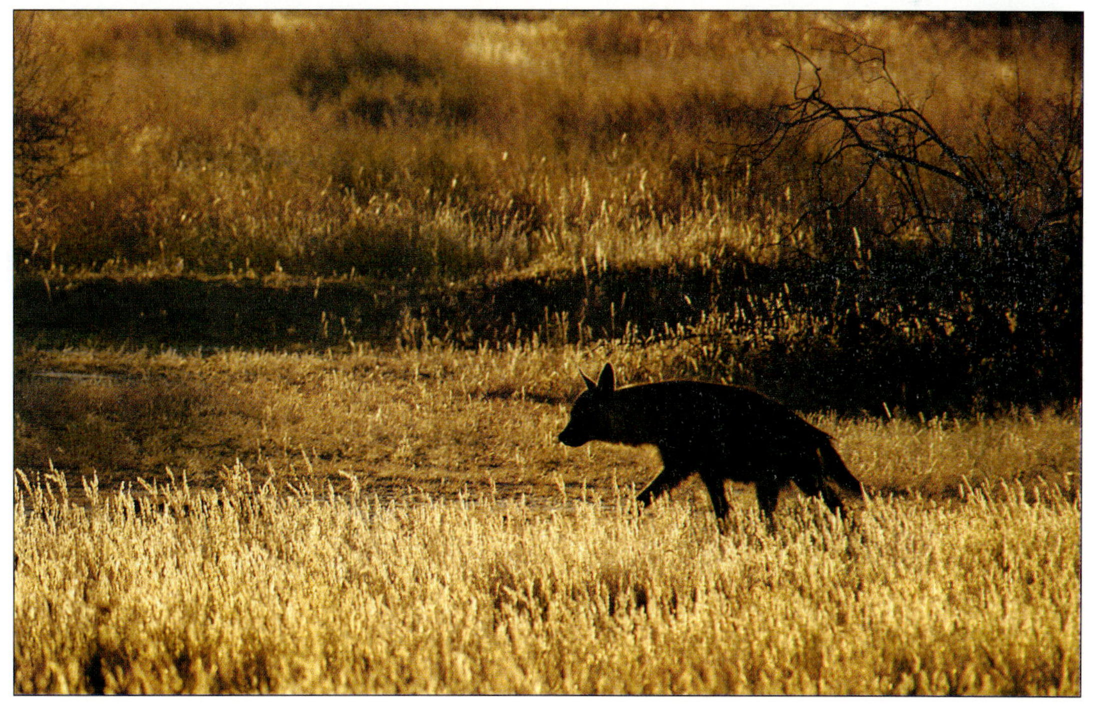

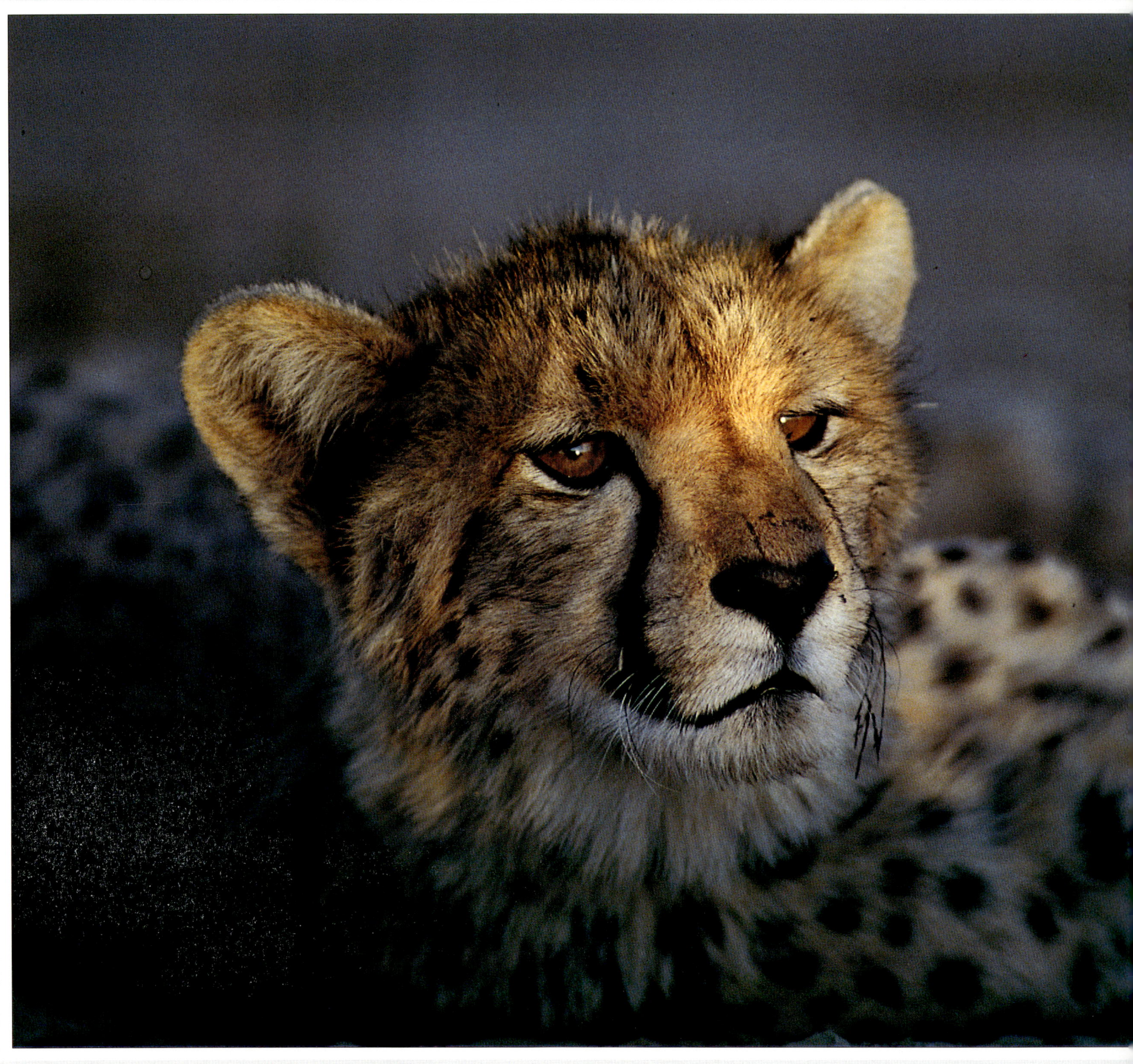

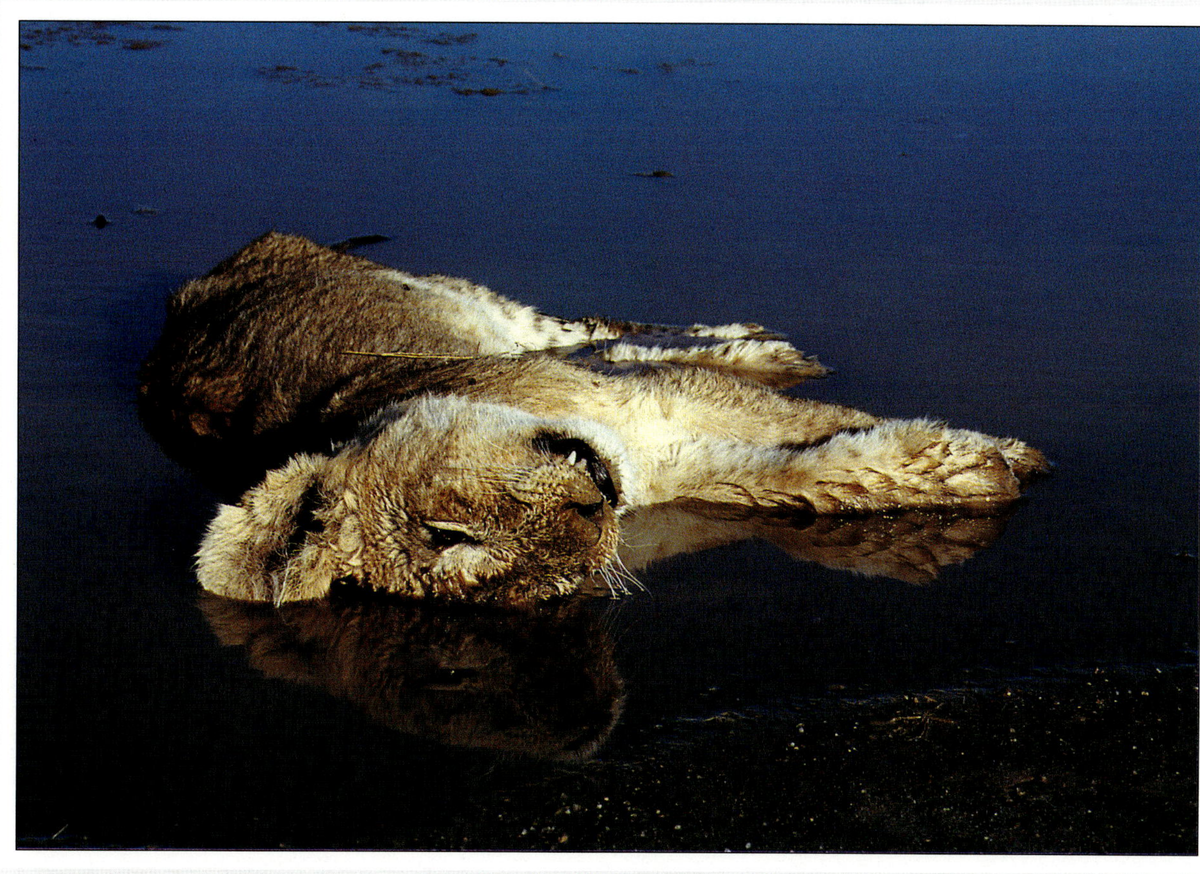

Reflection of death

"This three-month old cub had died of starvation. The glint of its eye reflected in the water gave it an almost life-like appearance."

Nikon 801S with 35-105mm lens; 1/60 sec at f16; Fujichrome 100 rated at 125

Cheetah

"I took this picture because of the way the late-evening light enhanced the cheetah's face."

Nikon 801S with 600mm lens; window mount; 1/60 sec at f4; Fujichrome 100 rated at 125

Young Wildlife Photographer of the Year

This section of the competition is open to photographers aged 17 years and under, and is judged in three separate age categories. Photographers can enter up to three images of any wildlife subject. The winner and runner-up receive cash prizes.

The overall winner of the competition, 15-year-old Louise Dean, received the British Gas award - a bronze sculpture of a scarlet ibis - a cash prize and the opportunity to spend a day on location with wildlife photographer Heather Angel.

Michael Hill, winner of the BBC *Newsround* award for the best picture telling an environmental story, won a cheque and a camera. Ross Hoddinott, winner of the WATCH award for the best plant picture won a cheque and a trophy. WATCH is a club for young wildlife enthusiasts and environmentalists with more than 1,000 action groups.

Louise Dean
United Kingdom
YOUNG WILDLIFE PHOTOGRAPHER OF THE YEAR 1994

Giraffe

"We spent many hours in the Tarangire National Park, Tanzania, searching for wildlife to photograph. When we came across this giraffe, the sun was quite high, but fortunately not too harsh. Though I have taken quite a number of pictures of giraffes in the past, I particularly wanted to get this portrait shot of one as it grazed."

Olympus OM2 with 500mm lens; monopod; 1/250 sec at f8; Kodachrome 200

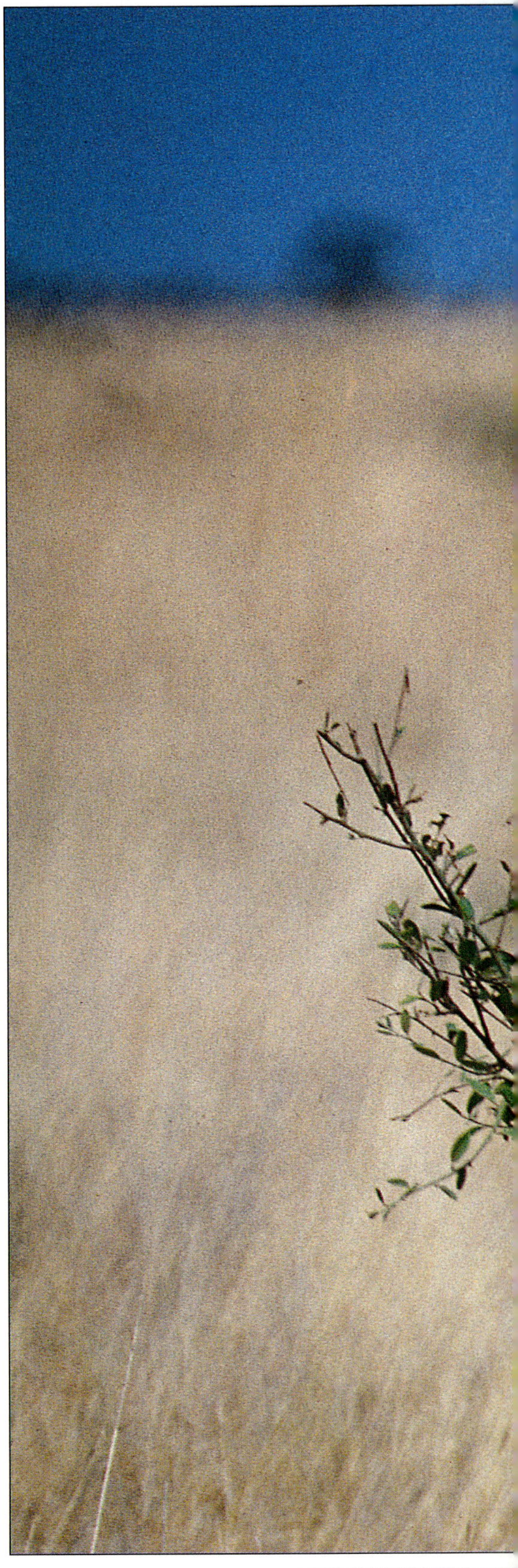

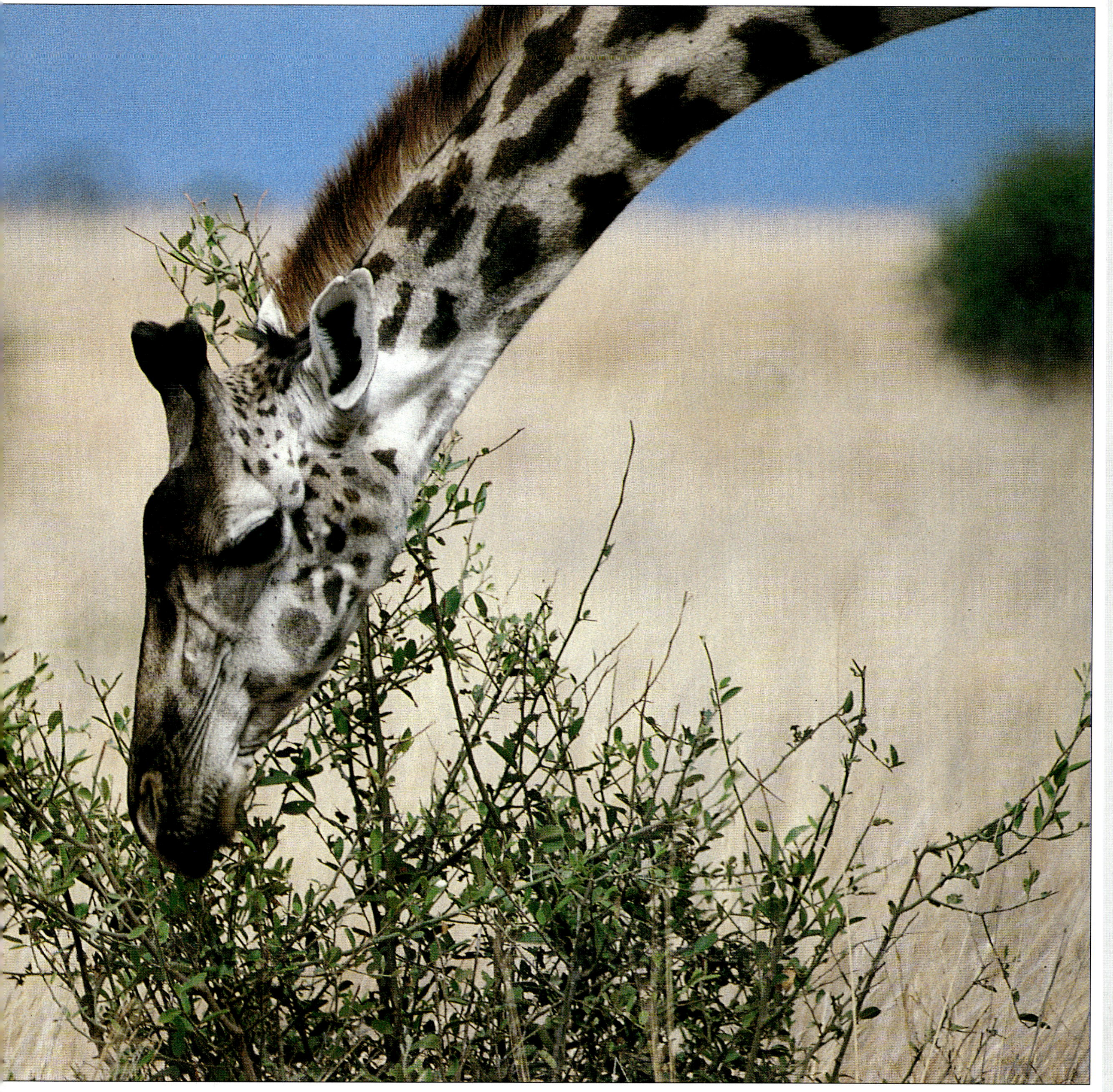

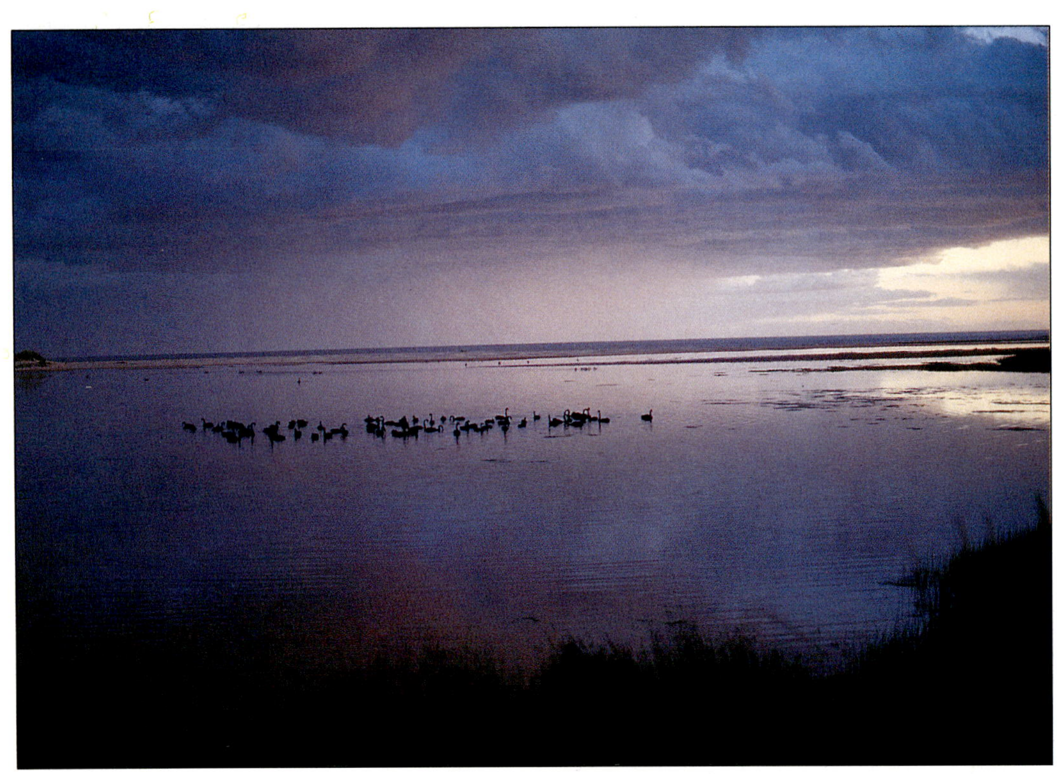

Gareth Westerskov
New Zealand
WINNER: 10 YEARS & UNDER

Black swans on lagoon

"I started taking photographs during the Christmas holidays and am allowed one film per month. I photographed these black swans swimming and feeding at sunset in Kaikorai Lagoon specially to enter for the competition."

Canon F1 with 50mm lens; tripod; 1/8 sec at f1.4; Fujichrome 100

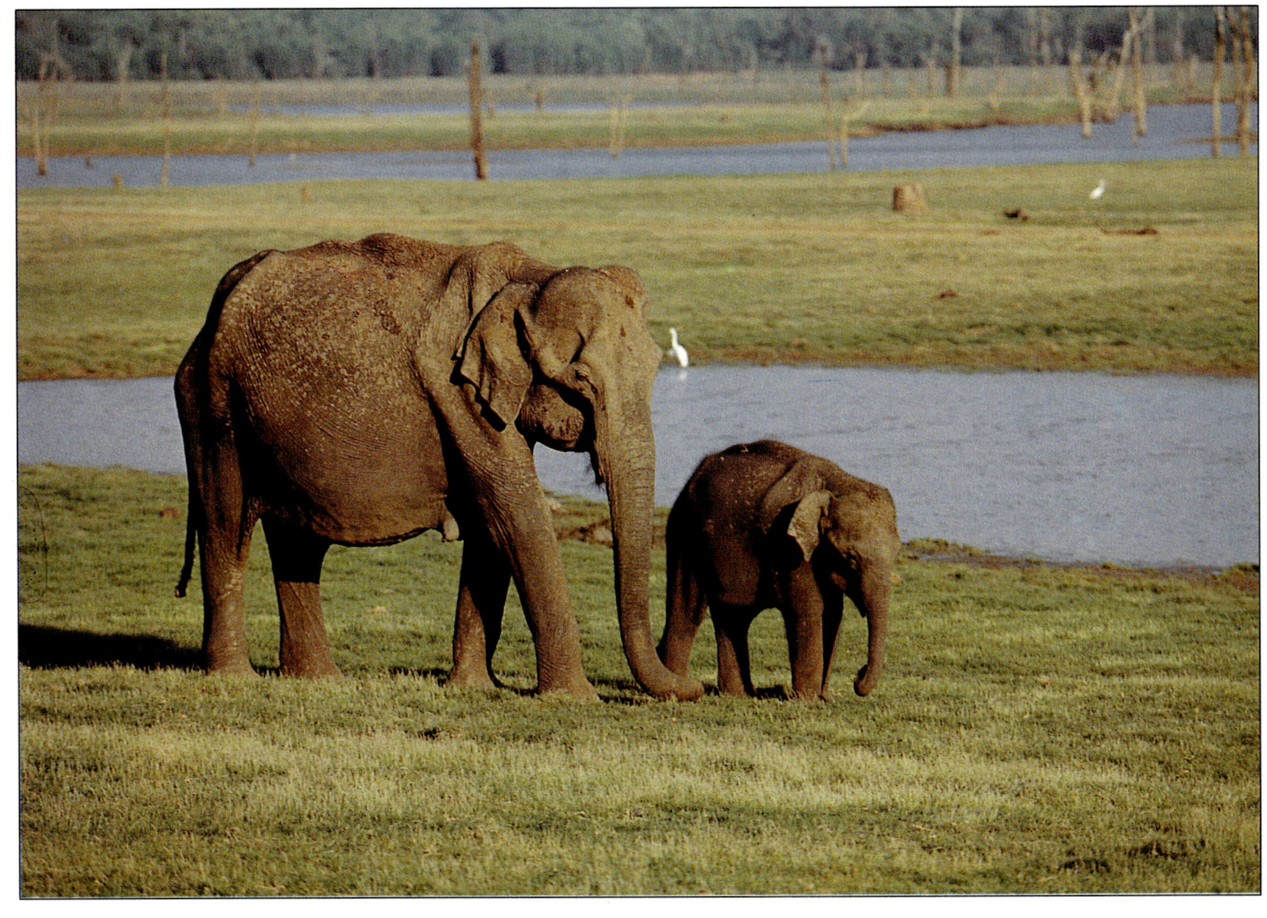

Jiwan Kaur
India
RUNNER-UP:
10 YEARS & UNDER

Indian elephant with calf

"I was on holiday with my father in the Nagarhole National Park when we came across this elephant with her calf. Now I have my own camera - a birthday gift from my father - I would like to spend all my holidays in the national parks of India, surrounded by nature."

Canon EOS5 with 80-200mm lens; Kodachrome 100

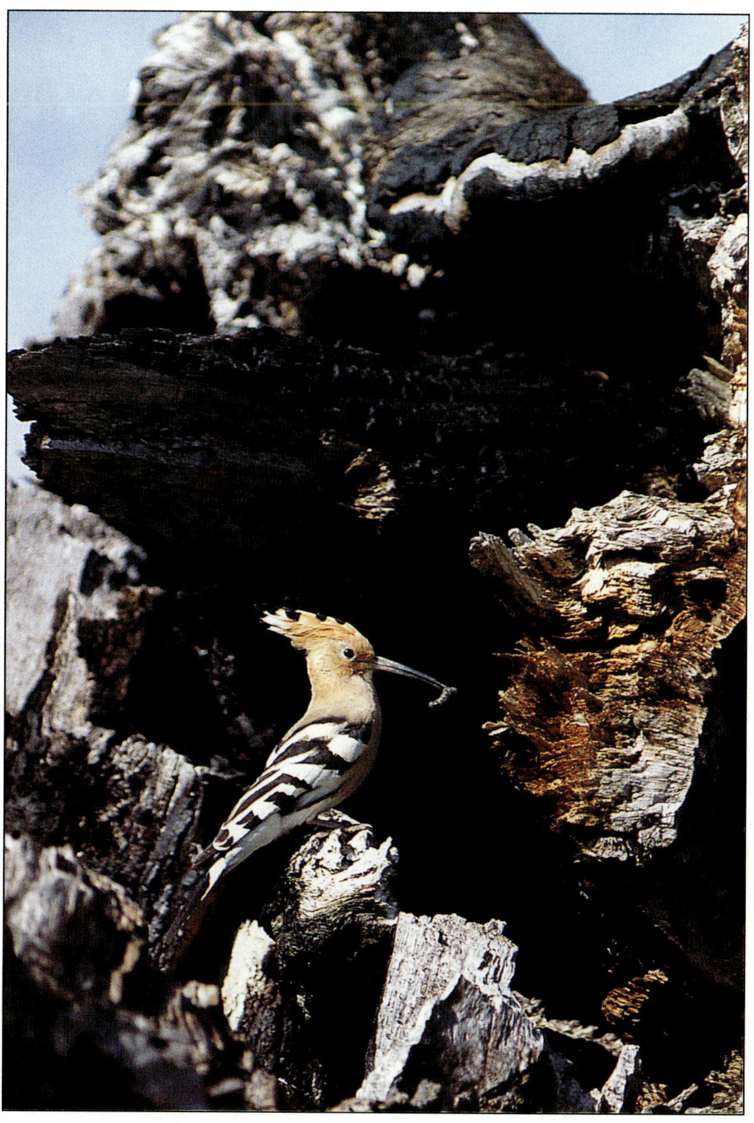

Malcolm Kemp
United Kingdom
WINNER: 11-14 YEARS

Hoopoe

"I saw a hoopoe flying from its nest in a fallen cork oak tree that had been struck by lightning, and decided to try to photograph it. I set up a hide 40 metres away. The next day I took half a roll of film of the bird coming and going from the nest."

Nikormat with 300mm lens; tripod; 1/250 sec at f5.6; Fujichrome 50

Rachel Hingley
United Kingdom
RUNNER-UP: 11-14 YEARS

Angle shades moth

"I found this well-camouflaged moth on a garage door just a few inches from the ground. I like to photograph all aspects of wildlife, except spiders and snakes!"

Contax 139 Quartz with 105mm macro lens; tripod; Fujichrome 100

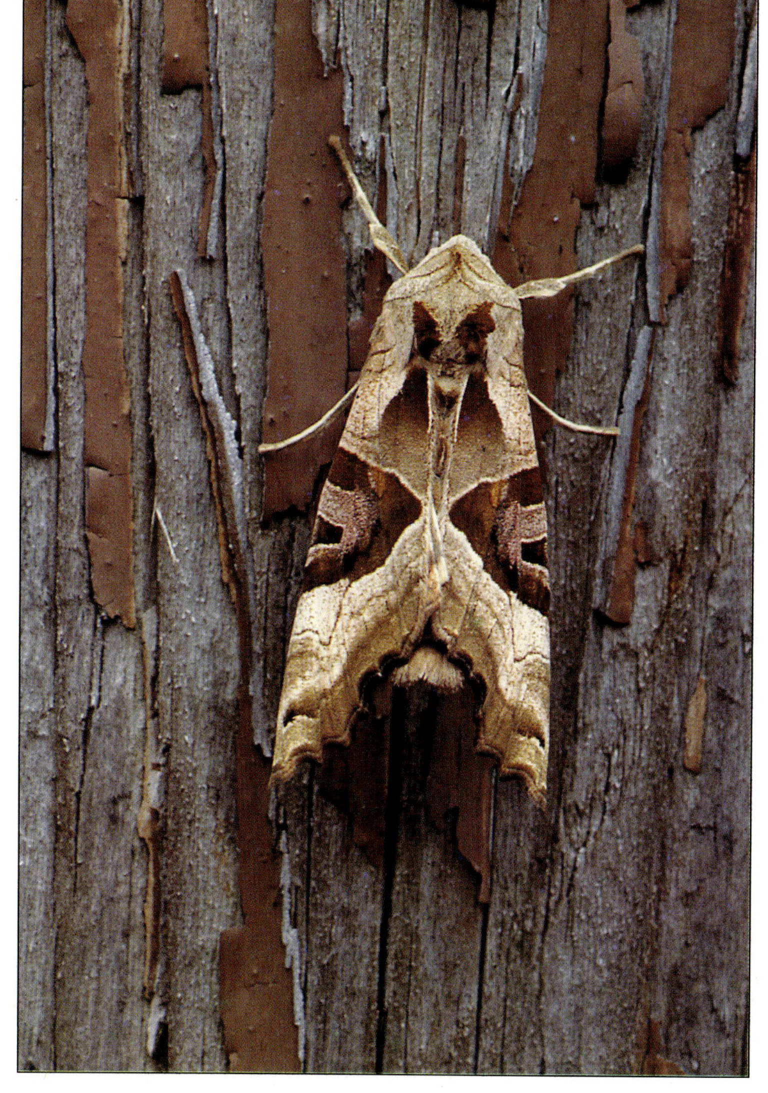

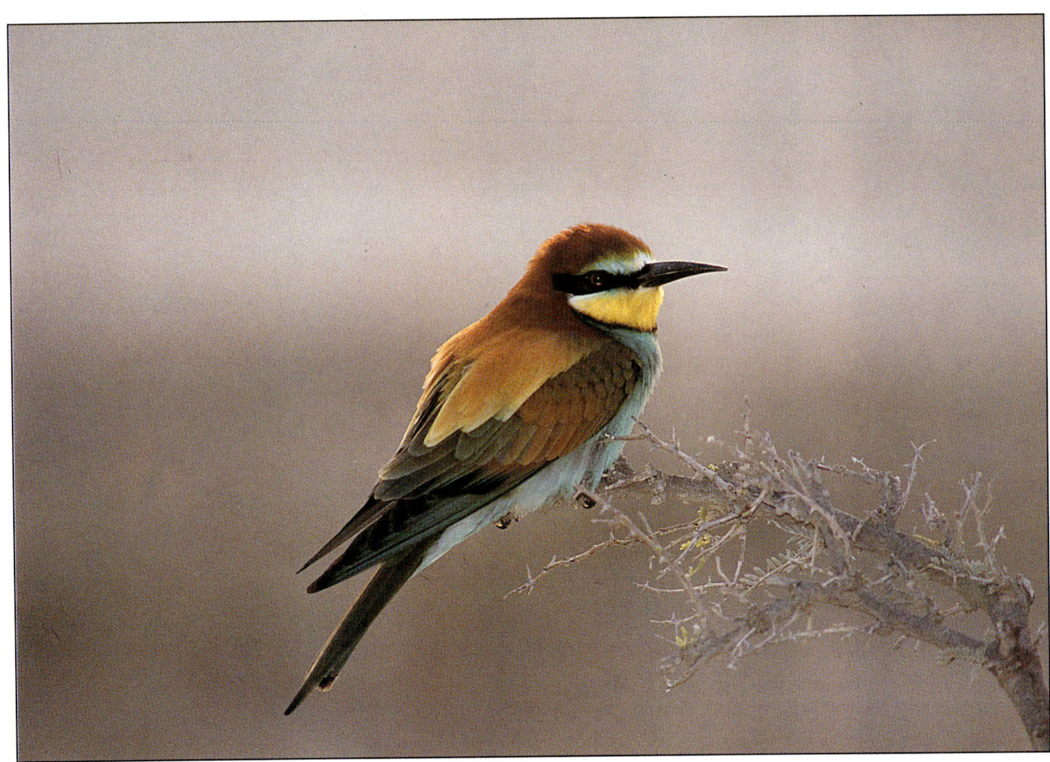

Michael Hill
United Kingdom
WINNER: 15-17 YEARS

Bee-eater

"Bee-eaters pass through Bahrain on their spring and autumn migrations. Though Bahrain is mostly desert, there are spots where trees have been planted, providing good resting points for bee-eaters to stop and feed on insects. We stalked the birds very slowly in the car until we were close enough to take photographs. The shot was taken in fading evening light."

Nikon F90 with 600mm lens; bean bag; flash; 1/125 or 1/250 sec at f5.6; Fujichrome Velvia

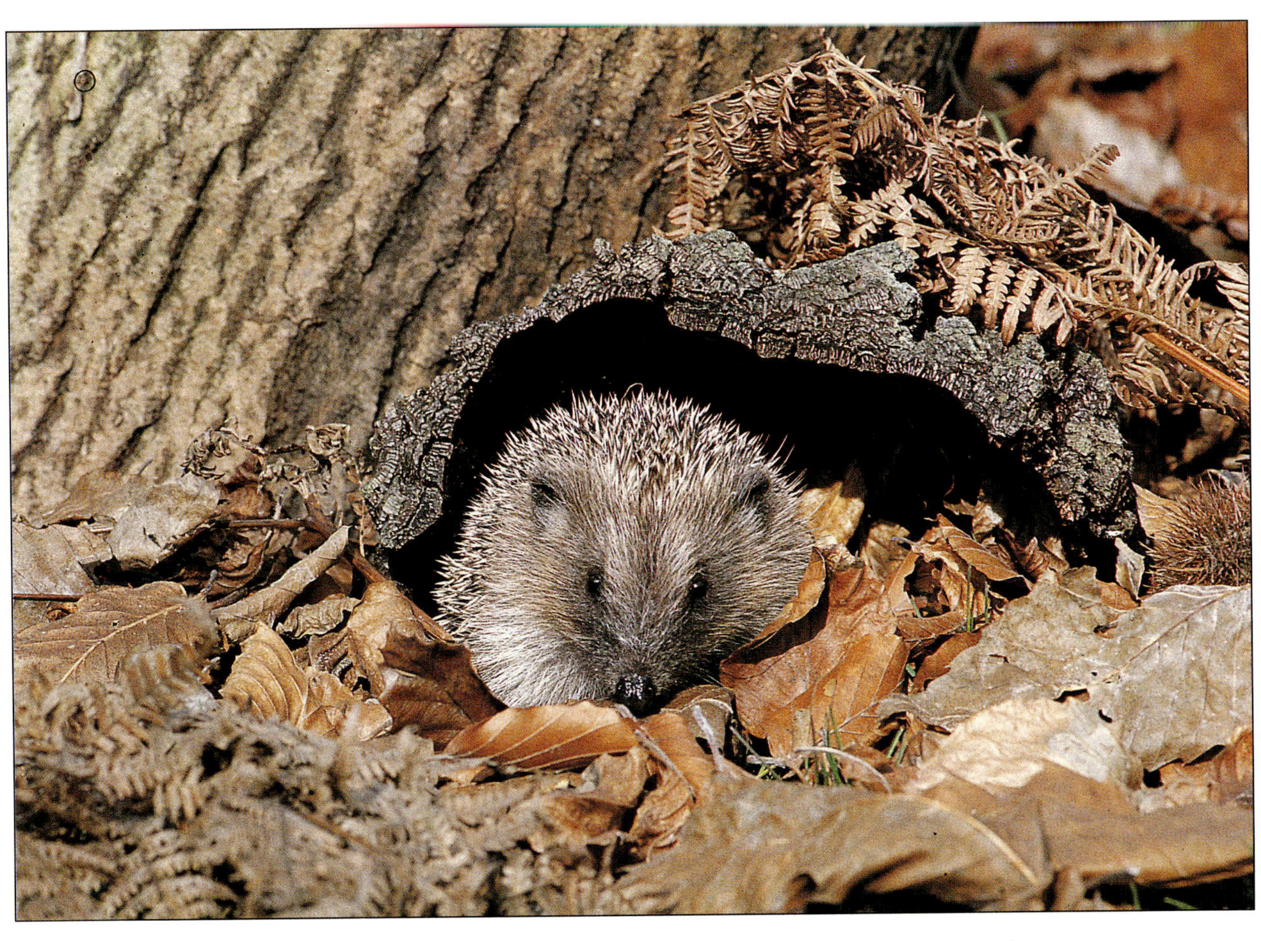

Tristan Millen
United Kingdom
RUNNER-UP: 15-17 YEARS

Hedgehog

"I am interested in wildlife and wanted a picture of a hedgehog for my collection of slides. I saw this hedgehog one day in my garden and rushed into the house to get some dog food to tempt it to stay there while I photographed it."

Nikon F601 with 100-300mm lens; tripod; 1/250 sec at f11; Kodachrome 200

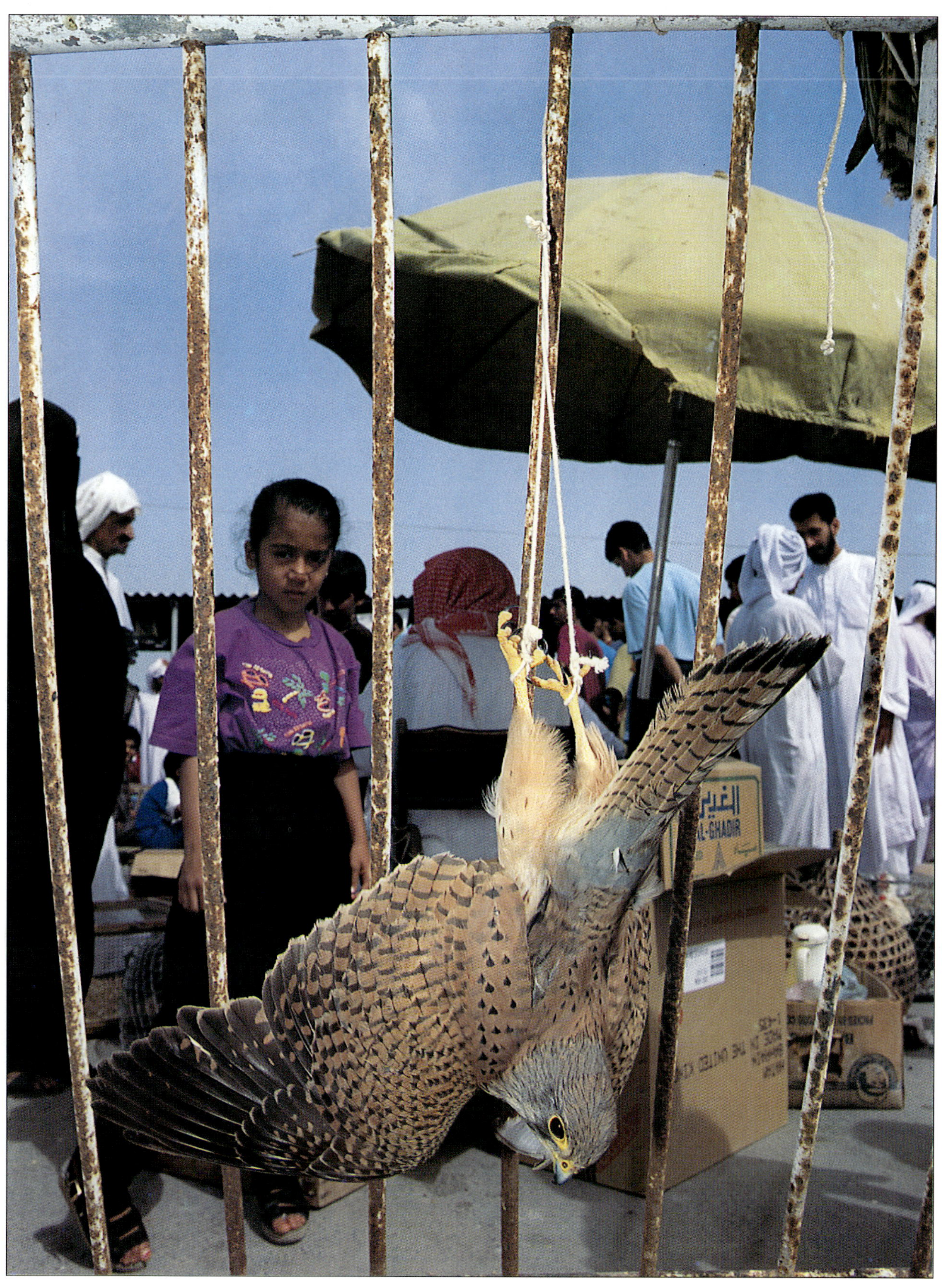

Michael Hill
United Kingdom
WINNER:
NEWSROUND AWARD

Kestrel for sale

"This picture was taken in the Bahrain bird market where many wild birds are sold. The trappers use a tethered bird of the same species to attract wild birds and then use a net to catch them. Sometimes as many as 10 birds are kept together in a small cage so they cannot move. Kestrels cannot be used for falconry, and so the birds are just kept for show and are often badly treated. I was tempted to buy one and let it go, but this would only encourage more trapping. I hope, by taking photos like this, to help to stop this practice. I have recently heard that there may be a law passed against the trapping of kestrels."

Nikon F90 with 24-50mm lens; 1/60 sec at f16; flash; Fujichrome Velvia

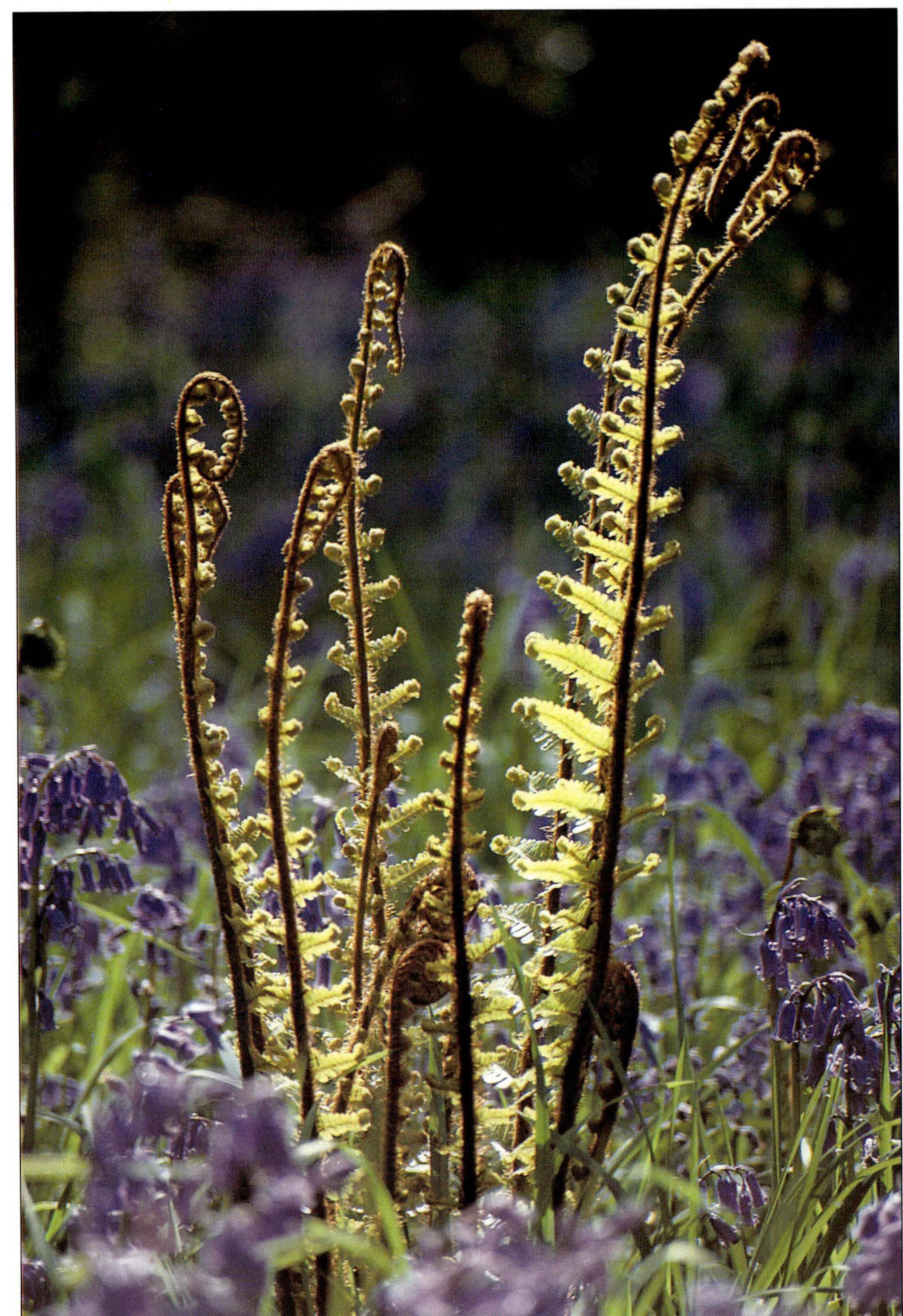

Ross Hoddinott
United Kingdom
WINNER: WATCH AWARD

Ferns and bluebells

"I took this picture in Marsland Mouth Wood in North Cornwall early in May. The spring light complemented the freshness of both the fern and the bluebells. I deliberately chose a small depth of field to blur the bluebells and so emphasise the fern."

Minolta Dynax 7000i with 50mm macro lens; f5.6; Fujichrome 100

THE NATURAL HISTORY MUSEUM

South Kensington London

The Natural History Museum, one of the most striking Victorian buildings in the country, was designed by the architect Alfred Waterhouse to house the ever growing natural history collections from the British Museum, bequeathed to the nation by Sir Hans Sloane, and opened to the public in 1881.

Central to the Museum's mission is furthering the understanding of the natural world. It is at the forefront of modern exhibition development making extremely effective use of the latest techniques such as interactive computers and robotics, which can be seen to great effect in many of its exhibitions. An annual highlight to its exhibition programme is the Wildlife Photographer of the Year Exhibition.

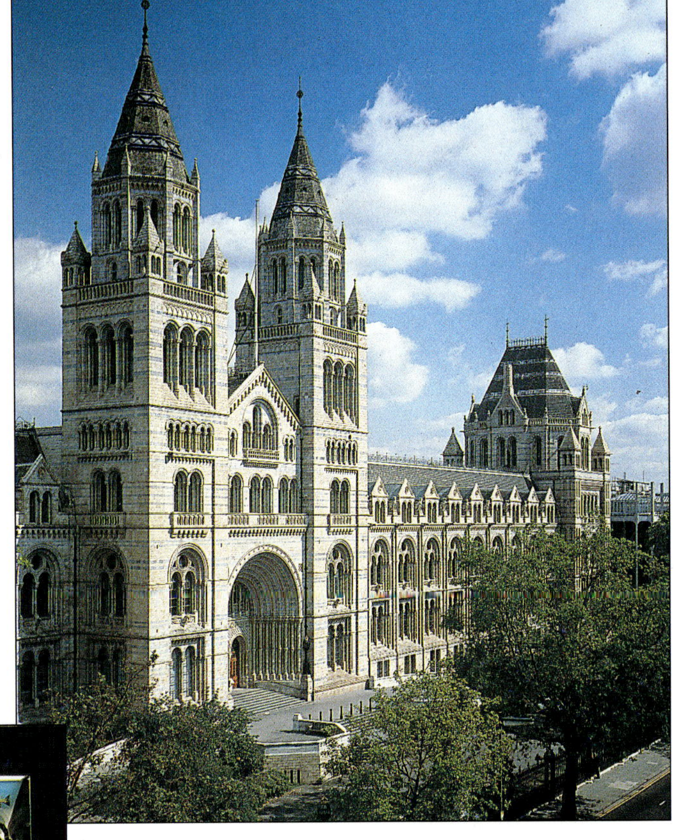

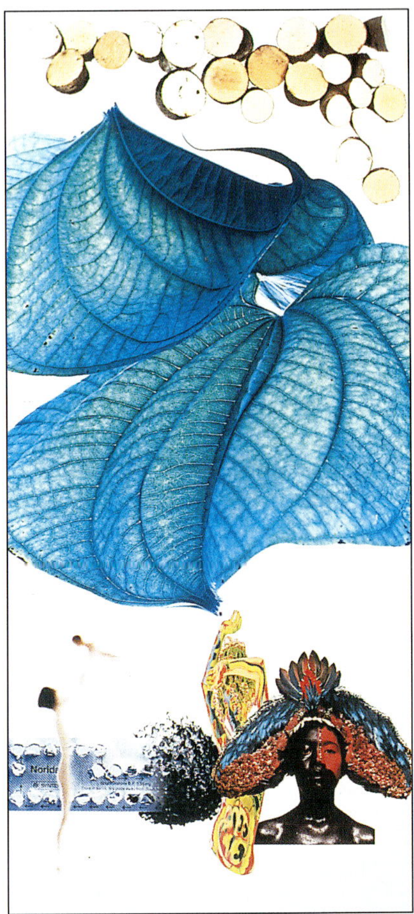

The Museum had in excess of 1.7 million visitors last year, illustrating its continued commitment to learning and enjoyment, as well as its contribution towards the public understanding of science. Many of the exhibitions are supported by literature, lectures, videos and study tours and the Museum was one of the largest contributors to the National Science Week programme in 1994.

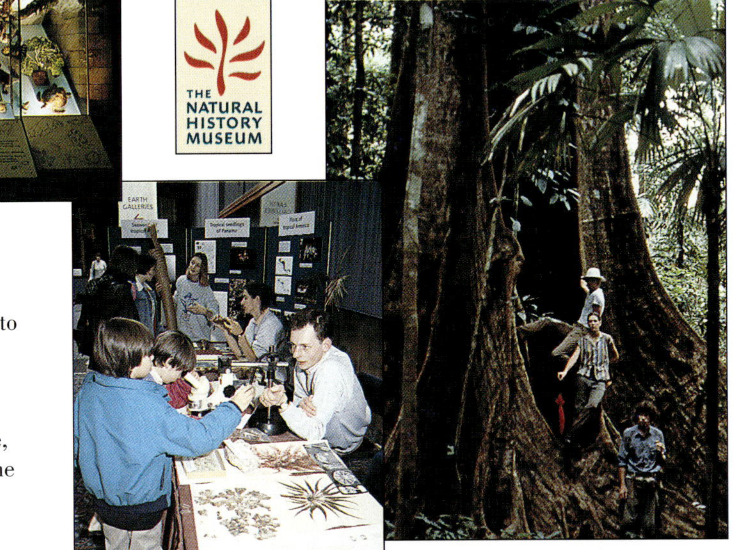

The Natural History Museum houses over 67 million specimens in its collections providing an unrivalled taxonomic database for the work of over 350 scientists. Scientists at the Museum are involved on a global scale helping to tackle many of the environmental, sustainable resource use and health problems which threaten our planet. There are ten research and curation programmes ranging from conserving biodiversity and improving human health to maintaining environmental quality and efficient use of mineral resources.

Index of Photographers

The numbers after the photographers' name indicate the pages on which their work can be found.

Markku K Aikioniemi
126/127

Palkisentie 5
98800 *Savukoski*
Lapland
Finland

Tel: 358 692 41357

Kelvin Aitken
70, 77

54 *Wilson Street*
South Yarra 3141
Victoria
Australia

Tel: 03 827 5111
Fax: 03 827 5333

Karl Ammann
39, 83, 132/133, 136

Box 437
Nanyuki
Kenya

Fax: 176 32407

Antonio Sabater Artús
111

Urb. El Bus, *nº* 58
41927 *Mairena del* Aljarafe
(*Sevilla*)
Spain

Tel: 95 476 84 44/71 61
Fax: 95 476 84 44

André Bärtschi
7, 60

Bannholzstrasse 10
FL-9490 *Vaduz*
Liechtenstein

Tel: 075 232 0338
Fax: 075 232 0339

Agent:
Planet Earth Pictures
4 *Harcourt Street*
London W1H 1DS

Tel: 071 262 4427
Fax: 071 706 4042

Erwin & Peggy Bauer
37

Box 987
Livingston
MT 59047
USA

Tel & Fax: 406 222 7100

Niall Benvie
98, 102

Heughhead
Friockheim
By Arbroath
Angus DD11 4TY
Scotland

Tel: 0674 674026

Agent:
Oxford Scientific Films
Lower Road
Long Hanborough
Witney
Oxfordshire 0X8 8LL

Tel: 0993 881881

Hal Beral
59

2600 *Michelson, Ste* 250
Irvine
CA 92715
USA

Tel: 714 863 1375
Fax: 714 863 9064

Markus Michael Botzek
62

Devensstr. 75
46238 *Bottrop*
Germany

Tel: 02041 66975

Pascal Bourguignon
41

Declic-Photo
77 *Rue de* l'Ecole *Militaire*
10500 *Brienne le Chateau*
France

Tel: 25 92 86 88
Fax: 25 92 74 98

Gary Braasch
94/95

PO *Box* 400
Nehalem
Oregon 97131
USA

Tel: 503 368 5091
Fax: 503 368 5075

Jim Brandenburg
7
(*Overall winner* 1988)
c/o Minden *Pictures*
24 *Seascape Village*
Aptos
CA 95003
USA

Tel: 408 685 1911
Fax: 408 685 1913

Dr Hermann Brehm
119

Spielbach 90
74575 *Schrozberg*
Germany

Tel: 07939 389
Fax: 07939 1346

Claudio Calvani
40

Via Metastasio 6
56028 S. *Miniato Basso*
Pisa
Italy

Tel: 0571 419684
Fax: 0571 43387

Laurie Campbell
13, 15, 131

Rosewell Cottage
Paxton
Berwick-upon-Tweed
TD15 ITE
Scotland

Tel & Fax: 0289 386736

Bruce Cantle
42

PO *Box* 40
Maun
Botswana
Africa

Tel: 267 660 375
Fax: 267 660 379

Bernard Castelein
92/93, 111

Verhoevenlei 100
B-2930 *Brasschaat*
Belgium

Tel: 03 653 08 82

Peter Chadwick
138 - 143

12 *Churchill Avenue*
Seaforth
Simonstown 7995
South Africa

Tel: 021 7861671

Martyn Colbeck
7
(Overall winner 1993)
Julian Villa
West Hill
Wincanton
Somerset BA9 9BY
UK
Tel: 0963 32443
Agent:
Oxford Scientific Films
Lower Road
Long Hanborough
Witney
Oxfordshire 0X8 8LL
Tel: 0993 881881

Daniel J Cox
39
16595 *Brackett Creek Road*
Bozeman
Montana 59715
USA
Tel & Fax: 406 686 4448

Bruce Davidson
65, 117
PO *Box* 65
Nakuru
Kenya
Tel: 254 37 210308
Fax: 254 37 44562

Louise Dean
144/145
"Tall Trees"
Ellesmere Road
Weybridge
Surrey KT13 OHY
UK
Tel: 0932 847418

Gertrud & Helmut Denzau
38
Memelstrasse 61
45259 *Essen*
Germany
Tel & Fax: 49 201 465188

Geoff Doré
106
c/o 56 *Jumpers Avenue*
Christchurch
Dorset BH23 2ER
UK
Tel: 0202 485174

Andrew N Drake
125
811 *Spindrift Drive*
Del Mar
California 92067
USA
Tel: 619 792 9362

John Eastcott & Yva Momatiuk
23
151 *Eagles Nest Rd.*
Hurley
NY 12443
USA
Tel: 914 338 4260

Jürgen Freund
75, 93
Riezlerweg 23
80997 *München*
Germany
Tel: 49 145479
Fax: 89 1411325

Luis Miguel Ruiz Gordon
136
Colombia, 6-4º B
Pinto
Madrid 28320
Spain
Fax: 1692 2747

Howard Hall
74, 76
Howard Hall Productions
2171 *La Amatista Road*
Del Mar
California 92014
USA
Tel: 619 259 8989
Fax: 619 792 1467

Asko Hämäläinen
116
Rinnetie 18
46920 *Anjalankoski* 92
Finland
Tel: 358 51 73238

Dr Mark Hamblin
135
63 *Waller Road*
Walkley Bank
Sheffield S6 5DP
UK
Tel & Fax: 0742 333910

Tony Hamblin FRPS
81
8 *Howard Close*
Bidford on Avon
Warwickshire B50 4EL
UK
Tel: 0789 772795

Hannu Hautala
44
Kiestingintie 12
93600 *Kuusamo*
Finland
Tel: 358 89 8511 056
Fax: 358 89 8523 031

Philippe Henry
110
2656 *rue Cuvillier*
Montreal
Quebec
Canada H1W 3B1
Tel: 514 528 1932
Agents:
Oxford Scientific Films
Lower Road
Long Hanborough
Witney
Oxfordshire 0X8 8LL
Tel: 0993 881881
BIOS *(France)*
Save Bild (Germany)

Pål Hermansen
110
Brubåten
Siggerudveien
N-1400 *Ski*
Norway
Tel: 64865515

Paul Hicks
14
26 *Bridgestone Drive*
Bourne End
Bucks SL8 5XH
UK
Tel: 0628 524996

Michael Hill
148, 149

Benson House
Wellington College
Crowthorne
Berkshire RG11 7PU
UK

Tel: 0344 780650

Dr Mike Hill
19, 114/115

PO Box 25005
Awali
Bahrain
Arabian Gulf

Tel: Bahrain 756292
Fax: Bahrain 753624

Rachel Hingley
147

19 *Mount Pleasant Road*
Norton
Stockton-on-Tees TS20 2HX
UK

Tel: 0642 531724

Asel Hjellbrekke
90/91

Vestvoll N/2323
Ingeberg
Norway

Tel: Daytime 62575486
Evening 62596437
Fax: 62575027

Ross Hoddinott
150

Higher Broxwater
Kilkhampton
Bude
Cornwall EX23 9RL
UK

Tel: 0288 321328

Dr Gyözö Horváth
52

H-1181 *Budapest*
Csontváry u. 46 III/16
Hungary

Tel: 36 1 290 5037

Mitsuhiko Imamori
54, 55, 68, 78, 107, 109

c/o Satoko Nakahara
Flat 2
71 *Warwick Avenue*
London W9 2PP
UK

Tel & Fax: 071 266 1271

Tim Jackson
36, 80

Mammal Research Institute
University of Pretoria
Pretoria 0002
South Africa

Tel: 012 420 2539
Fax: 012 43 2185

Alan Philip James
10

Cameras Underwater
10 *Kellaway Avenue*
Redland
Bristol BS6 7XR
UK

Tel & Fax: 0272 445443

Mike Johnson
73

7985 *Dormouse Court*
San Diego
California 92129
USA

Tel: 619 484 1740
Fax: 619 538 2916

Hans Christoph Kappel
53

Hugo-Preuss-Strasse 32
D-34131 *Kassel*
Germany

Tel: 0561 313943

Jiwan Kaur
146

c/o Thakur Dalip Singh
549-A, *9th 'A' Main*
Indiranagar
1st Stage, Bangalore 560038
India

Tel: 80 572288
Fax: 80 5588098

Herbert Kehrer
61, 129

Im Brühl 21
71404 *Korb*
Germany

Tel: 07151 31480

Malcom Kemp
147
Valley Farmhouse
Whitwell
Norwich NR10 4SQ
UK

Tel: 0603 872498

Richard & Julia Kemp
7
(*Overall winner* 1984)
See Malcolm Kemp above

Brian Kenney
79

9067 *Hilolo Lane*
Venice
Florida 34293
USA

Tel: 813 426 4284

Rich Kirchner
20

PO Box 1261
Bozeman
Montana 59715
USA

Tel: 406 763 4142
Fax: 406 586 0396

Jean-Louis Klein & Marie-Luce Hubert
34, 35, 38

49, *Chemin du Château d'eau*
Kogenheim 67230
France

Tel & Fax: 88 82 78 22

Dr P Kumar
51, 85

2/81 *Roop Nagar*
Delhi 110007
India

Tel: 91 11 2515852
Fax: 91 11 7137060

Agent:
Planet Earth Pictures
Lower Road
Long Hanborough
Witney
Oxfordshire 0X8 8LL

Tel: 0993 881881

Frans Lanting
7
(*Overall winner* 1991)
1985 *Smith Grade*
Santa Cruz
California 95060
USA

Fax: 408 423 8324

Kent Larsson
26

Kunturellst 6
Asbro S-69045
Sweden

Antti Leinonen
104/105

Koirisärkäntie 4 C 10
88900 *Kuhmo*
Finland

Tel: 866 551775

George D Lepp
33, 103

Lepp & Associates
PO *Box* 6240
Los Osos
California 93412-6240
USA

Tel: 805 528 7385
Fax: 805 528 7387

Brian Lightfoot
15

Wildlife Photography
Parkhead Croft
Balandro
Johnshaven
Montrose DD10 0PU
UK

Tel: 0561 362017

Charles Lindsay
47, 63

Q Photo International Inc.
2/F Ginza Building
Chuo-Ku, 9-15 Ginza 2 Chome
Tokyo 104, Japan

Fax: 813 3564 3578

Doug Locke
87, 102

1415 *Oakbrook East*
Rochester Hills
Michigan 48307-1127
USA

Tel: 810 656 1625

Martin van Lokven
124

Willem Barentszstraat 96
3572 PP Utrecht
The Netherlands

Tel: 030 722936

Renee Lynn
32, 88

Davis/Lynn Photography
PO *Box* 1278
Palo Alto
California 94302
USA

Tel: 415 327 4192
Fax: 415 322 5082

Seppo Määttä
45

692 Kuontila
93999 Kuusamo
Finland

Tel: 989 858638

Thomas D Mangelsen
8/9, 46, 97, 101, 102, 134

Images of Nature
PO *Box* 2935
2nd Level, Gaslight Alley
Jackson, Wyoming 83001
USA

Tel: 307 733 6179
Fax: 307 733 6184

Francisco Márquez
18, 108

Cervera, 2 6°
45600 Talavera de la Reina
(Toledo)
Spain

Tel: 25 82 41 22
Fax: 25 80 28 67

Marko Masterl
122/123

Rozna ul. 26
61330 Kocevje
Slovenia

Tel & Fax: 386 61 851 646

Mary Ann McDonald
16/17, 64

RR#2 *Box* 1095
McClure
PA 17841-9340
USA

Tel & Fax: 717 543 6423

Neil McIntyre
130

Ballinluig Cottage
Kinrara
Aviemore
Inverness-shire PH22 1QB
Scotland

Tel: 0479 810545

Agent:
Planet Earth Pictures
Lower Road
Long Hanborough
Witney
Oxfordshire 0X8 8LL

Tel: 0993 881881

Tristan Jay Millen
148

76 Gaze Hill Avenue
Sittingbourne
Kent ME10 4SJ
UK

Tel: 0795 475383

Mike Mockler
27

"Gulliver's Cottage"
Chapel Rise
Avon Castle
Ringwood
Hants BH24 2BL
UK

Sunjoy Monga
137

45-46 Madhurima
M.G. Road
Kandivli (West)
Bombay 400067
India

Tel: 91 22 8052148
Fax: 91 22 8063573

Peter Moore
12

Wildlife & Landscape Photographer
Poll Creagan
Newtonmore
Inverness-shire PH20 1BS
Scotland

Tel: 0540 673686
Fax: 0540 673342

Jussi Murtosaari
56

Tyyppäläntie 2 D 29
40250 Jyväskylä
Finland

Tel: 358 41 685045
Fax: 358 41 213905

John Neil
11

"Seaspray"
6 Mona Terrace
The Promenade
Castletown
Isle of Man IM9 1BH
UK

Tel: 0624 822969

William Neill
96

PO Box 162
Yosemite National Park
California 95389
USA

Tel: 209 379 2841
Fax: 209 379 2328

Dr Scott Nielsen
22, 84

Edge of the Wilderness Gallery
8008 South Dowling Lake Rd West
Superior
Wisconsin 54880
USA

Tel: 715 399 2160

Agent:
Bruce Coleman Ltd
Unit 16, Chiltern Business Village
Uxbridge UB8 2SN

Tel: 0895 257094
Fax: 0895 272357

Klaus Nigge
130

Ernst-Becker Strasse 12
D-4670 Lunen
Germany

Hijiri Okamoto
128/129

104-103 Otokoyama Takezono
Yawata, Kyoto
Japan

Tel: 075 981 7153

Tony Ord
42

The Chippings
Duckington
Malpas
Cheshire SY14 8LQ
UK

Tel & Fax: 0829 782262

Risto Petäjämäki
24, 25

Pihlajankaari 15
Joutseno Fin-54100
Finland

Fritz Pölking
43, 50

Münsterstrasse 71
D-48268 Greven
Germany

Tel: 2571 52115/2864
Fax: 2571 97098

Tapani Räsänen
86

Tasalantie 27
Joutseno Fin-54100
Finland
Tel: 358 5334929
358 534534929 (*from Jan* 1995)

Jeff Rotman
88

14 Cottage Avenue
Somerville
MA 02144-3019
USA

Tel: 617 666 0874
Fax: 617 666 4811

Jouni Ruuskanen
7
(Overall *winner* 1989)
Ratakatu 31 As 14
87100 *Kajaani*
Finland

Tel: 86 133026

Carl R Sams II
30/31, 82

2675 General Motors Road
Milford
Michigan 48380
USA

Tel: 810 685 2422
Fax: 810 685 1643

Jonathan Scott
7
(Overall Winner 1987)
PO Box 24499
Nairobi
Kenya

Fax: Nairobi 216528

Agent:
Planet Earth Pictures
Lower Road
Long Hanborough
Witney
Oxfordshire 0X8 8LL

Tel: 0993 881881

Anup Shah
21

Panthra Ltd
PO Box 44219
Nairobi Kenya
Africa

Agent:
Planet Earth Pictures
Lower Road
Long Hanborough
Witney
Oxfordshire 0X8 8LL

Tel: 0993 881881

Wendy Shattil & Bob Rozinski
99

PO Box 37422
Denver
Colorado 80237
USA

Tel: 303 721 1991
Fax: 303 721 1116

Warwick Sloss
103

8 Chantry Road
Clifton
Bristol BS8 2QD
UK

Tel: 0272 237144

Ralph Snook
118

Lydden Paddock
Ham Road
Liddington
Swindon SN4 OHH
UK

Tel: 0793 790851

Klaus Sudbrack
26

Am Rohland 17a
Hamm D-59071
Germany

Fax: 02381 28551

Charles G Summers Jr
7
(Overall Winner 1985)
Wild Images
6392 South Yellowstone Way
Aurora
Colorado 80016
USA

Tel: 303 690 6664
Fax: 3003 693 4750

Brenda Tharp
123

PO Box 1653
Ross
CA 94957
USA

Tel: 415 927 4579

Roberto Travesi
41

Ancha de Santo Domingo Nº6
Granada 18009
Spain

Tel: 958 222841
Fax: 958 521165

Jason Venus
100

24 *Central Acre*
Yeovil
Somerset BA20 1NU
UK

Tel & Fax: 0935 706834

Jan Vermeer
81

Wilhelmina Druckerstraat 343
7311 TD *Apeldoorn*
The Netherlands

Tel: 31 55 5224188
Fax: 31 55 5222313

Franklin J Viola
48/49

Viola's Photo Visions
9740 *Coleman Road*
Roswell
Georgia 30076
USA

Tel: 404 594 1086
Fax: 404 594 1087

Jürgen Vogt
57

Waldstrasse 5/1
D-72116 *Mössingen-Belsen*
Germany

Tel: 07473 4836

Kennan Ward
69

Kennan Ward Photography
PO Box 42
Santa Cruz
California 95063
USA

Fax: 408 462 8899

Adrian Warren
56, 69

Batch Farm
Panborough
Near Wells
Somerset BA5 1PN
UK

Tel & Fax: 0934 712556

Gareth Westerskov
146

20 *Greerton Road*
Tauranga
New Zealand

Tel: 64 7 578 5138
Fax: 64 7 578 1423

Dr Kim Westerskov
89

See Gareth Westerskov above

Art Wolfe
112/113, 120/121

6751 47*th Avenue* SW
Seattle
Washington 98136
USA

Tel: 206 937 5681
Fax: 206 938 3139

Konrad Wothe
28/29, 66/67

Konrad-Witz-Strasse 15
81479 *München*
Germany

Tel: 089 798675
Fax: 089 7914234

Agent:
LOOK GMBH
Fraunhofer Str. 5
80469 *München*
Germany

Tel: 089 2606320
Fax: 089 2606322

Norbert Wu
71, 72

165 *Ivy Drive*
Orinda
California 94563
USA

Tel: 510 376 8418
Fax: 510 376 8864

Ihász Zoltán
26

2315 *Szigethalom*
Jósef Attila 81
Hungary